D0919058

Letters on Familiar Matters

Aldo S. Bernardo is Distinguished Service Professor in the Department of Romance Languages and Literature at the State University of New York at Binghamton. He is the translator of Rerum familiarium libri I–VIII *(1975), also available from the Johns Hopkins University Press. The second volume in the series,* Letters on Familiar Matters: Rerum familiarium libri IX–XVI, *was published by Johns Hopkins in 1982.*

Francesco Petrarca

Letters on Familiar Matters

Rerum familiarium libri XVII–XXIV

TRANSLATED BY ALDO S. BERNARDO

THE JOHNS HOPKINS UNIVERSITY PRESS, 1985

BALTIMORE AND LONDON

This book has been brought to publication
with the generous assistance of the State
University of New York.

© 1985 The Johns Hopkins University
Press
All rights reserved
Printed in the United States of America
The Johns Hopkins University Press, Baltimore,
Maryland 21218
The Johns Hopkins Press Ltd., London

The paper in this book is acid-free and meets the guidelines
for permanence and durability of the Committee on
Production Guidelines for Book Longevity
of the Council on Library Resources.

Library of Congress Cataloging in Publication Data

Petrarca, Francesco, 1304–1374.
Rerum familiarium libri.

Vols. 2–3 have title: Letters on familiar matters.
Vols. 2–3 published by Johns Hopkins University Press.
Bibliography: v. 1, p.
Contents: [1] I–VIII — [2] IX–XVI — [3] XVII–XXIV.
1. Petrarca, Francesco, 1304–1374—Correspondence.
2. Authors, Italian—To 1500—Correspondence.
I. Title.   II. Title: Letters on familiar matters.
PQ4496.E29E23   1975   851'.1   75–2418
ISBN 0–87395–295–2 (v. 1)
ISBN 0–8018–2750–7 (Johns Hopkins : v. 2)
ISBN 0–8018–2287–4 (Johns Hopkins : v. 3)

To Marian and John

Contents

Book XIX

Book XX

Book XXI

Book XXII

Book XXIII

Book XXIV

Preface

The present volume completes the translation of the twenty-four books and 350 letters that compose Petrarch's *Familiares*. The same editorial principles obtain as in the first two volumes. The basic Latin text is again that of the definitive edition by Vittorio Rossi and Umberto Bosco, which is reproduced and translated by Enrico Bianchi in the first volume of an incomplete Sansoni series of Petrarch's works.[1] The paragraphing is based on the paragraphing in that edition rather than on the modern subparagraphs indicated in its margins. Despite its awkward bulkiness in English, such paragraphing serves the double purpose of allowing ready reference to the Latin text and of containing the length of the volume within reasonable bounds. This last criterion likewise remains the reason for excluding all annotations except brief identifications of correspondents not previously indicated or references to the initial appearance of identifications. Complete annotations of textual citations may be found in the Rossi and Sansoni editions, while more extensive annotations may be found in the Italian translation of the first eleven books by Ugo Dotti, in the Fracassetti translation of the entire collection, in the selected letters of the Ricciardi edition, and in the Cosenza translation of the letters to classical authors found in Book XXIV.[2]

As with the first two volumes, I found it useful to check particularly difficult passages against a number of Italian and English translations. In addition to the Italian translations by Fracassetti and Bianchi, these included the English translations by Cosenza, Bishop, Wilkins, and Robinson and Rolfe.[3] I also consulted a number of translations of classical, patristic, and biblical sources cited by Petrarch. The most extensive of these were from the Bible and from St. Augustine.[4]

For the sake of consistency, the present translation reproduces proper names as they appear in the Latin text, as in the first two volumes. Thus Virgil, Ovid, Horace, Juvenal, Seneca, Sallust, and Suetonius often appear as Maro, Naso, Flaccus, the Satirist, Anneus, Crispus, and Tranquillus, respectively. Most names with diphthongs retain the medieval form, viz., Anneus, Lelius, Sceva, etc., except for purposes of clarity or in commonly used names, such as Laelius (to distinguish the classical personage from Petrarch's friend), Caesar, Aeneas, Maecenas, etc. The same principle holds for Petrarch's spelling of Roman names ending in *ci*, for which he prefers *ti*, viz., Fabritius, Martia, etc. As for names appearing in the salutations, I once again generally observe the following criteria: names referring to persons of special renown have been anglicized (Charles IV, Clement VI, etc.), those of foreign correspondents are given in the language of their country (Jan ze Středa, Pierre de Poitiers, etc.), names of Italians retain their Italian form. The forms generally agree with Wilkins's list of addressees.[5]

Most geographical names retain the medieval Latin form, with the exception of a few ending in diphthongs which keep the classical form (Cannae, Baiae), and a number of others that, in my opinion, are more readily recognized in their modern forms (Aniene, Milan, Pavia). Book titles, with few exceptions, are likewise given as they appear in the Latin.

As I reflect on the past ten years of work spent in translating the entire collection of the *Familiares*, I experience not only a deep satisfaction at having communed with one of the great figures of the modern era but, even more, a profound sense of gratitude toward the State University of New York for having made it all possible. Through its program of faculty awards sponsored by its research foundation I received a sizable grant in 1968 that allowed me to initiate this work with the aid of the campus computer center, a process that eventually enabled me not only to expedite the translation but also to create and publish a concordance of the entire collection.[6] It was the only financial assistance that I enjoyed despite at least three subsequent requests to other funding agencies whose systems of peer judging repeatedly called into question the need for computer assistance, as well as the overly ambitious scope of the project. If this translation proves useful to humanistic studies, most of the credit must go to the willingness of the State University of New York to support such research. I am also grateful to the graduate provost of the Binghamton campus for the subventions granted me to assist in the publication of the last two volumes, to its Center for Medieval and Early Renaissance Studies for its generous allocation of computer time, and to the support staff of the computer center for its patient assistance.

A word must also be said about the willingness of university presses to undertake a project of this kind and scope. A large number considered the project worthy of publication, but balked at the problem of sales.

The Johns Hopkins University Press alone seemed to appreciate the importance of the project and showed little hesitation in accepting it. I extend my sincere thanks to the press for its highly professional approach to basic research and scholarship.

Finally, I must once again express my infinite indebtedness to my wife, Reta, whose assistance in polishing the translation, entering the entire text into the computer, revising, correcting, and proofreading it under the most trying circumstances, enabled us to complete this volume in the record time of two years. Her help was truly indispensable.

Notes

1. *Le Familiari*, vols. 1–3, ed. Vittorio Rossi, and vol. 4, ed. Rossi and Umberto Bosco (Florence: Sansoni, 1933–41); and Francesco Petrarca, *Opere*, trans. Enrico Bianchi (Florence: Sansoni, 1975).

2. Francesco Petrarca, *Le Familiari*, trans. Ugo Dotti, 2 vols. (Urbino: Argalia, 1974); *Lettere di Francesco Petrarca*, trans. Giuseppe Fracassetti, 5 vols. (Florence: LeMonnier, 1863–66); Francesco Petrarca, *Prose*, ed. Guido Martellotti, Pier Giorgio Ricci, Enrico Carrara, and Enrico Bianchi (Milan and Naples: Ricciardi, 1955); and Mario E. Cosenza, *Petrarch's Letters to Classical Authors* (Chicago: University of Chicago Press, 1910).

3. *Letters from Petrarch*, trans. Morris Bishop (Bloomington: Indiana University Press, 1966); Ernest H. Wilkins, *Petrarch's Eight Years in Milan* (Cambridge, Mass.: Mediaeval Academy of America, 1958); and James H. Robinson and Henry W. Rolfe, *Petrarch, The First Modern Man of Letters* (New York: Putnam, 1898).

4. *The New American Bible* (Kansas: Catholic Bible Publishers, 1971–73); St. Augustine, *The City of God*, trans. Marcus Dods (New York: Random House, 1950); and *The Confessions of St. Augustine*, trans. F. J. Sheed (New York: Sheed and Ward, 1942).

5. Ernest H. Wilkins, *Petrarch's Correspondence* (Padua: Antenore, 1960).

6. Aldo S. Bernardo, *A Concordance to Petrarch's "Familiares"* (Albany: SUNY Press, 1977). Microfiche. The Italian publisher, Antenore, is considering a printed edition.

Introduction

These last eight books of Petrarch's *Familiares* include 122 letters written for the most part between 1353 and 1361, following Petrarch's move from Provence to Italy. Most of the letters were written from Milan, with some thirty written in Padua and Venice between 1361 and 1365. The ten letters to classical authors found in Book XXIV span practically the entire lifetime of the collection, some dating as early as 1340 and others as late as 1360. The three actual missives of the last book not addressed to the ancients likewise contain a letter (No. 2) dating back to 1350.

Thus, these eight final books include letters written at a critical period of Petrarch's life, when his intellectual powers had reached a high point, as had his reputation and his determination to return to his beloved Italy.[1] His desire for continued independence together with his rekindled love for Italy led to a series of letters addressed to some of the highest ruling authorities of the time, starting with the emperor, Charles IV, and proceeding to the doges of Venice and Genoa, as well as a number of lesser rulers, all of whom Petrarch thought were irreparably harming Italy and humankind.

His unexpected decision to settle in Milan rankled some of his closest friends who had for so long admired his passionate love of solitude and spirit of independence. This prompted a series of emotional letters defending his actions and proclaiming his strong patriotism for the land of his birth, as well as his utter disgust with Avignon and the French papacy. It is nevertheless the sure hand of the man of letters that seems to dominate the tone of these final books. The most recurring theme in each one is the strong sense of the passage of time and the need to prepare for death, while more than in any other series of the collection one feels Petrarch's concern for maximizing the overall artistic effect of each book.

Such concern is reflected in the careful placement of the most significant letters at the beginning and end of each book, and is most clearly seen in the ordering of the highly original letters addressed to ten classical authors that form the bulk of the last book. Starting with three letters of moral indignation directed against two key Roman thinkers who had lived just before or in the time of Christ, Cicero and Seneca, and ending with three letters on the superiority of the ancient world in the realm of lyric and epic poetry as represented by Horace, Virgil, and Homer, the ten letters revolve around the great Roman historian, Livy, to whom he writes concerning his still extant works: "I busy myself with such few remains of yours whenever I desire to forget these places or times, as well as our present customs, being filled with bitter indigation against the activities of the men of our time who find no value in anything but gold and silver and pleasures." The *Familiares* thus end with a wistful look toward the distant past, a look that seems to reflect the same moral and intellectual concerns found in the troubled letter to posterity which was to close the *Seniles* as a final book in an obvious attempt to give artistic balance to the two collections. Similarly the first and last letters of the *Familiares* are addressed to the same friend, while the first letter of the last book consciously repeats the theme of the third letter of the first book, written thirty years earlier. The motif of fleeting time is thus dramatized in Book XXIV by placing the ten letters to classical authors between two letters that hark back to the opening moments of the collection.

The pronounced moral tone is quickly given prominence in the first three letters of the opening Book XVII of the present series. The initial two letters are addressed to Petrarch's two closest blood relatives, his monastic brother, Gherardo, and his truant son, Giovanni. The first letter acknowledges the unquestionable superiority of religious studies over secular ones; the second reflects Petrarch's strong desire to see his illegitimate and troublesome son succeed. The third and fourth letters initiate the theme of fleeting time and the fall of governments. The same moral tone permeates the remaining seven letters, which speak of his several missions in behalf of peace and his reflections on the pitfalls of life as contemplated from his new residence near St. Ambrose in Milan.

The dominant themes of Book XVIII include another appeal to Emperor Charles IV to be crowned in Rome (No. 1), as well as Petrarch's endless search for lost classical works and his dedication to friends. Book XIX contains a short-lived exuberance over the emperor's descent to Rome (No. 1), which evaporates by the twelfth letter, wherein he bitterly reproves the emperor for his hasty return to Germany. The book also launches the theme of Petrarch's patriotic concerns over the internal political rifts of individual Italian states, such as Venice (No. 9) and Pavia (No. 18). In addition to more criticism of the emperor and of the war between Venice and Genoa, Book XX contains an attack on contemporary mores (No. 1), an intimate and critical view of the legal profession and its history (No. 4), a strong defense of his stay in Milan (No. 14), and recurring expressions of dedication and loyalty to friends. Book XXI opens with two letters to high officials of the imperial court, the first on Petrarch's cultivation of truth, the second expressing his gratitude for having been named Count Palatine by the emperor and symbolically returning the golden boss decorating the diploma. The middle letters include the unique letter to Empress Anna, whose announcement of the birth of a daughter prompts a veritable history of the accomplishments of great women (No. 8); an apotheosis of Cicero (No. 10); an account of an incredible reception in his honor sponsored by a goldsmith (No. 11); two intimate glances at Petrarch's scholarly dedication and personal life (Nos. 12 and 13); and the famous letter to Boccaccio revealing Petrarch's attitude toward Dante (No. 15). Book XXII provides further insights into Petrarch's widespread popularity among the powerful and the intellectuals, as well as intimate glances into his personal life, especially his determined turn to sacred writers (No. 10), his problem with servants (No. 12), and his strong feelings against the use of mercenary troops (No. 14). Book XXIII contains no less than six letters to Charles IV (Nos. 2, 3, 8, 9, 15, 21), four to the imperial chancellor (Nos. 6, 10, 14, 16), one to the grand seneschal of the Kingdom of Naples (No. 18), and one decrying the decay of the royal family of Naples (No. 17). It also contains the important letter to Boccaccio on literary imitation (No. 19).

We see the collection's scope broaden as we reach the final book. From philosophical and spiritual concerns, Petrarch's interests turned increasingly to the European political situation. Following his return to Italy in 1353, he began directing his haunting preoccupation with the ravages of time to its implications for the future of humankind should Rome's centrality cease. The thought of a Rome abandoned by both pope and emperor had reached nearly apocalyptic proportions in his mind by the end of the collection. As a result, of the thirteen letters addressed to Charles IV throughout the collection starting with Book X, eleven appear in this series; of these, six appear in Book XXIII, which, as we have seen, also contains six others directed to some high officials of the imperial or Neapolitan court. The final appeal to the emperor is strategically placed as the last actual missive of the collection (XXIII, 21) just before the mostly fictitious letters of the closing book. Since the first two letters of Book XXIV were intended as introductions to the unique book—one being once again a "triumph of time," the other a justification of the book—the shocking contrast between the Roman world of the past and its decay in the present emerges full force. The deep sense of loss repeatedly expressed in the ten letters to classical authors, the obvious preference for ancient times, the possible irrecoverability of crucial ideas and masterpieces of the human spirit, when combined with Petrarch's moral criticisms of the personal lives of his favorite ancients and with his desperate final exhortation to the emperor, endow the collection with a conclusion that reflects the helpless outcries so forcefully expressed by the lyrical Petrarch in his famous canzoni, *Italia mia* and *I' vo pensando*. Perhaps more clearly than elsewhere in Petrarch's works, we see in this grand finale of the *Familiares* the merger of poet, scholar, and citizen of the world.[2]

Notes

1. In his book *Petrarch's Eight Years in Milan* (Cambridge, Mass.: The Mediaeval Academy of America, 1958), Ernest H. Wilkins presents a yearly account of Petrarch's life and works, as well as a useful summary of his activities after leaving Milan.

2. See *Francesco Petrarca, Citizen of the World*, ed. Aldo S. Bernardo (Padua and Albany: Editrice Antenore and SUNY Press, 1980).

Letters on Familiar Matters

Fam. XVII, 1.

To Gherardo, Carthusian monk, * *what is the true philosophy, what is the true law, who is the best teacher of both.*

From the hands of a certain religious, I have received your even more religious little book. I opened it, intending to read it the next morning since it was beginning to grow dark. It enticed me, as Seneca says, and so it was not laid down until I had read it all in silence; having thus deferred my body's sustenance until nighttime, my mind meanwhile dined most splendidly on its food and was delightfully refreshed. Dear and only brother of mine, I enjoyed it more than words can express, for it helped me understand not only the firmness of your holy purpose, which I had always expected of you, and your contempt for fleeting things, which for some time had been very familiar to me, but your unexpected and surprising abundance of literary ability, which you almost completely lacked upon entering that religious order so dear to God. Though salvation may not lie in literature, it still is and was for a great many men a way to salvation; furthermore, to have such a capacity without a teacher is a sign of excellence and of a mind disposed to rise on high. But to be perfectly honest, you certainly did not learn all this without a teacher since you have had the One who can not only cultivate, but actually impart, talent; I am not surprised that under Him you have learned so much in this brief time, for often more quickly than can be told He has instilled in many a man the highest power and knowledge, drawing forth many from the deepest shadows into the loftiest light with His merciful nod. Now, my dear brother, watching over you and having compassion for you, He has transformed you from an unlearned to a learned man, from a shipwrecked to a rescued soul. To Him, not to you, praises and gratitude are due, lest you perchance believe that you are now being flattered; but never having done so, I am not about to begin at this age. In antiquity men sought Cecropian Athens for the purpose of study, particularly before Rome became the fount of letters as well as of military and imperial matters; in our century they seek Paris or Bologna, which we too, you will recall, sought in our youth. All in vain, to be sure, it often caused us to complain about our friends' cupidity, yet we always considered that decision among the most valuable gifts of the Lord. Thus does human stubbornness eagerly undergo costly and difficult journeys, sparing no labor in seeking some remnant of an empty philosophy or the insidious loquacity of law, wasting an en-

*See X, 3.

tire lifetime in incredible squanderings without devoting any time to more important matters. In scarcely ten years you learned the true philosophy and the true law, yet I do not wish you to consider true philosophy what a thousand men in one city may now profess; it is not as common a possession as many believe. What else is this philosophy that we see prostituted before the multitude devoted to except the careful and uneasy consideration of insignificant little questions and word problems? Ignorance of such things is often no less helpful, perhaps even more helpful, than knowledge about them; thus does truth sink into profound oblivion, thus are good customs neglected, thus are scorned the very ideas in which resides the nobility of the philosophy that deceives no one; only empty words attract attention. The truth of this is revealed by the lives of philosophers who practice nothing of what they preach. As Cicero writes in one of his Tusculan disputations: "How many philosophers are so inclined and disciplined in their lives and in their ways as to behave according to reason's dictates, as to consider their discipline not ostentatious knowledge but the law of life, or as to listen to themselves and obey their own rules? Indeed a few can be seen displaying such vanity and ostentation that it would have been better for them not to have learned anything; still others yearn for money, hardly any for glory, while many are enslaved by their passions, all of which results in their words conflicting shockingly with their lives, a situation that for me personally seems shameful. For just as it is more shameful for the person claiming to be a grammarian to speak in a barbarous manner, or the person wishing to be considered a musician to sing off-key, since they fail in the very area where they claim knowledge, so the philosopher sinning against the rules of life is more shameful because of his faltering in the art in which he wishes to be a teacher. While professing the art of life, he fails in life itself." What is particularly notable in Cicero's words is that he calls philosophy not the art of words but of life.

My dearest brother, do you wish to know, if by some chance you do not, the substance of true philosophy so that, by understanding your great progress in this brief time, you may proceed with greater eagerness to what remains? Do you wish to turn your attention, denied to all those puffed up with the false name of philosophy, to me so as to listen to me alone, yet not really to me but to the prince of philosophers, Plato, and to Augustine, the philosopher of Christ, in the eighth book of his heavenly city? "At present," he says, "it suffices to mention that Plato determined the final good to be to live according to virtue, and affirmed that only he who knows and imitates God can attain to virtue—which knowledge and imitation are the only cause of blessedness. Therefore he did not doubt that to philosophize is to love God, whose nature is incorporeal. Whence it surely follows that the student of wisdom, namely the philosopher, will then become blessed when he has begun to enjoy God. For though he who enjoys that which he loves is not necessarily blessed (for many are miserable by loving that which ought not to be loved, and still more miserable when they enjoy it), nevertheless no one is blessed who does not enjoy that which he loves. For even they who love things that ought not to be loved do not count themselves blessed merely by loving, but by enjoying them. Who, then, but the most miserable will deny that he is blessed, who enjoys that which he loves, and loves the true and highest good? But the true and highest good, according to Plato, is God, and therefore he would call him a philosopher who loves God; for philosophy is directed to the attainment of the blessed life, and he who loves God is blessed in the enjoyment of God." Thus does Augustine report verbatim Plato's opinion, which was unique among all the schools of philosophy and quite similar to the true faith. Augustine, who esteemed him in this and in many other things, speaks of philosophy in that same book: "Its name if rendered into Latin means love of wisdom, but if wisdom is God who made all things, as attested by divine authority and truth, the true philosopher is a lover of God." To this I would quickly add that we who daily admit Christ to be our God must consequently and honestly conclude that the true philosopher can only be the true Christian. What credit do I ascribe to myself? I added nothing but the name of Christ; for what else did Augustine mean by these words, "If wisdom is God who created all things, He is without question Christ; for although each person of the Trinity is God, something which we are compelled to believe as Christian truth according to Athanasius, and each is therefore the highest power, the highest wisdom, and the highest good, still Christ is more particularly the wisdom of the Father through whom all things were made as may be seen in the gospel of John and in the symbolic service that the church of the faithful daily celebrates"? Furthermore, in dealing with the Trinity's operations in his *De uera religione*, the same Augustine says, "One must not believe that the Father made one part of all creation, the Son another, the Holy Spirit another; but that the Father simultaneously made all things and every creature through the Son with the gift of the Holy Spirit." This he often repeated even in other places and at the end of the same book: "God is one, from whom, through whom, and in whom we are"; and again, "God is one, from whom, through whom, and in whom all things are." The same concept occurs once again in the eleventh book of the *De ciuitate Dei*: "When any creature is asked who made it, by what means and why, its response should be: God, through the Word, because it was good, so that the Trinity itself may flow into us with its mystical loftiness, that is, the Father and the Son and the Holy Spirit." Later he says, "We believe and hold and faithfully preach that the Father begat the Word, that is, Wisdom by which all things were made, and the only begotten Son, one as the Father is one, eternal as the Father is eternal, and equally with the Father supremely good." There is no need to cite what follows since everything written about Christ confirms that all things were made through Him. If then this wisdom is God, and Christ is truly the Son of God, and philosophy is the love of wisdom, Augustine's words also must lead to the conclusion that the true philosopher is nothing but a lover of God and a true Christian. You, my dearest brother, happily learned this philosophy not in Athens or Rome, not in Paris, but on a sacred mount and in a spiritual forest, becoming a much truer and firmer philosopher than those who, again in Augustine's words, "prefer when it comes to disputation their mouths bursting with Plato's name than their hearts filled with the truth." If this is true even of the Platonists, preferred by our followers above other schools of philosophy, how much more applicable is it to those about whom the Apostle says, "Beware lest anyone deceive you with the philosophy and the empty seduction based on worldly values"; and who, I say, established countless sects rampant with infinite errors; but this is neither the time nor the place to enumerate them.

What do you think can now be said concerning laws? We do know of many lawgivers among various peoples; skipping the more obscure names, some outstanding ones include Phoroneus in Argos, Lycurgus for the Spartans, and Solon for the Athenians, whose laws underwent much improvement and amplification when passed on to the Romans. From these came the twelve tables and other laws, Senate decrees, plebiscites, the honorary oath of the praetors, and finally the edicts of dictators and rulers. Being of human invention, however, all these laws, as well as many others, suffered human change because of changing times and man's shifting passions and desires upon which they were based, for it is natural for one law to correct another. Would you like a law to be eternal? Then give it an eternal foundation. The law was given to the Israelites by God through Moses; certainly, then, it was quite stable, but do you think it eternal? Certainly, too, the law was given through Moses, but the grace of fulfilling the law was given through Jesus Christ; by not abolishing but instead by perfecting it, He put an end not to the law itself but to the many rites of the law. For this reason, Augustine says about Psalm 143: "You recall the many things that we read in the old law and do not observe, and yet we understand that they were proposed and set forth with a certain purpose, which was not that we refute the law of God but that we not celebrate the promised rites now that the promise has been fulfilled. For what they promised has come about, inasmuch as the grace of the New Testament was veiled in the law and is revealed in the gospels; we removed the veil and recognized what was hidden. We recognized it, however, through the grace of Our Lord Jesus Christ, our master and savior, who was crucified for us and at whose crucifixion even the temple veil was torn asunder." This testimony of Augustine I have cited lastly for this reason in particular, that you may clearly realize that the tearing of the veil about which we read in Scripture was a figure of a great and ineffable mystery, signifying by the ancient veil, which until that day concealed the mysteries of the law and which was rent by Christ's passion, everything revealed to a new and humble people, something that the older and prouder people had not seen with their swollen and blinded eyes. As the same Augustine notes in another place, "Although the Jews adored the one omnipotent God, expecting, however, only temporal and visible goods from Him, they refused to perceive in their writings, because of excessive self-assurance, the humble beginnings of a new people; they thus remained in the old man." And in yet another place, he says, "Although the old laws may be first in time, still the new ones must be preferred for their intrinsic value, since the old ones herald the new ones." Thus, to return to my point, the Mosaic law itself, although the most sacred of all human laws, yielded nonetheless in many ways to the grace, as you see, created through Jesus Christ. His alone is that law, unchangeable and eternal, that will yield to no other, to which all others will yield or have yielded; this is that "law of God that must be accepted," which Lactantius Cecilius Formianus treats at length in a certain place saying "that it leads us to the path of that sacred and heavenly wisdom that Marcus Tullius in the third book of his *De republica* depicted with nearly divine words. I shall cite them directly to avoid saying more: 'It is indeed the true law, true reason, harmonious with nature, widely diffused, stable, eternal, which calls to duty by so ordering, prevents evil by forbidding it, but which nonetheless neither orders nor forbids the virtuous in vain, nor fails to influence the wicked by forbidding or ordering. Nor is it permissible to repeal this law or any section of it, nor can the entire law be annulled. We cannot be released from this law either by the Senate or by the people, we need no glosser or interpreter, there will not be one law in Rome and another in Athens, one law at this time and another in the future, but for all peoples and for all times there will be one law, eternal and immutable. God will be the common master and the emperor of all, having been the inventor, the formulator, and the legislator of this law. Whoever does not obey it will be denying himself and scorning human nature, and for this very reason will undergo the greatest sufferings, although he will escape the others called punishments.' "

This then, my dear brother, is the law of God according to Cicero, which he, I shall not say with Lactantius "far removed from awareness of the truth," came to know through the revelation of Christ, whom he did not know, which he expressed so distinctly that no one else could have done so as exactly or briefly, even among the initiates of the sacraments of the true faith. Without doubt—and in this I am in agreement with Lactantius—one must believe that he did so through the inspiration of some divine spirit. But do you know why divine law is immutable? Because it was given by Him who remains always the same, whose years never cease, whose concern is not for transient or mutable matters but eternal ones; and although it does at times address transitory things, nevertheless in the mind of the Legislator Himself everything refers back to the eternal life beyond which nothing exists. Thus it is necessary for a law concerning immutable and impossible things from One who is infinite and immutable also to be infinite and immutable in the eternal republic. Christ is the author of this law, that "immaculate law of the Lord that converts souls" about which the Psalmist speaks, that "faithful witness of the Lord who instills wisdom in children." You learned this law, my dearest brother, not amidst the rumbling of scholarly hordes but in solitude and in silence, something that you would not have done had you not been a child. And know that by children is meant humble beings, as is attested in these words, "Allow the little children to come unto me, for of such is made the kingdom of heaven"; and in those other words, "You concealed these things from wise men and from prudent men only to reveal them to young children." But scarcely new to you is this passage in particular, "The Lord is the keeper of children," to which is soon added to show clearly who these children may be, "I humbled myself and He freed me," as if to say, "Since the Lord watches over small children, I have made myself a small child in humility so that He may watch over me as well." Your willingness to learn was supplemented by a very appropriate teacher who was not Aristotle or Pythagoras or Plato among the philosophers, not Papinianus or Ulpianus or Scevola among the lawmakers, but Christ. With such a magnificent teacher, your devoted and humble intelligence easily bore fruit in both arenas; love Him, honor Him, and give yourself to Him in a much more dignified fashion than did Eschines to Socrates, since you possess nothing more worthy than He, and He will return you to yourself a better man, endowing you with what Socrates promised his disciple. Always render gratitude to Him for the many things that He has bestowed upon you, but especially for this spirit that you lacked before He gave it to you; have no fear of rendering too much gratitude to Him, or that by praising and loving Him you may exceed His kindness, which you can never equal even in imagination. To this alone Terence's saying, "Nothing in excess," cannot apply, but rather those more appropriate words, "Never enough." So as not to be perhaps astonished at Christ's supreme magistracy, since you made under Him more progress in a brief time than would have been possible during your lifetime in Plato's academy or in the schools of philosophers or jurisconsults, note that whatever greatness man may possess is as nothing in comparison to God. Plato was a great man, as was Pythagoras, Aristotle, and Varro; I say that they were great if considered in themselves. They say that Augustus Caesar was not of great stature, yet so elegant that he easily redeemed his small body with his charm; this was no longer the case, however, when someone taller approached him, for then his shortness, ingeniously disguised, would reappear. Do you want to know the true greatness of these men who seem the greatest? Compare any of them, or rather all of them, as well as the many who preceded, followed, or will follow them until the end of time, compare any of them to Christ and you will see that their names may be exalted, but empty, that what you had greatly admired is to be disdained, once the truth is known. Their splendor will immediately vanish when the sun of justice, Christ, has dawned. Although you need no urging to believe this, I should like you, as you consider the matter, to recall these words in the Psalms so as to believe an older man with greater confidence: "Their judges were cast down over the crag," or to use an ancient version, "Their judges were cast down before the crag." The crag, as we know, is Christ. Consequently, Augustine says in commenting upon this passage: "Let all the earth from east to west praise the name of the Lord. What do the few who argue otherwise do? They are the judges of the wicked. But what does it matter to you? Note what follows, 'Their judges were cast down before the crag.' What is meant by 'were cast down before the crag?' The 'crag' was Christ. 'They were cast down before the crag,' by 'before' is meant compared to; the 'judges' are the great, the powerful, the learned. They are called 'their judges' as if judges of conduct and proclaimers of verdicts. Aristotle said thus and so: compare him to the crag and he is cast down; for who is Aristotle? Let them learn that Christ said thus and so, and he trembles among the damned. Pythagoras said thus and so, and Plato too: compare them to the crag, compare their authority to that of the Bible, compare those arrogant men to the crucifix; let us say to them, 'You composed your letters in the hearts of the proud; He affixed His cross to the brows of kings; afterward He died and rose again; you are dead and I do not want to ask how you may rise again.' Therefore, the judges were cast down before the crag; they seem to be saying something until compared to the crag." These are Augustine's words. Today, more than ever, as you can see, I have cited other sources, although we have gleaned from learned men that anything well said becomes ours through usage, for a right of ownership comes with usage in the verbal arena just as in the business domain. I have done this, however, so that you may have greater trust in my words since they have been confirmed by all this testimony. I admit, however, that in this area I have always carried great authority with you without any external support, not really through any merit of mine but because of your brotherly love. So much for the response to my happy astonishment at the unexpected wealth of learning in your letter, my dear brother. Nothing more shall I add except that everything contained in that little book of yours—and there was a great deal—I embrace with great approval and praise, and with sincere assurance I declare it to have been as helpful to my spirit as it has been enjoyable. Farewell, O you who are an honor to me.

Monza, 7 November.

Fam. XVII, 2.

To an unknown correspondent, * *a rebuke to an undisciplined youth.*

So far I have received only bad reports of your insufferable conduct, and each day they seem to worsen. I used to suffer in silence, and while preparing further punishment, I would chastise you with deadly silence, though you deserved worse and there was no lack of more subtle punishments. Because the distance separating us made me unable to chastise you with the rod, I have stopped the flow of my customary liberality since I had been too generous with you. I shall not return to my former generosity until you turn from the downward path of your adolescence toward the straight path of virtue, nor shall I believe anyone concerning your behavior except public report or personal experience. What makes me briefly interrupt my silence is this friend of ours who, if he would love you less, would enjoy greater trust from me. But granting that what he says of you is true—since human nature is such that everyone easily believes what he desires—persevere and apply yourself so as to compensate more speedily for your past laziness; but if what he states is false, behave so that it may begin to be true. I admonish and implore you for your own sake, if you have any concern for yourself, any love of honor, any fear of a bad name; for all that ever reaches me about you is nothing more than the first blossoms of hope, an uneasy expectation, and perhaps dubious promises for the future. If you trust in me, after I am gone you will gather the sweetest fruits from your present efforts and from this stage of your life.

*Presumed to be Petrarch's illegitimate son, Giovanni.

Fam. XVII, 3.

To Guido Sette, Archdeacon of Genoa, * *concerning the many difficulties in human affairs, and the unfortunate fate of the Genoese.*

The very complexity of human affairs causes me neither to approve nor disapprove of your plan. For who can give approval to your unexpected change of mind and your settling in the worst and most detestable of all lands? Yet on the other hand, who can blame you, things being as they are, for dreading the spectacle of your beloved homeland, and for preferring anything to beholding the people's misery? When you cannot offer assistance, what is better than to avert your gaze so as not to see your people's misfortunes? You would have to flee beyond the world not to perceive the events that you learned about with such sadness, that neither your strength allowed you to cope with nor your well-known humaneness and love of country allowed you to remain untouched. What would you like me to say except my usual words? Often have I given my opinion on this subject, and in the repetition have made it mine: "Nowhere on earth is life peaceful." In one place there is war, in another a peace sadder than war; in one place there is infected air, in another an even more fatal infected morality; in one place there is desolate famine, in another a flowing abundance more dangerous than famine; in one place there is wretched slavery, in another an insolent freedom worse than slavery; in one place there is thirst and a desert region, in another a widespread raging of rivers; finally in one place there is heat, in another cold; in one place attacks by beasts, in another the deceits of men; in one place a vast and horrible solitude, in another a rough and troublesome crowd. Thus the spot that we seek is nowhere. What are we to do? Depart more swiftly from this life? That is not allowed for any reason; it is not permissible. Let Anneus Seneca remain silent, for Cicero's opinion is better: "Both you," he says, "and all pious men must keep your soul in the body's custody, nor must you leave human life against the will of Him who gave it to you." Noble words and equally noble the reason when he adds, "lest you seem to flee the duty imposed on humanity by God." Words truly powerful and admirable. For if a soldier assigned a post by a temporal commander does not desert it except at his commander's order, or if he knows that he will lose favor by abandoning it, and thus fears shame and prison, lashes and death, what must we think of disobeying the orders of an eternal king? Thus clearly we must do nothing precipitously; patience overcomes difficulties, and the Psalmist

*See V, 16.

advises us best in telling us to wait for the Lord and to behave manfully so that we may respond fearlessly when He does call for us. In the meantime, silently and patiently waiting, let us try to become worthy of Him so the Lord will call us to sit at His right hand. We should listen to Cicero's advice that all the while "we cultivate justice and practice a piety that is good when directed toward our parents and neighbors, but finest when directed toward our homeland since this is a way of life that leads to heaven." What does he mean by these words if not, as our own writers state, that we are wayfarers who must climb to our native land in heaven on the wings of good works and with the steps of good thoughts? This will happen more readily, as he himself is pleased to note, if now while in the flesh we stand apart from it, and contemplating what is outside, withdraw as much as possible from it. To me, these seem sound counsels of holy and learned men regarding a serious problem. Yet Seneca's advice is rash and strange; while fleeing temporal tribulations, he falls into eternal ones, something that otherwise learned man did not see. All of these writers, then, come to one conclusion: the prison in which we exist must not be loved, yet release from it must not occur before the proper time lest, as happens to many, in the escape from this prison we perish in the precipice. We must so live in this prison as to deserve a happy departure from it at our appointed time. Doubtless insofar as the state of present life is concerned, to return to my point, I deny that any place exists under the heavens where countless troubles do not weary the noble spirit; thus, no one is so fortunate, no one so desirous of life who may not be overcome by losing control of his patience because of his hatred of life and at times his desire for death. Moreover, just as it is wretched to be on earth, so it is difficult to rise to heaven under the weight of our sins; and just as it is forbidden to depart hence of our own accord, so it is impossible to remain here even for a moment against the will of heaven. Therefore, wherever you turn, all things seem difficult, thorny, rough, and miserable. And yet, how great our blindness! While we often invoke death's assistance against life's weariness, still, all things considered, whether the apprehension of the conscience or the attraction of pleasures or the profound horror about death, we desire nothing more than to be here. At least for now let us desire to be elsewhere; and although guilty let us trust in divine mercy and wish eventually "to be set free and to be with Christ." But until that day comes, which is so desired or ought to be desired, I pray that we live with our minds in heaven and our bodies on earth, in moderation, in patience, in humility, and that we compensate for the wretchedness of places with peace of mind.

I was eagerly expecting you in Italy, as God is my witness, and was upset at your delays because the mild days of autumn arrived before news of your coming. For I had forgiven you, indeed had pitied you, when I left you behind ill at the height of the summer, nor would I have expected you, even when healthy, to expose yourself to Phebus's heat without any urgent need, nor to subject your delicate body in my company to the dust and perspiration resulting from the madness of Cancer and Leo: to such things was I born, as though to some fatal unmilitary destiny. Yet when the sun had already crossed into Virgo and was nearing Libra, I marveled at your slowness, and as I viewed the delightful Italian countryside and the tranquil heavens, I often said to myself: "What is he doing now except wasting away in Babylon's filth, unmindful of his promise and forgetful of our friendship? Why does such a lover of liberty and upholder of moderation voluntarily frequent homes of arrogant men? If he is attracted there by ambition, nothing is more vain; if by greed, nothing is more foul. What, then, is his purpose? Is it to quench his cupidity by accumulating possessions? In the search for them, desire becomes increasingly enflamed; remove wealth, and you will have removed the foundations of greed. For the poor man desires only the few things necessary for living, while the rich man, who has seen mounds of money, who has learned to admire grandiose and useless things, continuously yearns in his greedy mind for mountains of gold and rivers of silver. Wherefore, if we desire great wealth to limit or mitigate our greed, we are proceeding backward: it increases with our successes and stealthily steals upon us, and not simply greed will increase, but any need that may have been avoided. What is more, no effort will prove successful until one begins to understand that all these chains can be removed by contempt for riches, and not by riches themselves." Thus was I pondering, angered at you and at my fate, when suddenly an even sadder report of the unsuccessful Genoese war struck my ears like frightful thunder. Stunned, I stiffened and turning to you in spirit, said, "Alas, O friend fortunate even in your misfortune." For either you had foreseen that event, proving your great power of deliberation, or you happened to be absent without foreseeing any such event, and fate was at least rather kind in sparing you the spectacle of its onslaught. There is little question that, whatever the situation, slowness was better for you than speed; for at least you will not behold the misfortunes of your wretched country. What can I now honestly say, what words can I use to describe the magnitude of the event? What I feared has happened; if I say that, I shall be lying, for in truth what I scarcely believed possible has happened. The sea beheld the flight of the Genoese fleet and was stunned, for if rarity makes a miracle, what is rarer than the Genoese defeated at sea in actual battle array? However, neither the battlelines nor the fleets were fairly matched; instead there was a multitude of foreign troops and several nations against a single one, a greater army on one side, and a battle with the winds and the enemy that was certainly unevenly matched. Yet I cannot cease, nor will I ever cease, to marvel at the thought that never, since the days of our forefathers, has the valor of the Genoese and the distinguished banners of that city-state been known to fail in any maritime war, even when they were outnumbered. "But what am I saying or where am I?" to use the poet's words. This is the customary trust placed in fortune; we spend our lives on earth where good fortune never was, and never will be, of any duration. What makes us happy and sad are but dreams; God arouses us as we dream; His judgments are an abyss, while the depth of his counsels are infinite, and their loftiness immeasurable. Perhaps it was fitting to check with unexpected adversity an arrogance engendered by lengthy prosperity; often one brief hour can punish the abuses of many years, and so often nothing has proved more useful to fortunate peoples than the reminder that they are not exempt from fortune's whims, though presently blessed by fortune. Africanus's words, recounted by Panetius in Cicero's *De officiis*, come to mind: "Just as horses that have become wild through repeated struggle are wont to surrender to their trainers in order to be managed with greater ease, so must men, who have become unrestrained in their search for possessions and in their confidence, be led, as it were, within the province of reason and learning so as to understand the fragility of things human and the fickleness of fortune"; not much different than the shorter saying by the Psalmist: "Let nations realize that they are men." Excessive good fortune causes many to forget their human condition; when this happens, the whip is not merely useful but necessary to rouse them, thus making them feel that they are men and not gods.

Inflated by many errors, and especially by the false opinion about his divinity to the point of believing his court flatterers that he was the son of Jove, Alexander the Macedonian was given warning by a wound received in India that he was a man, not a god. This he openly confesses in Seneca, "All say that I am the son of Jove, but this wound proclaims that I am a man." Wise words, indeed, coming from a man accustomed to believing in fate rather than in reason. If military victories made Mars believe himself the god of war, if the accomplishments by the founders of certain arts earned for them the names of divinities, why, after so much success and so many victories at sea, should one not believe that the Genoese were gods of the sea? Now events have taught us that they are men of the earth. Their prosperity has perished, but not that alone; for with it has also vanished error, the companion of prosperity. When a certain quantity is removed from one of two contrary things, the other necessarily increases by the same amount; consequently, while their good fortune has diminished, their reason has increased. And it is she who must be summoned for deliberation that her enemy, prosperity, did not allow until now; she will alleviate our incredulity and our sorrow; she will show us the ways and constancy of fortune. How many times did Hector or Hannibal or Pompey emerge the victor? And yet each was ultimately conquered. Perhaps for this reason Julius Caesar, we read, ever zealous in combat, began to be more cautious toward the end of his life; he whom nature had endowed with the greatest gifts and skill, whom long experience had made most learned, knew the roots of his good fortune, and knew through experience, as is written about him, "that he looked down upon everything from heights not stable but shaky, and that he stood upon uncertain ground." And so, bearing in mind the many dangers endured thus far, he calmed the fervor of his great spirit with prudent moderation. We err in a variety of ways in this area; for what seems fortunate is not, while what we hope will be long-lasting is not, and what disappears does not return. Nothing remains the same for long, nothing ends as it began; everything passes, time flows on, years fly by, the days hasten on, the hours fly on; the sun pursues its vaulted path, the moon daily changes and is always other than it was, never beholding her brother with the same eye. Whence come the very attractive variety and varied attractiveness of the seasons: thus the rose soon blooms where the snow was lately frozen, the tree trunk recently barren and parched is soon decorated with branches, while heavy rains solidify and make fertile the field reduced a short while before to dust by the summer. All things change their condition: lands and seas, the heavens themselves, and man, the most industrious and noble inhabitant on earth; his destiny is continually shaky, his mind agitated by emotions and his body affected by locations, his spirit daily diminishes, his memory ages and his talent grows dull, his health is uncertain and his strength impaired, his agility becomes sluggish and his beauty wastes away, his youth perishes while death pursues him and his life takes flight. Although this dizzying change does apply to everything, the swiftest of all is fortune's fluctuation, something apparently noted by the thinkers who made the revolving wheel one of her attributes. And still we marvel that she continues her usual ways? The vanquished can conquer when victors can be conquered; war is necessary both to conquer and to be conquered. Let whoever undertakes a long journey realize that at some point he will fail; if it happens differently, he ought to recognize that he has enjoyed good fortune above other wayfarers, and that it will go otherwise for him if he proceeds for too long. Know that those men whom you read about as perennial victors avoided adversity either by retirement from military service, which perhaps happened to my Africanus, or by an early death. For many, and especially for Alexander whom I mentioned a short while ago, this inspired great admiration among the unlearned and the ignorant. Livy says of him: "I do not, to be sure, deny that Alexander was a captain of consummate merit; but nonethless he became more illustrious because he alone died young while his fortune was still on the rise and he had yet to experience serious reversals. For, to bypass other celebrated kings and leaders who afford examples of the decline of human greatness, what else but a long life could have subjected Cyrus (whom the Greeks in their panegyrics exalt beyond all others) to the caprice of fortune? And the same was, lately, true of Pompey the Great." These are Livy's words.

Those who aspire to untroubled happiness must desire this assistance afforded by a brief life against a changeable and unstable fortune. Perhaps it does happen to kings or captains, but not to kingdoms or cities, which I would not with Cicero call immortal, but enduring. Therefore, in such a period of time, such as the extended life of a state, it is most difficult to imagine its people, though victorious, not having occasion to behold the two faces of fortune, and not having to feel the shame of defeat. How often was Rome conquered, though a conqueror of all? The days of calamitous battles, which in histories are called cursed and black, unpropitious, unmentionable, and funereal, bear witness to this; as do such places of sad memory as Allia, Cremona, Ticino, Trebbia, Trasimeno, Cannae, and Thessaly, where Rome defeated herself with her own hands. Had we borne this in mind before recent events, we would have realized that Genoa too could be conquered. But so it goes; bitter considerations offend the sensitivity of an infirm mind, and rare is the person who willingly ponders the causes of grief; for the mind readily turns to more pleasant thoughts. I too must confess to not anticipating this day, not because of my lack of knowledge of fortune's revolving wheel, but because of my belief that proven valor could impede it; comparing you with all other foreign powers dwelling by the sea, I was convinced that you would enjoy continuing success. This I confess was my expectation, this I have said, this in short I put in my writings. Do you wish to hear this writer's great boldness? So far I do not regret having written it, although the fact does remain that I had written and hoped for something false. Can it then be that I have no shame at having lied? Certainly I would be ashamed if I thought myself a liar. But in this instance I have always expected victories and uninterrupted good fortune, provided the unity of civic harmony had not been shattered, but instead it was. Some men maintain that soldiers willingly allowed themselves to be vanquished out of hatred for their leader; if so, this is nothing new since from history we know of such happenings. Others say that the commander surrendered out of hatred for his soldiers; if we accept this, there is no need for an example of such a disgraceful action. The one reason for my sadness and profound astonishment was the spectacle of your spirits confused and crushed by fortune's first blow; I once thought that your spirits would remain undaunted, even if an enormous catastrophe destroyed all the heavens. It was dark when the calamitous news suddenly reached me from nearby, and the dark shadows of night seemed to deepen for me; I shuddered in body and in mind, and upon recovering sadly seized my pen. There was much to write about; my grief and indignation prompted many ideas, and many words of consolation occurred to me. My simplicity gave me the necessary confidence to strengthen your wavering spirits with my words, just as from the beginning I had always tried to discourage an Italian war and subsequently applauded your seeking victory over an external enemy. But now I see lying prostrate and conquered a people who had never feared misfortune while they stood firm and unconquered. In addition to rationalizations and encouragements, I had in mind and had already begun compiling examples of virtue from every past nation, particularly from the Romans, who were foremost in every virtue, but above all in military valor. After many defeats, especially after Cannae (which historians call "almost the final wound of the Empire"), with their strength diminished but their spirits improved because of the calamity, they continually returned to do battle until finally defeating their victors with a glory all the greater because they had seemed so distant from any hope of victory. I added that indomitable people, the Spartans, so similar to the Romans in their largesse of spirit, because after their defeat at Thermopylae by an enormous Persian army and their subsequent crossing into Asia with an avenging fleet, they often emerged victorious after moments of utter despair. I included the Athenians, who had undertaken a war with the Spartans and reached the extreme of misfortune with the loss of their leaders, the annihilation of their army, and the destruction of nearly their entire fleet in the sea near Syracuse; yet they preserved their courage, which was all that they had left, and shortly thereafter magnificently avenged themselves on land and on all the seas. Nor did I overlook the Carthaginians, courageous although faithless and changeable, who had often borne arms and overcome misfortunes, but preferred in the end to perish rather than to become enslaved. So as to have exemplary individuals follow exemplary peoples, and to shame an entire people for not daring what a single man had done, I included Marcus Claudius Marcellus; after he had

held his ground against a persistent enemy throughout an entire day only to be defeated on the next, he returned to the fray on the third day
to defeat Hannibal, who had defeated him. Caesar was cited because,
after his defeat at Dyrrachium (though he was not actually present), and
after his reform of the army and the loss of his bravest captain, he was
soon victorious in the great battle of Thessaly. Furthermore, so as to
counter masculine cowardice with feminine virtue, I called to mind the
glorious deed of Thamyris, queen of Scythia; after suffering tremendous defeats at the hands of the dreaded Persian king, Cyrus, she still
refused, with her army destroyed through deception and with her only
son dead, to submit to womanly dismay. Instead, in an equally skillful
attack upon the victorious king, with good fortune complementing her
valor, she slew the king and 200,000 Persians, thus exacting a revenge
that will remain in eternal memory.

Although I first began dictating these and similar deeds with great enthusiasm, by early morning I learned that fancy words were useless, that
the defeated people's spirits had seriously fallen, and that they were considering plans that I still know not whether to call too modest or too
cautious; I shall await the end, when judgment will be simpler. At that
moment, however, I do admit to feeling enraged; throwing down my
pen, I said to myself, "What am I to do? Am I forgetting the saying
that 'words do not produce valor'?" That city's glory is now finished,
and one must accept it. What people can enjoy immortal valor when
Rome's was mortal? Cities age as does the earth; they decline and die; all
things hasten to an end, the common lot of creatures and of all things
must be borne with courage. "All things that are born die, and those
that grow become old." Even had Sallust not said this, we still would
know it, but we would conceal it with self-deception; and yet when we
do observe the inevitable, we lament in astonishment, as though we did
not know it. I am really not lamenting what has happened, but I do
grieve that it happened in our day, even though such mourning is not
manly or courageous. What does it matter how you come to know that
all things perish, when you do realize it? Some Romans prophesied the
end of the Empire, whose real end we have yet to see but whose condition is worse than the end; they thus foresaw something about to perish
that we have already seen do so. Even though we had never seen this
fate befall the Genoese, we still could not be unaware of it, judging
from the past and applying its lessons in the future, nor were we unac-
quainted with human diversity and inconstancy. Proud Babylon fell,
and that celebrated power that threatened heaven can now be scarcely
recognized in its remains scattered over the earth. After flourishing some
1,300 years, the Assyrian rule was passed on after the death of their

effeminate king through the prefect Arbatus to the Medes and the Persians; after a short while, however, it was seized by Macedonian armies and taken to the Peleian stronghold from which it departed even more swiftly. For although many years elapsed between the beginning of Macedonian rule and the last king, nevertheless between Alexander, the victim of ambition for the monarchy whom the Greeks called the Great, and Paulus Emilius, who brought the kingdom to an end, leading in triumph the captured Macedonian kings and taking his name from badly defeated Macedonia, which he had reduced to the level of a province, exactly one hundred years elapsed, unless my calculation is faulty. The kingdoms of the Medes and of the Persians lasted twice as long. Lest the South perhaps envy the East and the North, that part of the world also suffered its misfortunes and ascended through many periods of hardship before its final collapse. Search for Carthage, and you will find not even its ruins. Valerius says: "Where are the lofty ramparts of proud Carthage? Where is the maritime glory of that famous port? Where is the fleet dreaded on every shore? Where are the numerous armies? Where the great cavalry? Where those spirits unsatisfied with the immense expanse of Africa? All of this was the result of the good fortune of the two Scipios." But I ask you, O Valerius, where are the famed conquerors of Carthage whom you mention? You will answer, "They were men, and death exercised its rights." But where, I ask, is the Roman Empire, the last and strongest of all, which the Assyrian king's vision depicted in iron, the metal superior to all others? Indeed, after gold, silver, and bronze had been shattered by the unyielding stone, the iron mixed with clay—as may be seen in the last section of the vision—was not destroyed by anything other than the rustiness of old age, as is characteristic of iron. But to conclude with a final and convincing argument, great consolation can be found in so many examples. I am not snatching all hope from you, but I am sprinkling caution with my words: scorn the flattery and threats of fortune, and prepare yourself not so much for what cannot be avoided as for what can happen, for it is doubtless inevitable. We are at war with a powerful and implacable enemy; we cannot hope for peace, but we can hope for victory unless we surrender, unless we yield to false opinions. Foolish is man to hope for anything eternal on earth, when we see that kingdoms are mortal. Farewell.

Fam. XVII, 4.

To the same correspondent, * *concerning the same matter.*

Waiting is a punishment, so I have determined to set you free forthwith. A few days after the first announcement about the defeat, a solemn legation arrived, showing what I would call a dignified sadness, "bearing the great majesty of their misfortunes," as Statius elegantly puts it. Their eyes revealed the shame of their suffered disgrace, the grief of public injury, and pity for their homeland; mingled with these smoldering feelings were also bitter indignation and a burning spark for revenge. The negotiations were lengthy and need not be described here. At last a day was set for a final meeting; at dawn we were all summoned, and I was requested to remain with those waiting for our lord; I readily obeyed because of my desire to learn directly from witnesses the sorry tale being publicized in various versions by the multitude. We convened in the royal palace in the great hall with walls and beams sheathed in gold, so marvelous in its remarkable splendor. After many courtiers had gathered, I found myself by chance next to the head of the legation, a prudent man knowledgeable in letters. Given this occasion, I conversed with him on various subjects, and among the first was you, whom he knew well; the next was his country's state of affairs, a much sadder and prolonged discussion, which can be summarized as follows. The entire blame for the unsuccessful battle falls upon the commander, whom he wished had rather been a Carthaginian leader, for we know that they crucified not only frightened or rash leaders but even unsuccessful ones! The cause of all this dismay, I learned, lay not in the fear of an enemy who had to pay with much bloodshed for its empty victory and not in our soldiers' lack of confidence, for even now they feel confident of their superiority over the enemy. It lay instead in what we feared from the beginning: the danger and fear of internal discord since the foremost leaders who ought to have pitied the oppressed masses were suspiciously seeking excuses to take advantage of the shameful situation in order to establish a tyranny. Beset on one side by the enemy and on the other by citizens even worse than the enemy, the terrified people turned for assistance to this truly righteous prince. During these lengthy discussions, everyone was introduced to our lord, including a sizable group of famous men. Then the head of the legation spoke thus: by order of his people, he committed himself to our lord's service together with his city and its citizens, its fields, sea, land, towns, hope, resources, and well-being,

*See V, 16.

and finally all things human and divine from Corvo to Porto, which, some believe, was sacred to Hercules, and was once called Meneco but now is popularly called Monaco. In the surrender he included both boundaries, adding other conditions too tedious to enumerate, which were then written down by a notary and publicly read in a distinct voice. In the evening some council members asked me to respond to the envoys' words and to deal with matters of great import since it would be highly pleasing to our lord. Although I did entertain many possibilities—whether to speak mournfully or splendidly, or whether to restore hope or deplore the calamity—and although that evening would have more than sufficed, nevertheless, knowing very well the difficulty of giving adequate expression with my own words to others' feelings, I used as an excuse the lack of time for so important a task. To this I added that one word from our lord to the pathetic legation would mean much more than another's words. And I was not mistaken, for he so responded that no one could have been more effective, although others might perhaps have been more eloquent. The tenor of his reply suggested his lack of trust in his own powers and virtues, but his faith in divine assistance; with no desire to extend his borders, yet out of compassion for a friendly people he would accept such a demanding and difficult undertaking. Thus he would offer them his protection with the promise to give whatever advice and influence at his disposal, their republic as much aid as possible, extensive assistance to their suffering people, and justice to all; then too he would pray to God and to all the saints (a considerable portion of his speech had a large listing of the more celebrated ones) in the hope that they would happily bring to pass what he had proposed with devotion and faith. What can I say? In the name of our friendship I swear that, as he spoke, I could not check my tears; and I believe that others were affected in much the same manner, judging from everyone's steadfast gaze, attention, and silence. To such an extent did that great man sympathize with the tribulations of the Genoese, appearing ready to assist them with such magnanimity that if he lives long enough—for on this do all things turn—real hope may exist for a great victory or an honorable peace. For if we have seen the fortunes of war often fluctuate at a change in commander, what else do you think is to be expected with so many legions and such military power? If, indeed, he were to realize our hopes, he would forge for himself eternal honor and immortal glory from others' calamities; but if some whim of fortune thwarts his praiseworthy inclination, he will personally deserve considerable credit for his pious intent.

Even though I have said much in these two letters, there still remains more to say. You have heard me recount past events and present conditions; if you were to ask my view of the future, I would not dare put it in writing, lest perchance fortune in her usual fashion would go on a rampage; then I would suffer censure by the multitude, which will be unaware of my opinion if I remain silent. To pass over other things, then, that raise my hopes more than usual, this much is certain and corroborated by wise men, namely, the best kind of state is one governed justly by a single man. But in preparation for any eventuality, I shall end with Augustine's words; he says: "The city that begot us in the flesh remains. May God be praised! Would that it could beget us spiritually and pass over into eternity with us. But the city that begot us in the flesh does not endure, the one that begot us spiritually does. Did the Lord in erecting Jerusalem lose His handiwork by sleeping or let the enemy enter by not watching over it? Unless the Lord watches over the city, those who watch over her do so in vain. And what city? He who watches over Israel does not sleep nor is sleepy." A few lines later, he adds: "Why are you terrified that earthly kingdoms perish? So that you would not perish with earthly kingdoms, a heavenly one was promised you; for it is foretold that the former would perish altogether; nor can we deny that prediction. Your Lord whom you await said to you, 'Peoples will rise over peoples and kingdoms over kingdoms'; earthly kingdoms undergo change, and He will come concerning whom it is written, 'And His kingdom will have no end.'" I am not going to try to persuade one whom I know is persuaded even without my speaking. You know that it is particularly characteristic of a man and of a noble spirit who despises human things to be prepared for anything that can happen to man; this applies not only to those uncertain and, as they say, fleeting goods of fortune, but also to his own body and those of his loved ones, and even to his friends and to his homeland, which is dearer than life itself to the good man, but only if his spirit is secure which, as it seemed to saints and philosophers, cannot be harmed by others, but only by itself. All other things must be borne with magnanimity, for if there is no flight from the uncertainty of fortune and if evil, though light, grows heavier with impatience, what expectation remains except that of patience? Farewell.

Fam. XVII, 5.

To the same correspondent, * *in praise of the rural life.*

You have heard about the hope and comfort that public misfortune offers; now it is time to turn my writing to happier ends. I have heard that, because of pressing tasks, you have fled the city for the country. Whenever possible I unconditionally praise this practice, indeed in the past I have written at great length about the sufferings resulting from urban concerns and the peacefulness of the solitary life. Even though I have often spoken on this subject, it is an area about which I shall say much more if I am permitted to live so long. I am speaking as does the multitude, for truly nothing in human affairs is enduring, not merely joys or fleeting prosperity, but even grief or the laments that begin and end with us. And yet in these obviously narrow confines of life, what is more worthy of constant repetition than something that will always be on my mind until death? I speak of my quest for tranquillity and solitude concerning which I have already published separate treatises more for others than for myself, lest perchance a forgetfulness resulting from silence turn my mind to new cares. That does not seem likely to happen now, since my conviction has so grown with time, becoming hardened and tough, that it has become a habit. But to bypass what is common knowledge in order to arrive at the reason for this letter despite my many incumbrances, I hear that you stayed for several days at my country place at the source of the Sorgue, and that the pressure of your responsibilities was alleviated by its lovely tranquillity. This gives me pleasure, and I commend your action; for unless love for my possessions and the influence of my long-standing habits deceive me, that rustic retreat is truly a dwelling of peace, an abode of leisure, a refuge from toil, a hospice of tranquillity, a workshop for solitude. Nowhere, in my opinion, can exceptional works of the mind be molded more magnificently: I speak as an expert, provided, however, something of exceptional distinction can emerge from this paltry and limited talent of mine. There, indeed, can be found a welcome relief from anxiety and an enjoyable diversion for the busy mind; there can be found silence and freedom, untroubled joy and joyful security. Banished are city cares, heated controversy, and the clatter of revelers; there one cannot hear the clash of arms, the empty joys of victory, or the unjustified sorrow born of the contrary winds now afflicting us. In the crystalline gorge silvery fish sport, oxen scattered in the meadow bellow at a distance, wholesome

*See V, 16.

breezes murmur as they lightly strike the trees, multicolored birds in their branches sing in various modes, and if you will allow me to use my own verses, "in the night Philomena laments, the turtledove weeps over her friend, and the river murmurs as it issues from its source." Moreover, the peasant silently concentrates upon his rustic chores, and stooping over the ground, produces sounds and sparks from his mattock worn by toil; in short, the dwelling is joyful, heavenly and divine. Therefore, if you place any credence in my words, as often as possible flee there as to a port from the storms of the Curia, since there, just as in the port of Brindisi, you can moor the restless ship of your mind with but a quivering hawser. Make use of my books, which too frequently mourn their absent master and their changing guardians; make use of my garden, which, as far as I can determine, is unique in all the world, and implores assurances from you and from our Socrates not to let it suffer in my absence. I shall indicate for you the appropriate time for planting trees that perhaps differs from that of other farmers because of the different soil. I have heard the old men of my village and especially my overseer, a worthy man experienced in agricultural matters, say that anything planted there by 6 February takes firm root, never suffering the adverse influence of the stars. I beg you, therefore, especially if the moon is favorable, to plant something new; then perhaps, if fate allows us to spend a placid old age there together, the site may be more pleasing and the shade thicker because of your labor. Make use of the small trees—the oldest were planted by Bacchus and Minerva, the younger by my own hands to have shade not only for our descendants but for ourselves. Make use of my small home and my simple bed, which will not miss my presence once it has received you into its bosom.

"But where are you now getting this extensive description?" you will wonder; your wonder would cease, however, if you knew the place from which I write. Nearly in the center of Cisalpine Gaul is a most fertile and lovely hill on whose slope struck by Boreas and Eurus stands the castle of San Colombano, celebrated for its location and very well protected. The base of the hill is washed by the Lambro, a small but limpid river navigable for small craft, that flows through Monza and empties into the Po a short distance from here. To the west, there is a pleasing solitude and delightful silence as well as an unencumbered view; never do I remember seeing such a splendid and impressive landscape from so slight an elevation. One slight turn and Pavia, Piacenza, Cremona, and many other celebrated cities can be seen, at least according to the inhabitants; how true this may be, I have been unable to determine on this cloudy day, but I do believe it of those three cities, having seen them with my own eyes. Behind us lie the Alps, which separate us from

Germany with their snowy peaks touching the clouds and the heavens; before us lie the Apennines and countless towns, Casteggio among others, famous for its historical connections with the days of the Punic War, as well as the banks of the Po where Marcellus, the Roman commander, killed King Viridomarus of the Gallic Insubres in a vicious and uneven battle, and returned for the third time with the splendid spoils of enemy generals; beneath us lies the Po itself dividing the fertile countryside with its serpentine course. When I first stood on this hill, what do you think were my thoughts or desires? You may perhaps think that they were how I might subjugate those cities, or how many plows I could use to till the soil, how many herds could fill these delightful pastures, how many ships could transport foreign goods up the river, how many legions could trample those green fields, or what pleasures I could enjoy in this lovely countryside? It was none of these; I have set different goals for my life. And so? You must know that I never look upon lovely places without a quick return in memory to my country home and to my friends with whom I would very gladly, God willing, spend the brief remainder of my life. Thus, thinking of you and of that country abode, I meanwhile committed to memory all the things that I wished to write you since I had no writing materials, and when I returned home my memory faithfully restored them to me. I am thus writing you at night, from a bedroom worthy not of a philosopher or poet but a king, all those things that I thought about before sunset while standing alone on a grassy knoll in the shade of a huge chestnut tree. Farewell.

21 October, from the castle of San Colombano.

Fam. XVII, 6.

To Bernardo Anguissola, Governor of Como.*

Customarily a lazy horse is prodded by both spurs; my slowness is whetted by triple ones: the sight of a new place, my desire for a sweet friend, and the fulfillment of my promise. Certainly I am as eager to behold Como, that nearby city encircled by the airy hills of Cisapline Gaul, lying at the foot of the Alps and overlooking a celebrated lake, as I was to see Campanian Cumae so often. But much more readily would I see a friend such as yourself, for I firmly believe that nothing gives greater pleasure to my eyes than to behold the face of a much-desired friend. Added to my twofold desire is the sacred pledge of my word, for I did indeed promise to come, and have no regret at having made the promise, only shame at not having kept it. I admit that each goad taunts me, all three gnaw at me; but, O most excellent man, what am I to do? Do you not behold Aquarius violently pouring raging rain from his brimming urn? At present rushing down from the heavens is not rain but rivers; every road has become such a raging torrent that wayfarers must swim rather than travel along it. But what am I saying? I must be mad! So eager for tranquillity, I tremble at the thought of one day's journey, let alone a journey of several days in the dead of winter across the Alps, which are perhaps too well known to me. The person who orders me to go is probably the same who orders you to remain, though you are eager to depart; thus scarcely any living being is satisfied with his lot. I shall nonetheless obey since my wish is to deny nothing to the one requesting my departure, and all the more readily because, to speak honestly, he is not commanding but requesting, thereby surpassing his enormous authority with his celebrated kindness. Moreover, however much I may dread the difficult road and harsh winter, I am just as delighted at the reason for my journey, inasmuch as I go to reestablish peace between the two most powerful nations of Italy. Would that I could accomplish that as successfully as I go willingly! When I return, however, together with temperate springtime, my priority will be without a doubt to behold that remarkable spot and to visit once again my fine friend, thereby keeping both my promises. Farewell.

*An official in the government of Galeazzo Visconti of Milan, and the governor of Como. That his friendship was very close may be seen in the fact that Petrarch announces his death in his beloved Ambrosian Virgil, referring to him as "an outstanding and unusual soldier among my rare and truly close friends."

Fam. XVII, 7.

To the same correspondent, a recommendation for a friend crossing the Alps.

I am sending you, as usual, something requiring work rather than enjoyment; you probably wish that I were living in another part of the world from which I could demonstrate as much love for you but make fewer demands. The fellow whom you see before you is a foreigner by birth but a friend in spirit who loves and cherishes not me alone but whoever he knows loves me; therefore, consider him a friend; his face is unknown to you, but the man's spirit, believe me, is full of kindness. I ask you to show him the way, as you recently did for others, so that his journey over the Alps into lower Germany may be safe and brief. He had come with the apostolic legate to spend a year in Italy, but love for his country and for his family overcame him, and the year seemed longer than a century, thus preventing him from completing the twelfth month; he is thus returning, driven on the one hand by boredom and on the other by his yearning. He has an aged mother; he fervently wishes to arrive home before her last day and thus fears too much delay. Among his other qualities we find this admirable filial devotion, and by measuring his mother's wishes by his own desire to see her, his becomes even more consuming. You too can easily imagine his mother's state of mind if you recall your own mother, and your compassion will match his devotion when you consider that he is the only child of an aged widow. For even precious things usually have little value when abundant and enduring; in this instance, however, they all concur to become priceless, for he is a son, an only child, and his very appearance testifies to the kind of man he is. Even before coming to Italy, he was far from his mother, but now his innate patriotism and his friends' expectation, but especially his mother's age and solitude, hasten him onward. Do assist as you can such a pious and truly burning desire, and claim for yourself a portion of such devotion, though it be in a foreigner. Return a son to his mother, return a citizen to his beloved country, lest we consider foreign hearts incapable of feeling the sweetness of their land, and are tempted to limit such feelings to Italians or Greeks. In any event, inquire of anyone you please, not only those considered more cultivated because they live by the Rhine, but those from backward countries flanking the Danube or even the Don; they will tell you that nothing is more pleasing than their native skies, nothing more agreeable than their lands; but beware of making comparisons, for they will call Italy barbarian. Farewell.

*See XVII, 6.

Fam. XVII, 8.

To Brother Matteo of Como, * *that the desire for knowledge grows more honorably by learning than does the desire for possessions by amassing them.*

I truly rejoice and exult each time I meet a man of letters desirous of learning. Usually greed is aggravated by amassing possessions, becoming all the more enkindled with success; why this is so I know not, since, assuming the presence of reason in human counsel, he who has the most ought to desire the least. Sleep is driven away by sleeping, weariness by repose, and hunger by food, while thirst is quenched by moderate drinking. Astonishing as this may be, greed alone is whetted by acquiring, and Horace seems to be singing to deaf ears when he says, "Let there finally be an end to seeking wealth, and when you have acquired more than most men, may you fear poverty less, and begin setting limits to your toil once you have what you craved." Sound advice, if it penetrated the mind. But we mortals, filled with immortal cares, especially begin to fear and to toil as we approach the end; the desire for money grows as our money accumulates. Alas, how much more dignified and better would it be if our desire for knowledge and passion for letters were to increase with learning, particularly since the goal of accumulating possessions is limited and defined, whereas learning and progressing have no limit until we reach our end. Let no one believe that he has made sufficient progress, for that man never strives to reach the summit who thinks he has reached it. He who arrives at his destination overcomes the journey's labors, as does he who believes that he has arrived; he would therefore stop, and would not only not progress but even regress. Unlike the wealthy merchant who, at journey's end, has heaped and stored money in his home, the scholar who has put an end to his reading and thinking cannot consign it to memory as to a moneybox. For it is untrustworthy and contains many cracks and, if not constantly stuffed with some substance through study, daily loses something. Therefore he who does not learn forgets, and whoever neglects his memory, as if it were full and overflowing, will be astonished at its emptiness when he subsequently returns to it. Continually and without interruption one must study until the very end of his life; a few from the many celebrated examples may serve as reminders of this. Even Socrates, who might be called the father of philosophy, learned to play the lyre in his old age, while Cato devoted himself to Greek letters; when Pythagoras wished to become more learned, he did not

*Nothing is known about this correspondent except that he was a churchman.

fear toil, nor did Pliny fear death nor Democritus blindness. Cicero, the prince of eloquence, is said to have excused himself at the point of delivering an oration because he had not read anything in three days; and Plato, the prince of philosophy, had beneath his head on his deathbed at the age of eighty-five not sacks of money, witnesses to an old man's greed, but books, witnesses to philosophical study, as though silently saying, "On these books that supported my mind during life, I can now at least rest my body as I die, since there is nothing else I can do." We know that Carneades in his extreme age, with his limbs growing cold, often became negligent of food because of his incredible mental ardor and his implacable thirst for learning; had it not been for a maidservant's devotion, he might have died of starvation. Yet, of all the examples at hand, none is more famous than Solon, the great lawgiver, who raised his head from his deathbed when surrounded by disputing friends on his last day; his response to his astonished admirers about the reason for such an unexpected movement was that he desired to learn from their discussion; and then he died. Nor was he undeserving of dying as he learned since, as we have read, he used to boast that he had grown old by learning something daily. O noble passion of renowned minds! As elders they wished to learn, not to become wealthy. Furthermore, Tullius justifiably berates those elders "who seek more provisions, the less road they have to travel." For that reason I like, and have often praised, the popular saying: "O happy mankind, if each man were as satisfied with his inheritance as he is with what he knows!" But we, questionable judges of our own affairs, seem quick to deem ourselves learned and wise, but never truly wealthy; from this derives the perversity that makes us both hungry for wealth and contemptuous of honorable study. Why, I ask, if not because we seek what we lack, and we neglect what we believe we abound in? This is hardly unnatural inasmuch as a false judgment precedes our choice. For money is useless and often fatal to many, whereas wisdom is never so deeply entrenched that more is not needed. Therefore, I congratulate you, my dear friend, for despising wealth not only in spirit but by profession, that on the contrary you are most eager for knowledge and for letters in which you are very learned, and that you zealously search for them wherever you can. Whence it happens that, though wealthy, you even knock at my door in the manner of a poor man, most worthy of being heard except that my poverty cannot satisfy your desire, forcing me then to say to you, "Go in peace, seek elsewhere, and approach a wealthier dwelling, for here what you seek is without doubt unavailable." Farewell.

Fam. XVII, 9.

To Marco da Genova,* that those who love intensely make poor judgments.

You are mistaken, my dear friend, if you believe my writings will please everyone as much as yourself. I am not the same in everyone's eyes; love is blind, lovers are blind, lovers' judgments are blind. "You are not the first to say this," someone will say; "it is an old saying." "It may be old, but it is true," is my response; "truth does not age, and its author was perhaps more gifted but not more truthful." What does it matter that someone else said it? Is it any the less true because many have said it? Someone else did say it, but being in agreement with it and considering it the truth, I yield to another's opinion. This being the case, I ask you to take care lest your indulgence, unrestrained in my praise, pose serious danger to both our reputations, lest you then appear an unperceptive judge while I, who might have found greater safety by remaining in hiding, may be subject through your doing to harsher judgments. But I have little fear that any new opinion will ever cause you to change your old one. Whatever happens, let us hope that the doors of our friendship always stand open to your friends; I wish nothing to be concealed from them regardless of their judgments. I shall confront them, and if by chance you and the others have differing opinions, I certainly hope that they will not love me any the less. In short, I would prefer them to accuse you of blind judgment, which love can easily pardon, than to accuse me of pride, which is an inexcusable evil, especially since I possess so little of those things in which men are wont to take pride. Farewell.

*See III, 12.

Fam. XVII, 10.

To Giovanni Aretino, * *why we do one thing while wanting another.*

Your recent letter has strengthened and reconfirmed three deep-seated opinions that I have long held concerning you, and has at the same time provided proof of your wisdom, virtue, and friendship. You so clearly set before my eyes what I swear to God is always there: the flight of time, ever so brief and uncertain. On the one hand you compile and enumerate with such seriousness my past activities, which you regard as praiseworthy, on the other my present ones, which you see as conflicting with my former ones and as antagonistic to the quest for glory. You then so kindly urge me to flee and, upon regaining my liberty so generously being offered me, not to forsake the foundations of a better life but rather to strengthen them, and to add wings to my mind and spurs to my pen in view of the dangers of prolonged delay. Consequently, impossible as it may appear, you now seem to me wiser, better, and more friendly than I had heretofore known you to be. But what do you think my response will be? Do you think I can say no? No indeed; perhaps with words I could, but not with my heart. I am truly convinced, there is no need for spurs; the truth is violent, it controls minds. Moreover, why should I not honestly confess to you what I dare not deny to myself? As I began reading your letter, I immediately said to myself, "This bears with it the bonds of truth; I am captured." How, therefore, can I now escape? With what skills can I set myself free? With what astuteness can I liberate myself? What shall I say except that mine is a fault held in common with all mankind? For what man has not done harm to himself, who could not profit from that old saying: "O foolish man, you have brought all these evils upon yourself"? Elegant and astute is John Chrysostom's treatise, which may seem to contain falsehood at first reading, but upon further consideration contains as much truth as any other. It is entitled *Nisi a semet ipso neminem ledi posse.* Hearing this, the multitude, that enemy of truth, will immediately become enraged, but if it were willingly or unwillingly to take reason's path, it would admit this truth. We suffer the evils that we have committed, and punishment falls back upon the doer. We are not struck down from the outside, nor is it even necessary; for believe me, there is no need for well-trained troops or machines to attack the walls or secretly dig tunnels. Each man possesses within himself a destructive enemy, his companion amidst his pleasures, whom he surprisingly obeys and obstinately sup-

*See VII, 8.

ports against himself. You will perhaps say, and before you do, I agree with you, "This is not a cleansing of one's fault, but rather having others share in it; accusing others is no excuse for ourselves; a partner in crime makes a guilty party more guilty, certainly not more innocent." Forgetting others, then, I return to myself. I see you, my dear friend, armed with the truth, an easy victor in this battle, should I resist. For nearly simultaneously with the blows of your arguments upon my brow, a transalpine friend in a touching but courteous letter struck my defenseless back, so to speak, likewise asking why I, so taken with rural tranquillity, have willingly fallen, in his opinion, into so many urban affairs. Moreover—take note of his ingenious artifice—so that his question perhaps not offend me, before asking it he wonders why he too detests Babylon's subterfuges and yet cannot flee them. So here we have two similar ways of thinking, prompting two friends from different regions of Europe to engage me in a similar kind of battle. But what would either of you say were you to know the state of my affairs, especially now as I write? While all the stars in heaven conspire to strike us not simply with rain but a flood, while winter continues harsh and unrelenting, I am being compelled to cross the Alps, which we all know so well; perhaps you will ask by whom. By whom do you think, except by myself, who am so devoted to a certain person that his sweet entreaties and, in Laberius's words, "the gentle, kind, and flattering speech of a distinguished man" have the power over me of an absolute command and the force of imperial majesty? Thus, nothing is more vile to man than himself, nothing more venal than liberty. To my other friend I shall respond in person, if I ever do arrive there alive and well—for his inquiry is somewhat difficult and, I believe, has much in common with yours. But with trepidation I am answering you in writing, not in order to seek pardon, as I have already confessed is impossible, but in order to defend myself, if I am allowed, not with examples from the indolent, ignoble, and unintelligible multitude, but with the glory and splendor of illustrious companions. What does the Apostle Paul, the greatest of men in every respect, what, I ask you, does he say? "I do not the good that I wish to do, but rather the evil that I do not wish to do." My dear friend, what can others say, if Paul speaks thus? You already know what follows, and the excuse he uses: "If I do what I do not wish, it is not I who bring that about but sin dwelling in me." Surely a dangerous and profound conclusion, one that I do not deny can be used against me. I cannot linger over this; yet I do want to indicate the reference in case you should become involved with such subjects. It is Psalm 118; and the difficulty near the beginning of the Apostle's text is certainly resolved by Augustine. Now let us proceed to less weighty matters. How did father Augustine himself act on the day of his conversion and during his salutary and difficult spiritual conflict, when he wished to go on to a better life and did not do so? What torments agitated him? What goads drove him? And yet, destructive restraints prevented him from crossing over when the only necessity was the will alone, not a lengthy preparation. Flaccus elegantly jokes about this, "A turbulent laziness disturbs us; we seek ships and chariots to live well; yet what you seek is here present." I enjoy recalling Augustine's difficulties and the internal warfare of his spirit: when his worst side had finally been vanquished, it gave his better side, as was fitting, a bright and eternal triumph. With still greater pleasure do I recall it since it occurred in this city where I am now experiencing something similar. Only the basilica of Ambrose stands between my dwelling and the tiny chapel where Augustine, at length the victor in the secret battle of his internal conflicts, was freed from the anxieties of his past life when the famed Ambrose baptized him. Immediately thereafter, the old and the new friend of Christ, both exultant with a great and sacred joy, together intoned to God their famous hymn of reciprocal praise and gratitude that was composed here and soon spread to all churches. Now with your permission, I shall cite Augustine's words about himself since it is nearly impossible to render as effectively that great battle within such a mind. He says: "In the torment of my irresolution, I did many bodily acts; sometimes men will to do bodily acts but cannot, either because they have not the limbs or because their limbs are bound or weakened by illness, or in some way unable to act. If I tore my hair, if I beat my forehead, if I locked my fingers and clasped my knees, I did it because I willed it; but I might have willed and yet not done it, if my limbs had not the pliability to do what I willed. Thus I did so many things where the will to do them was not at all the same as the power to do them: and I did not do what would have pleased me incomparably more to do—a thing too that I could have done as soon as I willed to, given that willing means willing *wholly*. For in that matter, the power was the same as the will, and the willing was the doing. Yet it was not done, and the body more readily obeyed the slightest wish of the mind, more readily moved its limbs at the mind's mere nod, than the mind obeyed itself in carrying out its own great will, which could be achieved merely by willing. Why this monstrousness? And what is its root? Let Your mercy enlighten me, that I may put the question: whether perhaps the answer lies in the mysterious punishment that has come upon men and some deeply hidden flaw in the sons of Adam. Why this monstrousness? And what is its root? The mind gives the body an order and is obeyed at once: the mind gives itself an order and is resisted. The mind commands the hand to move, and there is such readiness that you can barely distinguish the command from its execution; yet the mind is mind, whereas the hand is body. The mind commands the mind to will, the mind is itself, but it does not do it. Why this monstrousness? And what is its root? The mind, I say, commands itself to will; it would not give the command unless it willed; yet it does not do what it commands." Thus does Augustine express his astonishment about himself. If this could happen to him, why am I surprised that it could happen to me? Yet, as you see, I am evading and rambling, withholding a brief, clear response to your, and my friends', stupor as well as my own – for I do not wish you to think that anyone marvels more than I at my errors and at the monstrousness of my spirit that desires one thing and does another. Why is it then that Paul, Augustine, countless others, and – to attend to our immediate question – why, I say, does our friend, myself, and perhaps you desire one thing and do another when clearly no one compels us to do so? Paul's answer to this is rather obscure, as I said; yet simplicity is the friend of truth and intimate discourse; let us, then, listen to Augustine's way of ending his astonishment. "The mind," he says, "does not totally will: therefore it does not totally command. It commands insofar as it wills; and it disobeys the command insofar as it does not will. The will is command-ing itself to be a will – commanding itself, not some other. But it does not in its fullness give the command, so that what it commands is not done. For if the will were so in its fullness, it would not command itself to will, for it would already will. It is therefore no monstrousness, part-ly to will, partly not to will, but a sickness of the spirit to be so weighted down by custom that it cannot wholly rise even with the support of truth. Thus, there are two wills in us, because neither of them is entire: and what is lacking to the one is present in the other." This is the naked and pure truth, my dear friend: we all truly wish to be happy, and we cannot not will this in any respect. Such a desire was implanted in us at birth, and is absolutely indestructible; I say that we all wish to be happy, but we all do not do what is necessary to be happy. In point of fact, very few wish to pursue that very special and narrow path to happiness, nor do they truly desire to pursue it, but rather they believe that they desire it rather than will it. This is the destructive sluggishness and perplexity of mind, about which I have already said much, afflict-ing those who do one thing when they seem to will another. Yet if they truly wished it, they would do it at any cost rather than what they do. If we wish, then, we can achieve happiness, that is, do what we know will lead to happiness and to true freedom of the spirit. But such would be the case only were we to wish it truly, fully, firmly, and in good faith. But perhaps to wish this is not exclusively dependent upon our free will, for although we do accept it as free, we so suppress freedom itself by the weight of our sins and by the bonds of terrible habit that without God's powerful assistance it cannot rise to noble things, so numerous are the obstacles restraining it and blocking its path. As Augustine says in the same work, "For I had but to will to go, in order not merely to go but to arrive: I had only to will to go—but to will powerfully and wholly, not to turn and twist a will half-wounded this way and that, with the part that would rise struggling against the part that would keep to the earth." Such are the anxieties, very similar to mine, that those extraordinary and great souls experienced; this is my response to you, my dear friends, as many as you may be, who are upset and concerned about me in my present difficulties. One thing does greatly disturb me: that I may not want wholly what I wish in part and, unless I am mistaken, what I desire to will fully. I say that I do want it, and I do not fear to say so with Christ as my witness; but I consider it fitting that what I sought unworthily I shall experience with bitterness and not with pleasure. The burden of fame disturbs my peace and my leisure; and it truly makes no difference whether it be a false or a true fame. How astonishing that a premature, let alone precipitous, fame is prejudicial to itself, and that an abundance of false fame hinders the growth of true glory! Had I not received before its time what I did not deserve, I could perhaps have deserved in its own time what I desired. Yet such is life; this is the source of all my agitation and restlessness, but even that is good since the experience is nothing new; for often celebrated lakes are disturbed by fishermen's nets, often famous forests are invaded by barking dogs. O blessed is the man, if there be one, able to hide amidst noble studies, shunning the multitude's clatter and man's persistent curiosity! Whoever has thus remained hidden emerges more celebrated, and will first begin to live when he seems to be dying. I know not whether my sinfulness or my misfortune envies me such a sweet hiding place; thus far, as often as I have attempted flight, my fame has always made me appear more loquacious and more mendacious than I wished. And thus, I, the great lover of solitude and of the forests in my youth, toil in cities amidst hateful crowds now that I am older; and that is bad for me. Often there comes to mind the words of the divine Vespasian, who, oppressed by the procession's slowness on his day of triumph and by the wearying crowd, declared himself justly punished for having sought, all the more shamefully because of its lateness, an honor undeserved by him and his ancestors. A profound and modest judgment indeed! Only one excuse can be presented in my behalf, namely, that although I do not deny my desire for true fame, I nonetheless do not recall any desire for the pomp that is now destroying me. In my eagerness to converse with you, I may have digressed a great deal. Here I come to the end of our discourse, and hope that you understand that, although labors follow upon labors for me and amidst these labors I daily find new occasions and causes for labor, nevertheless, even in fetters, if fortune condemns me to them, I continue thinking of liberty, and amidst the cities I continue thinking of the country, and amidst my labors I continue thinking of tranquillity, and finally, to reverse that worn saying by my Africanus, amidst my occupations I continue thinking of leisure. Meanwhile, know that it was granted me either through skill or nature after persistent and powerful meditation to consider vile what I am unable to achieve and pleasant what I am unable to avoid. Remember me and farewell.

Milan, 1 January.

Fam. XVIII, 1.

A response to the letter of Charles IV* offering excuses for his delay, and the weakness of his excuses.

You will find it astonishing that your imperial handwriting reached me nearly three years after leaving you. And yet it is so; not merely for you or your legions, but even for your messengers and your letters, O Caesar, the Alps are impassable. Just as I truly grieve over this, so I rejoice and personally congratulate myself, I must confess, that it did not happen without my saying something. Indeed I did cry out to no avail, nor were my two letters heeded; though written in a style perhaps too unadorned for your ears, they contained a great deal of truth, their writer's sincerity was pure, and the time seemed most opportune for action as the entire Roman world will testify. Now once again I am crying out, and it is up to you to decide whether I do so in vain or with effect; as for me, whatever I do in good faith is not in vain. For though it may profit no one else, it will certainly be to my benefit to have fulfilled my duty and satisfied my obligation. I have received an enormous reward for my affection, and truly there can be none greater for man: the testimony of Your Majesty that rewards my sincerity with high praise. My advice may not actually be taken, but I prefer my sincerity to remain firm without prudence than my prudence without sincerity. As long as my good faith and devotion are appreciated, I do not strive to be considered clever, and I shall patiently accept my lot, whether my advice is rejected or deferred; in fact, I shall also rejoice, rightfully boasting that you surpass not merely myself but all mortals in imperial dignity and in keenness of mind. I advised you and indeed believed that I had persuaded you of the necessity for hastening with your plans; but while it appeared so to me, it did not to you. You hold the reins and control the helm at sea, and therefore all depends on your judgment. It shall be said that I spoke in good faith, which suffices for me; prudence is required of those who profess prudence. Nevertheless, if you will allow me to explain my words, I urged speed in order to drive off your sluggishness, not to swing you to the other extreme. For I knew that, while haste is harmful in all matters, it is shameful in the government of the greatest empire; therefore I urged haste, a haste that was not precipitous but measured. "Moderate your flight," says Maro, which Macrobius glosses as "flight seems contrary to moderation"; and shortly thereafter he adds,

*See X, 1.

"Moderate your flight, meaning that it be neither swift nor slow, but at a middling and measured pace." Concurring with this opinion, Caesar Augustus "used to warn that in order to bring an undertaking to fruition, a diligent speed and a slow diligence should be observed at one and the same time; from these two opposites is attained moderation." Other analogous opinions are found there, but I shall return to the matter at hand. If then, O Caesar, you dislike this advice, let the good faith that prompted my suggestion please you. What do you think I will say? Certainly I have no additional advice to offer, but I wish for every decision that you do make to enjoy the favor of God Almighty, that He render your delay useful to the world and glorious for you; and in the Psalmist's words, "May He concede all things to you according to your heart and give strength to all your deliberations." But since I have not performed my duty until my tongue gives expression to all that my mind conceives, I shall now answer your letter, O Caesar; thus you may understand that I have laid aside my advice not as much for the reasons given in your letter as for the majesty of your name. For what person of sane mind would dare to think differently than Caesar, especially in imperial matters? If the discussion were about poetry or literature, I would perhaps make use of the freedom of the poet Accius, whom we learn usually did not rise in the presence of Julius Caesar when he frequented a poetic gathering, not out of contempt for the ruler, but out of confidence in his own art. Since the present matter concerns the empire, who would not rise in your presence, who would not yield to you, except an insane man, forgetful of everything? I speak, then, not to refute you but to answer your letter, not to oppose you but to open myself completely to you and to uncover whatever lies hidden in the shadows of my mind.

Your first excuse for the delay is the changing times, which you exaggerate with so many words that I am compelled to admire and praise the writer's skill rather than the Emperor's spirit. What is there at present, I ask, that did not previously exist? Indeed, what proportion of labors and dangers do we face in comparison to those of our forebears when Brennus, Pyrrhus, and Hannibal ravaged Italy? Is there any comparison? Every fatal wound that we may suffer is caused not by human destiny but by our own weakness; we mourn what our ancestors used to laugh at, we are horrified and benumbed by any difficult obstacle, whereas no intervening age and no people were ever more prompt in inventing excuses. You say, "Once upon a time the Roman Republic was wealthy." Who, I ask, produced that wealth if not the virtue of its citizens, their striving for moderation, their cultivation of justice, and their discipline in warfare? What do you consider greater, to have erected amidst many fierce and hostile peoples, amidst forests and thorny hills, an empire, a name unheard of and detested at that time, or to restore it from the ruin of old age while its foundations are still standing and the reverence for its name is still spread throughout the world? If anyone were to use the argument of changing times, I would not listen or, if I did, I would laugh. For believe me, O Caesar, the world is as it has always been, so is the sun, so are the elements; virtue alone has waned. Indeed some of the cities and buildings created by man have prospered while others have declined, some were overthrown early while others have risen in our day: ancient indeed are the vicissitudes of human affairs. What is your conclusion? Once again I ask you to believe me: if that Rome from which you assume your title and if that Caesar whose name and, hopefully, spirit you possess, were alive today, they would attain world dominion and the pinnacle of empire much more rapidly than in their own day. For at that time there was great opposition, serious peril, and enormous sacrifices for our people; now the road is level and easy, but the wayfarer is missing. Extravagance and laziness reign far and wide, shame dominates the world, which would quickly yield to Caesar's weapons, indeed would even take your side. For would not your name, supported by the few good men and lovers of virtue and the empire, easily win every battle against indolent extravagance and defenseless arrogance? Do you wish me not only to show you but to prove this to be so? Here it is. A few days ago, a man of low station rose above all others. He was not a Roman king, not a consul or patrician, but a Roman citizen of little fame, having no titles of his own and no statues of his ancestors, in short, not exemplary at that time for any virtue, and yet he declared himself the avenger of Roman liberty! A splendid declaration for an obscure man! At once, as you know, Tuscany eagerly offered him her hand and recognized his rule; gradually all of Italy, and then Europe, were following suit, and the entire world was on the move. What need is there for more? This we did not read but saw, and already justice seemed to be making its return together with peace and their companions, cherished faith, peaceful security, and finally traces of the golden age. Yet in the very flowering of events, he withered. Do not blame him or anyone else; I do not condemn the man nor do I absolve him; I am not his judge but I do know what I believe. He had assumed the title of tribune, the most humble of Roman honorary titles; if the title of tribune could achieve so much, what might the title of Caesar accomplish? But if you delay, if you hold back without considering time's flight, which I have placed before your eyes, the die is cast; the empire is ruined, liberty has perished. Do not, O Caesar, read this with distaste; what I have served you is perhaps less sweet than you would like. Do you not realize that bitter remedies alone are of any assistance in dissipating thick bile? I have not feared to tell you the truth, since I know that you love truth and despise flattery. This you do wisely, excellently, magnificently: such flattery is the poison of kings, the derision of the powerful, the death of rulers, and the weapon of deceivers. But we really do not know "what a monster the Empire may be"; this was the second of your excuses. I am astonished that you attribute this statement to Augustus when it belongs to Tiberius, unless it is because your preoccupation with present events is perhaps obscuring your memory of antiquity, or because by extending the title's meaning you call any emperor either Caesar or Augustus. Perchance you knowingly did it so that the title you opted to use would gain authority by coming from a famous source, aware as you were of the difference between Augustus and Tiberius: the first being the wisest and best of rulers, the latter repulsive and wild, and as a writer most fittingly said of him, "He was but mud mixed with blood." Yet you also know the occasion on which that statement was made; if you are somewhat forgetful amidst your many pressing concerns, you may read it in Tranquillus. Indeed, Tiberius said it when, following Augustus's death, he brazenly succeeded him, though truly unqualified for the office; but with ambiguous words and deceitful dissimulation he declined the title in an attempt to earn the false image of modesty, so much so that, as he wavered, a certain writer mocked and jeered him to his face, saying that while other men are late in accomplishing what they promise, he was late in promising what he had already accomplished. But even admitting that the statement was made by a good ruler, and assuming that it was spoken in all sincerity and that Augustus may have been its author, what then? He said, "You do not know what a great monster the Empire may be." But really we know it very well; it is an extremely powerful monster, but one that a skilled hand may control; it is an enormous but manageable monster, untamed only if not handled with care. Be bold, act, seize the reins in your hands and ascend the throne that is yours; if you are fearful, it will find other occupants. Julius Caesar, whose name you inherited, as I just said, rode a horse raised by him and impatient of other riders, which he held in great esteem; and you flee the throne that not only tolerates no other occupant but was held in the past by many princes and thus covets you as an occupant. It is certainly true that "all measures ought to be tried before turning to the sword"; this is your final excuse, which makes me wonder whether you had forgotten the words of Terence's braggart soldier: "It behooves the wise man first to try all things with deliberation before turning to arms." Your only defense of this opinion is that physicians advocated it and rulers learned it. You conveniently equated two disparate things since we know that rulers are wont to heal a sick world. Now they too are sick along with the others, the sick world lacks a physician, and universal death is at hand.

Do tell me, O Caesar, what have you not tried? Words, pleas, threats, flattery, armaments? What remains except to fall on your knees as a suppliant before the empire's enemies? If that is loathsome and unbearable to your ears, there remains the sword, that extreme remedy for unhealed sores. What more do you expect? That the Po return to its source? It goes where it is accustomed to go and the years flow with the river; to add nothing that you have not heard from me before, old age will replace your youth and death your old age. You will bring with you nothing more than whatever good or whatever evil you have done; you will leave behind nothing except the memory of your name and a bloodless little body, it also not yours but belonging to the earth and to the worms, which spare neither rulers nor commoners, which indeed devour nobler bodies with greater relish. What will become of the other things that appear to be yours? It is surely unavoidable that you must leave your wealth and your empire to another, and you know not to whom: this is the human condition from which no Caesar, no Roman pontiff, in sum no ruler or man is exempt. Now then, now is the time to show your concern for what you will not always be able to do, to wit, how you wish those things to be that are irrevocably yours: your soul and your reputation. Between audacity and laziness, I know not which to prefer; often audacity has proven the better course. I take no pleasure in extremes, I seek the mean; but, alas, I fear—and may I say this with due respect to you and to all who preside over an empire, thus assuming the responsibility of public office—that what I constantly repeat may be only too true, namely, that each defect has its own particular excuse while inertia has them all. Had Africanus deliberated a long time, Italy would have been deserted by its inhabitants and belonged to the Africans; had Nasica deliberated a long time, Roman liberty would have succumbed to the efforts and boldness of the Gracchi; had Claudius Nero awaited, not to mention other lengthy and useless things, but a single recommendation by the Senate that seemed necessary and brief, Hasdrubal and his brother would have trampled the Roman name. Why linger over minor examples? Had Julius Caesar himself, whom I have often named, been a procrastinator, he would never in so brief a period have founded and erected this powerful structure called the Empire, which now is barely being sustained with great enthusiasm. If you hesitate over everything and linger over individual obstacles, I shall make this prediction, perhaps quite displeasing to you but certainly rooted in my good faith (and I hope to turn out to be a false prophet): there will be no end to difficulties, obstacles will continue to increase, Italy will never see you and you will never see Italy, yet outside Italy I know not where you can seek the capital of the empire. I honestly believe your words that you were not drawn by ambition in aspiring to the empire, but fully cognizant of the difficulties involved you obeyed a divine bidding, for I do know your prudence and modesty. But note that this should have been your first and greatest goad for haste, given your trust in divine aid. Moreover, satisfied with your father's kingdom, you could have delegated to others the burden and honor of the empire; but the infallible Father, master and defender of all things, wrested it from others who desired it and placed it upon your shoulders. You obeyed. Not to have accepted the empire would have perhaps been a sign of magnanimity, but scholars will determine that; surely, too, it could have been rejected without infamy, but once accepted, it could not be neglected without infamy. For God—and I am certain that you will agree—God Himself, I say, and not your labor or ambition is the creator of the empire. Do you fear to proceed under His aegis when Abraham was about to slay his only son at His command, and Moses, a solitary shepherd, was unafraid of approaching an arrogant and obstinate king? This I do know: many things disturb you, and when they are resolved, still others will continue to emerge. Do you believe, O Caesar, that you could lead a life without care in ruling an empire, as does a shepherd in his hut? What are those excuses that you find so soothing? Is it not true that the number of blotches upon your personal reputation equals the number of public disasters throughout the world, that the many excuses that you try to extract from them are simply arguments you furnish against yourself? For upon whose honor do the kingdom's misfortunes weigh, if not its ruler's? You say that the empire's freedom has been destroyed: you, as father of the empire, will restore it; that the Romans have been subjected to the yoke of slavery: you will remove it from their backs; that justice has been prostituted in the brothel of greed: you will restore it to its sacred chambers; that peace has fled the minds of mortals: you will return it to its proper abode. For you have been born to it, destined to this office, so that you might do away with the republic's ugliness and restore its pristine face to the world. Only when you have fulfilled your duty will you appear to me a true Caesar and a true emperor; without doing so, neither a ruler nor a private citizen can expect any praise.

But you add—to my astonishment—that in those days of yore discord was unknown in Italy. When was that, pray tell? I can find no such period in annals, nor do I believe that it can be found. I maintain silence about the city's ancient origins and the first city walls moistened with fraternal bloodshed as well as the crowns sought through wicked crime. Once liberty was won, the number of times the indignant masses seceded from the patricians is attested by Monte Sacro, the Janiculum, and the Aventine. Pyrrhus crossed through Italy to bring aid to the rebellious Tarantines; in the same period there were revolts of the Brutti as well as the Lucani and other Italic peoples, all of whom had to be crushed by war in order to be returned to the fold despite their unwillingness. Hannibal followed; Capua remained unfaithful and ungrateful notwithstanding the great kindnesses by the Romans and, to speak frankly, the freedom that they enjoyed thanks to the Roman people. Who indeed did not revolt in those days? Reread your histories: eighteen colonies throughout Italy remained faithful, "through whose assistance," according to the great historian Livy, "the Empire of the Roman people at that time held its ground, and gratitude was expressed to them in the Senate and by the people." What good comes from recalling the rebellious Hernici or those perpetual enemies, the Volsci, or the Equi? How many near-civil wars with the Latini (when they seemed part of the Empire), how many cities overthrown, among the very first Alba itself, the mother of the Roman Empire! And what brought this about, if not the fear and recollection of rebellions? How often was there fighting with uncertain outcome against the Sabines, the Umbrians, the Samnites, the Etruscans, the Ligurians and the Boii and the Insubrian Gauls where now stand the cities of Milan and Pavia. But why look so far? Tivoli, Tusculum, and Preneste, three near-suburbs of the city of Rome, provided the causes and reasons for war when they not only abused their own power but rendered aid and refuge to foreign enemies. To these must be added Veio, which was barely destroyed in ten years, Fidena burned to the ground, Faleria conquered out of admiration for her loyalty, Naples captured by force, Brundisium, Corioli, Fregelle, Sora, Algidus, Corniculum, Sutrium, Boville, Veroli, and Fiesole, which provided the foundations of my homeland. It is with sincere regret that I include minor events with major ones, but just as nothing was difficult for a city already powerful and strong, so no thorn was too small for a weak and barely developed republic. Add the lengthy and difficult siege of Syracuse and that celebrated city's destruction, which moved even the enemy commanders to tears and commiseration; add Fermo and Ascoli and the Piceno, which was totally subdued, as well as the Vestini, the Marsi, and the Peligni, and among all these external conflicts, the internal discords, the Senate's arrogance, the tribunes' madness, the violent riots against the agrarian law, not to mention others that I cannot enumerate. Once power was returned to one man, add the countless conspiracies and the ambushes so often set, though in vain, against this venerable leader, not to mention the men who perished by poison or by the sword. Add the famine of Perugia and the siege of Modena and the rebellion of the colony of Cremona, which alone had been among the faithful few, as I mentioned. For too long I have pursued a historical journey, and I shall now cease. Every age witnesses many Italian secessions and rebellions so that a strong mind well-versed in antiquity is not unduly alarmed, and will view Virgil's words as truly fitting and as emerging from the bosom of Nature: "Italy, pregnant with empires and roaring with wars." For thus it was from the beginning, thus it is today, thus it shall be to the very end. But poverty, all too powerful, is delaying you. What does poverty have in common with Caesar, or how can he be poor who enriches others? It is attitude that makes the poor man and the wealthy man. "I am poor": and Julius was poor before the Empire; after the Empire he was not wealthy, for, in Anneus Seneca's words, "no one used victory more liberally and retained less for himself save the power of giving." Finally, "I am poor": poverty forced many into war and gave courage to many, especially when the opponent was wealthy, since, to be sure, war brings wealth to strong men. But "the scarcity of followers concerns me": war provides a following. "The multitude's opinion frightens me": sometimes certain tiny things have a great name, and often fame is more terrible than reality; opinion does not change reality; what your eyes do not see is seen by your followers' eyes not because they are keener but because they are nearer; many things feared by those viewing them from a distance appear ridiculous to those who are closer.

See how much I have written you in three letters, O Caesar, in the hope that you will perhaps listen after this threefold summons, and that, since you cannot do otherwise, from them you may perceive my feelings. I would prefer to be able to meet you with armed legions, prepared to obey your commands; instead I turn to the only things available to me, my spirit and my exhortations, and now I know not what else to say, nor do I understand what else I might add, should this not suffice. In you, O magnanimous Caesar, in you, I say, must be that flame that we hope would aid us and our tepid justice; if perchance it is extinguished, in vain do we blow into the ashes. As a wicked man said who nonetheless spoke the truth on this subject: words do not increase virtue; exhortation can arouse it but not provide it. Thus I shall say nothing more, save the principal thrust of the entire matter: all things, O Caesar, require deliberation, but nothing requires inertia, and there are times when it may be advisable not to deliberate too long. Farewell.

23 December.

Fam. XVIII, 2.

To Nicholas Sygeros, Greek praetor, * an expression of gratitude for his sending a book by Homer.

Yours was a noble gift from a noble spirit, as was fitting; for the acts of man are images of his spirit, and a man's character is revealed by the nature of his actions. Something unusual behooved your character, for truly you are an extraordinary man, far from the common crowd in your every effort. If you were part of the multitude, you would have done as the others; now instead you have magnificently revealed your true character, and in a single act demonstrated your friendship and nature. From Europe's furthest corner you have sent me a gift, one that could not be more worthy of you or more pleasing to me or more noble in itself. Antiochus, the great Syrian king, as some believe, or Attalus, the Trojan king, as Cicero prefers, "sent Publius Scipio some splendid gifts from Asia all the way to Numantia," gifts that the illustrious man did not conceal but "accepted in the presence of his army," as the same author states. His grandfather, the elder Africanus, gave magnificent gifts to King Masinissa for his meritorious service because he had given extraordinary aid in wartime to the Roman army. Others often did the same; but my purpose is not to enumerate either public or private generosity but to list a few so that you will understand my forthcoming words. Some people bestow gold or silver, dregs of the earth that are perhaps very desirable but also very dangerous; or they give booty from the Red Sea and the spoils of its rich algae, precious stones and gems, which, like comets, often reflect a mournful and bloody color; some give necklaces and belts, the glory of sooty artisans; others give strongholds and fortresses, the labor of filthy builders. But you, O best of men, have given none of these things that might display the wealth of the giver and the greed of the receiver. What is it then? A rare and pleasing gift that I wish were worthy of me but certainly is worthy of you, as I have said. And what would an intelligent and eloquent man give except the very source of wisdom and eloquence? You gave me Homer, whom Ambrosius Macrobius deservedly calls the source and origin of all divine invention, and even were everyone to remain silent, the book would speak for itself;

*A high-ranking official in the court of Byzantium, Sygeros was sent in 1348 by the Emperor, John Cantacuzenus, to Avignon on a mission to Pope Clement VI regarding the possible unification of the Greek and Roman churches. He met Petrarch during his stay and promised to send him whatever manuscripts of classical writers he could find in Constantinople. The resulting gift of a Greek Homer was one of the earliest and best manuscripts of its kind in Italy.

but everyone admits it. From among all of them, however, I have mentioned the one witness whom I thought would be the best known of all Latin writers to you, for we readily believe those we love. But to return to Homer. This you gave me as a gift, O kindest of men, mindful of your promise and my wishes, and to mention something that adds even more to the gift, you gave it to me not in another language as though wrested from a violent riverbed, but pure and unspoiled from the very springs of Greek eloquence and as it originally flowed from that divine mind. Moreover, I have received a supreme and, if its true value were asked, an inestimable gift, one that nothing could approach unless along with your Homer you would honor me with your presence. Under your guidance I would penetrate the difficulties of this foreign language, happily taking delight in your gift, and in astonishment I would perceive that light and those splendid wonders about which Flaccus speaks in the *Ars poetica*, "Antiphates and Scylla and Charybdis with the Cyclops." But alas, what am I now to do? You are too distant from me, blessed in your singular knowledge of both languages; death snatched away our Barlaam and, to tell the truth, it was I who first banished him from my presence. While seeking honors for him, I was inflicting harm upon myself that went unnoticed; thus in helping his climb to the bishopric, I lost a teacher under whom I had begun to serve with great expectation. I admit a tremendous difference between you and him; for you have been of great assistance to me, and I do not know how to reciprocate. He, on the other hand, while teaching me a great deal in daily lessons, admitted that he too had acquired much from our meetings, including considerable earnings. I know not whether this was out of courtesy or the truth; but he was as learned in Greek as he was poor in his knowledge of Latin, and though possessing a nimble mind, he would nonetheless have to work hard to express his feelings. And so, in turn, with trepidation I would approach his field under his guidance, and often he would wander after me within my field, though with firmer steps. For this too there was a different reason: his knowledge of Latin was greater than my knowledge of Greek. At that time, I was laying foundations while he was somewhat more advanced since he had been born in Magna Grecia. Being older than myself, and having once availed himself of the knowledge and skill of the Latins, he returned more readily to his usual ways. Death snatched him from me, as I lamented a short while ago, while distance, not that dissimilar to death, deprived me of you; for although I delight in having such a friend wherever you may be, I still cannot hear your voice in person, and thus my thirst for learning with which I admittedly burn can neither be enkindled nor soothed by you. Without it, your Homer is silent for me, rather I am deaf to him. Still I take pleasure in his mere presence and with many sighs I embrace him, saying: "O great man, how willingly would I listen to you! But death has blocked my one ear and detestable distance the other." Nonetheless I thank you for your magnificent gift. As you know, recently from the west—surprising as that may seem—the prince of philosophers, Plato, arrived at my home. I do not fear that you, with your stature, would protest this appellation, as the scholastics are surely wont to do, when neither Cicero himself nor Seneca, neither Apuleius nor Plotinus the great Platonist, and finally neither Ambrose nor our Augustine would object. Now at length, through your gift, to the prince of philosophers has been added the Greek prince of poets. Who would not rejoice and glory in such great guests? I do possess whatever of each of them had been translated into Latin; but to behold Greeks in their own dress, which perhaps may not be useful, is truly a pleasure, nor indeed have I lost any hope at this age of making some progress in your language in which we know Cato made such strides in his old age. If perhaps you wish something from me, show in turn a similar confidence in me and make use of my services as is your right, just as you know I make use of yours. And since the success of one request leads to boldness in requesting others, send me at your convenience a Hesiod, send me a Euripides, I beg you. Farewell, O distinguished man, and if you will, attempt to make my name, which without any merit and with the mysterious favor of men or of fortune is now well known in the West, known to the oriental court as well, and to its illustrious members, so that what the Roman Caesar finds appealing may also please the Emperor of Constantinople.

Milan, 10 January.

Fam. XVIII, 3.

To Giovanni Boccaccio,* an expression of gratitude for sending Augustine's book on the Psalms of David.

You delighted me with your splendid and unusual gift; now I shall sail David's sea with greater assurance, avoiding the reefs, unafraid of his waves of words or collisions with mysterious meanings. I used to attempt the high seas under my own power, and at times waving both arms, at others supported by some chance object, I would so keep my exhausted mind afloat through the resisting waves that often, while beginning to sink, I would exclaim with Peter, "Oh Lord, save me," and often with him I would rise with the assistance of Christ's hand, which He extends to supplicants. Amidst such storms you have sent me Augustine, a powerful and diligent skipper of divine intellect whose immense work—usually divided in three parts by the multitude and into even more by others, and contained in several large volumes—is complete in a single volume. With joyful surprise I welcomed it, saying to myself: "Now is not the time for laziness; if I did have any leisure time remaining, this will destroy it, for my illustrious guest must be attended to with great sumptuousness. He will not permit sleeping throughout entire nights; in vain, O eyes of mine, do you become pale or blink—you must remain awake, you must work by night, futilely do you think of repose; you must begin toiling." I shall tell the truth: none of my friends viewed that book without admiration, and with one voice they all bore witness that they had never seen such an enormous book, something I myself, scarcely an amateur at such things, admit; nor is there a greater work of such tremendous literary merit or wealth of content. It is impossible to imagine the greatness of his intellect and his learning, whence came that holy man's fervor, his passion for writing, his knowledge of divine things, in one who had been long involved with earthly pleasures, finally that dedication to toil in old age, that productive idleness in a bishop, that skill in the Roman tongue in an African, although as he clearly implies in one of his works, some Africans knew Latin in his day. You may well say about him what he borrowed from Terence to say about Marcus Varro: "From any perspective a most learned man is Varro, who read so much that we marvel he had the time to write, and wrote so many works that we believe scarcely anyone can read them all." But bypassing other works of his genius, whether they be the many I already possess or still lack, or those he himself mentions in his *Retractationes*,

*See XI, 1.

or those that were perchance forgotten or omitted or overlooked in that work, or had not yet been written and would require at least a lifetime to read, who would still not be astonished that he could write this one work, though he had done nothing else? I know of no work of comparable magnitude by a single Latin writer, except perhaps his other book on the Epistles of Paul, that seems to approach the same magnitude, unless my opinion is flawed and my memory failing. Or perhaps one could recall the huge work on Roman history by Titus Livy, which was divided into sections called decades not by him, but as a result of readers' laziness. The value of such a gift from your friendship is increased not only by the size of the work of which I am speaking but by the book's elegance, the majesty of its calligraphy, and its truly modest ornamentation; consequently, since I first set eyes upon it, I am unable to look away, like a thirsty leech, until they have had their fill. Thus are my days slipping away without eating and the nights without sleeping. How much this generosity of yours has added to my pleasure, which now resides almost exclusively in reading literature, can never be easily imagined by the multitude who enjoy only bodily pleasures. But you will readily understand and will not be astonished that I have been awaiting with eager anticipation this book's arrival. You know that a brief wait is a long time when something is desired, while any kind of haste is slow; but if a mad lover in Naso's work can say, "The seventh night has passed, a period longer for me than a year," how do you think I feel when during my waiting, as the same writer has another character say, "the moon has four times hidden itself and four times reappeared throughout the world"? The flame of desiring noble things is usually more serene but not more sluggish. I am, however, of the opinion that it deliberately happened this way, not through any fault of yours since you were so solicitous in sending the book, but rather through fortune's whim, which made the delay serve as a spur to my desire and increase my gratitude. And so that you may not perchance believe that this letter's contents or any one day is indicative of the extent of my gratitude for your gift, know that it will have no boundary other than the day I put an end to my reading and living. Farewell, and remember me.

Fam. XVIII, 4.

To the same correspondent, * *another expression of gratitude for sending books by Varro and Cicero.*

My pen, I see, is subdued by your graciousness; and I shall weary of your favors before you weary of your generous acts. Once again I have received from you a book by Varro containing some choice, indeed rare, short works by Cicero; nothing could have happened more pleasing to my intellect, nothing more desirable or more delightful. The book's charm was enhanced by being in your hand, and this in my opinion made you worthy of a place among those two giants of the Latin tongue. Please do not be embarrassed about being included among such celebrated names, "and do not repent of having wearied your lips on the reed pipe," in the poet's words. For while you may admire those whom antiquity, mother of all culture, produced, and rightfully so since you properly admire what the multitude despises and despise what it admires, there are yet to come those who perhaps will admire you. The present age has already begun to do so, though ever envious of and unfriendly to outstanding talents; you certainly know how much their own age stole even from the ancients, which the following age gradually restored, and because of this one thing it became known as more just and less corrupt. Moreover, you acted most nobly in joining two men whom the fatherland, time, intellect, love, and studies had united. They loved one another with mutual respect, they wrote much to each other and concerning one another; they both were of one mind and had the same teacher; they frequented the same schools and lived in the same Republic, although they did not enjoy the same honors: Cicero rose much higher. What more need be said? They dwell together harmoniously and, believe me, few of their ilk from all centuries and different peoples could you have so joined, even though one was more learned and the other more eloquent. I accede to their reputation. Oh, were I to dare to speak! But which gods or what man has made me a judge of such great minds, or would listen sympathetically, were I to dare pass judgment? But since my spirit so moves me, I shall whisper only in your left ear whatever I have to say. Although both men are truly great, Cicero is greater in every respect unless love and familiarity deceive me. Oh! What have I said, or to what purpose and what abyss have I approached? But I have said it, I have committed myself, and I only hope that I have addressed the matter with as much discrimination as boldness. Farewell.

*See XI, 1.

Fam. XVIII, 5.

To Gherardo, Carthusian monk, * *that often the books of learned men are more incorrect than those of others.*

As companion to this letter I am sending the promised *Confessiones* of Augustine, which perhaps you expect to be entirely correct because the book was mine; I know of your persuasion that I am more than an ordinary man. Love, the greatest of persuaders, whispers this in your ear; but do not believe it, my dear brother; do not, I ask you, deceive yourself, and do not allow anyone to deceive you. If love says this to you, it is lying; if another, he is ignorant of me; if it is you yourself, I could believe you if you did not love me. And so? Believe only me, for although I do love myself, I still despise my ignorance, and between hatred and love I can give a just opinion. What indeed would you expect me to say? Until now, I am one of many, although I try with the greatest zeal and persistence to be one of the few. If this were to happen, it would be a good thing, for my labor will have borne fruit; otherwise I shall at least have improved myself through my own effort to rise above the common crowd. "When," you say, "do you expect this to happen, if it has not already done so, since you may now be whatever you were supposed to be?" My dear brother, no age is unsuitable for the pursuit of wisdom and virtue; whenever it may be, it is never too late provided one makes the attempt. But enough about myself. What shall I say of others who not through kindly conviction but through clear and uncorrupt judgment have become learned? Such men are ever a rarity, but in our age a truly rare species indeed! Not even from them may you always expect perfectly correct manuscripts: they deal with greater and nobler matters. An architect does not mix the mortar but orders it to be mixed; a military commander does not sharpen swords, a ship's captain does not plane a mast or the oars, nor did Apelles saw boards or Polyclites ivory or Phidias marble; it is the work of the ordinary intellect to prepare materials needed by the noble intellect. Thus among us, some scrape parchment, others write books, others correct them, others, to use a common word, illuminate them, others bind them, others adorn the covers; the noble intellect aspires to higher things, foregoing the humbler ones. And so, you may be certain that the books of the learned, just as the fields of the wealthy, are less cultivated than others, for abundance produces peace of mind, peace of mind laziness, and laziness neglect. Hence, those who suffer with the gout, either being afraid or

*See X, 3.

recalling a minor fall on a road that they usually travel, cleanse it of even the smallest pebbles, while those who do not suffer from it disdain the sharpest stones; hence, invalids enclose every little window with glass, while healthy people enjoy the clear air and the blowing of the cold north wind; hence the ignoramuses, whom a single syllable or letter often leaves perplexed, correct everything with great accuracy so as not to err repeatedly, something those more confident in their minds or more involved in more important matters overlook. All this I have expressed generally. But as regards this book, its very cover will warn you of what to expect: new and naked, it has yet to undergo careful correction. It was handwritten by my helper whom you saw there with me last year, a young man more skillful with his hands than with his mind. Yet you will find in it bad spelling rather than glaring errors; in short, it may perhaps contain something to exercise your intellect, not to impede it. Peruse it with care and persistence; this book, which can enkindle lukewarm readers, will enflame your spirit. You will see, as happens in the fables about Biblis, Augustine transformed into a fountain of devout tears. I beg you to ask his intercession in my behalf with our common God. What more need be said? Let yourself weep as you read; in weeping you will rejoice, saying that you have found in his words a truly fiery eloquence and "the sharp arrows of a warrior with consuming coals of brushwood." Farewell.

Milan, 25 April, at eventide.

Fam. XVIII, 6.

To Forese, parish priest, * *how great the diversity of nature may be in one and the same species.*

Your truly elegant style has conveyed more sweetly than flattery your complaints to me, O great man. Astonishing and infinite is the diversity of things, their variation utterly amazing; the pleasant person oftentimes becomes unpleasant and the unpleasant pleasant, something we do not admire in other species. For who is surprised that a lamb be gentle and harmless, a wolf raging and greedy, or a lion untamed and ferocious? The bear, the boar, the panther, and the tiger couple at times at the bidding of Mother Nature; yet they flatter their beloved consort in a frightful manner and happily murmur something violent in their shaggy ears. On the other hand, the nightingale, saddened at the loss of its nest, laments sweetly and pleasantly, while the swan, they say, sings an exceedingly sweet song at death's approach. But in one and the same species we observe such things with amazement. For who does not marvel that some men's flattery is irksome and offensive, while other men's insults are sweeter than honey? Here is an example of each that I found close by. In my own house lives an old fellow who, though born at the fringe of the inhabited world beyond which there are no men, is still a man, possessing a man's soul and appearance; but he behaves so inhumanly that he either growls like a bear or snarls like a wild boar when he wants to show affection. In short, his behavior is so rough, so thoroughly barbaric that he seems to bite when he licks; you would consider most appropriate for him not the great prophet's words to the effect that his eloquence flows like dew, but rather those of the comic poet that he speaks with words of stone. Stone, I say, which is bare and hard, with which he strikes the mind in an incredible fashion, wearying and saddening the heavens with his awful thunder. On the other hand, I have friends, a precious, dear, unchangeable possession, who charm me when they chide or scold me. One of them is you, whose gentle complaints, I confess, sprinkled me with sweetness by deploring on the one hand your misfortune in a mild and friendly manner, on the other my insensibility or better still, believe me, my laziness: heaven forbid that I be unmindful of you or of myself. I recall the beginnings of our friendship, which you cast with such pleasant reminiscing into

*Little is known of this friend of Petrarch's except that as a clergyman he was part of the Florentine circle of admirers of Petrarch whom he first met during a visit to Avignon as part of the entourage of the Bishop of Florence.

my face as something I had forgotten that I rejoice in my guilt; and although I would not wish to give just cause for complaint, still I am happy that something did happen for you to complain about. At times it is useful to irritate minds, and often a small offense leads to virtuous results. Indignation, grief, and fear have forced many to speak out; if one of Cyrus's soldiers had not violently attacked Cresus, then Atys, the son of Cresus, would have forever remained silent. By my silence, I too made you speak, something which words probably could not have accomplished; in fact, I rejoice that you have spoken, and regret that my silence has been troublesome to you. I shall take care that it never again proves so bothersome, or that you never again feel that you have written me in vain, or that, should you not write, you have no occasion to lament my overlooking you in my letters, or at least in my letters to friends. But let this suffice; have compassion on my exhausted pen, forgive my weary fingers, spare my busy mind, and farewell.

Milan, 15 March.

Fam. XVIII, 7.

To Francesco of the Church of the Holy Apostles,* that unpolished works are often more pleasing to the intellect.

Your letter, written in haste and on the spur of the moment, was nevertheless pleasing to my eyes and mind, indeed even more so; its appearance was like that of a rather disheveled woman to her eager lover. I sighed, saying, "What would this have been had it seen itself in the mirror!" It bore witness to its hasty stuffing into an everyday dress and to its command to come to me in that fashion, as you were rising from dinner with Ceres and Bacchus struggling within you, to use your joking phrase. Yet its style revealed a sober and fasting author: nothing could be more modest or abrupt; the seriousness of the ideas was suitable for the occasion, the tone of the words sweet and tender. It behooved many women caught unawares to make use of shame, a trembling voice, uncombed hair, ungirt breasts, bare feet, and casual dress; often a casual simplicity has been preferred to fancy dress. Thus did the disheveled Cleopatra sway the imperial firmness of Caesar's spirit; thus did Hippolytus's roughness, unkempt hair, and light covering of dust on his remarkable face attract Phaedra's eyes; such, I believe, was the conquered Sophonisba when she vanquished her victor Masinissa, as once happened in Africa and as now occurs as a pathetic moment in my *Africa*; such, I believe, was Lucretia when she enflamed the heart of Sextus Tarquinius, resulting in the end of royal rule and the beginning of Roman liberty. Yet while these may be viewed in this fashion, it is still common custom for a handsome person to lament his ugliness, for nothing seems lofty to the mind aspiring to pre-eminence until it attains its goal. Your letter's brevity was the only indication of its being hastily written, since you customarily are not so frugal with words in writing to me. So as not to stifle its exemplary brevity with excessive verbosity, I have included in a separate letter news about everything in my modest home; for I am so removed from those concerns that what I write about domestic affairs I consider unworthy of me and believe it to be absolutely foreign to my nature, although in that letter I do make special mention of my books, for which I shall not deny my excessive attachment. Since my youth this passion has shadowed me, and someone could perhaps say, "It is silly." For what is more foolish than to seek anxiously something that, once attained, you know not how to use, as in the example so fittingly ridiculed by Flaccus: "He purchases and collects lutes with-

*See XII, 4.

out knowing anything about the lute or the Muses"? You know the rest, and where it can be found. If I have a passion for books, this will not astonish anyone who has ever read Cicero's letters; for from his intellect issued as from a pure and overflowing fount nearly all the celebrated works in which ancient Latin culture glories, yet he nonetheless seems not only to yearn but burn for works by others. But enough of this. I know that several of my letters addressed to you have not reached you. This is caused by the insolent and insatiable thirst for my letters, similar to that felt by persons who covet harmful drinks when burning with fever. Thus whatever slips from my fingers they thirstily intercept and do not abstain from doing harm to scholars while passionately drinking what they can barely digest, thus causing nausea in them and in others. These I call not so much men of letters as frivolous and empty pedants and, in the poet's words, "fair-weather friends." Born under an evil star and at all times lovers unloved in return, they pursue fleeing letters. Enough too about these. Once again I am sending you some of those letters, not so much because they may be necessary and proper, but so that you may know that in my leisure I often do think of you, indeed never forget you.

Milan, 1 April, in haste.

Fam. XVIII, 8.

To the same correspondent,* that sincerity suffices for corresponding with friends, and that no special style is necessary.

You may believe that I too am concerned about making my letters elegant, and that after a few days I either succeed in this responsibility or assign it to you, quite like a vain youth who examines not only his face but his back in the mirror. Believe me, nothing could be less true; whatever I say to friends is in large measure spontaneous. I do hope that they know me, nor do I despair of pleasing them even when unkempt; for the person offended by his lady friend's disheveled hair cannot love her very much. I do, however, expect pardon from the others; if they would consider who is speaking, to whom I speak, and what I say, perhaps they will not pay attention to the style. Useless toil I flee; if I succeed in the essentials, I am satisfied. Certainly it is true that great love needs no artificial eloquence. Who does not consider a lady friend eloquent? Who does not delight in hearing the stammering of his infant son? Who seeks ornamentation when speaking to himself? The old saying goes, "A friend is an alter ego," while Cicero elegantly states, "What is sweeter than to have someone with whom you dare express everything as though to yourself?" Thus, let no one expect from his friend what he does not expect from himself; otherwise he is not speaking with his friend as he would with himself. Every friend's language I truly understand as though it were my own, and not merely his speech but his silence and his gestures. For what does it matter provided I understand what he wishes or does not wish, since we have agreed that we have the same likes and dislikes? Nevertheless I do welcome a friend's eloquence if he has it, just as I welcome his other charms; but I do so because of my pleasure in seeing his speech reflect his mental qualities, not because I have fastidious ears toward friends. I prefer a friend to be eloquent rather than stammering, as I prefer him to be healthy rather than ill and handsome rather than ugly, not because I love the ill and deformed less but because I am happier when he is healthy and handsome. Similarly I prefer him to be wealthy rather than poor, not because I am considering taking advantage of him, but because it brings me joy and him abundance, without which my friend cannot enjoy security. The foundation of friendship is virtue, and its continuance needs nothing but mutual affection; it is uncomplicated and sincere, requiring nothing from without. Though many advantages, even when unsought, may derive from it (for who

*See XII, 4.

can enumerate friendship's benefits and delights?), love nonetheless needs no incentives, being self-sufficient, its own stimulus and reward; if it enjoys added benefits, it is due not to friendship but to fortune. Thus, the man who finds a gem inside a fish is not a better, but a more fortunate, fisherman, and the man was not a better hunter who in ancient times, if the story is true, caught in the northern regions a stag with a golden collar on which presumably was written in very old lettering, "Let no one capture me," and which Julius Caesar ordered freed. The farmer who while tilling the soil happened to discover under the Janiculum seven Greek and seven Latin books and the tomb of King Numa Pompilius was really doing something else; often there came to me in Rome a vinedigger, holding in his hands an ancient jewel or a golden Latin coin, sometimes scratched by the hard edge of a hoe, urging me either to buy it or to identify the heroic faces inscribed on them; and often while putting in supports for a sound foundation a builder has discovered a golden urn or a treasure hidden in the ground. Which of these with their unusual treasure became famous for his artistry or talent? For these are the gifts of fortune, not the laudable merits of men. Much more worthy of the name of artist is the man who is stopped short, while performing his rightful labor, by a serpent sliding from a cave than the man working blindly who is happily bedazzled by the unexpected brilliance of hidden gold. The same can be said about friendships: I have prudently chosen a friend, I have fervently loved him, I have carefully cherished him, I have offered him my trust to the fullest. The friendship brought me hardships, anxieties, and dangers: this is not the fault of friendship but of fortune. He in turn treated me in the same manner, but he gained honor and wealth because of this friendship; as I have said, he was perhaps a more fortunate friend, but not a better one. Another person, instead, pretended to be a friend and, feigning loyalty, acquired advantages and many other benefits. As Laelius says in Cicero, "For benefits are indeed often received even by those who had cultivated and flattered at the opportune time under the guise of friendship." Would you like to know my feelings about such a person? I would say that he is an expert vendor of deceit and an accomplished liar; as regards his friendship, I would give him the name of imposter rather than friend. As Cicero remarks in the same work, "For in friendship, nothing is feigned, nothing simulated, and whatever is, is true and spontaneous." Briefly, in friendship one must seek only friendship; a true friend thinks of nothing but his friend.

But if I know that I was always the same to my friends and they to me, I believe that they should not expect from me, especially in friendly letters, the eloquence that I direct to others, nor should they view it as a defect if I happen to speak with my friends as I would with myself. This has made me so careless that I become negligent not only with words but even with content. Whence it has often happened, and I mention this as an aside, that I was accused of inconstancy by those who believe that, even in speaking with friends, everything ought to be weighed so as not to permit discord either in language or in subject matter. They say: "What manner of speech is it to say something to a friend or to ask for anything today whose opposite you would say or ask tomorrow? One must first clarify his thinking and then offer it to friends; only in this way does one attain uniformity of words and action." This I do not deny is useful in other areas, but in friendship it is overdone. And so I answer them—"for the controversy is still under consideration," and I do not reject you as judge—that I say everything to my friends as to myself; indeed with myself I often deal with matters not only weighed and approved but more often ambiguous and uncertain, and I strive for the truth by hesitating, pondering, and deliberating. Therefore, as befits one who deliberates, at times I accept one opinion, at other times another, as does even Virgil more than once, through his praiseworthy hero: "Now hither, now thither does he hastily draw his undecided mind and compel it in various directions and still he remains uncertain." But if I direct only firm and tested ideas to my friends, perhaps I will seem more cautious, and if I were striving for the empty title of consistency, the reason for my choice will be justified; yet that does not mean having your friends participate in your deliberations but simply making them aware of them. I shall offer my friends not only my deliberations but the thoughts and movements of my mind, which are called spontaneous; nor will I write merely summaries and conclusions, but the particulars of their beginnings and their progress; to the friends whom I meet I shall relate early in the morning whatever occurred to me during the night. If upon sitting at table I change my mind, upon arising I shall tell my friends, and I shall take pleasure in seeing my opinions struggle until the better wins. This will more easily occur if my loyal friends are allowed to participate in my deliberations from the very beginning. As I was saying this and similar things in defense of my daily routine, I happened by chance to come upon Cicero's letters, a magnificent book replete with great variety and with this kind of friendly discourse. In it I read a similar defense and was delighted that, whether because of similar reasoning—which I would like to believe but dare not hope for—or simply because of similar subject matter, I had expressed what that great man had long ago stated without my knowing until that moment, I swear to God, that he had said it; I was delighted too in having, as he says in one passage, followed in his footsteps. To make this still clearer, I shall cite Cicero's very words; while writing to Atticus, he changes his mind many times and then adds, as if speaking to himself, "Don't you change your opinion as often?" And he replies as I said: "I speak with you as with myself. And who would not be in disagreement with himself in such an important matter?" Adding yet another reason, he says, "At the same time I wish to elicit your opinion so that I may be more certain of mine if yours is the same, or agree with yours if it has changed." His final point does not concern me. I am not that cautious, I apply no skill to friendship except to love greatly, to have complete trust, to feign and conceal nothing, and to reveal to my friend everything as it is in my mind. But I return to the point. Although I do not intend to deceive your ears any more than my own, I still find myself more effective when speaking with rousing and moving words than when speaking with restraint. Then do I feel that, having changed roles, I am communicating with my friend no differently than I do with myself; then am I a little more attentive in my discourse and in my desire to rouse rather than to deceive or to flatter with empty dexterity. This happened as I recalled my last letter to you and the hasty manner in which I had dispatched it, and decided that certain thoughts could be added to it, whereby its main point might become more effective and eloquent. I wrote them separately to you as they occurred to me; if they meet with your approval, insert them in the letter and let your hand supplement mine. Farewell.

Fam. XVIII, 9.

To the same correspondent,* that being unknown to the multitude is a sign of virtue.

I have replied to your letter as it seemed best, and I have sent it with a messenger from our republic who happened to be here and with whom I spoke at length about you. What especially pleased me in those discussions was learning that you are little known in your homeland and to its citizens, and for that very reason better known, more famous, and dearer to me. I have always expected much of you but now I cease hoping; for hope applies to an uncertain and future good, while for me there is no longer any uncertainty about you. The most learned of cities, Athens, had Epicurus and Democritus, citizens celebrated throughout the world but unknown to her; and we marvel that our city of merchants and wool-spinners does not know you? Until now you held the uppermost place in my friendship; and lo, he whom I considered unsurpassed by anyone has now surpassed himself, something I thought impossible. Thus did that messenger hear me speak about you whom he knows only by sight, and as though I were speaking about the Indian philosophers Dindymus or Calanus, he stood astonished and hesitant, with his eyes fixed upon me and his hair standing on end as at the dreadful sight of a new monster, while I paid homage not to you but to the truth. On the other hand, I was amazed at the stupor of a man who is anything but foolish, and as the saying goes, I silently rejoiced, repeating to myself, "How great my friend must be if this man has seen only his body, but not his head!" I reckon so, for it was bound by clouds as usually occurs on the highest mountains, and had really gone beyond the clouds. If this be true of Mount Olympus, how much higher must be the part of the soul that has gone beyond the clouds of passion to that place where steadfast serenity dwells, a place that the rabble, half-blind and surrounded by great mist, looks for in vain! Let us not dwell on this too long; be convinced of this much, that no eloquence has served to increase my high esteem of you as did that man's silence and amazement. Farewell.

*See XII, 4.

Fam. XVIII, 10.

To the same correspondent, * *Varro's rules for dining.*

What a happy and joyful gathering it must have been, which at my messenger's arrival had brought together three such compatible friends to celebrate at your house! In Marcus Varro's book on rules for entertainment, he suggests among other things that the number of guests must be neither more than the Muses nor fewer than the Graces, lest the affair degenerate into a crowd or into a state of loneliness, although in my opinion solitude is always to be preferred. You know what his rule further requires for the gathering to be perfect in every respect: "That charming men be assembled." This he says, I believe, because a gathering of intemperate men nearly always disrupts tranquillity just as the billows in a stormy sea. To this he adds, "That the location, the time, and the preparations be carefully considered." He also suggests that it be neither disorderly because of garrulity nor quiet because of silence, but somewhere between the two; that it be adorned with pleasant conversation, useful and interesting discussion without contention or quarreling, upset or trouble; that it be marked, in short, by an agreeable intimacy and affability. Easy things to say, but not easy to attain, unless a gentle and steadfast serenity marks the faces and words of those present. What can I say about his other points? What norms shall I set for servants and the banquet host except that the former be few, humble, and solicitous, while the latter be liberal but moderate, joyful but modest, and finally considerate, sophisticated, and eloquent; yet he must know how to remain silent, how to sow, according to the nature of his guests or the circumstances or the locations, conversational seeds among his table companions, and how to listen to others' discussions. These and similar qualities I believe were indeed present at that Attic and truly philosophical gathering of yours, except that you were perhaps more sumptuous than our rustic antiquity knew how to be, even though I know your sumptuousness was laden with exceptional sobriety and moderation. But where was I at that time? The very fortune that had certainly decreed my absence saw to it that I too was present in the only manner possible, for in the midst of that dear gathering arrived my letter, which you say caused your delight to double. I do believe it, nor does the sincerity of our faithful friendship allow me to suppose otherwise. Farewell.

*See XII, 4.

Fam. XVIII, 11.

To the same correspondent. *

I know not whether our common friend is still in Bologna. I prefer him to be in the Academy or on Parnassus, I prefer him to be guided by Plato or Homer rather than the willing followers of Ulpianus or Scevola, and involved with the Muses' chants rather than with legal knots. But I cannot oppose the multitude alone. It is enough that I have managed to escape the torrent of common opinions—if indeed I have managed to avoid them—without being immersed and dragged along with thousands of others. I would like, I admit, to take my friends with me; but if I cannot rejoice over their being saved, nothing prevents me from lamenting over their being shipwrecked. In any event, I know not whether he still lives in Bologna because of his zeal for learning, which he feels almost equally for all kinds of studies, or whether he has returned to Florence, compelled to leave the university and to return to his native land because of the serious rebellions in Cisapline Gaul. Because of these, as you know, amidst the upheaval of nearly all of Italy and Germany, the powerful armies of the Ligurians and the Venetians do battle, and thus that unfortunate city, once famous for its delights but now the somber abode of sadness, has lately been punished for its boldness. By its actions and with its own blood it has demonstrated the truth in the words of the poet of Cordova: "Whoever is controlled by the people's authority will see liberty perish because of liberty." And so I say that wherever he may dwell amidst these rebellions, please see to it that Cicero's little book that belonged to him, the one I once accepted from him in your presence, reaches him as soon as possible. Being uncertain of the state of affairs, I decided that it was best to send this to you since I knew that you would not readily leave your nest; I have added an accompanying letter because it seemed unlikely that this unattended and unarmed Cicero would arrive safely through the clash of arms and the flashing of swords, being, as some say, "a man born least of all for war." And yet, if I am allowed to jest with the dead, he would perhaps be ill-pleased to hear this, since, surprising as it may be, he seemed to exhibit in a letter to Atticus so great a desire for winning. Farewell, and remember me.

Milan, 14 December.

*See XII, 4.

Fam. XVIII, 12.

To Jacopo Fiorentino, *that it is much more harmful to be deprived of the books of learned men than the words of the pagan gods.*

Your Cicero was with me for more than four years. The cause for such delay is the great shortage of intelligent scribes, which has resulted in an incredible loss to learning, since those books that were naturally obscure ceased being intelligible, and having lately fallen into universal neglect, have perished. Thus have our times gradually been deprived of the richest and sweetest fruits of literature, and wasted the vigils and labors of famous intellects. I would not hesitate to maintain that there is nothing more precious on this earth. I even venture to say with great confidence that for our age this loss is greater and more deplorable than the silence of the Delphic oracle which Lucan laments in his day and calls a unique gift of the gods and the greatest of all gifts. It would have been better had the oracle always been silent, and its tenant, Apollo, forever mute; for he is condemned not only by the prophets' testimony, for whom "that people's gods are all demons," but even by his own words, if it is really true (such is the power of truth!) that "he admitted to being the devil" when questioned as to what he was. Surely no one will deny that it is worse to be deprived of the sweet consolation of literature than the false and deceitful discourse of the devil. But putting aside my complaints about the disappearance of learning, I return to your Cicero. Since I did not wish to be without him and was not allowed to possess him due to the laziness of scribes, I turned from undependable, outside assistance to my own devices, setting about working with these weary fingers and this exhausted and battered pen. And I used a system of writing that I want you to know as well, should you some day perchance attempt a similar undertaking. I read nothing before writing. Someone may ask: "What was that? You were writing without knowing what you wrote?" At the beginning it was enough for me to know that it was the work of Tullius and that it was extremely rare. But as I reached particular passages, I experienced so much pleasure and was drawn with such force that, reading and writing at the same time, I became aware of one difficulty: my pen did not move as rapidly as I wished it to. I feared that my pen would outstrip my eyes, that my compulsion to write would diminish by reading. Thus did I proceed, with my pen checking my eyes and with my eyes propelling the pen; and not only did I find delight in my toil, but in the writing I learned a great deal and commit-

*See VII, 16.

ted much to memory. Since writing is slower than reading, it impresses more deeply and clings more tenaciously in the memory. I shall confess, however, that as I wrote I reached a point where I felt overcome not by mental fatigue—for that is hardly likely with Cicero—but by manual weariness; and reconsidering my project, I was regretting having undertaken a task properly not mine when suddenly my attention was drawn to a passage where Cicero recalls copying someone else's orations; just who it was I do not know, but certainly not Tullius, for there is but one such man, one such voice, one such mind. He writes, "Those orations, O Cassius, which you recall being in the habit of reading when you had nothing to do, I have copied," and joking as was his wont with his adversary, he adds, "roughly and crudely so as not to be totally unoccupied." Upon reading his words, I blushed as though an embarrassed soldier being chided by a respected commander, and reproached myself: "So Cicero copied others' orations, and you do not wish to copy his own? Is this your intellectual ardor, your enthusiasm, your esteem for his divine intellect?" Fired by such goads, I continued, but with renewed determination; and if from my shadowy existence anything can accrue to the brilliance of his celestial eloquence, it will probably be mainly due to the fact that, seized by ineffable sweetness, I began the naturally tedious labor of copying so eagerly that I barely felt that I was doing it. Now at length your Cicero gladly returns to you and thanks you in my name. Quite willingly too does he remain with me, and I remind him in a friendly way that never would I have so dedicated myself to almost any other ancient author as to take the time to transcribe another's words in the midst of the many unavoidable difficulties of life and in the midst of much concern for my studies, for which even a long life is too short. Perhaps in the past I seemed to dispose of more time and had not learned how stealthily it slips away. But the riches of time still remain the most uncertain and most fleeting of all possessions. Now the situation has clearly reached an impasse; my time cannot be wasted, I must use it with great care for it may already be too late; yet Cicero is so great that I have gladly allotted some to him, though it be minimal. Farewell.

Fam. XVIII, 13.

To Croto, grammarian from Bergamo,* a comparison of the labors of Hercules with the study of Tullius.

Rumor has it that of all Italians you are the most knowledgeable about and hospitable to Cicero, and that you have in your possession a great number of extremely rare works by that genius. How fortunate you are to have such a guest, certainly much more fortunate than was Evander with Alcides! But what does eloquence have in common with the labors of Hercules? "Though Hercules may have pierced the bronze-footed deer or appeased the groves of Erymanthus, and caused Lerna to tremble because of his bow," you will find that if you seriously seek the truth, however celebrated the labors of Hercules, he exercised the body, while Cicero exercised the mind; he was strong in muscle, Cicero in speech; for the Greeks he was a victor over monsters, for our people Cicero was a victor over ignorance, the most deadly of monsters. But lest praise of that praiseworthy man be found wanting and perhaps annoy you by declaring something already well known to you, I turn from praise to plea. I now ask you, though I do not know you personally, to allow me in whatever manner seems best to share so great a guest. Perhaps he would not shudder at being my guest, nor will you be ashamed of aiding my studies; in any case our common friend will convey what my pen has failed to say. Farewell.

---

*The only information concerning this correspondent is in this and the following letter, which credit him with being an avid collector of ancient manuscripts, especially of the works of Cicero.

Fam. XVIII, 14.

To the same correspondent, * *concerning Cicero's book known as the "Tusculane Questiones," and concerning that writer's fame.*

What joy to learn that my plea so effectively touched you that not only was it not turned down, but granted without delay. Cicero himself could scarcely convey my pleasure in beholding your Cicero in my home. Either by chance or because of your good judgment—for there is nothing I do not expect from your intellect—it was that same book of Cicero that first made fast with iron nails my earlier opinion, whether old or new, expressed in my previous letter. Although Hercules, wanderer and peacemaker in distant lands, freed the groved forest of Nemea from the lion, the hills of Erymanthus from the wild boar, the Aventine mount from the fire-setting bandit, and the swamp of Lerna from the many-headed serpent, and although he ascended to the highest heaven on the wings of glory, as they say, because of the liberated peoples' gratitude for these and similar deeds, nevertheless still greater are the accomplishments of our Cicero within the tiny space of five books. This can be easily demonstrated. The first section slays the fear of death, which threatens mortals everywhere with its terrifying bellowing; the second overcomes the harsh and cutting pain of the body; the third quells mental illness, burning with its blinding vapors; the fourth plucks by the roots the poisonous and manifold passions of the spirit. Do these monsters perchance seem any less significant than those that brought Hercules fame, simply because they are invisible while the others assumed horrifying physical forms? On the contrary, for me there is no more threatening enemy than the one who does harm but cannot be seen. Finally, in the fifth he displays his logic sparkling like starry lights as he proves that virtue alone suffices for the blessed life. For me, what else could this section be except a portrait of the Ciceronian heaven where the luminous and lofty mind finds repose after subduing far and wide the countless monsters of error? Thus, let the pagans admire and revere Hercules, I shall revere and admire, yet not adore, our Cicero, and not as a god but as a man with a divine intellect. I am truly astounded that in our age some scholars are wont to make other great men his equal, whereas I consider them very inferior to him. Although I respect freedom of judgment for others, as I hope they do for me, still I know what I think, and I hold it so firmly that nothing can dislodge it. Even Demosthenes could not, were he to return for a time from the nether world to devote himself with persistence and with all the power of his eloquence to this

*See XVIII, 13.

one task; nor could all his rivals who during his lifetime and beyond tried to envelop his reputation in mists of envy, all the more so because they had no need to fear his towering eloquence and availed themselves of the favor of a wicked and bloody enemy; nor did his death mitigate their wrath or destroy their envy. I shall instead trust in myself, in universal fame, and in the many great writers, whom I would enumerate were they not countless. Still I shall mention two non-Italians, lest love for my origins render my evidence suspect; they were truly great and celebrated Spaniards who—to make my words more believable—were adversaries and had long held conflicting opinions; they did agree, unless I am mistaken, only in their praise of Cicero, something that is neither useless nor irrelevant to learn. Anneus Seneca, that illustrious man, says near the beginning of the first book of the *Declamationes*, "Whatever Roman eloquence has to offer in contrast or in preference to insolent Greece, bloomed around Cicero; all studies that illumined Latin letters were born with him." Further on, he says: "I seem to have heard all those celebrated for their eloquence except Cicero; yet it was not my age that kept me from him, but the madness of civil wars that overran the entire world in that period. I remained in my own colony; otherwise in that small atrium, where he says two noble pupils were wont to declaim with him, I could have seen and heard that genius whom alone the Roman people considered on a par with their greatness, and I could have heard a truly living voice, which the multitude finds in many others but which is to be found only in him." In the *Institutio oratoria*, Quintilian, a most perceptive and learned man, after saying a great deal about Cicero and the preeminence of his eloquence concludes: "He therefore was deservedly said by everyone in his age to rule supreme in matters of judgment, and indeed it happened that posterity considered Cicero's name not only the name of a man but of eloquence itself. Thus, let us contemplate this man, let us propose to use him as an example, and let the person who finds Cicero truly pleasing know that he has made some progress." If these last words are really true, by Jove I rejoice that I too have made a little progress, something I otherwise did not dare hope. But now I am really straying. And so, this Cicero of yours, known as the *Tusculane Questiones*, which preserves the name of the city long since laid waste and destroyed, was well known to me from my earliest years. Now you send it to me carefully corrected, accompanied too by other Ciceronian gems and by your truly friendly and polished letter. I thank and beseech you, in the name of our recently established friendship, to lend ever greater support to my burning passion that doubtlessly has been brought to your attention through my letters or viva voce through a friend. Farewell.

Milan, 1 December.

Fam. XVIII, 15.

To Giovanni Boccaccio,* that no arrow of fortune can reach the stronghold of reason.

From your many letters that I have most recently read, one thing stands out: you are mentally disturbed. This astonishes me, and makes me indignant and sad. For what, I ask, can possibly disturb a mind firmly rooted in study and in the solid foundations of art and nature? I have read and understood the meaning of your allusions to Syracuse and Dionysius. But what of it? What does it matter whether it is death that attacks, or tribulations, prisons, exile, or poverty? These are very similar to the arrows of fortune; but which of these can ascend to the loftiest and most fortified stronghold of the mind unless you willingly open the gates to the enemy? I admit, though, that this is somewhat easier to say than to do, and easier to teach than to learn. You are angered among other things that I call you a poet in my letter. How surprising, for you wished to be a poet and yet tremble at that name, whereas many seek the name without deserving it. Perhaps the reason you cannot be a poet is that your brow has yet to be adorned by the Penean frond? But if no laurel tree existed in the world, would all the Muses be silent, would one not be allowed to weave a sublime song in the shade of a pine or of a beech? But seriously hampered by the lack of time, I shall not quarrel at greater length with you. You may call yourself whatever you wish to be called; I have long since determined my opinion of you. How you view yourself is your affair; how I view you is mine. I have received the books that you gave me, and also those that you returned. The fact that my letter expressing gratitude has not reached you is not surprising since we daily tolerate such happenings, which have become for me a source of perpetual complaint. As for other news, this young man who loves me and wishes to know you has accepted the responsibility of conveying everything to you in person. When you have heard him, not only will you know what I do, but what I think and what I believe you must be thinking and doing. I wish you well.

Milan, 20 December.

---

*See XI, 1.

Fam. XVIII, 16.

To Andrea Dandolo, Doge of the Venetians, * *an attempt to dissuade him from war deliberations.*

You will hear nothing new, you will read nothing unusual, except words with which I have often wearied your ears and your eyes. I believe that you will recall, O illustrious leader, that nearly three years ago before the dark-blue sea reddened with blood when deadly Mars was already arming two celebrated peoples with lethal weapons, fearful not for myself but for Italy, where I confess my temporal salvation also lies, I sent you a lengthy letter, full of love and anxiety and fear. Although you may perhaps have forgotten it—for it was not composed so carefully as to make it worthy of such remembrance—you surely cannot have forgotten your eloquent and thoughtful response. Already two battles had been waged, already two seas had been bloodied after two massacres of our people, already it could be reasonably expected that flames of anger would slacken under the bloody rain, when the greatest of Italian princes recently sent me, faithful but ineffective, as an envoy of peace to you and to your people, than whom there is nowhere a more prudent leader or more peaceful people. However many my words before the council over which you preside or to you alone in your private chambers, I believe that it was all so recent that your reply may still be ringing, so to speak, in your ears. But all in vain, for the heat of battle and the din of arms as well as remnants of old hatreds and the recollection of pride over the recent victory had hardened the hearts of your counselors and even your own, astonishing as it seems, despite sound warnings and justified entreaties. Yet this is scarcely new: for wrath, as Cicero says, is hostile to all deliberation, and victory is by nature haughty and arrogant. A slight breeze of new developments had approached from the north, which, though contrary to what I had in mind, blew in, confirming my fears; still, if you will allow me to say so, these should not have diverted you from the gravity of the moment or caused you to overlook sounder advice. How long will we wretches seek foreign aid with which to strangle our fatherland and perpetrate public murder? How long will we continue to employ those who will strangle us? With a clear voice I shall say what I feel: among all the countless errors of mortals, none is more insane than the fact that we Italians so diligently bring to Italy those who would destroy her. What would she be in the hands of lovers and cultivators, when—O what great pity and

*See XI, 8.

implacable grief! – even in the hands of savage pillagers she has far excelled for many centuries all countries on earth? But why waste time with words, especially since what I am saying is very well known to you? Sadly I then sensed the tricks of fortune, and not only did I learn that she whom I had believed to be nothing for educated men *is* something but I was forced to admit with Sallust that in some way she dominates all things, with Cicero that she is the mistress of human affairs, and with Virgil that she is omnipotent and irresistible. Thus, with many words wasted hither and yon, I left full of shame and fear, as I had come full of hope. For I mourned the people's destiny, ashamed too that I had been chosen and proved unequal to the great task and that not as a simple participant in the distinguished legation but as its leader by special appointment (though I vigorously tried to be excused) in preference to more honorable and learned men who far surpassed me in valor, I was to bring back not the fruits of a noble endeavor but the testimony of my ineffectiveness. And this despite the fact that my colleague, unless my affection for him deceives me, very eloquently addressed in one of the final meetings the military problems about which I knew little. But neither our eloquence nor perhaps that of Cicero could open your tightly closed ears or move your obstinate spirits; it takes great eloquence, or rather none at all, to force unwilling people to listen. Fearing this very thing, at the beginning of my solicitous speech, I even used Cicero's words in remarking about the need for an open mind. But this too proved as useless as the rest. Obviously I feared what I now perceive your rigor is leading to: a large-scale war and an excuse for a serious crisis. If such possibilities had proved as displeasing to you and to the other princes of your state as they have to me, who am deeply devoted to tranquillity and solitude, Italy, at present almost enslaved, would be happy and even now be ruling over all the outlying provinces.

But because great love emboldens me, making me unwilling to abandon the remains of sweet hope, I shall try again and again, and from a great distance I shall confront you, O most prudent of doges, should I perhaps be more fortunate in my absence than in my presence and more powerful with my pen than with my tongue, or should my second letter be able to surpass the first. You certainly know, O most excellent man, that hope is the last of all human matters to be laid aside, and only at life's end with our last breath; and not even then is it abandoned but rather it turns to better things to reach its ultimate goal. But I am speaking of human affairs. She alone therefore now heartens me; in her alone do I find refuge, weary as I am of the many public ills and frightened by fortune's menacing face; I shall cease living if I stop hoping. Moreover, were you to ask me what I hope, it would be what I desire: a sane mind and more mature judgment, proceeding perhaps not from reason but certainly from experience. As an expert, you know what peace and war each bring; you have seen the two faces of fortune; you have been defeated and you have defeated, although you would perhaps deny the former, so indomitable and fond of victory is man's mind. I do not wish to argue; even had you always been victorious, what, I ask, has victory brought you, what has it brought the state: less gold, less blood, and, what is worse, more crime and more ills? If these things happen to victors, what must the vanquished expect? I beg you, begin now to open your eyes in this matter, your eyes otherwise so watchful and keen. If war brings more harm than advantage, more evil than good, more disgrace than virtue; if indeed in war there is no virtue, no good, no profit, but instead a pile of opposites, resist, I beg you, and, since Trojan blood flows within you, consider directed to you as well, the Trojan commander's words: "Lay aside your arms, O blood of mine." Do not allow the Venetian and Ligurian states to do battle during your reign; for already, as you can see, war is not staying within its boundaries since it is clearly contagious. It creeps among nearby neighbors and gradually extends to distant ones, overcoming many who previously seemed immune to it, and like a torrent engulfing them in a flood of hatred and divisiveness. Once you believed that you were involved only with the Genoese, something that in itself was terribly lamentable and wretched; now you see that you are waging war with all of Liguria, and to mention an evil that I would not place last, you even disagree with this exceptional man, this lover of peace, whose virtue is as admirable as his fortune, whose spirit is as great as his kindness. Among distinguished men, even though unknown to each other, there customarily is a certain intimacy and feeling of good will, since nature joins similar spirits; for likeness engenders friendships and practicality nourishes them. The fact remains that you are both upright, both prudent, both high-minded: so what is the cause of your disagreement? Peace is useful for both of you, indeed it is necessary for everyone, except for those who live on plunder, making small profit on much bloodshed. A monstrous race of men are they, if they can still be called men when their only human characteristic is their face, who lead miserable and worthless lives for shameful pay, who rightfully therefore fear peace and the hunger that accompanies peace, but love war, and like wolves and vultures delight in the slaughter of men and the sight of cadavers. Will you wish to deal with such monsters? They are equally hungry for the flesh and for the goods of the slain, and thirst equally for their blood and for their gold. I beg you not to allow a flourishing state, entrusted to your care, and this wealthy and beautiful region of Italy lying between the Apennines and the Alps to fall prey to foreign and famished wolves from which—I never tire of repeating this—thoughtful Nature separated us so well with those same Alpine peaks. We can blame no one else, for it was our impatience that opened the way for them; while we take vengeance upon our own people for some unimportant matter, we allow foreigners to graze and fatten without punishment on our flesh. Ah, how much better for them to have been consumed by starvation and rage! This will happen as soon as Italian shepherds begin to recover their flocks; a shepherd's foresight means a wolf's death.

This, then, is what I hope you do before the others, indeed you may have already done so. For unless my presentiment is faulty, you are now becoming irritated and disgusted at the mercenaries' insolence and greed. Why then do you wait? Listen to your heart, and if foreigners displease you, love your own people. If, however, some rust or hatred perhaps lingers in your heart, cleanse yourself of it with your love of homeland and with compassion for our common ills. And be not convinced that Venice will be secure after Italy perishes, for she is part of it; for it is in the nature of a part to follow its whole, whether it subsists or falls into ruins. As you mull this over, do not allow matters, O greatest of doges, to reach an extreme where to be defeated is terrible and to conquer is wicked, and for that very reason more terrible than to be conquered. It is far better for these weapons to be turned against our enemies, who are certainly numerous, than against ourselves; it is better for this wealth to provide protection in necessary wars or beautification in peacetime than instruments of a willed cruelty. Hasten as quickly as you can; since you cannot remedy past ills, at least cope with the present ones. And do not wait until the great cloud of war around our heads begins to thunder or until all of Italy overflows with its own blood; since at that time there will be no room for deliberation, but for tears; rouse yourself, rally your citizens, and reveal the public danger to them. Do this before all things perish, before all of Italy becomes either a desert or a foreign country. Since nature made you mild and peaceful, as well as all your people, whose increased well-being rests upon the foundations of peace and justice, not of war, beware lest you seem among those who, in the Psalmist's words, "mulled over iniquities in their hearts and planned battles throughout the day"; beware lest his curse perhaps strike you: "Scatter those people who desire war." In my opinion, nothing is more hateful to God than to squander His care and trust so that while He has endowed you with a gift of unique virtue, you willingly remain wicked from a kind of perverse pleasure. For this reason, I insist and I cry out again and again: follow not the multitude's madness, but your own nature, which always directs you to pursue the path of righteousness and to ever better things. And if perchance you have, because of the multitude's tendencies, fallen into something unbecoming, even now while you can, draw your foot from the edge of the precipice, while banners have not yet collided, while dreadful Mars thunders but has not yet begun to hurl his bolts, while amidst the bitter and dreadful threats of war can be heard the sweet name of peace, and finally while hope, alone not yet destroyed by countless fears and the only light amidst deep shadows, is still present; it perhaps will never return, should we hold it up to scorn. Seize it while it is present, so that you may be called the founder of Italian peace and may transmit to posterity your name, glorious for many great deeds but in particular for this one. I am advocating only what is within your power: follow your reason and not impulse, avoid dragging all things with you into the precipice; for while this may be shameful for everyone, it is most shameful for you and certainly unworthy of you. What good would literature do, or the study of fine arts—which fame, which does not lie, maintains you possess in greater abundance than all other doges of our age—if while foreseeing what is best you pursue the worst? May such wrongdoing remain distant from your spirit; and so as to delimit this letter, already too loquacious in my opinion, I beg you, I entreat you, I implore you, I adjure you, I beseech you for the love of virtue and the studies in which you excel, for the love of country in which you surpass all others, and finally in the name of the five wounds inflicted on Christ, from which His most sacred and innocent blood flowed and through which we were redeemed, that if you believe that I have spoken well, piously, and faithfully, you not deny me your ears and your mind, and if my advice pleases you, you not despise its author. Otherwise Our Lord Christ, who sees all things, will join the present letter to attest for all time (to borrow from the philosopher Plutarch, and to look upon you today as my Trajan) that in the destruction of Italy not only did you not follow the advice of its author, Francesco, but you opposed it, as he struggled with all his power, being able to do nothing else, to restrain you with deep sighs and great groans of his spirit. Farewell.

Milan, 28 May.

Fam. XIX, 1.

To Charles IV, * felicitations on his arrival, though late.*

Overwhelming joy is wont to impede one's words; yet what if it is such as to leave one breathless? Thus am I, so often loquacious in the past in urging you onward, now so terse in my congratulations. For what shall I say? Where shall I begin? You have emptied my heart of its many torments and filled it with joy, and what the Psalmist says, "Your very presence fills me with joy," has been fulfilled by your famous name alone. What therefore will your imperial presence, what will your majestic countenance accomplish? Throughout my anticipation I prayed for patience and resignation; now I desire to be equal to such happiness and joy, now for me you are the king not of Bohemia but of the world, now you are the Roman emperor, now you are truly Caesar. Beyond doubt you will find what I promised, for everything awaits you: the crown, the empire, immortal glory, and easy access to heaven, in sum, whatever man is allowed to desire or hope for. Now I boastfully rejoice for having roused you with a few modest statements; now I mentally hasten to you as you cross the Alpine heights, and indeed I am not alone; there is an infinite group with me. The common mother of us all, Italy, and its head, Rome, with loud voices address to you en route these Virgilian words: "So you have come at last. The love that your father relied on has won through the difficult journey." May the pretext of Germany not cause you to dislike or spurn this mother, with whom you spent the early part of your life, and with whom you will spend its close if you prize your dignity. As I said from the start, we consider you, O Caesar, an Italian wherever you may have been born, nor does where it was really interest us, but for what purpose. Stay well and farewell, O Caesar, and make haste.

*See X, 1.

Fam. XIX, 2.

To Zanobi da Firenze,* a description of a frigid winter.

My great desire to write is limited by lack of time, while frigid air checks the ardor of my mind. It is a year without precedent, with the harsh winter already viewed by the multitude almost as a miracle, as they are wont to say with religious superstition. O tranquil Parthenope and Campania, praised by great intellects, to you apply those words of Maro: "Spring is perpetual and summer holds sway in unusual months"; but of course the poet's motherland, icy Mantua is not thus, subject to bitter cold and beset by Alpine snows and the Apennine peaks, nor is Liguria. And yet the present year, which has even astonished elders with its strangeness, may perhaps derive from a more hidden cause: namely, the new Caesar from the German territories has brought to our heavens such cold air as to astound even the Germans themselves. In fact, the day before yesterday in Mantua, where I went after many invitations to visit Caesar—I was often so honored by that very kind prince who is no less Italian than German in his language and in his ways, and whom I had never met except by letter—I heard him remark in an informal conversation that in Germany he had scarcely ever experienced such weather. I responded that perhaps it was an act of heaven so that the German soldier not be frightened by a sudden change in weather and by the mildness of the Italian climate. But let me continue; winter will yield to the west wind, summer to the north wind, and all things to old age. The day will come that will put an end to all days and a stable eternity will put an end to this variability in weather; so, let nature do her work while we do ours. Indeed no frost lying on the Riphean mountains or on the Meotic swamps could block my desire to write at length, had I received your letter in time. But when that illustrious man arrived here, I was absent from Milan, as I said. Upon my return, I found your impressive letter and the messenger who was planning to leave, and it seemed useless to begin something that I could not complete; therefore the rest must be left to another day that will perhaps be longer and less hectic. In this brief and confused moment I shall say only that none of your letters has reached me during these past two years, and I am not surprised that it should astonish or even anger you: our letters encounter robbers en route, but we must tolerate what cannot be changed. But who knows? Perhaps, my dear friend, we motivate many men with our studies and possibly inspire many others with in-

*See XII, 3.

centives for glory. Let them go, let them double our labor, and let them delay and intercept our letters, provided they love us and admire what they steal.

Written with numb fingers, 27 December, before dawn.

Fam. XIX, 3.

To his Lelius, * that one must not seek false glory, just as one must not scorn true glory.*

Naso says that love is credulous, nor is he mistaken; experience bears witness for both sides, whether good or bad. How favorable and well-disposed is the love of friends for the grandest hopes and the most noble opinions? Or what can be conceived as so pompous that a lover does not readily believe it when spoken by his beloved? I think that no one believed the labors of Hercules more than Philotetes, and that no one received the news of defeated Carthage more joyfully than Laelius. Our friends' ears are open: they hear everything before others do; great is the faithfulness of friendship: it believes everything immediately, nor is it satisfied with simple belief unless it adds something of its own to what it had heard. On the other hand, burning jealousy, one of love's companions, is ever so hasty in believing everything displeasing. It is terrified not as much by circumstances as by shadows and dreams. But I return to that devoted credulity of friendship about which I was speaking. To the best of my knowledge there were once in Rome two Laelii, a name dear to the Scipios; one was close to the grandfather, the other to the grandson; the one saw Carthage in slavery, the other saw its destruction. I too have my own Lelius, whom the same city, old but not yet barren, has produced after many centuries. Are you surprised? But love deceives you too; you perhaps too quickly believed the words of the first person to speak to you about me without considering how much trust should be placed in him. For who is so reasonable, not to say strong, as to reject willingly something that gives great pleasure, particularly when such delight is sincere, when under the covering of friendship the error may not only be excusable but commendable? You thus put your credence in someone—for I scarcely dare suspect that rumor, though often false, lied so openly—who said that I, specially chosen to negotiate an Italic peace with the new Caesar, had happily met with success, and was now returning home to great glory after securing peace for the republic. I do not wish you to remain in error or to gain empty pleasure from your error, for that is not the way it is, my dear friend. Such a tremendous undertaking does not call for a single man; the most eminent citizens were sent. For if we read that illustrious Greeks were once sent in search of the golden and perhaps fabled fleece, was it not much more fitting that the most eminent Italians be sent to procure a truly golden

*See III, 19.

peace? With little hope, and in a vast and stormy sea, those Greeks reached barbarous Colchis under the rule of the unknown king, Oethes; should not these emissaries, drawn by a great and nearly inestimable reward, have gone over so short and smooth a road to Mantua where Caesar, known throughout the world, had already arrived? They did go, and as the outcome proved, with happy and joyful omens; and as the Greeks carried back to their homeland a celebrated and magical sorceress, so our men returned with a delightful prize. I was not, however, among their number; let no one flatter you with falsehood. But although I was far unequal to the immense task, the kind opinion of the men sending the emissaries would have made me eager to accept the noble undertaking, had private interests not conflicted with public wishes; about these it would be best to keep silence. But in truth so that my words perhaps not lead you to think me a despiser of all glory, but instead to understand that if I reject false glory, I am also unafraid of true glory, I shall tell you what happened some days after our legation's departure when nearly everything had been agreed upon and signed. In the interim Caesar had expressed the desire to see me in order to come to know personally someone whose mind, character, and works he already knew.

By now winter had become extraordinarily severe, yet showing no concern about my affairs or labors, he still sent an official messenger, and he who rules over kings asked me to hasten to him; he also sent his request to someone whom he thought I could not refuse, nor was he mistaken. What could I do? At the one's summons and at the other's urging, I set out, and never did I more clearly understand the meaning of Augustine's words, "the icy Italian soil." I set forth on 11 December, when the road was more like diamond and steel than earth, when the danger of ice was lessened only by the snow that had something about it more terrifying than usual. We sought nonetheless to find a spot where our horses, uselessly shod for the ice, might gain a foothold in the snow, and thus the constant fear of falling made us not feel the journey's hardship. The severe weather was intensified by an icy and cold fog, the worst in memory, as well as a desolate landscape and a dismal solitude that you would say suited Mars and Bellona more than the Muses and Apollo. Everywhere stood abandoned homes without inhabitants, smoking farmhouse roofs, thorny meadows, and on all sides armed men bursting forth from the shadows, without doing us harm since they were our own, yet still causing a sense of terror since they were vestiges of the ongoing war. But I had to submit to my usual fate and proceed amid difficulties and perils. On the fourth day after leaving Milan, indeed on the fourth day of continuous darkness, I arrived in Mantua, where the successor of our Caesar received me with a welcome that was more than

Caesarean, and a gentility that was more than imperial. Omitting the usual amenities, we went on speaking and conversing in private from the torches' first lighting into the dead of the night. In short, nothing is more pleasant than the prince's majesty, nothing more human: this you must know; as for the rest, since "one must not trust in appearances," according to the Satirist, I dare not render a definitive judgment. We shall wait, and to what degree he is a true Caesar we shall learn not from his words or his looks, unless I am mistaken, but from the man's actions and their consequences.

This I did not keep even from him, for when his imperial conversation turned to a request for some of my works, primarily the one entitled *De viris illustribus*, I replied that it was unfinished and in need of time and leisure. Moreover, when he expressed the desire to have it in the future, I had recourse to that frankness I am wont to use with important people, which nature conferred upon me, which approaching old age has now intensified, and which will be even greater when old age actually arrives; I said to him, "I promise it to you provided your virtue persists and my life as well." When in astonishment he asked the reason for my words, I replied: "As far as I am concerned, for a work of that magnitude a lengthy life is necessary; scarcely any enduring work can be completed in a brief time. As for you, O Caesar, know that you would be worthy of this gift and of the book's dedication if not merely with the brilliance of your name or of your meaningless crown, but with deeds and a valorous spirit you enroll in the ranks of illustrious men by leading a life that posterity will read about as you now read about the ancients." That he was in agreement with my words could be seen by the serene twinkle in his eyes and the cheery nod of his venerable brow. And thus, the time seemed most opportune for me to attempt something I had long considered doing; taking advantage of the occasion offered by his words, I gave him as a gift some gold and silver coins bearing the portraits of our ancient rulers and inscriptions in tiny and ancient lettering, coins that I treasured, and among them was the head of Caesar Augustus, who almost appeared to be breathing. "Here, O Caesar," I said, "are the men whom you have succeeded, here are those whom you must try to imitate and admire, whose ways and character you should emulate: I would have given these coins to no other save yourself. Your prestige has moved me; for although I know their ways and names and deeds, it is up to you not only to know but to follow their example; it was thus fitting that you should have these." Giving a brief summary of each man's life, I intermingled my words as much as possible with goads intended to make him imitate their valor and zeal; deeply touched, he appeared to accept my modest gift with the greatest pleasure. Why detain you with particulars? Many of the things that we said I am omitting, except one that will perhaps surprise you. He wished to have a chronological account of my entire life from the day I was born to the present time—I still cannot believe it—despite my protests that it was too long and very dull. So intently did he listen to me with his mind and ears as I spoke at some length that whenever I omitted anything either through oversight or through a desire for brevity, he would at once supply my omission, often knowing my affairs better than I, as though my fame (astounding as it may appear!) had wafted across the Alps with some breeze, thereby catching the attention of someone intent on the world's problems. Finally as my narrative reached the present day and I paused a little, he inquired as to my future plans, saying, "Tell me your intentions for the future and the plans you have in mind." "My plans, O Caesar, are ambitious indeed," I replied, "although I have yet to give final polish to my actions; for my impetuous past habits are more powerful than my present intentions, thus swaying my heart against my new purpose just as the sea pushed by different gusts of wind is driven against a new obstacle." He responded, "I believe it is as you say, but my question was not that: what kind of life would you like to lead?" Without delay my undaunted response came forth: "The solitary life, which is more secure and tranquil, happier than any other, which I can attest transcends the glory and magnificence of your empire. I shall seek it, if allowed, in its own abode, that is, in forests and on mountains as I often have already done, otherwise, I shall do so to the extent possible even in cities as I am doing at present." He smiled, saying: "This I knew, and thus knowingly I slowly led you with my questions to this admission. Although I approve of this opinion in others, I do not in your case." Thereupon a serious debate arose between us, with me often interrupting to say: "Be careful, O Caesar, of the risks that you run; you are truly fighting an unequal battle since in this debate not you alone but even Chrysippus, with all his syllogisms, would succumb. There is no subject I have meditated on at greater length, and my head is full of arguments and examples; experience, teacher of all things, is in agreement with me, while the silly and unteachable multitude is against me. Do not take its side. I shall defeat you, O Caesar, before any urban judge provided he be just; and indeed so immersed am I in the subject that recently I composed a small work about one small aspect of it." He quickly interrupted to say, "This too I know, and if that book ever reaches me, I shall consign it to the flames." In reply, I said, "I shall see to it, O Caesar, that it does not reach you." Thus our dispute continued in lengthy and humorous conversations, so much so that I must confess that among all opponents of the solitary life whom I have known, no one ever argued more effectively against that way of life. It ended—if it can be said or believed that a Caesar could suffer defeat—with him being defeated, I believe, by my words and arguments, but yet considering himself not only undefeated but clearly victorious, he made a final request that I accompany him to Rome. He then explained his primary reasons for summoning me, so desirous of tranquillity, in such foul weather: he desired to see that great city not only with his eyes but with mine, so to speak, and he also needed my presence in certain Tuscan cities about which he spoke so knowledgeably that you would have thought him an Italian in heart and mind. Although it was certainly agreeable to me—for those two pleasing names of Rome and Caesar had so much in common that nothing enticed me more than to go to Rome with Caesar—I still refused for reasons in part justifiable, in part dictated by necessity. Whereupon this sparked another controversy that continued for many days without being settled until our final parting when, having accompanied him at his departure from Milan for five miles beyond Piacenza's walls, I finally tore myself from him and from our great battle of words. At that moment a Tuscan soldier from Caesar's suite made a solemn and sincere statement. While holding my hand and looking at Caesar, he said: "Here, O Caesar, is the man about whom I had often spoken to you. Were you to accomplish anything worthy of praise, he would not allow your name to be forgotten; otherwise he is capable of remaining silent or speaking out."

But I shall return to the beginning. I do not, then, flee any glory offered me because it is hateful, but because truth is dearer to me than all else; I was not a minister but a lover of peace, not a seeker but a supporter and praiser of peace, I was not present at its beginning but at its end. Since a durable peace rests upon public solemnities, Caesar and fate wished me to be present at the conclusion of the negotiations. Certainly, too, no greater tribute in matters of this kind has ever been paid to an Italian—to be summoned and requested by Caesar, to joke and dispute with Caesar. According to Pliny, "The tyrant Dionysius sent a garlanded ship to meet Plato, the prince of wisdom, and he came to meet him, as he disembarked on the shore, in a chariot drawn by four white horses"; this is reported as a splendid tribute to the glory of Plato. You now see, O my beloved Lelius, in what direction I am tending and how I overlook no occasion that might reflect true glory. What would I not dare when I have no fear of comparing myself to Plato? But far be it from me to compare myself to him to whom in the judgment of the wisest men, especially Tullius and Augustine, not even Aristotle could be compared; my comparison is not one of intellect but of circumstances. The tyrant, perhaps observing Plato's arrival from his castle, sent a decorated ship for the short distance of the strait to meet him; but Caesar sent his noble and valorous envoy laden with pleas to me on a journey of several days; the former received his man as he came of his own accord; the latter pleaded for me to come. Compare the two situations: the decorated ship with the armed envoy, the four-horse chariot of Dionysius with Caesar's courtesy, and finally the Sicilian tyrant with the Roman ruler, and I believe that you will admit that my good fortune surpassed Plato's. Now I have sought enough glory in jest; and this itself would be mere levity, were it not that I speak with you as I would with myself. Along with this letter, you will receive the letter that you wished from me to Caesar about you so that you could approach him with greater confidence and familiarity; both hasten to you in Pisa, where you will meet the emperor. I hope that it, and even more your own merit and the recollection of our heroes, will open Caesar's doors to you. Farewell.

Fam. XIX, 4.

To Charles IV, * *a recommendation for his Lelius.*

See how much hope and courage your kindness affords, O Caesar; so much indeed that I dare recommend to your clemency not only myself, something I have always done, continue to do, and do so most vocally when seemingly most silent, but also other people; although to speak truthfully and properly, it is not another whom my devotion now recommends to you, but another me, as they say. This man, O greatest Caesar, who comes to your feet with my letter is a Roman citizen and of noble blood, yet even more noble in virtue. It would require much time to sing his praises (for copious and abundant is the subject matter offered me were I to speak of his prudence, fidelity, industry, eloquence, versatile foresight, and other virtues), but I have decided to entrust him completely to you and to your opinion, O most learned of princes. While my words may fail to do him justice, you will judge him exceptional if you deign to consider him with the profound and infallible intuition of your luminous mind. You will then judge him in your own way; but if you have any trust in me, O most invincible Caesar, know that he is a good man, possessing many good qualities either by nature or through study, a true man, in short, worthy of your favor and your benevolence, unless love deceives me. I might add that he has always been very loyal to your holy empire and to your name, and above all dear to your followers. Indeed the magnanimous and remarkable Stefano Colonna—whose devotion to your glorious grandfather, the Roman emperor, is well known throughout the world, who was unable to see your day and you whom he used to await as Simeon did Christ, overcome as he was by old age and death—loved this man as a son, and all of his noble family loved him with a brotherly love. Giovanni Colonna, grandson of the great Stefano, a most noble and valiant young man who died tragically after too brief a life, loved him as a father. I learned of your great esteem for him from the events of nearly seven years ago when Divine Providence first elevated you to the Roman throne and you came to the Roman Curia, now lodged on the Rhone after its abandonment of the Tiber. Though unknown to you, I was then living there and saw Your Majesty publicly lean upon his shoulder in a friendly manner and embrace him with affection. What more need be said? They all sought his favor equally, vying for his affection; he gave of himself and knew the secrets of all, with them he spent his

*See X, 1.

childhood, his boyhood, and his adolescence, and with them the flower of his youth; with them he had resolved to grow old and eventually die, and he would have done so except that within a brief period premature death snatched away the family so devoted to you. Imagine that all of them, who supported you while on earth and even now, wherever they may dwell, are no less devoted to you and wish you a long and happy life and success for your empire, have now gathered at your feet, confidently pleading with you to accept this man who was theirs. Furthermore, he was even esteemed by and friendly with the Roman pontiff, Clement, who loved you above all as a father and whom you loved as a son. He was on equally familiar terms with the French king who is in turn related to you by blood and in friendship, and with the bishop of Porto who illuminates with the splendor of his family and of his mind the College of Cardinals of the Roman Church, who through his priesthood is a father to you and through his affection a brother. Now amidst so many brilliant names, what place remains for mine? And yet—behold the great confidence that hope creates—I shall dare include myself among them as a night owl among eagles and a mole among lynxes, and prostrate I entreat you first to become acquainted with this man whom his own virtue and the love of so many commend to you, and then, if he is deserving, to cherish him. His name is Lelius, who among the ancients, according to Cicero, was a wise man distinguished for his faithfulness and friendship; among us he has acquired a reputation in both areas. The ancient Laelius had Scipio as a friend: I am not Scipio, but I am his friend, and as a suppliant I intercede with my lord in my friend's behalf. Farewell, O Caesar, and live happily, conquer and rule, and remember me.

Milan, 25 February.

Fam. XIX, 5.

To Moggio da Parma, grammarian,* an invitation to share in his studies.

Our young man has written you; I know not what he has written, indeed I know not the words or the manner, but I do know the subject. He has not written to burden you with requests, but to search your mind to see how inclined it may be to join us. Nevertheless, you perhaps wish to hear from me what you have heard from him so as to preclude all doubt owing to his youth, capable as it is of going headlong in pursuit of its desires. Listen, then, and generalizing from my few remarks, consider this letter official proof of our social contract. I do desire to have you with me, knowing full well that the courts of the powerful and the great are open to you; but if I truly know your spirit, it would be better, I am convinced, for you to live in my poverty than with their riches. For sweeter is honest poverty shared with a friend than enormous wealth under a lord, especially for the person eager for freedom, tranquillity, and frugality, as perhaps you are by nature or surely as a result of your studies. Lest the word, poverty, cause misgivings, know that just as there is here nothing sordid and no room for painful want, so too worrisome and burdensome wealth is kept at a distance. The comparison is based solely on the common opinion of wealth and poverty; if you were to compare anyone who constantly complains of his lot with futile outcries and lamentations to Caesar's Amycla, you would consider him wealthy. And if you were to compare any one of the fortunate people who are proud of their questionable gold or position to the wealthy Marcus Crassus or to Cresus, the Libyan king, then he will appear poor. Without question, the spirit alone and not public opinion makes the truly wealthy man; which of these you embrace is known only to you. Here with me are offered to you the best of possibilities, moderation and freedom; I call you not to servitude but to friendship, for never, and indeed nowhere, will you be as free as you would be with me if my invitation is accepted. If you question the reason for the invitation, the response has already been given: to enjoy friendship and a common life. And lest you fear being summoned to a life of idleness, I would like you to do things, but that depends exclusively on your own

---

*Teacher of Petrarch's son, Giovanni, when a child, as well as of the two sons of Azzo da Correggio. Petrarch's high regard for his ability and learning may be seen in his invitation to come and live with him and his son in Milan, where in addition to tutoring he could also do some copying for him and share in his studies.

will. If you would like to undertake something or to go somewhere, no one will push with spurs or words, no one will restrain you with a bridle; you will control the direction of your life and your moments of repose. And you will make this young man better and more learned if he proves to be deserving; for he will learn either from you or from no one; since childhood he has learned to admire and love you above all others, and friendship, love, and admiration contribute much to learning. Moreover, you will transcribe some of my trifles if you wish, and as much as you wish, for yours will be the decision as to whether they are worthy of wearying your pen already occupied with your own affairs. Come and participate in my studies; my works will have greater value for me if written in your hand; I also hope that whatever escaped me through forgetfulness or carelessness cannot escape your hand and your notice. In exchange, I promise you not mountains of gold or fancy dress, not palaces embossed with marble or ivory or ebony, but something that I imagine will be more to your liking: substantial but modest nourishment, very near, though I dare not say equal, to a philosopher's, and in addition leisure, solitude, and freedom. How extraordinary that I promise you this last thing when I cannot find it for myself, but often a weary doctor bestows health on another when he himself does not have it. Caught in the chains of an inconvenient, useless, and annoying fame, and in the bright and vain renown of my name, all of which I openly confess are undeserved, I am able neither to be free nor to hide. In a foreign country you will find no lack of peace and freedom and pleasant retreats, at least until you begin to be known. These then are the rewards for your coming. I should like to add that by participating in some of my studies as you transcribe them, you will perhaps derive further pleasure, but this too will depend on you. One further reason I shall add that may be the last in this letter, but surely is not among the last attractions for you: Ambrose will be nearby. Farewell.

Milan, 1 May, in haste.

Fam. XIX, 6.

To Francesco of the Church of the Holy Apostles,* a recommendation for a friend going to Rome.

This man whom you see is a humble little man devoted to Christ, a true despiser of the world and transitory things and zealous for eternal things, and what is more—a tiny addition to so much praise but your love for me will make you consider it very large—he is also very dear to me, and he is on his way to Rome. And so, look upon him as you would me; he possesses a good soul. I know the man; we have served in the same army and have not yet been discharged, although our common commander has been killed. If he needs advice or any favor in order to complete his pious pilgrimage, I believe that you would comply without being asked; nevertheless I do ask you. For what could be more acceptable to Christ whom you serve, or to His apostles who are your guests, than for you gladly to give assistance and advice to this devout man who has left behind the court's deafening roar to make his way to their silent dwellings. If you wish to learn anything about me (surely there will be much that you will wish to know), although our different interests may mean that he does not know everything about me, he will still be able to tell you something of my private life, and nearly all of my public life. This letter I have written in haste from a remote corner of Milan, from a secluded section in the convent of St. Ambrose on the day and at the hour when a living light from earth shone upon a world immersed in shadows and upon blind mortals. Farewell, and remember me.

*See XII, 4.

Fam. XIX, 7.

To the same correspondent,* an expression of gratitude on the same matter.

To me something different happens than happened to Manlius, the painter who painted lovely images with his hands and yet fathered ugly children; when asked why he could paint so much better than he could procreate, he charmingly gave a humorous response: "Because I procreate in the shadows, while I paint in the light." For me, on the contrary, what I create in the shadows of my mind is either more beautiful or certainly less ugly than what I write with these little fingers in full daylight. This occurs not because I find light in itself harmful, since it proves troublesome only to the half-blind or to evildoers, but because it opens the way to hateful preoccupations that friendly and silent shadows prevent. In short, after having thought of many things during the night to write you, my pen with the coming of light scarcely wrote anything because of the many knocks at my door, the many swarms of daily concerns, the many requests of friends, the many laments of servants audible on all sides. For many, Bootes is sluggish, for me it is swifter than the wind since it rotates its wagon so rapidly even on these cold nights. For Naso, night is the greatest foster mother of human concerns, while for me daylight is the father of troublesome and gloomy cares, whereas night fathers silence and repose. And you marvel that I am liked by the few when I agree with the few, when I see all things differently from the multitude, from which I try to remain as far as possible, preferring whatever path is distant from it? But to show that the day's perversity does not force all my nocturnal ideas to miscarry, know that your letter so similar to its father and to its sisters has arrived, know too that I have found it most delightful and friendly. Through it I have perceived what I once learned through experience: the way you would receive me, judging from your reception of my friend on his way to Rome, but I am unable to follow him, as he led you to hope, because of the riots in Liguria. I shall wait and see whether the autumn is more peaceful; stormy weather certainly threatens this region, and flight is the only kind of remedy against it. Alas, what have I said? For what kind of flight can surmount the assaults of fortune? I am thus of this basic opinion, that I ought to seek that peace I have vainly sought outside of me within the most intimate shadows of my soul, and since it is not of this world, let us request it of the Lord. Farewell, and remember me.

*See XII, 4.

Fam. XIX, 8.

To Guido Sette, Archdeacon of Genoa,* who is flattered to be mentioned in his letters.

Considering it wonderful to have your name mentioned in my letters is typical of you; for that results not from my merit but your indulgence, nor do I consider it proof of my talent but rather of your friendship. In writing to his Lucilius, Seneca says, "That you should wish me to send you my books I consider no more an indication of my eloquence than I would consider your seeking my portrait an indication of my handsomeness." Elegantly put indeed, for who does not prefer a painting of an ugly friend to one of a handsome enemy? Its value lies not in itself but in what it expresses; that is, it results not from looks but from feeling. Now too you seek a place as much in my letters as in my memory, nor do you give heed to the quarters where you live but to its host; and surely no one is so ambitious as not to be more willing to enter either his own place or the dwelling of a poor friend rather than the courtyard of an unknown king. You see how eagerly the shepherd returns to his hut, the bird to his nest, the wild beasts to their lairs, the flocks to their stables, you see how goats return of their own accord to their shelters, in Maro's words, seeking their own places, not more beautiful ones. This instinct, no doubt natural and inculcated not only in men but in all animals, is similar to the desire to see your name inserted in friends' writings rather than in those of learned men. I satisfied your wish in the past, and if my life permits, I shall continue to do so, calling your attention to King Evander's words to his guests when he invited Aeneas into his poor palace; reminding him that another famous guest had already been there, he says, "The victorious Alcides entered through these portals, and this palace welcomed him," as if to say, "Do not disdain my poverty or scorn this humble dwelling which Hercules deemed worthy." I say the same to you and, to address everyone in the same manner, to my other friends whose names I have included in my writings. Forgive me and bear with me, I beg you, if the place where I include you is not commensurate with your fame, and your ears and eyes are horrified at my style's roughness and inadequacy; no one has any doubts that you deserve a better place, yet consider not your merits but my ability. I mention you not where I ought, but where I can; my love is very great, but my dwelling is small; if I were Cicero, I would place you in Cicero's letters, now I place you in mine; even had I

*See XVII, 3.

wished to do so, I could not place you in others' writings, and I know that you value not your host's renown but his friendship. Finally, so that you find comfort for the dwelling's darkness in the splendor of your company, I place you among generals, kings, Caesars, pontiffs, and finally, in my opinion, among even greater men, philosophers and poets, nay, among the greatest of all, good men. Farewell.

Fam. XIX, 9.

To the same correspondent, * *traveling in France, news from Italy, especially on the death of the Venetian doge who was executed by his own republic.*

Without doubt you have your daily fill of news from Italy, news I wish were more infrequent or less grievous! So plentiful and violent and clamorous it has now become as to be heard not only in neighboring France but even among the Indians and the Arabs. Great are the riots, great the rumblings of war and the collision of empires and chariots, great are the rumors resounding not only over the Alps but over the seas; and while these present ills may always be great, even greater is the expectation of future ones. Thus we are losing what is most difficult to maintain in any adversity, namely hope, which is our consolation in moments of extreme trouble. Are we always to continue destroying one another, are we to continue filling the ears and mouths of all peoples with the sound of our squabbles, are we always to give the world something to hear and rumor something to say? Not only for his own age but for all centuries, then, Flaccus rightly asserted that "the sounds of Italy's destruction were heard by the Medes." Let fortune behave as she will, let her complete what she began whether she receives her power from her own force or from our cowardice, since we abandoned the only weapons with which she could be opposed, the weapons of reason. Let her, I say, act as she wishes, let her rave and thunder, and hurl lightning bolts particularly in this region of the world where she has always been kept busy working both sides; let her continue and insist, press and goad, and when the spirits above and below are agreeable, let her complete what she has begun, as I already said. But I fear that this present preface, like a sign of imminent doom, may have perhaps disturbed your loving spirit, making it fearful and concerned because of its love. Lay aside your fear: I am not experiencing any adversity in my private life, just as I am not experiencing any solace in my public life.

For what comfort can men find, or rather what does not make them sad and wretched, with freedom dead and buried for which many often gave their lives with great pleasure and glory? This is especially so because along with freedom have perished faith, piety, and chastity; and with the worst now holding sway, nowhere is there room for justice and moderation. Since this could not have occurred without mankind's consent, the angry and indignant mind mourns the public fate as much as

*See XVII, 3.

it does its own. Hence, again and again my grief bursts forth into futile laments that do no one any good and even hurt me. This, then, you should know, is the origin of my preface. Now, not to keep you any longer in suspense, I shall disclose my thoughts; and omitting the rumors constantly and loudly resounding in your ears, which in my opinion no chronicle could ever hold, I hasten over the revolts in Pisa and Siena, the direction in which Bologna has turned, the state of my homeland, which I wish were always as productive as it was flowering, why Rome weeps, what Naples fears, how its name of Land of Labor befits the events there, the fires of hate with which sulfurous Sicily burns, what is happening in Genoa, what Liguria is preparing, what Emilia or the Piceno is plotting, how sleepy and troubled is Mantua and how frightened Ferrara, how miserable is Verona, which, like Acteon, is being torn to pieces by its own dogs, how Aquileia and Trent are ever subject to foreign incursions, and finally—greatest of shames—what kind of mercenaries are ravaging Italy so as to transform her from a lady of the provinces to a province of slaves; and now I move to the Venetian corner, to use Livy's words, and to events about which you probably have not heard. Those who undertook a war against the Genoese—or shall I say brought it into the open, since I believe that a latent war has been going on between them—and who were in short order first defeated and then victorious have once again been defeated in a major battle. In their defeat I truly feel sorry for them as men and as Italians, but personally I am pleased since I foresaw and predicted all these ills for them, and I did so not by using the stars or prophecy, which I despise and reject, but through a certain mental foreboding and distressing conjectures, whereby my opinion was so firmly entrenched that I then seemed to see what I now really see. Would that the doge Andrea who presided at that time over the republic were alive today! I would annoy him with letters, striking him with all my arrows and using all my freedom, for I knew him as a man of integrity, truly devoted to his republic and very friendly to me, learned and eloquent, prudent, courteous, and kind; in one area only did he shock me—he was fonder of war than behooved his nature and his character. Indeed while he was alive I spared him neither words when in his presence nor letters when not in his presence, and certain of my good intentions, he bore it all most patiently; but because of his elation at the recent victory he rejected my advice. Death so showed him consideration that he did not see either the harsh destiny of his homeland or my biting letters: for he was wont to entrust himself to the ways of fortune, seemingly having no doubt that the more successful his cause, the more just it was. And thus, he would often appropriate the words of Scipio Africanus, who said to Hannibal, "The gods are my witnesses who decided that war's outcome according to justice and divine law, and are deciding, and will decide, the outcome of this one," and also those words of Caesar: "This war, with fortune as witness, will prove who armed themselves more justly, this battle will show that the guilty suffer defeat." Would that he had lived a little longer so that I could turn those arguments against him, proving with fate as witness, that he was the guilty party for having based his innocence on the testimony of fate! A few days before his death he received my letter, which I confess was harsh but full of a great deal of affection. It so disturbed him that he was quite anxious to respond—so I learned from those who were present—as if he thought it most shameful not to be capable of equaling my style, something that was very simple for him, learned and eloquent as he was. He paid no heed to what I believe was most difficult, that is, to rebut and refute my opinions; armed with eloquence and with the experience of speaking, he was unafraid of a verbal contest. But what can you do against reality, how can you respond to manifest truth save by silence or assent? You may arrange words, you may be either equal or superior to another; but you must remain inferior to reality, for very often naked truth defeats armed eloquence. Thus, after a futile and lengthy struggle, finally on the seventh day, he dismissed my messenger without a letter, promising a reply through his own messenger. He never did send it, nor did he subsequently respond, prevented either by an illness of body or of mind. For in those days against his own, and all other, expectations, the Genoese fleet, which he considered totally destroyed and frightened, boldly approached the Venetian shore, causing an uproar in which the armed doge intervened contrary to his custom. Nor did he do much of anything after that day, as though hastening to remove himself with a timely death from the threatening misfortunes, although some maintain that he did reply in some fashion to my letter, a reply that never reached me because of his intervening death. Shortly thereafter, near the island of Achaia, also known as Sapientia, the Venetians were overtaken by that same wandering Genoese fleet and routed in a great battle. Fortune granted that great doge the kindness, as I have said, of not being alive to see his country's defeat that had long been protracted. Certainly I believe that divine intervention caused the defeat in that particular place since the island's name served to admonish subsequent doges that they should follow wisdom rather than fortune, and should draw their arguments from reason rather than from the sequence of events. But am I not breaking my word since I promised you fresh news and instead am presenting old information? But wait, for here at the end I am keeping my promise. You had heard what I have thus far said: what follows is new.

The distinguished young doge was succeeded by an elder who had taken his country's helm when it was late but before it was necessary for him and for his country. He was a man long known to me as a friend, and yet my opinion was mistaken, for he was more courageous than prudent; his name was Marin Falerio. He was able to serve but one year in high office, having assumed it under an ill omen. For the Venetians have recently decapitated in the courtyard of his palace this Venetian doge, an officer considered inviolate throughout the centuries, and always held in high esteem by the city's early residents as a kind of god. To speak openly, I cannot explain the reasons for this action, as poets usually do at the beginning of their works, so confused and varied are they. No one excuses him; all say that he wished to make some change in a government handed down from the past; and thus all things are so coming to pass that, to use the words of Flaccus, "the beginning, middle, and end are in harmony." For something happened to him that I think would scarcely ever happen: on the bank of the Rhone while serving as legate to the Roman pontiff in peace negotiations that were futilely attempted first by myself and later by him, he inherited the office of doge without his seeking it, indeed without his knowing it. Upon returning to his homeland, he considered something that I believe no one had ever done before; and he suffered what no one else had ever suffered in the most celebrated, famous, and beautiful place that I have ever seen, where his ancestors had often accorded copious honors with triumphal pomp. Dragged thither by a throng of nobles and divested of his ruler's insignia, he fell, decapitated, with his blood defiling an entrance to the church and the approach to the palace as well as the marble staircase, often the place of honor either for solemn festivals or for enemy spoils. The place I have revealed, and now I shall reveal the time; it was the year of Our Lord 1355, the day was, as reported, 18 April. The uproar over the event is so enormous that whoever considers the city's laws and customs or the extent to which the death of a single man threatens social upheaval (although several of his followers, I understand, have either suffered, or are awaiting, an identical punishment) can only conclude that there has scarcely been in our day a more sensational event in Italy. At this juncture you are perhaps expecting my opinion. I acquit the people, if report is to be believed, even though it could have vented its rage with less violence and avenged its grief with greater moderation; but it is not easy to restrain a just and overwhelming anger, especially in a great people, when the rash and flighty multitude incites the spurs of anger with impetuous and indiscreet outcries. I both pity and condemn that unfortunate man since I have no idea what he intended doing, following the bestowal of the unusual honor, in the last years of his life; and his misfortune is even more serious because, with the rendering of public judgment, he will seem not only wretched, but mad and foolish, having acquired over the years with fatuous skills the false reputation of a wise man. To the doges who will assume office I make this declaration: they should know how to place a mirror before their eyes so as to see themselves not as masters but as doges, indeed not even as doges but as honored servants of the state. Farewell, and since public affairs are in a state of flux, let us devote ourselves to governing our private affairs with the greatest moderation.

Milan, 24 April.

Fam. XIX, 10.

To the same correspondent, appointed Archbishop of Genoa, his uncertainty as to whether to rejoice with him or to offer condolences.

I have long been in doubt as to whether ultimately I ought to be sad or joyful for your success. On the one hand, I was concerned about your tranquillity, on the other about your glory; I noted that the first was now being wrested from you in your time of greatest need while the other was being imposed upon you at an age when it is particularly appropriate. I was not sorry that a glorious task had been bestowed upon you, knowing that true glory can be achieved or preserved only with toil, but I was fearful that your freedom, which you had always loved, was endangered and that the honor would doubtless entail an onerous burden. For the higher one's station, the more difficult is the control of one's life if one fears ill fame, since heights are always more visible. What else could I do? The love of freedom and tranquillity as well as the advantage of living in privacy was influencing me to the point of feeling sorry for you when I happened to think that even previously you were not free, weighed down as you were by oppressive and endless responsibilities, perhaps the worst kind of slavery. Now from a servant of many men you have become the servant of the one God: a fortunate change with cause for rejoicing. What this situation requires of you, or what guides you must use amidst the waves and reefs of this stormy office, I am not in a position to suggest, nor are you in need of such advice since you have spent all your time in those disciplines especially befitting this position. A recent bishop, you have been so experienced since youth in the duties and rites of such offices that what is difficult for many is simple and easy for you. But so that he who once was my beloved brother and now is my father may not lack my advice or encouragement on such a sea, or at least my personal good wishes as he unties the line, I shall cry out those words by Horace: "Go, my good man, where your virtue calls you, go with happy gait." To be sure, your very nature will take you where others are scarcely driven by the spur of constant advice; you need not be compelled, urged, or even begged; advice itself is almost superfluous save that it shows the good faith of those offering it. In sum, in order to reach your desired port, follow your good nature; to her entrust the helm of the ship plowing the narrows. Should a storm of affairs cause you any doubt, you should seek advice from the stronghold on high and from that uppermost part of

*See XVII, 3.

the mind that remains ever serene and tranquil, inaccessible as it is to earthly tempests. Taking upon yourself no responsibility for bringing your work to conclusion, fasten your anchor of hope in God and as the Psalmist says, "Reveal your path to the Lord and hope in Him and He will give you assistance." This is all I shall be saying today about this great event, although my aroused mind wished me to say much more; but I have barely been able to do so with your messenger chafing at the bit. Farewell.

Fam. XIX, 11.

To Benintendi, Chancellor of the Venetians,* that he who is affected by others' praises must find refuge in the stronghold of reason and in his own conscience.

It was a stroke of good fortune that your letter found me alone though in the midst of a populous city; had I received it in the presence of others I would have blushed, but being alone, I have blushed to myself, saying: "What is it that you cannot do, O mighty love? What can you not do when you dull the eyes and judgment even of such a man?" In your letter, O excellent sir, I recognized two opinions from the ancients: that great is the power of love and great the power of eloquence, and that there was reason for saying, "The judgment of lovers is blind," and "The orator can do all things." First of all, you, my dear friend, doubtless deceive yourself in your opinion of my achievements; secondly, I would have been somewhat less prone to begin viewing myself as you do—so firmly do you hold your reader's heart in your hand, holding sway over your writing paper as though it were a royal palace and handling your pen as though it were a sceptre. But feeling manipulated, I escaped into the stronghold of my reason, repeatedly asking myself the truth of what was being said about me in such elegant and sweet-sounding words. I know my heart's silent response, and consequently I beg you henceforth to spare my modesty and not weigh me down with undue praise. My request is not for you to rid yourself of an error that gives me pleasure, but rather for you not to drag me with the hook of your eloquence into a much more serious error. For your error is ingenuous, a noble witness of your love, whereas mine, if it is such, would only be foolish and ridiculous, although hopefully I have taken measures not to fall into such error. I have something to cling to, my conscience, from which I shall not readily be separated unless by others' chatter, for in it there are only the purest air and the spirit of truth. In short, rest assured that I can believe everything that you say save what you write concerning me. Had such flattery come from another, how do you think I would have received it? But by now your sincerity is well known to me; whatever you say or do receives my approval, and whatever appears derisive coming

*Grand Chancellor of the Republic of Venice with whom Petrarch struck a close friendship while in Milan and often asked for special favors for acquaintances going to Venice. Benintendi in turn was an avid collector of Petrarch's letters and provided a special copyist to transcribe substantial portions of the epistolaries. The two became inseparable during Petrarch's later stay in Venice in 1362–68.

from others' mouths seems pleasing and sweet from yours. In sum, whoever I am, I am yours, and the doors to my friendship, which you are trying so hard to open with the keys of your eloquence, are now open. Enter whenever you wish, and believe me, there is no need for effort or skill; what is more, my spirit stands ready, happily welcoming you at the threshold, and will not shut you out until death cuts down this soul of mine. I really want you to be convinced that it is as I say. Few are the things of which I boast, and even in these I am wont to be uncertain; but without hesitation I can say this much: I do not recognize temporary friendships, and if we were attracted to them not by the shaky argument of empty gain but by immortal virtue, then such virtue would not allow such friendships to be mortal. I confess to a slowness in initiating friendships and an inability to end them; but I am certainly inclined to enter into this one. Moreover, lest you think this accidental, know that I have been favorably disposed toward you for some time, and thus you appeared to me sufficiently worthy and desirous of being numbered among my friends. Beyond your modest desire for friendship, you also deigned to request a portion of my personal writings that for various reasons daily slip from my pen. I marvel that you thirst for the half-dry and muddy streams of your neighbors when at home you have a living and clear spring, except that I have long understood your mental ardor. So great is it that it scorns no waters of the intellect wherever they may be, and deeming insufficient whatever your highly creative heart produces in abundance from its perennial fount, it drives you, though wealthy in your own right, to knock on the doors of the poor and to beg from others. Continue doing so, for you have worthy models as predecessors: Socrates or, if you prefer, Plato. The first, as is written, was poor in learning but very capable in teaching; the second gathered learning from the entire world, which he then disseminated throughout the world. With a reliance on these exemplars and with this journey begun, you too cannot fail to rise to the highest riches. As for my trifles, you are simply adding love to your longing for me and for my works. Love is blind, as I have said, and always a bad judge; the multitude is wont to say: a popular singer always sings well. The origin of your pleasure lies not in me or in my writings but in yourself. How much I wish to satisfy your desires with these works since they delight you, or with greater ones if fortune allows me to write them, as well as what I wish from you in return if possible, you will learn from the person delivering this to you. He is a man capable of charming the ears with his sweet music and of rousing the spirit with his fingers, and though great himself, he has given birth to a still greater son, though not born from a marriage with Thetis. Now desirous of peace, they have both chosen from the entire world Venice in which to settle. I beg you to welcome them as is your wont; they are my friends, and therefore they wish even more to be yours since thereby they will not appear to belong to someone else. Finally, know that I read with joy but not without tears the letter of that illustrious man, citizen, and doge who now dwells in a better homeland, whom I wish we had been worthy of knowing a while longer. From the grave, indeed from heaven, he appeared to be answering me, in order to renew my grief but even more to prevent me from responding to many of his points, were he still with us; but now, I believe, he understands me though I am silent. Farewell, and remember me.

Milan, 26 May.

Fam. XIX, 12.

To Charles IV, Roman Emperor,* upon his departure from Italy, a rebuke.

When you recently entered Italian territory over the barricades protecting our world, I came to meet you in spirit and by letter, and shortly thereafter in person at your summons. As you depart, once again I follow you in spirit and by letter, but with this difference: then my spirit was as joyful as my letter, now all things are sad. Therefore, O Caesar, after gaining without labor and bloodshed what your grandfather and countless others had attained with so much bloodshed and toil—an unobstructed entrance to Rome, an easily obtained sceptre, an undisturbed and tranquil empire, a bloodless crown—either through being ungrateful for so many gifts or being an inappropriate judge of events, you turn your back on it all and—how difficult to change nature!—again return to your barbaric kingdoms. I dare not tell you outright what my mind and the present circumstances prompt me to say, lest I sadden with my words you who have saddened me and the world with your deeds; not because having once deserved invectives and satires you now deserve a eulogy, or because of a fear to speak the truth for any reason, but because with this precipitous departure, which I must say so resembles a flight, I believe that no one cuts a sadder figure than you. And thus, more and more your resolution astonishes me, making it difficult to see how fortune could ever view it with favor; and surely reason and virtue, all good men and the entire empire, if it could speak, are against your decision, while only evil men and insurgents applaud it. Go then since you have made up your mind, but I do wish you to impress this too upon your memory, to remain with you as a small souvenir from one who takes his leave: no prince ever willingly abandoned a prospect so great, so glittering, so ripe, so honorable; nor in truth did it behoove any Roman prince to show less resolve than the Macedonian king who, leaving his home territory, wished to be called not the king of Macedonia but of the entire world; you who are the ruler of the Roman empire long only for Bohemia. I ask you, Would your grandfather ever have done such a thing? Or your father, who, though not himself an emperor, in mere remembrance of his father's empire sought jurisdiction over a number of cities? Valor is not hereditary although I do not believe that you lack the ability either to govern or to wage war; you lack his will, which is the fount of all deeds. Oh, if only you were to meet your grand-

*See X, 1.

father and your father on the Alpine summits, what do you think they would say? I believe that you can hear them even in their absence: "An outstanding deed have you performed, O great Caesar, by coming to Italy, a journey delayed these many years, and by your hasty departure; take home that crown of iron and the other of gold along with the empty name of empire; you may be called Roman emperor when in fact you are only king of Bohemia. Would that you had never been even this, so that your valor would be compelled to reach greater heights, and domestic need would urge upon you the cultivation of your neglected patrimony." But let my pen wearied by this brief sally stop to rest, and indeed, as I hope, bring silence to exhausted ears. My Lelius brought me your words of greetings, which were for me a double-edged sword producing a fatal wound, together with a figure of Caesar carved long ago that would cause you, if it could speak or could be seen by you, to desist from this inglorious, indeed infamous journey. Farewell, O Caesar, and consider what you are leaving behind and where you are headed.

Fam. XIX, 13.

To Francesco of the Church of the Holy Apostles, * concerning his embassy to Caesar.

O harsh lot of mortals, O truly "heavy yoke upon the sons of Adam," as it is written, "from the day they emerged from their mother's womb until the day they are buried in the mother of all." Here I was seriously thinking about solitude and repose when amidst the great clamor of preparations and servants, against my custom and my will, I am now being sent almost to the Arctic Ocean. Who would believe that the Rhine that I as a young man saw at its aged mouth would now be seen again at its youthful source by that same man in his old age? Indeed long ago when my years were on the increase, I was near the river's fork, where it begins to divide in two; now in my waning years a journey is taking me to the foot of the mountain where it springs forth and grows, then beyond that to the ends of the earth. A great effort indeed, yet not burdensome if useful, particularly for one who has such conflicting desires; for no personal toil should seem difficult if in behalf of the public good. For this reason alone, sent by the Ligurian ruler I hasten to Caesar; how effective I shall be as his representative in the appointed task, only the results will show. As for me, I shall do what I can with voice and presence to have some effect on the man with whom I have accomplished nothing through correspondence. I shall dispute and reprove him, I shall take him to task for his shameful about-face and for his flight so unworthy of imperial conduct; and should this journey of mine prove futile, I shall at least have been an ambassador for myself. For I first shall mention the mission entrusted to me and then separately my feelings about the matter; I shall avail myself of my liberty and of Caesar's patience, and thus take vengeance at least for myself as well as for Italy and the abandoned empire. Please pray for my happy return, after which I hope to immerse myself so completely in solitude that no laborious task—O what hope is there before I die?—and no envious investigator of noble retreats may find me. Farewell, and remember me.

Milan, very hastily and amidst the bustle of my baggage packers, 19 May.

*See XII, 4.

Fam. XIX, 14.

To the same correspondent, * *concerning his return from Germany.*

I thought of you at my departure, I am thinking of you upon my return; but my pen that then needed but a few words does not suffice for the many things preoccupying my mind. And thus my mind requests a delay that I cannot deny, pressed as I am by the lack of time. It suffices for you to know that I have returned and, what is more, that I am safe and sound; even more than my return and my safety you will find of interest that the more I travel throughout the world, the less I like it. If there is anything attractive—unless loves deceives me—it is in Italy, to which all climates, if they could speak, would yield and silently surrender except for the fact, and this is said with sadness, that the turmoil and envy of its inhabitants spoil its mild climate. Often have I said many things in her praise, and I shall continue to do so while I am alive; but in the meantime I have decided to say something about my journey and return while it is fresh in my memory. As for the rest, the man from whom you will receive this letter, a fellow citizen and friend of ours—for I fear not to say ours for what is mine—will tell you much about my situation (I shall not add "if he is allowed") since I know your inextinguishable and perpetual thirst for news about me. Farewell, and expect very soon longer letters from me unless responsibilities prevent me.

Milan, 20 September.

*See XII, 4.

Fam. XIX, 15.

*To the same correspondent.**

You request me not to deprive you of the letter in praise of Italy that it seems I promised you. In point of fact nothing pleases me more than to speak often with you about many things, nor do I deny that as I recently traveled through foreign lands, a number of thoughts occurred to me while riding along that might be said in her praise. So it happened that I never understood my own land more clearly than during this journey; in short, it was in Germany that I learned how beautiful Italy is. And this was the basic idea of a letter that upon my return I began with enthusiasm, but soon abandoned, burdened by the weight of events and distracted by their variety. Since that time, I have hardly had a day's peace and no time to breathe; this would not astonish you in the least, I think, if you consider the turmoil in Liguria and the state of affairs in these times. On a ship tossed about by countless storms, I could perhaps be a fearless helmsman but certainly not without being shaken. You recall Augustine's words about himself and about this very city in speaking of a similar state of affairs: "Though still cold, we were nonetheless roused by the warmth of your spirit in the midst of an astonished and troubled city." If this happened to him a stranger and while still cold, as he says, what do you think could happen to an Italian whose spirit has not yet grown cold, thank God, and in fact has been burning since youth with a kind of love for the Italian name superior to that of all his contemporaries? But now through heaven's favor, this city has emerged with great glory from its many storms and has entered into the port of its desired tranquillity. As for the rest, in both prose and poetry I have often happened to write much on the subject that you request of me, which I hope you have seen; and if perchance I should now write something more, you will see it before anyone else. Farewell.

Milan, 31 May.

*See XII, 4.

Fam. XIX, 16.

To Guido, Archbishop of Genoa, * *a detailed account of his state of affairs.*

I know you, and I know how you are always anxious and concerned about me; certainly, too, one does not love without being fearful. You express the desire to hear about my state; yet if the word *state* derives from *standing still,* man does not have here on earth a single state but perpetual motion and slipping, and ultimate collapse. Nevertheless, I do understand what you wish: not how my affairs "stand" but how they are evolving, whether happily or unhappily. According to circumstances, I have often answered this question in various ways for inquiring friends. Why not repeat what I have previously said, or repeat any change in my circumstances or opinions? I know that my affairs have long been well known to you; unless I am mistaken, you are now asking for particular details and day-to-day information: what I do during the day, what plans I have for the future, although I have the suspicion that wherever I may be you naturally know not only what I am doing but even what I am dreaming. For what shall I call men's actions and thoughts but dreams whose vanity the Lord knows, as the Psalmist says? In fact, I do not consider it in the least troublesome or difficult to let you know what I am doing. Once the storms of youth were bridled and that flame was extinguished thanks to the maturity that comes with age—oh, what am I saying when so many lecherous and foolish old men can be seen everywhere, a shameful spectacle and example for the young—after the fire was extinguished, rather, by celestial dew and Christ's assistance, the tenor of my life has nearly always remained constant, nor have I altered it despite my frequent changes in location. No one knows this better than you since I was your guest for nearly two years. Imagine me now as you saw me then, except that the farther I proceed, the more I hasten; and like a weary wayfarer at eventide I sigh at the thought of the long road still before me, but yet I spur myself on, shake off my weariness, double my pace, and forget the countless distresses of life. Thus by night and by day I read and write, finding relief in alternating my work so that one labor serves as repose and solace for another. I find no other source of pleasure, no other joy in living; this one occupation so absorbs and immerses me that, were it removed, I would scarcely know where to seek work or repose. Meanwhile, my labor steadily increases, and as life passes by, still others constantly appear; and yet, to tell the truth, the great amount of work that I have undertaken in

*See XVII, 3.

this brief life fills me with dismay. The outcome is seen by God alone, who knows my inclinations, which He will abet, I hope, if He considers them salutary for my soul; in any event, my good intentions will be their own reward, even though empty and stripped of all success. In the interim, I sigh, keep vigil, sweat, seethe, and struggle against adversity, and the thicker the hedge of difficulties, the more eagerly I face them, aroused and driven onward by their very novelty or arduousness. My labor is certain, the results uncertain, an evil held in common with others who enter this contest. While I am intent on such things, my remaining days flow on, and I am carried along with them toward my end; thus I, a mortal, am closely pursued by immortal cares. My pen wearies my hand, my wakefulness impairs my eyes, my concerns weaken my heart, every part of me has already become hardened and calloused, to make use of our Cicero's words. If perchance I do arrive where I should like, it will be all to the good; otherwise my intentions will be worthwhile: the first would be fortunate and the latter praiseworthy since the first depends on others, but the latter on myself. On this, then, I shall insist: no day or night, no labor, repose, or pleasure shall sway my mind from its noble intention, and furthermore I shall accept my lot not merely with patience but with uplifted spirit. If I am known and admired by posterity, why should I not rejoice? If not, it is enough for me to be known to our own age; and if I do not seem to achieve even this much, it will suffice for me to have been known to a few or even to myself alone, provided that I know myself as I am and that I be as I wish to be; a great accomplishment indeed, easier to covet than to carry out. Thus, I live amidst such cares, often praying to God in the meantime that whatever He decrees concerning my studies and my fame lead to something good and simple and pleasing to Him, and that He not abandon me in the end after rescuing me from countless perils. With many sighs I often whisper to Him those words of David: "Abandon me not in my old age; when my strength is failing, do not forsake me"; or again: "You have taught me from my youth, O Lord, and unto old age and senility do not forsake me." Nothing, however, do I pray for with greater frequency and sincerity than that He not abandon me at death.

This, my dearest brother, summarizes what you call my state and I call my journey or more truthfully my decline; but since you wish greater details about particular events, here is more. My body is still so vigorous that neither increasing sobriety nor more tranquil years nor any kind of abstinence has subdued it, nor has the war I have declared against it as though it were a stubborn and rebellious slave or, more fittingly, a kicking ass. It will at length be tamed by Christ our master, without whom I would doubtlessly succumb as in the past; and so it does often summon me from my winter quarters to do battle, still compelling me to do so for freedom's sake. O cruel fate of those born to this life, to do constant battle not only against foreign enemies but internal ones and to waste their limited time on uncertain self-trials. My first and last hope is Christ; with His aid I shall overcome the enemies who very often defeated me in my younger years, and I shall so curb this ass with a sturdy and unbreakable bridle that he will not disturb my sweet dreams and my mental tranquillity with his wildness. In other matters, which are called fortuitous, my way of life is very pleasant, as far as possible from extremes: distant from misery and want, distant from wealth and envy, with a safe, sweet, comfortable moderation always at hand. So do I appear to myself, but perhaps I am mistaken. In one thing alone does moderation not accompany me, and it would not be surprising if this perhaps exposed me to envy: I am more honored—I might better say burdened—than either I wish to be or is necessary for one who always desired tranquillity. And not only does this greatest of Italians or his officials but (may I say this for the greater glory of the people) all the general public honor and love me more than I deserve. It is now a full four years, as you know, that I have remained in Milan, indeed it is the beginning of the fifth. Never, I swear, did I even slightly foresee this, nor did you or any of our friends. But this is a fact of human existence; just as nothing that we hope is certain, so there is nothing that cannot happen to a man beyond his hope. Let no one deceive himself or say, "Here I shall die, there I shall live," for the event does not bear him out; after you have weighed many factors and meditated a long time, there is always one thing that will deceive you; and after you have made your plans, fortune will invoke her rights, overturning in the wink of an eye whatever plans you have made. In this city, then, where I have spent the equivalent of a Greek olympiad, indeed where I am beginning a Roman *lustrum*, the kindness not merely of the rulers about whom you have surely heard, but even of the entire populace, as I said, probably serves to bind me in perpetuity to the foremost citizens, to the country and its air, and in a particular way to the very walls of the city and its ramparts. I enjoy general favor, and everywhere feel stares and hear words of praise. Thus, passing over individual friendships that need too much time to treat, I know the multitude admires me. Why I do not know, save that fame too follows its own pathways, and between my own concerns and everyone else's they have had no occasion to know me more intimately, or I to be better known; consequently, at least until now the multitude is mistaken and I remain hidden. Furthermore, my dwelling is far from the urban tumult, save when a traditional religious rite brings weekly worshippers to the western corner of this great city. I am the guest of Ambrose. Though many men often say that they are coming here, whether they know me or are eager to meet me, they are prevented by some business or by the distance. Thus, just as my most saintly host affords consolation with his bodily presence and, I believe, spiritual consolation, so too he helps me avoid much boredom and annoyance. Good wishes and visits, praises, compliments, and flatteries are all torments from which such a host delivers me, and I behold as from a bluff storms over the sea and hear the din but remain untouched by the waves. And if ever I am drawn outside by a desire to take a walk or by my duty to visit my lord, something I rarely do willingly or out of courtesy, glancing to right and left, I silently greet people at a distance with a bow, and after their greeting I go on my way, allowing nothing to weary me as I go.

As for the rest, the story is both shorter and better known to you. Lest you think, however, that with the change in fortune I have also changed, as happens, my way of living, I am as I once was. You know my eating and sleeping habits, for no circumstance will ever lead me to indulgence; instead, day by day, I cut down and have reached the point where I can scarcely cut down further. In short, were royal wealth mine, it could not banish frugality from my table or bring lengthy sleep into my room. My bed never sees me well and awake, but only when ill or when tossing in my sleep; as sleep leaves me, I leave my bed, for I consider sleep a kind of death and the bed a tomb. When the last sleep steals upon us, we shall lie enough, indeed more than enough, in our bedchamber of earth or stone; and so with this thought, I scorn my little bed, returning to it only when in urgent need. As soon as I feel myself free of nature's bonds, I immediately tear myself away to take refuge as to a stronghold in my adjoining library. At midnight sleep and I part company, but when perchance either a shorter night or longer vigils prolongs my repose, dawn certainly never finds us together. In short, I strive in every respect to let nothing interfere with my more important concerns except for the needs of imperious nature, that is, sleep, food, and a short and modest recreation suitable for invigorating the body and refreshing the mind. This I tell you because it does properly vary with the change in time and place, and thus you cannot know what it is like now unless I tell you. I love solitude as is my wont, and I pursue silence save among friends, none of whom are as talkative as I; probably the reason for this is that I am rarely in the presence of friends, and rarity enkindles appreciation. For a year's silence, then, I often compensate with a day's loquaciousness, and at my friends' departure, silence once again descends upon me since it is tiresome to speak with the multitude or with any man with whom one feels no ties of love or learning. But following the custom of those who, as Anneus says, provide for life in its individual parts rather than in its entirety, in anticipation of the upcoming summer I have obtained a pleasant and salutary lodging; named Garignano, it is located about three miles from the city. Rising above the plain, its land is surrounded by streams that, while not comparable to our transalpine Sorgue, are modest and limpid, so gently intertwined and meandering that one can scarcely tell whence they come or whither they go; they join and diverge, then reunite and finally flow through many channels into one river bed. You would say that amidst the meandering waters were bands of nymphs and dances by maids. Now I am here, and I have told you what I am doing, something you would know even were I silent. I follow my old habits, except that I am enjoying greater freedom in the country; it would be a loss of time to describe the boring urban cares that I avoid, the rustic pleasures that I enjoy, even how my humble neighbors eagerly bring me fruits from their trees, flowers from the meadows, fish from the streams, ducklings from the brooks, birds from their nests, hedgehogs from the fields, as well as hares and goats and wild pigs. Here, too, is a new but imposing Carthusian charterhouse that provides me at any hour with any holy joys I desire. I had entertained the thought of retiring into the monastery, but it was uncertain as to whether it would have been more pleasing to those holy men or to me. And I would have done so, with no fear that my presence would have in any way bothered them, but upon considering that I cannot be without horses and servants, to which I have become accustomed, I was afraid the servants' drunkenness and rowdiness would interfere with their religious silence. I thus preferred a house nearby from which, assisting at their office without disturbing them, I may participate as one of them in devout services of their pious family. Their holy door, ever open to me, keeps out my servants and strangers, save for a very few whose way of living makes them worthy of their hospitality. This is surely the way one ought to seek another's solace so as not to impose upon those whose aid you seek; often one is guilty of thinking too much of himself without any consideration for others. Here I miss nothing, you may be sure, save my old friends, in whom I truly abounded because of good fortune and their virtue, who have become fewer through death and now through absence. For although such absence separates bodies but not spirits, my desire for their physical presence is still strong. Know, then, that my desire would be alleviated if fortune would restore you and our Socrates to me, something I confess has long been my desire and my hope. I do not really wish to accuse anyone else in an attempt to excuse myself; but if you continue resisting, if there is no other remedy, I shall find comfort in the imaginary presence of my friends, and from these holy and simple friends of Christ I shall elicit whatever conversation I can, which will surely not be literary and eloquent but humble and devout. With them I enjoy occasional meals, frequent conversation, perpetual charity, and I hope to find in their prayers substantial assistance in life and in death. I beseech you to add yours to theirs, so that the Holy Spirit, to whom this day is consecrated, may descend upon me to enkindle this dark and cold heart. Farewell.

Fam. XIX, 17.

To the same correspondent, * *concerning the same matter.*

I thought that you had your fill of me and of my affairs, but love is never satisfied as long as something remains for it to obtain. Now you ask whether to believe the rumors that I have become wealthy; if you had any faith in me, you would not have asked such an obvious question of one who openly preaches moderation. Since the question of my wealth has come up, I realize that your faith in my preceding letter is wavering. Considering the entire matter, I shall be brief since good faith is often denied to the man who is too loquacious, and less credence tends to be given to the person who labors to convince. Thus, I do not deny that my wealth has increased a little, but my expenses have increased even more, believe me. You know my ways: I was never either more wealthy or more poor, not because I lack anything—indeed I have more of everything than usual—or because the nature of wealth is such that with its increase the thirst for it also increases, which, in turn, represents even greater poverty than the lack of or desire for wealth; for the thirst for wealth is indeed the ultimate poverty while the lack of riches is the foremost wealth. For if the truth were known, there is no greater want than to desire many things, no greater wealth than to be content with what one has. In fact, it cannot be either that one does not greatly need what one greatly desires or that one needs what one does not desire. Need derives from the verb *to be in want*, which means the same thing as *want* or *poverty*; thus this is not what makes me needy. I dare in this case to grant myself a unique quality, thanks to Him alone from whom everything derives, if there be anything that is good in me or in any man. How I would act with great wealth or how my mind would react to it, I know not, but to this day the more I have had, the less I have desired, and the more abundant my possessions, the greater the simplicity of my life and the smaller my desires, anxiety, and cares. Nor do I find it difficult to believe that it might have been otherwise had I attained great wealth; for just as a ship sails smoothly with its proper cargo but sinks under undue weight, just as excessive light bothers eyes that see well in moderate light, so would I have been overcome by the immoderate weight of wealth, as I believe others are; I have thus far not succumbed because of moderation, although I do believe that for many people, perhaps even for you, this would seem rare and unbelievable. If this, then, is not the cause, which appears usu-

*See XVII, 3.

ally associated with this evil, you will perhaps ask what else it might be. I shall answer so that you may more readily see the nature of the matter as well as my own: it is also an eternal and unalterable law of wealth that with the constant increment of riches the number of parasites increases. I knew this to be Solomon's opinion, but we scarcely believe what we have not experienced, whereas we do not believe but know what we have experienced. Now I do not believe this, I am certain of it. Gold has learned to slip through my fingers without clinging to them, something that truly pleases and delights me. For this reason was gold sought, found, mined, purified, and stamped: not to nourish men's passions by accumulating, but to alleviate needs by passing from hand to hand. By Jove, he who scorns gold in moderation, who neither seeks it nor hopes in it, is for me a truly wise man who did wonderful things in his life and whom Scripture seeks out and praises. He who distributes it usefully and honestly is its master; he who serves it with anxiety is its servant, and he who loves it is mad; he who fears it is a slave, and he who worships it is an idolater. Where I fall in this classification I know not, nor do I believe in classifying myself since we willingly and openly deceive ourselves. This I do know, that gold does travel from my house and moneybox, never staying put; consequently among my heirs there will be no struggle, or very little. But enough about myself.

Concerning our pupil about whom you also inquire, and justly so since he is in a certain way part of us, I am in doubt as to what to say. His ways are mild for a young man and his possibilities are not to be scorned for these times; what I hope from such possibilities, if you ask me, is simply that he be a good man; for I know that he is already gifted, yet what good is intelligence without study? He hates books as he does snakes. It is sufficient, however, if he becomes good; he who dies a good man is not born in vain. I delight in his intelligence, but often become angry since he lets it wither out of idleness; entreaties, flattery, threats, or the rod do no good, for his stronger nature has overcome my efforts. But so be it if it cannot be otherwise; I admit the title of man of letters to be splendid and glorious but difficult to acquire, wherefore it may well be that a defect in eloquence or knowledge is more tolerable than a defect in virtue inasmuch as the former applies to a few but the latter to everyone. And though this boy of ours may belong to the few, what can be done if he continues to be stubborn? I have done my duty, I shall await the outcome, willing to bear all things provided he develops into a good man. As truth is the object of the intellect, so goodness is the object of the will; and he who does not have this will has no one to hold responsible or to blame, being thus unworthy of pardon because he willingly sins. Not everyone can be a Cicero or a Plato, a Virgil or a Homer; but all can be good unless they do not wish to be. Even the plowman and the fisherman and the shepherd will have his value provided he be a good man; and finally, if one or the other must be missing, to use Themistocles' actual words concerning wealth, I prefer a man without letters to letters without the man. Farewell.

Fam. XIX, 18.

To Brother Jacopo of the Augustinian Order, Tyrant of Pavia, *
a harsh and lengthy rebuke.

Often have I admonished you, O brother, to devote yourself to the work of peace by recalling your position and your office. Once you have removed this goal, what else is man's life but death, what else this world but a workshop of unending toil and danger? I intermingled pleas and supplications so that, should your reason not move you, your friend's love would. I beseeched and begged you by all the saints and particularly by the sacred and venerable name of your father Augustine, whom I too, though a sinner, serve in spirit and seek his assistance in Christ. I prayed that at last, once the flames of hatred were quelled and controlled, once the tumor of pride that had closed your eyes and ears to more rational advice was checked, you might direct your keen intellect and your heavenly eloquence, which, if I may say so, you have thus far directed to inciting your citizens' minds for the sake of applause rather than for the public good to better things and to something more worthy of you, namely, devoting your religious soul to peace efforts. I was not asking something strange and difficult from Augustine's soldier and disciple when I urged him to work for peace, especially when you hear your mentor and master so often speak of peace, particularly in a section of his book on the laws of the heavenly and eternal city where he writes, "Peace is so great a good that even in earthly and mortal matters, there is no word we hear with such pleasure, nothing we desire with more zest, or find to be more thoroughly gratifying." Shortly thereafter he says, "Just as there is no one who does not wish to be happy, so there is no one who does not desire to have peace, for even they who make war desire nothing but to win, and thus desire through war to achieve peace with glory." Again he says, "Thus wars are waged for peace even by those who take pleasure in exercising their warlike nature in command and battle, whence the conclusion that peace is the desired end of war; for every man seeks peace by waging war." In this even Cicero concurs by saying that wars must be undertaken "so as to live in peace without injustice." I shall not pursue the ideas that Augustine's

---

*An Augustinian monk whose talents and acumen enabled him to take control of the government of Pavia after having ousted the Visconti, at which time he became virtual tyrant of the city. Petrarch, presumably at the request of the Visconti, urges him to return to his spiritual duties. By 1359 Bussolari's behavior during a siege caused Petrarch to accuse him of "wicked inhumanity."

divine intellect draws together in the same work since they are well known to you, and too I must beware lest, in my desire to cover them all, the abundance of arguments exceed my letter's limits. Nonetheless, he concludes that all earthly affairs should be directed to the enjoyment of earthly peace in the earthly city and of eternal peace in the heavenly city.

Such being the case, I admit my hope to be that just as every animal, though wild, especially that animal man, capable of reason, in whom humanity resides, so you, even more than other men, who ought to be more reasonable with your unique religious spirit and piety, would love peace and seek peace; that you would really believe that David's words that you so often sang applied to you, "Seek peace and follow after it," unless perchance your reply is that you certainly have pursued it since, as we see, you have compelled it to be driven into exile from your lands. But what do we say to that royal prophet's cry: "Pray for the peace of Jerusalem"? Knowing full well that in peace is every good, all justice, all the pleasure and tranquillity of saintly souls, he then adds, "And may those who love you prosper," and again, "May peace be in your virtue"; in one place he mentions, "May prosperity be in your towers," and in another, "Justice shall flower in his days, and profound peace," and still elsewhere, "The meek shall possess the land, they shall delight in abounding peace," and again elsewhere, "In peace I find sleep and repose as soon as I lie down." A lengthy process it would be to search for the individual passages speaking of peace as the only spring of all good and desirable things; and once this dries up, poverty, weariness, and toil follow. Yet what are we to say to Jeremiah, whose voice I marvel is not ever ringing in your ears: "Seek the peace of the city, and pray to the Lord for it, for in the peace thereof shall be your peace"? From these and similar testimonies in Sacred Scripture, in which I considered you most learned, I came to think highly of you, O brother, convinced that you too were a friend of peace. But I was mistaken, as I see: for you, under Christ's cloak, reveal yourself consecrated to Mars and more devoted to Bellona than to Mary, hiding under a religious habit a warrior's intentions; nor do you simply conceal them, but reveal them in your words and deeds—astonishing as it may be to think and terrible to say; you believe that in this lies the height of good deeds, happiness, and glory: that our age might see, and posterity might hear, that you fomented a war harmful to many people and to nearly all of Italy, fatal to your people, perhaps even a war to end wars, by so inciting it with your advice and so enkindling it with your eloquence that it may well be said of you, whom I considered an agent of peace and a proponent of well-being, what was once said inappropriately about Jeremiah: "This man is not interested in the welfare of the people, but in their ruin." Alas, dear brother in Christ, how deeply I fear that the wise man's words in Proverbs also apply to you: "The wicked man dredges up evil and on his lips is a scorching fire; the perverse man sows discord and in his loquacity separates princes"; or another's words in Ecclesiasticus: "The passionate man enkindles strife and the sinful man will trouble his friends, and bring in strife among those who possess peace." For if you can listen to the truth from a friend with understanding and a tranquil mind, who will doubt that, were it not for you alone, the many thousands of men who inhabit not only this region of Italy—the most beautiful and striking of all—but the entire world would now be living in tranquil and desired peace. And who will doubt that the arms or banners scattered throughout squalid and uncultivated fields, the fires that are ablaze in deserted dwellings, all the terror or exodus or periodic uprisings that strike in turn large and noble cities, and finally all the bloodshed that has occurred and will continue in this war, all of this originates in the dark springs of your deliberations and in the recesses of your fertile imagination?

O happy are you to have attained glory in military matters without the use of arms, simply by sitting and speaking, so that you appear one who, in the Psalmist's words, "devise evil in their hearts and daily stir up wars"; and so that you know the words most apt for you even though you do not go forth into battle, there follows not the words befitting warriors, "they put on arms, mounted horses, marshaled troops," but instead, "they make their tongues sharp as those of serpents; the venom of asps is under their lips." Alas, dear brother, how much better, how much more worthy of your profession to have devoted your tongue to God, using it to proclaim divine praises rather than senile blandishments and vain exhortations of peoples. You have, because of such actions, befouled yourself not merely with one crime, as others have, but with all of them; you have become a partner in the crimes with which war usually abounds, not only as a participant but as its leader! Is then the glory of empty eloquence sufficient for you after your neglect of your conscience, so that for its sake alone you wish to be called the source, origin, and cause of all these ills? For in any age, who will either remember or discuss this war without placing your name at the opening of his tearful account? Who will depict this story, which is already painted in princely halls and courtyards, without including your figure among the advisers and even among the fighters? An astonishing spectacle, indeed one never seen before, to behold amidst the helmets and shields, flashing swords, and resounding weapons a small friar in black robes corrupting minds with his poisoned breath and initiating wars with his words! Rejoice, therefore, and exult, for having earned two of the three praises bestowed upon the great Cato and Scipio Emilianus, since you surely are a commander and an excellent orator, leading an army with your nod alone and a people with your voice. But to avoid your yielding in anything to these greatest of men, who can prevent you from appropriating the third praise as well, that of being an excellent senator, when the entire fortune of your country and all the judgments of its foremost citizens depend upon your counsel? For it is said that those two ancients were distinguished for the three greatest qualities a man could possess, namely, "that he be an excellent orator, an excellent commander, an excellent senator." But take care, I beg you, lest the desire for glory drive you to this through crooked pathways, for no senator or commander is good, and surely not excellent, unless he provides and accomplishes in peace and in war what is beneficial to his people and his army, not what is appealing to him. Who cannot see how very far you are from achieving this since you have drawn your country into an unpleasant and dangerous war after rejecting the sweetness of peace? There remains only the title of orator, which you really do not deserve by advocating evil and injury since, according to the greatest orators, an orator is defined as "a good man skilled in speaking." You perceive the narrow quarters in which I am confining you, for of all the titles to which you aspired I have not conceded you even one, except in small part. Although I do not deny your skill in speaking, I do deny that you are an orator; you are not a good man and cannot be one as long as you oppose the public good, as you do, and plans for peace. O how much more useful you would be to yourself and your country by being silent rather than by having so zealously sought a destructive eloquence! If you knew not how to speak or were incapable of speaking, Italy would be neither in pain nor in mourning; the root of public woe, then, lies in your tongue, and if you loved God and your neighbor, your country, and yourself, it would behoove you to bite it to pieces and throw it away so as to be of use to ravens or dogs rather than do harm to men.

But you act, strive for, and cultivate the following: like a birdcatcher, you charm your listeners and catch the credulous multitude in your snares; you allow your fame to increase daily by way of new tribulations and destruction, all of which have now reached a limit within your wretched country. For it suffers externally the unfortunate devastation of a hostile army drawn to it, so to speak, by your hands, and internally the battering and unyielding power of your tongue. You have acted as did Amphion, son of Dirce, but in reverse; with his eloquence he built Thebes, with yours you are destroying Pavia, an admittedly old and noble city, one that would have been fortunate indeed had it not begotten you under an evil star, but is instead wretched with you as a citizen and most wretched with you as its leader, save that you relieved your besieged city by exiling a great part of its citizenry and destroying many of its dwellings, that as a dreadful solace during the siege you built numerous squares although it was content with only one, providing throughout the city a gloomy solitude and places of refuge that good citizens find unpleasant. Is this, then, the sole reason, I ask, why you daily entreat God to open your lips? Please note what you request and what you promise. You are asking that He open them, I think, not for your mouth to announce the destruction of men but rather to proclaim the praise of the Lord. Consider to what an extent you accomplish this; He truly proclaims peace and you its opposite, perhaps taking this scriptural saying literally: "I have not come to bring you peace but the sword." Why not consider instead the ones proclaiming the naked truth without an allegorical veil: "My precept is that you love one another"; "Love your enemies, be kind to those who hate you"; "May peace be with you." And when He healed a person, He would nearly always release him with the words, "Go in peace," and when He approached His disciples, He would use this greeting, "Peace be with you," giving them instructions to do the same. Finally when near death, He gave and left peace as almost His greatest gift to those whom He greatly loved and had loved. I know not what you will be leaving your people at your death, but surely during your lifetime you have heaped upon them war, toil, debts, and various dangers. How could you have forgotten everything that could lead to salvation, and above all, the Savior's parable that you perhaps disdain because Luke alone reports it! It tells of the man who, whether building a tower or entering a war, would first estimate the cost of the work or of the army before beginning the project. This negligence, this haste that makes you not consider the things necessary for peace but rather makes you attempt undertakings beyond your strength will destroy you, as I hope. That will be truly just provided the fall of one man does not affect an undeserving people whom you prevented from hearing the Apostle's words to the Hebrews with which it could have remained safe and innocent: "Follow peace and sanctity with all, without this no one will see the Lord." O what an incredible esteem for lesser things you have, that you should allow so many disasters in order to appear eloquent, and that the false glory of a single tongue should lead to so many deaths and wounds! But why seek the reason for present evils with empty and inane conjectures? If it were correct, it would doubtless partake more of vanity than of villany; for there is another cause, truer and more serious, and you aspire considerably higher than to the mere glory of eloquence.

But consider Roman and foreign leaders: you will find none among our own with such intentions, none with similar boldness. For who ever dared such an undertaking depending solely on an unarmed tongue? Perhaps you may cite Cicero, who admittedly, as we know, with his all-powerful eloquence terrified and drove Catiline from the city, but he was armed with the office of consul and senator, enjoyed the citizens' consent, and sought the Republic's liberty rather than a private empire. You may cite the Athenian tyrant Pisistratus, who, though I know of his great eloquence, compelled his country to serve him, armed as he was with both tongue and sword. Of them all, only Pericles, who later succeeded him, seemed to have an experience similar to yours, if it is true that his unarmed eloquence was as useful to him as was an armed one to the others; through his eloquence was thus ruined that flourishing city, the highest honor of Greece. But here, too, there is a tremendous difference: being of noble descent he was bound by no bonds of religious service, whereas because of your humble origins and your vows of poverty and obedience, you know yourself to be the servant of the poor, yet you desire to preside over the wealthy. What is more, in order to satisfy this shameful desire, you make use not so much of your charm—do not take too much comfort in this—but of the wonderful simplicity of your citizens, whom you have snared by the hooks hanging from your mouth, dragging them into places from which you will not easily retrieve them, believe me. What can I say? Surely if you loved your city, your mother and nurse, you would rather subject yourself to her than her to you. Now just as you perceive the opposite course as shameful, so do you perceive your accomplishments as astonishing. So rejoice; you alone, unexcelled in any land and in any century, unattended, naked, poor, and obscure, with new and unheard-of skills have formed a tyranny, and what was once the royal palace of the Lombard kings is now the seat of your rule. Only a hardy people can endure such a master! I rejoice too in your military successes, I rejoice that your giantlike exile, illustrious for his triumphs and victories, has been recalled by your prudent citizens, following your advice; as another Alcides, he will face not twelve but a thousand labors, crushing with heroic deeds all the monsters on earth. I rejoice too that near the castle of Nazziano where the glowing power of your spirit and your powerful effort were especially manifest, fortune at least performed as she ought. See to it that you carefully assume the demanding custody of your garrison and that you show compassion for your prisoners. This befits your greatness, which I do hope will not beget insolence; but may your clemency appear distinguished and notable to your prisoners whom you will lead before your triumphal chariot.

But laying aside all jest to conclude what I began, I beg and implore you, my friend, once you have returned to yourself, to weigh not what helps but what behooves you, not what you wish to be but what you are as well as what you have become through nature and fortune, your profession and your previous way of life. Unless I am mistaken, you will then understand that there is no room for ambition and bragging, no room for an improper and unworthy tyranny. Each time your desire to dominate is enkindled, I do not say that you should look up to heaven, as upright and temperate men indeed do when pressed by temptation, but you should turn your eyes inward and focus on your sandals, your cord, and your habit. You will see no trace of purple, everything indicates a servant of Christ and not a ruler of men. In brief, if you cannot be persuaded by any argument or warning or entreaty to renounce your ridiculous appetite for tyranny, at least adopt a love for peace in order not to become either an exile from the society of men of good will to whom the angelic herald proclaimed peace, or appear disinherited and bypassed in the testament with which Christ bequeathed peace to His followers. If you are wise, continue doing what you do with commitment. If you desire to rule, rule over those who are desirous of serving you; rule, O brother, rule over those who wish to be ruled, but in peace, which alone has the power to increase small things, to bring together scattered things, and to revive lifeless things; rule, but over a secure city, or, since that cannot be, rule more gently over its ruins, and permit no further destruction through implacable savagery, after it has been so ravaged. Do not always arm your tongue as a sword, but proceed happily with prudence and eloquence, and when you and your citizens so desire, rule and await the consequences, "for through truth and gentleness and justice," which are all sisters of peace, "your right hand will wonderfully serve you." Remember that when Gideon heard from the Lord, "Peace be with you, do not fear," he erected an altar to the Lord and gave it the name of Peace of the Lord. Do not through your wars raise a temple to Mars, as Julius Caesar presumably thought of doing toward the end of his life; for this befits a Martian ruler, the other a peaceable friar. Finally, if you like the example of Caesar and prefer to be a ruler rather than a friar, though there has been nothing more monstrous in centuries, if the stars still favor you, indeed if the Lord permits, be a ruler, but gentle and kind and a lover of peace; thus was Caesar according to those who read his letters from the period of the civil war. Listen to this final advice as though it were from heaven. Try to do good for yourself rather than evil to others, and beware lest with goads of hatred and envy you drive the people subject to you into the extremes of wretchedness, which is already at hand, and to ultimate destruction. Try not to bring shame or trouble with your tyrannical and civic arrogance upon your noble order, which is founded on the glorious name of Augustine, on the sacred charms of the solitary life, and on the humble devotion of many religious men—for this you should have already seen to if you were wise. But in recalling that the venerable relics of Augustine himself are under the same roof with you, as well as he himself who was always concerned and attached to his order, and by imagining him a witness, as they say, to whatever you do or say or even think, let yourself at length fear to sin before such a witness or to commit those acts so offensive to your master and teacher and to Christ, the master and teacher of all men. Farewell.

Milan, 25 March.

Fam. XX, 1.

To Neri Morando of Forlì, * *a curse against the present age and a prediction of things to come, and the great power of gold.*

Weighed down with cares, overwhelmed by affairs, hating everything that I see, and longing for solitude and silence from which I am chased by the barking of pursuing hounds, as though a weary and thirsty stag at a shady spring, I found your letter a temporary distraction, which I wish had been lengthy enough to make me forget forever, as it briefly did, all present concerns. For you must know that I am such an admirer of our century that in my opinion hardly any other age was more wretched or worse. My one consolation is that, if we had to be born (and it was certainly necessary for inexorable Clotho to force us over the hard threshold of this life) and could not have earlier come forth into the light, it was much better for us to have been born now than later, so negative are my predictions for the future. I am, I hope, deluding myself in this troublesome prediction, but such is the hope that our youth offers with its character, ways, desires, and studies; in comparison to them, even our mad elders will appear enviably wise to you, and fortunate for having been born earlier. Thus the world drags all things toward a worse condition as it falls headlong to its destruction. But I am omitting what a later age will do, seeing that, to cite what Tiberius Caesar supposedly said about Sergius Galba, "This has nothing to do with us"; and too I must take care not to exaggerate my complaints with my imagination lest perhaps Seneca's words apply to me, "Every age laments its ways." I believe this; yet unless I am mistaken, no other age was ever more justified in complaining about its customs. I have not overlooked what can be used as counterargument by those who love themselves and admire all their possessions. I am aware of Italy's wounds suffered in the present and in the past. She has become hardened to misfortune, developing callouses over frequent scars, although not only Italy but the entire world from the beginning has suffered countless disasters. What else is this brief life if not a prolonged death? What else is this earthly existence if not a foul prison of painful slavery and a dark house of perpetual sadness? I realize this, but it is one thing to be besieged, oppressed, pressed, burned, and ravaged by enemies,

*A high official of the Republic of Venice during the reign of Doge Dandolo, he subsequently joined the staff of the emperor, whom he accompanied on his coronation trip to Rome. Accomplished in both literature and arms, he helped court the favor of Charles IV in a number of requests made by Petrarch in behalf of friends.

and still another by vices. Sometimes an external enemy withdraws, becoming exhausted in harassing others; further, every human assault is brief, no mortal war is immortal; it necessarily ends with the loss of its leaders and with the quenching of their power. But over the space of time vices multiply and gain strength, and thus the more harm they have done, the more they will continue to do. No one is more cruel than one who has long been cruel, no one succumbs to dissipation sooner than one who has often done so. Habits are formed by repeated acts, and by succumbing to habit we become stooped, and with this inclining it is easy to be thrown to the ground. Thus does avarice increase with time, thus does ambition become more persistent with old age, thus also do all the other vices increase, while the intemperance of the ill causes their prolonged illness. With enemies such as these we must cope, yet not only do we not resist them but favor them, placing the sword to our own throats of our own accord. In fact, amazing as this may seem, if vices begin to weaken, we incite them as though the greatest unhappiness is to become less wretched. Today we see this to the point of disgust among old people—and under the sun there is nothing more repulsive—and we can read about others in histories. Among the foremost examples is Tiberius, whom I mentioned a short while ago; may his gods and goddesses torment him with evil even in the nether world. My stomach sickens and my bile convulses each time I read about that old man's shameful and shocking practices; among others was one that I am even ashamed to mention, whereby he would arouse his failing lusts, in the words of Tranquillus, by attending spectacles of monstrous copulation. Whence our elders' ridiculous and shameful complaints because they are stimulated less than usual by pleasure, or because they no longer experience seductive tickling and youthful itching, or because they have been robbed of the charms of the throat and of sleep and of the stomach, and finally because their bodily strength has failed when participating in slaughters and carnage.

Yet it is still worse to want to be bloodthirsty than to be so, although he who wishes to be evil is already evil to excess; nor is anyone worse than the person eager for sin and boastful about his shameful acts. Indeed to delight in doing evil is natural for nearly every evildoer, whence Cicero calls the habit of sinning very pleasant. To experience some remorse in the midst of dishonest pleasures and to feel a kind of rein on one's passion is also common among evildoers, but primarily among those inclined to improve, whom we have seen reach a safe haven after freeing themselves from their great storms of lust. To wallow in evil, to be carried away by pleasure, to exult in it, to strive for it, and, worst of all, to boast about it, are near-signs of an extreme and hopeless perversity. Yet the entire world is full of such people and we must live among them; it is good for us to live among them without joining them, although to no one is association with the wicked more irksome than to those who reject them because of their marked difference in behavior. However it is, we have lived among these men, and as the kingly Psalmist laments, we have grown old amidst our enemies; I would call it still more unfortunate that we must die among them. For where can we take flight, where shall we go, where will the hordes and banners of the wicked not precede us, where has their empire not been promulgated and rooted in their terrible practices? One would have to cross the ocean, were it not that we must assume our vices have long since spread to the Antipodes. It would be better to fly to heaven, except that we are pressed to the earth by our own weight; if we desire to be saved, we must free ourselves of that weight. An easy accomplishment indeed, were we not oppressed by the examples of the wicked that enrich our own age, as I said, and will enrich posterity even more. Our ancestors fought against the Carthaginians, the Cimbrians, the Teutons, the Britons, and barely defended Italy from Hannibal or the Capitoline from the Senones, but they were victorious over all because of their true and indomitable valor. If by calling upon celestial aid for protection we succeed in defending the stronghold of our Capitoline from the great army of barbaric vices enveloping it, if we resist with steadfastness the clamoring misdeeds of the multitude, we shall be stronger than Manlius, Marius, and Caesar himself. For a wall, and sometimes a fortification, separated them from the enemy, and they often rested at night and found relief from winter's rigor in their winter quarters. For us there is no repose, no time without danger, no winter, no truces, no night; nothing is ever secure and peaceful, we continuously strive for our salvation, we are always in the battleline, we are tested, besieged, and driven. The enemies are inside the walls, already armed, and approaching the stronghold of reason; they make use of their shelters, they direct their battering rams, they set fires, they climb towers; nor are the ladders raised against the walls any differently than at Troy, the ladders of crime against the walls of the soul. What do you expect me to say? They intrude even at our tables and in our bedrooms, they take us by the throat, and, what amounts to our near destruction, all the rabble armed with errors fights in the enemy's behalf. In this uncertain and difficult battle there is no hope for victory unless it be from heaven; from there let us seek it, my dear friend. But meanwhile noting where I am, I cannot avoid being disturbed, and sometimes so gravely that I am nearly overcome with gloomy anguish at my impatience with my fate.

I seem perhaps to have strayed from my point; my argument has swept me along, but now I return to it. Today, then, while involved in these cares created by the noise and annoyance of all the clamor about me, as I emerged from my bedroom, I was met by your letter, brief indeed and girt as one who arrives from a lengthy journey. Although it was late in reaching me for reasons certainly unknown to me, although it also contains news known to me for some time (indeed our Caesar, about whom it speaks before his arrival, has in the meantime not only been crowned but stolen away from us like a shadow or a dream, in a departure that I attacked with a sharp and fervent letter), my love for its sender and its own sweetness led me to view the letter as though it were announcing something new. Indeed with few words it covers much, as do weary and hastening people, and you can well imagine how sympathetically I read each word and especially the name of my Lelius, whom I beg you, whenever you can, to associate with willingly and to hold dear, for you each are worthy of the other. As for what follows in your letter about the Pisans, surely you ought not to be surprised at their upset and suspicions about our people's arrival, for no people is more suspicious; you know that this terrible vice, this viper that grabs a man with his teeth and makes him bleed, may also arouse suspicion in those who feel secure. In this I praise Caesar's foresight in providing for the citizens' fear and for the soldiers' honor. What you write about my native land I had previously heard with much joy, but I read with even greater joy that she is not refusing obedience to the Roman emperor, and that if at present there be in the entire world any concern for loss of freedom, it is in my native land.

Finally I was not at all surprised at your facetious criticism of the power of gold, for I do know that what Flaccus says about it is very true: "Gold loves to circulate among accomplices and to shatter stones with blows more powerful than lightning." In his *Metamorphoses*, Apuleius makes a similar statement: "I know well the fragility of human loyalty, and that all difficulties yield to money, and that even steel doors can be shattered with gold." How widespread and well known is this opinion, held in common by both philosopher and philosophizing jackass! You have read, I believe, in the third book of the *Cosmographia* of Pomponius Mela that the Ethiopians are very rich in gold but poor in brass; as a result, by basing the value of objects on a different scale of scarcity and abundance, their ornaments are made of bronze and their chains of gold. With us, my dear friend, all things are now made of gold—our spears, shields, chains, and crowns; with it we adorn and gird ourselves; because of it we are rich or needy, happy or wretched. Gold defeats the free and frees the defeated; gold sets free the guilty and condemns the innocent, makes the mute eloquent and the most eloquent mute; for gold Metellus delivered a harangue against Caesar, for gold Demosthenes the orator refused to speak; gold makes rulers of slaves and slaves of rulers, instills fear into the bold and boldness into the fearful, concern into the indolent and indolence into the concerned. It arms the unarmed and strips the armed, defeats undefeated leaders, oppresses great people, scatters powerful armies, ends lengthy wars within a short time, makes and snatches away peace, dries up rivers, traverses lands, agitates seas, levels mountains, opens approaches to strongholds, attacks cities, captures fortresses, and demolishes towns. As we read in Cicero, there is no place strong enough that "a donkey laden with gold cannot enter." Gold purchases famous friendships, important clients, and noble marriages, and causes its possessors to be generous, strong, learned, attractive, and—what is most shocking—saintly. Thus, the wealthy are called good men by the citizenry and in them alone do they believe; no one has confidence in the poor man because he has no money, and thus the Satirist's saying is really true: "A man disposes of as much confidence as the amount of money locked in his coffers." In short (this I say unwillingly but truth impels me), gold is not only powerful but nearly omnipotent, with all things under the heavens yielding to it and subservient to it: devotion, chastity, loyalty, in short all virtue and fame, even our God-given intellects—how shameful!—are dominated by this sparkling metal, the dregs of the earth. It unites rulers and pontiffs, it appeases men and, as they say, the very gods themselves; nor with gold is anything unconquerable or unapproachable. Knowing this full well, Jupiter transformed himself into a golden shower in order to strip the captive girl of her chastity and break open the iron doors of her prison, an undertaking worthy of such a god. Our God, however, whatever His successors may do, loves chastity, scorns gold, and detests greed. My best wishes for continuing health for your body and mind.

Fam. XX, 2.

To the same correspondent, * *that the Roman empire is everywhere more prosperous than in the north.*

I had not yet affixed my seal to the previous letter when another one unexpectedly arrived, forcing me to lay aside my signet ring in order to take up my pen once again; and although your letter is longer than the previous one, a shorter response will suffice. For there is no need to repeat my complaints about our times (since even my silence speaks out, and the situation cries out for itself), nor am I prevented in this letter from referring to what I said in the previous one. For my grief is no less today that it was yesterday or the day before, nor is the comfort afforded by your letter of today any less effective than that of yesterday. Moreover, I dare not openly speak my mind about what you just wrote me, nor does this mean that you know any less what I may feel or what I may say; often silence is more powerful than speech in expressing mental concepts, and Niobe through her silence expressed the sorrow implanted in her spirit no less than Hecuba with her barking. And thus, though the story goes that the first was transformed into a stone and the second into a dog, the silent image of the former expressed her wretchedness just as well as the querulous madness of the latter. But on one matter alone I shall not remain silent: I know that the fate of the Caesars has enjoyed fortune's favor more in the west, and indeed in any other place, than in the north; there all things are cold, lacking noble fervor and vital warmth for the empire. Restore to us, O Fortune, if the fates allow us to have the Roman Caesars, at least the Theodosii of Spain, the Severii of Africa, the Philippi of Arabia, and the Alexanders of Syria. Alas, what would that great architect of the monarchy now say, seeing his successor competing in humility with a lowly priest, recalling too that once the proud king of the Gauls, according to the historian Florus, "came as a suppliant into the camp and threw his decorations and arms at Caesar's feet," saying, "Take these, O strongest of men, you have defeated a strong man"? Many similar examples come to mind, for the subject is rich while indignation makes me loquacious; but I shall restrain myself and would not even have cited the few here except that anger compelled me to speak. As for the encounter between Caesar and the envoy, I am in agreement with what you foresee, indeed I seem almost to behold how it will go; all these things against which I have often argued do not really upset me, but

*See XX, 1.

I base what will occur on experience. I am not troubled by the fact that the emissary's horse tried to kick Caesar since I know that minds can also throw kicks and that every authority is impatient with partnerships. If ancient examples do not offer sufficient proof, I fear that a recent event offers a good example: the Roman pontiff has forbidden the Roman emperor to stay in Rome, something indicated both by reports and by the flight of Caesar, who has abandoned Italy more readily than he sought it. Indeed it seemed to me unnecessary to expel someone who fled so willingly and could be retained only with great effort; as I now understand it, the principal reason for it all was his desire to assume Caesar's crown in his own city, really the only thing for which he still seems to have some reverence. But the successor of Peter, more secure than the successor of Caesar, is not concerned with such matters, and pays no more heed to his crown whether it be on the Tiber or on the Rhone. Not only does he allow but even orders the emperor, who is satisfied with the imperial crown and title, to leave Rome, thus allowing him to be called emperor without letting him reign. For him—O marvelous human wiles!—he opens the church containing the crown, but seals the fortifications and the city, seat of the empire. But enough of this. I am pleased and not surprised at Lelius' friendly reception by Caesar, for nothing attracts more rapaciously and tenaciously than virtue, which captures and overwhelms minds, thereby keeping them forever in bonds. I never entertained any doubt that he would be loved as soon as information about him was available, and not simply by the most courteous of princes but by anyone who still treasures virtue, even though he be of a harsher nature. For who is so boorish as not to love Lelius, a name conspicuous for its praise of wisdom and famed in friendship? But if the mere reputation for virtue makes us love the ancient Laelius, whom we have never seen, what can the virtue and presence of our own Lelius accomplish? I believe that each of your points has been answered; in a separate letter I shall respond differently to your letter's final section about my domestic affairs. Furthermore, I thank you for your clear memory of matters that I had so consigned to oblivion as to think that I had not even spoken to you about them; you obviously are more curious about my affairs than I myself am, something astonishing and almost incredible, if it were not that your wonderful charity loses somewhat in value because of my well-known negligence. A cordial farewell, and remember me.

Fam. XX, 3.

To the Genoese Galeotto Spinola, * *an appeal to seize control of the republic.*

Nothing, O magnanimous man, nothing, I say, can I imagine with greater pleasure than your serene brow so worthy of reigning, which reflects the noble concerns of your indomitable intellect; nothing do I recall to mind with greater enjoyment than your magnificent words resounding with a quality not merely superior to the vulgar and ordinary but even to the human and mortal. And nothing gives me greater delight than to have deserved, though tardy, the courtesy and kindness of a great man whose personal traits I had previously tasted in his illustrious brother. What is more, I feel joy and gratitude for your brief exile that for a time drove you to this city, since it allowed me to enjoy the sight and presence of a friend whom I held dear even before knowing him. Finally, I expect nothing to be more pleasant than to behold through your prudence and authority the restoration of your city, which God, your virtue, and your bloodline have given you to rule, and which is presently upset over foreign incursions. Now, then, as you have often done in the past, reveal to the world who you are and how great you are, all the more so because it is you who have made yourself greater, more famous and more illustrious. True virtue does not feel the onset of age, it is immortal; instead of waning, it so steadily increases with age that, while it may have blossomed in youth, it bears fruit in old age. You too were rooted in firm and fertile ground, not in sterile or marshy soil, and thus owe the rich fruit of your past life and your fully developed glory to your homeland. She is calling you, her hope rests with you, she seeks your aid. Make haste; let not your age bridle you; Aratus freed Sicyon from slavery, Trasibulus freed the city of Athens and Camillus the city of Rome when each was older than you. An honorable undertaking it is, one particularly fitting for your present age, to restore harmony to your native land by the rule of the good over the wicked. If the opposite occurs, it is unavoidable for the body of a kingdom or of a city, as with the human body, to wither because of constant diseases. Already your country seems ill and in danger; prove yourself a distinguished citizen, a physician, and a father. In order to say no more than the matter requires and to appear not to distrust your valor, I shall add nothing to this; silent yet not alone, I shall note the

---

*A noble Ghibelline high in the governing bodies of Genoa, he played a key role in the political vicissitudes of that city.

results of your natural excellence. Take action, I beg you, O great man, with righteousness as you must, with strength as you are wont, with fortune as we hope, and use me as you can, if in my small way I can be of any assistance in this great undertaking. Continue in good health, remember me, and farewell.

Milan, 18 December.

Fam. XX, 4.

To Marco da Genova,* an appeal to persevere in his studies, and a comparison of ancient orators and lawyers with advocates of our own age.

I have a number of brief letters from you, all having the same subject: you ask my encouragement in order to persevere in your studies of civil law, in the belief that the power of my words would somehow serve to settle your mind, which is so upset over this recent undertaking and so anxious about its enormity. What you hope from me is prompted on the one hand by your affection for me and on the other by your humility, that excellent endowment of the spirit that is the first step toward virtue and true glory. I admit that it was not by chance but intentionally that I witheld my reply, in fact I would have avoided a response had you allowed it. The subject is difficult, perhaps more difficult than you realize because it was either dangerous for me to speak or questionable for me to remain silent; for I am in such a predicament that all my words on this matter may be taken as an indictment, my silence as contempt, my statement of truth as hatred, and my humor as derision. They call me a deserter who, after being initiated on a sacred altar, later violated and neglected it, and then spread about the secrets of Eleusinian Ceres. As a boy, my dear friend, I was destined to such study by my father when I was barely twelve. Having first gone to Montpellier and then to Bologna, I wasted seven entire years in such study, learning its rudiments as much as my age and intelligence allowed. If asked today whether I have any regrets at having spent such time, I am embarrassed, for I would like to have seen everything possible; I do regret losing so much time from my brief life, and I shall regret that as long as I live. During those years I could have been doing other things more noble or more suited to my nature; one does not always select as a way of life what is nobler but rather what appears more suitable to the chooser. Otherwise all men would purse the same profession since, as in everything else, there is always one superior to the others. Yet if all men were to focus on this one pursuit, what would become of the others? If everyone aspired to philosophy or poetry, what would happen to navigation, agriculture, and the others that provide assistance to mortal life? Imagine the world consisting only of Platos or Homers, Ciceros or Virgils: who will be the plowman, the merchant, the architect, the smith, the cobbler, the innkeeper, without whom great minds would

*See III, 12.

go hungry and be distracted from the heights of their noble studies for lack of food and shelter? It was good for there to be such variety in human interests and endeavors since the greater ones offer adornment and support for the lesser ones, and the lesser for the greater.

I am not unaware, my dear friend, that in the past many men sought great glory through the study of civil law, particularly in the age when men truly cherished justice, when, according to Sallust, "they valued justice not because of the law but because of natural inclination." Yet even at that time the infinite variety of affairs and man's short-lived memory made laws necessary whereas today they serve to check boldness and to restrain passions, and are honored mostly because mankind cannot survive without them and not because of any respect for virtue or the law. Hence many codifiers, interpreters, and teachers of these laws attained fame among various peoples; but to speak of them in too great detail would be a lengthy undertaking. Most celebrated of all was Solon, the Athenian lawgiver, who turned to poetry in his old age, it is said, after having established sound institutions for his native land, a famous source of philosophy and eloquence. Had he done this with controlled deliberation, imagine how much the studies deserted by such a man would have been misconstrued! And who would not prefer that field to which he turned at a time when he did not lack the light of the intellect or an abundance of learning or a prolonged experience with life? But it could happen, nor is it far removed from the truth, that not through comparing different studies but through delight alone and in order to avoid toil, that distinguished elder yielded to his inclination and exchanged a difficult and weighty occupation for sweet idleness; thus he should not so much be an example for young people, born to serve the state, as an excuse for deserving elders who, being similarly tempted, might want to seek out a noble idleness following his example. But on such a doubtful matter, I have no way of reaching a definite conclusion. For who can guess what prompted Solon, especially since, though we know much about him, no written testimony still survives with which to form an opinion? In such a doubtful and ancient matter, it would be ridiculous for me to suggest a weak hypothesis without any evidence to support it; thus, the entire matter must remain in doubt, affirming only what is certain: at one time lawyers and orators enjoyed great fame. But these were always very rare indeed, even rarer than outstanding poets, whose rarity is surely well known. What great talent must a man possess who can join the power and beauty of skillful speech to a knowledge not only of civil law but of nearly everything that the orator must address in rendering judgment or other decisions involving such law (once an immense field before being reduced to manageable size, something that Julius Caesar began but death prevented him from completing, and Justinian then realized)! Yet still today the field remains hopelessly confused and uneven due to the great variety of barely distinguishable legal cases. This I believe to be the greatest and rarest miracle of the human intellect and memory inasmuch as it is insufficient merely to have acquired knowledge; one must also have everything in readiness and, to use Caesar Augustus' words, at one's fingertips because of unexpected and sudden attacks by adversaries and because of the dangers inherent in legal suits. Ultimately, not even this suffices unless all you have learned with the intellect and through study or have diligently preserved in the memory is used effectively in order to persuade, as the rhetoricians call it, with an eloquence befitting the matter at hand, effective, adorned, and capable of arousing minds. No one should be surprised that there has always been a dearth of men with such ability, for they must exhibit not one quality but numerous ones, and these not as other men do but in a different, unique, and personal way. Yet more important than all such qualities is an exquisite eloquence that, if considered only in itself, "is a vast and complex subject that until now has not been compliant enough to reveal itself entirely to anyone," if we are to believe Severus Cassius. Thus, the men who have excelled in the art of oratory, consisting of various elements, have enjoyed great glory and were justifiably said to control events through their eloquence and to hold sway over the minds of men. Of this type were Demosthenes, Isocrates, and Eschines among the Greeks, and Cicero, Crassus, and Antonius among the Romans, and even several others, but these three were easily the most prominent, although beyond any doubt Julius Caesar reached the summit of such glory, something even his enemies do not deny, or surely would have reached, had he not been distracted by his involvement in numerous affairs, by the toil of war, and by the burden of command.

Subsequently, since a stay on the summit is often brief and descent always easy, it happened that they too had to descend, and abandoning the heights of eloquence, they acquired a basic knowledge of the law in which they then distinguished themselves; in such law it is common knowledge that Greece yielded to Rome. Here then are names in your profession worthy of respect, names that are usually considered ancient, whereas they are almost new and recent: Iulius Celsus, Salvius Iulianus, Neratius Priscus, Vindius Verus, Salvius Valens, Volusius Metianus, Ulpius Marcellus, Iabolenus, as well as Scevola also known as Breviloquus, to distinguish him from others before him with the same name who were also outstanding for mental ability or prophecy or as high priests. Under Scevola studied Papinianus, who, if my memory is correct, they say had the sharpest mind in civil law; what is more, the historian Elius Spartianus calls him the "sanctuary of the law and stronghold of royal learning." The first three are known to have flourished under the divine Hadrian, the next five under Antoninus Pius, the ninth under the philosopher Marcus Antoninus, the most prudent of princes; the tenth lived under Antoninus Bassianus, a cruel monster who eventually killed him because of his unwillingness to excuse the emperor's parricide. After these Iulius Paulus and Domitius Ulpianus, able lawyers and assessors to Papinianus, lived in great honor under the Emperor Aurelius Alexander; indeed they were held in such esteem that the emperor was considered outstanding primarily because he governed the Republic by acting upon their counsel. I shall not mention others; let it suffice to have cited the more illustrious. I have done so with great care simply because a large portion of the pettifogging lawyers in our day care little or nothing about the origin of justice and the first lawmakers, for they are satisfied with learning how to be careful about contracts, decisions, and wills, thereby making profit their professional goal, whereas a knowledge of the beginnings of their art and of its authorities provides intellectual pleasure and strengthens the understanding with the knowledge of what must be done. Furthermore, profit is peculiar to the mechanical arts, while the goal of the noble and more honored arts is more liberal and respected. If you now reconsider what was said, you will note a further decay in your profession, one that is much greater than the first. Nor will you be surprised if you also view this part of the universal nature of things; once they have begun to slide, they rush downward, hastening their collapse under their own weight, so that the fall from the midpoint to the bottom is easier and more serious than from the top to the midpoint. Just as the first stage was from the heights of a complex discipline and heavenly eloquence to a single discipline of equity and civic law, so the second stage proceeded from that point to loquacious ignorance, whence, in my opinion, we can now be quite certain about the likelihood of falling even further. Indeed what can be lower? Either they do not understand or they forget the laws laid down by our fathers with such seriousness and facility, thereby dishonoring the justice so zealously cultivated by our predecessors. What a venal merchandise they have created! For them, their tongue and hand, their intelligence and soul, their dignity, reputation, time, loyalty, and friendship, in short, everything is for sale, and not at a fair price. What a difference in times and customs! Our predecessors armed justice with sacred laws, these men prostitute it, stripped and defenseless; our forefathers greatly valued truth, these value deception; the former used to give the people clear and precise answers, these nourish disputes with deceits and cheap tricks; with the legal shafts they acquired for destroying opponents, they desire to become immortal. But why continue? Whoever has succeeded in twisting the reluctant and resistant law to his whim is thought to have fulfilled an attorney's duty, thus deserving the reputation of a learned man. But if a person, scornful of such stratagems, were to take the path of naked truth, he would not only be cut off from honors and fees but suffer the shame of being considered an uncultivated, stupid man.

Having chosen this course late in life, you now ask my encouragement as if you were aware of the difficulties of a late start. I know not the words with which to address this, but I shall make an attempt. Laws are not in themselves bad, yet though established for the common good they are often directed toward its destruction; so too gold is not an evil simply because it was the cause of sin or of danger for many. Nor for that matter is iron evil; even though originally intended to be of service to man, for tilling earth and protecting one's native land, it has often caused the death of individuals or civil war. In general, if everything that man misuses were evil, what would ever not be evil? Not the bodily senses or intelligence, not wealth or the foods that we eat. Many men abuse even the mercy and patience of God, and often those things that are excellent by nature are put to the worst use by our perversity. Laws are certainly good, not only useful but necessary to the world; but those who administer the law can be either good or evil, and the more they are evil, the greater is the glory of those who are good. In human actions the intention of the doer is of prime importance, as is the purpose for which one undertakes something; it is not the matter in itself but your mind that deserves praise or censure. That is what converts good into evil and things that appear evil into good, and what directs one and the same thing to such different ends that the thing no longer appears as one but as two totally opposite ones. The priest goes to church to perform his sacred offices, the adulterer goes to further his lusts; a person may be lustful before the altar and pure in a brothel. King Saul saved King Amalech, and for this clemency deserved the inexorable wrath of God; Phineas pierced an Israelite and a foreign woman with a sword, and his cruelty, pleasing to God and useful to the people, gloriously earned for him a perpetual reputation for justice. Here you have murder, a monstrous crime, being acceptable in the judgment of not just anyone but of God, and kindness disapproved by that same judgment. I could list a thousand such examples if needed, but in this one you have the taste of all. Desire for gain leads one man to a school of law while another goes for love of injustice; God, the judge of minds and the discerner of intentions and the distributor of intelligence, will cause the first to emerge as a mercenary and ambulatory loudmouth and the second as an eminent professor of the good and a supporter of justice. From these examples you can see where I am leading. If you were to ask my advice about the entire matter, giving me complete freedom to counsel you, I would suggest that you carefully consider many things, weighing on accurate scales your qualifications and your inclination. As with other things, there are degrees of intelligence; some are suited to certain ends while others are suited to others. I would also suggest that you consider your age, for generally a strong and early beginning is required for anything to bear timely fruit; a tree that does not flower in the springtime will not bear fruit in the autumn. Thus, although some tend to discount the age of infancy, the mind destined for great success must be shaped, in the opinion of truly learned men, not only from infancy but from the wetnurse's lap. I would point out many other difficulties: chiefly the marital yoke about your neck, which is truly unlike Hercules' and which is in need not of further burdens but of relief. Great, indeed, is a strength of mind and body that can support both scholarship and a wife. I would also say that you should give some consideration to the costs as well as the labor since no other profession offers less pleasure and more tediousness. And finally I would counsel you not to overlook your reputation, which, because of the present state of the legal profession, may perhaps enjoy some greatness but not for long. I could list lawyers in our time whose names were very celebrated not long ago, yet today are obscure and unknown. But since you are not asking advice on what to do, but assistance in accomplishing it, together with the comfort of my words, which I alone seem able to offer, I urge and suggest that you persevere in this field to which either your will or your fate has driven you and not start a new way of living every day. Nothing is worse for a wayfarer than not knowing where he is going, nothing more shameful for a man than not knowing what he knows. In vain do you raise the sails when you have lost the rudder; for you will go wherever fortune, and not your reason, leads you. From the beginning we must have fixed in our minds where we wish to go, lest with continual changing we think, as happens at night when the path is lost, that we are going forward when we are going backward. This is why we see decrepit old men with childish minds, behaving as though they were returning to the threshold of life at which they had begun, being deceived by the shadows of error and wearied by the bewildering change in their plans. In recent years I have seen you cast about by a constant flux of plans and exhausted by the blows of varying advice. I beg you, begin in good faith to desire one thing; when your prow is directed to a particular shore and your sails to a single wind with your helm under control, then at last will your voyage be certain, then will you really make progress, perhaps not as much as you wish, but as much as heaven will grant. You will go forward, I say, and not turn back: for nothing is so contrary to repose and nothing so near to vertigo as going in circles. In sum, here is my thought on it all: if to have excelled among the first orators were a supreme accomplishment, and to have excelled among the second-level experts in law were a great one, so too, given these times, it is no little accomplishment to excel among our third-level lawyers; nor do I deem it unworthy of praise, provided this be the spirit of the scholar and this the purpose of his studies, namely, that once he has attained his goal, he not become a promulgator of lies and an accumulator of riches as the rest, but a defender of justice and the state, a terror against lawyers' audacity, a check on judicial greed, in short, a port for the wretched and a reef for the wicked. Farewell.

Milan, 28 May.

Fam. XX, 5.

To Barbato da Sulmona,* that he be more cautious.

Never, I swear, have I received your letters without their bringing some reason for rejoicing or some solace for my cares; this is just what your last letter did with more than its usual power, for it rid my mind of the fear and suspicion, typical of all lovers, that your absence and your lengthy silence had produced. My pleasure was heightened too by your mentioning that fine and dear man whom I particularly love and find surprisingly refreshing despite my never having seen him, save that by seeing you, I seem to see him; thus does love make two persons into one. As for those two whom you mention as having unexpectedly come to see you last year with the pretext of being close friends of mine, I do know the one from Bologna, but the other from beyond the Alps I scarcely know at all. In the future, then, I beg you to be more cautious and not to give money indiscriminately to anyone with my name on their lips. So widely known is our friendship that if you submit to these kinds of flattery, all is lost: not only will they empty your purse, but your moneybox and your home. Were the person, the one whom I said I do indeed know, to return here, he doubtless would give me much news about you; but while he was away — and you must not be angry with him but rather have compassion on him — he suffered an unexpected and miserable death. Hopefully from his hands you received my *Parthenias* that you requested, copied by my own hand, as well as a brief poem that serves as proem to the letters dedicated to you. But of my remaining writings what shall I send you and what shall I not? I was hoping to go to Rome, drawn by an insatiable desire to satisfy my eyes and my mind, where finally I could put an end to my travels, not to say my wanderings; this I would have done two years ago were it not for the tumult in Liguria that kept me chained beyond the Po. I shall nonetheless go, as I hope, bearing with me some of my trifles that I recall you were always so eager to have. And then, I shall either send for you in Rome, availing myself of certain prerogatives, or I myself, in order to fulfill a long-standing desire of mine, shall come among the Peligni if at all possible. In the meantime, give my best to that distinguished man who bears my name and is of one mind with me, and farewell.

27 August.

*See IV, 8.

Fam. XX, 6.

To Francesco of the Church of the Holy Apostles, * *a complaint on the interception of his letters.*

Here, in brief, is the reason for my lengthy silence for which your letters chide me in a way that could be called either bitter or sweet, respectful or frank. First of all, for many days I was hampered by fervor for my studies, with which I would like nothing to interfere, and by my zeal in composing, which usually is as furious as it is beguiling, but also likely to cool down at the least reason. To this also add your journey, which left me uncertain for a long time—and I continue to be so—as to where my letters might find you; then there were few messengers, surprisingly as common an inconvenience in the midst of cities as it is for one living alone in the country. Nor shall I deny that, throughout this silent period about which you rightly complain, I had written some things that I decided upon rereading not to send for the simple reason that they seemed too true and too unrestrained: for in our century nothing is more hated than truth and freedom. Thus, it seemed preferable to offend by silence you alone, in whose good graces it would always be simple for me to return, rather than to wound outrageously with the sting of my words the many thousands whom truth alone has long made my enemies, several of whom still bear the bloody scars and still feel the pain of old wounds. Nor should I forget to mention—my frequent lament—that the graceful style of your letters has been an obstacle to their reaching me untouched and only after a long time. In fact, not only their style but the rare and unusual beauty of the calligraphy serves to enchant the mind and eyes on the one hand with elegant concepts and language, quite natural to your talent, and on the other with the unusual hand-penned ornamentation. I do not know, however, what prevents my letters from reaching you (since they wish to do so), although I do know that many of mine were stopped midway, like proper matrons who unwillingly suffer violence at the hands of foul adulterers. Thus not only has freedom of action perished but even freedom of expression. During my return trip from Padua, where I had lately gone on business—having first been to Venice for some relaxation—I came upon two beautiful letters of yours, twin creations in a single birth from your fertile mind; they were in the hands of certain men who were not evil, yet I was really more surprised at their having them than I would be at a mole purchasing a mirror, a bull with wings, a jackass with a lute,

*See XII, 4.

a monkey with a chaplet, or a raven with rouge. And what do you think happened? I came away happily when by agreement of the enterprising group they kept one letter and gave the other to me, who was the only one named in your insciption. And thus, my dear friend, I have kept my promise to reveal the reasons for my silence; I would now write at even greater length were it not for the lack of time, which I have brought upon myself, and also for the pleasant company of our common friend, which, save for its brevity, lacks nothing but your presence. Without my noticing it, the enticing and silent days have slipped by; but what I cannot tell you by pen, he will convey in person. Listen, then, to him in full confidence since he knows everything I am thinking and doing, what my life is like, in short, all of me with all my trifles and small hopes. Farewell, and remember me.

Fam. XX, 7.

To the same correspondent. *

I really feel as though I am reading not your letter but Flaccus's, to whom Caesar jokingly said, "You seem to fear that your books are greater than you." Certainly your stature is moderate and elegant, something he lacked, but if he could jokingly be excused, what is your excuse for such brevity? Yet what am I saying? You have already given such an excuse by blaming the lack of time. By heaven, I believe you, for I too have the same problem quite often, so that when I would like to write at length, I must be content with writing very little. As to whether I have received your letters, you will learn that from my next letter and personally from that friend of ours (to whom I send my regards); to his long tale of hardship I now add nothing except my sorrow, shame, and compassion for having allowed such a man to leave me and my house, indeed his own, in such foul weather. But his wishes compelled me to yield, for I did not feel that I could oppose him, though I did see and pointed out to him the threatening weather and heavy skies, the dark clouds and the drenched fleece of the Ram, which usually delights in vegetation and flowers. What could I do? Neither Lycomedes nor fabled Apollo departed with greater sadness from Neoptolemus or from Phaeton than I did; but what could I expect from a friend that neither the former could from his grandson nor the latter from his own son? I thus yielded and when part of my mind had departed, I was distressed until learning from his letter that he had completed a considerable portion of his dangerous journey, having crossed the Po and its tributaries, now raging more than usual at their swollen sources. I shall not rest until I have learned from his or your letter that he has arrived in his native land; for though he has crossed the king of rivers, there remain the Apennines, the king of mountains, and I pray for his successful crossing to Him who alone "beholds the earth and makes it tremble, touches the mountains and makes them smoke." I must now explain my silence in these recent days, which you rightly lament, although I do believe an adequate explanation was given in my earlier letter. If you calculate the duration of our friendship, either I am mistaken or you still are my debtor in the number of letters that we have exchanged. Indeed among my trifles—some call them letters—that I am now collecting with the help of a gifted man and friend, almost no name appears as frequently as yours despite the fact that our des-

*See XII, 4.

tinies and the immoderate and foolish thirst of some scholastics dissatisfied with their own drink have, I hear, caused a delay in receiving many of your letters directed here to me and mine to you. Stay well, and farewell.

Milan, 11 April, in haste.

Fam. XX, 8.

To Agapito Colonna the Younger, * *an excuse with an expression of admiration.*

I happily read the beginning of your letter, but the remainder sadly, the conclusion with uncertainty, and the entire letter with such amazement that I seemed to be reading it almost in a dream. Your style turned my attentive mind in so many directions that as I read I could not foresee your reason for writing, or where you were leading your puzzled reader. What do you expect me to say? I still seem not to be awake, I still seem to be dreaming, nor do I know what sense to make of your words. You so mingle the bitter with the sweet, the happy with the sad, the bright with the dark, the certain with the doubtful, that I suspect I have drunk bile mixed with honey or nectar mixed with wormwood, or if such a thing exists, a mixture that leaves an uncertain taste. But if possible with these words I shall digest in any way possible this medicine with which you watered my soul, which expected something more pleasant from your springs. The first section of your letter brings me back in memory to my youth and to your boyhood or adolescence, recalling with affectionate and mindful care how much I then tried to prod and nurture your fine character, encouraging it in any way that I could, and how eagerly and skillfully I weaned you from your diet of milk to solid food, and finally how I always held you in highest esteem. But while I admit to yielding to no one in my love for you, I claim no credit for your success. Whatever you have of greatness—I rejoice that at present it is considerable—I did not cause, save perhaps by rejoicing and admiring and praising, which are wont to be sharp goads for noble minds, nor to my knowledge did anyone else, except divine providence, your own hard work, and the burning power of your intellect. This being the case, I nevertheless am glad that it seems otherwise to you, and willingly accept the credit that you offer me for such glory though it is based on false premises. Therefore, whichever may be the case, nothing could have been more pleasing or sweeter to my mind than your affectionate commemoration of things past and your testimonial in my behalf. The bitterness that I later found sprinkled on this sweet moment I would state more directly, were I not speaking to you who provided me with both in one letter. I shall nonetheless make an attempt. What you say, then,

*A junior member of the powerful Colonna family in whose youthful education Petrarch had a hand and who at the time of this letter, c. 1359, found himself in difficult straits.

in other words but obviously with this meaning (and it is so expressed that you seem to be joking except for making your point in a style that is much too firm and serious) is that in the natural course of vacillating and revolving human affairs, having come by great riches, a somewhat loftier position, and a lovely and elegant home, I have spurned, fled, and forgotten you. And furthermore you say that by the same harsh destiny you have become an exile and a poor man after falling from greater heights, but that you are satisfied with modest nourishment and humble dress, a roof that protects you from the rain, and a small home; having been cast ashore from the tempestuous seas of the Curia, in which we were tossed about for so long, as if from a serious shipwreck, you have found refuge on the shores of the University of Bologna. Nor did this suffice, for you had to add that I, and this is even worse—I cite your own words so as not to alter any of your accusation—"cast lots on the innocent garment of the unjustly accused," a crime that admittedly I cannot comprehend despite much mental effort. So too, I do not understand your saying that I had designed a tree of vanities in which you have heard your name is included. I truly know nothing of having ever designed any tree of vanities, although if we are willing to recognize and confess the truth that whatever we write or read, whatever we think or speak, whatever we do or desire, in short, all of this life, or at least a great portion of it is vanity, as that author says who with all his wisdom did not publicly deny the charge of vanity: "Vanity of vanities and all is but vanity." On this theme I had long ago begun to write a short work in a style between elegant and ordinary as is my custom, and I certainly would have completed it except that the subject seemed to deserve more extensive treatment since man's life daily brings something new and something vain, whence my little book may turn out to be longer and fuller. But neither in it nor in others have I ever included your name since there was no occasion to do so, despite my willingness; and yet if illustrious men of our age were to be included, I would certainly not have remained silent about your uncle and your father, leaving aside yourself lest I would seem to be flattering you in your anger when I did not during our friendship. But I was unwilling for the sake of so few outstanding names to have my composition stray so far and through so many shadows; and so, economizing in both subject and labor, I decided to set as a limit to my account a period long before this century.

Since, then, as I have said, I do not grasp the double accusation of garment and name directed against me, I shall leave them aside to respond to those that I do understand. As for your words about my good fortune, take care lest someone has been making a fool of you or you of me. I cannot deny that my annual income has increased somewhat, and that by remaining idle and still, I have accumulated what is denied many busy and hard-working men. But they who measure with a prejudiced eye only the growth of a person's patrimony do not consider the losses incurred, which always seem paltry to them. I shall say nothing more to those men since they are victims of envy, but to you, to whom I wish to relate the tenor of my life, I shall also say this: the greater the income, the greater the expenses, and at year's end my purse is more worn, dirtier, and emptier, not fuller. Thus despite having already spent so much time among riches, I am in no way richer except for an increase in years and a readier contempt for perishable things; this is my wealth, not that proclaimed by envy, and it is much greater and indeed, in your judgment and mine, more certain. Do not, however, take this as an expression of displeasure with my fortune, or in the manner of the multitude, as an attack of vain laments against her. Among the rabble she is thought to be a great power, but I have trusted in the opinion of the great writers that she is really nothing in herself, and that fortune rests exclusively on Him alone to whom I have always said with the Psalmist: "You are my God, my destiny rests in your hands." Abundantly, plentifully, although perhaps not in accordance with my desires yet surely in accordance with my needs, have I been provided for, thanks to that God who, much more truly than that Virgilian god of Tityrus, "granted us this repose" so gently and so equitably that neither arid want nor excessive abundance wearies my mind, wherefore I rejoice because I seem to remain equidistant from both extremes. My riches thus far suffice for myself and for my friends in need, and—something that is a significant advantage of wealth—they consume and torture the envious. Cicero calls moderation best, and what is more, Flaccus calls it golden, perhaps so as to make it seem most desirable to men of the persuasion that nothing is better than gold. Thus, this finest of things, this truly golden possession has been granted me with God's assistance so that at least you who have loved me and my virtue should rejoice in this condition rather than insult or disparage it. But were I not happy even with this lot, to whom would I turn? Where would I set my goal? Or what would be left for me, save to join the Arimaspi in order to wage war with one eye, or better yet blind, against the northern griffins? Let this suffice regarding my wealth, which I never really intended to discuss. If deceptive rumor has perhaps caused your opinion to stray from the truth, it is not surprising because the time, the place, and the very nature of the matter could have caused the error. For conditions in Italy have long kept us apart; what is more, even among neighbors, estimating a family's worth is wont to be all the more difficult the easier it is for mortals to brag or complain, and pride feigns false riches or avarice bewails false poverty.

Insofar as the remainder of your letter is concerned, I cannot help being astonished and amazed that you can be so forgetful concerning either myself or yourself. For you say—would that you had implied it so that I would have been free to forgive your words, something I would have gladly done, but you do say it clearly—that because of your poverty, which I find difficult to conceive considering your lineage and virtue, I have come to have contempt for you; and you ascribe this, God willing, to my riches, which I, as you have heard, neither lack nor abound in, yet I gradually seem to possess in even lesser quantities since my indifference to earthly things daily intensifies as the journey for which they were needed becomes shorter. Alas, how true are proverbs, particularly the one saying that many measures of salt must be eaten in order to fulfill the duties of friendship. Did I then deserve your insulting opinion that my riches, regardless of their amount, have made me arrogant, whereas I really have incurred more obligations and am more readily subject to envy and to a more serious fall because of my loftier position; or do I deserve your opinion that I have come to despise not so much you, whom I have greatly esteemed of all your contemporaries, but anyone else because of poverty? On the contrary, time and again I disdained those who had become wealthy, whom I had previously esteemed and cherished, not because wealth in itself should be scorned, or poverty loved, since philosophers had taught me to consider them unimportant, but because through long observation I have learned that for many men adversity was the father of virtue and prosperity the father of vice. But now I am as weary of writing as I am of inquiring what prompted these remarks so foreign to your writing and to my behavior, unless you wished to reproach with such punishment my silence, which I do admit has been too long. How justifiably you do so I refuse to discuss; every reproof from a man such as yourself is just, indeed not only just but pleasing and agreeable and pleasant. Had you remembered me who you claim has forgotten you, then you would not have been convinced that I had been transformed by some mysterious riches, as if by Circe's poisonous drink, nor would you have ascribed my silence to scorn but to my nature. For some time now, you have known of my laziness as well as my responsibilities and cares that at day's end, believe me, usually become more serious for the wayfarer.

Add to this the lack of messengers, for although you mention to my amazement an elegant dwelling and unusual munificence, still to this day I am Ambrose's guest; and thus hidden in a remote section of the city, and often even in the country, I know not what transpires in the world. So farewell, for now, and if you can, be convinced that I am neither wealthy nor poor, and that whatever I may be, even though I were to become deaf and dumb, I shall be yours.

Milan, 13 April.

Fam. XX, 9.

A response to a letter from three friends. *

Your threefold letter written with three fine pens and colored with three inks I have joyfully looked at three times, and more. My only response to your letter is that there is nothing an ingenious eloquence cannot accomplish, and if I wished to pursue the many proofs of its power, I would need more time than is available for writing this, it truly being so brief a period of time that my original intention was to write nothing rather than so little. But with your letter you have accomplished something that I would have deemed utterly impossible: to make me envious of Babylon's inhabitants. Yes, I envy you who live in the worst of all cities, but in an honored dwelling free of evil desires and inaccessible to Babylonian mores, very similar, in short, to the Elysian fields that are said to be full of happiness amidst the pains and afflictions of Avernus. This I write at one and the same time to all of you to whom I had often written individually, amidst haste and drowsiness, amidst the anticipation and fear of dawn, the cold and a cough, while even paper and pen and oil lamp seem to rebel.

12 January before dawn. Live happily, farewell, and remember me.

*The three friends were Socrates, Guido Sette, and Francesco of the Church of the Holy Apoostles.

Fam. XX, 10.

To Giovanni Aretino,* felicitations on his condition, and news about his own.

Lay aside any expectation of a lengthy letter, usually frightening to a reader but delightful to you because of your desire to speak with me. Everything here prevents me from rambling : the hour, the cold, sleep, work, and things that I must do all hold me in check. To these must be added the small sheet of paper that I purposely chose so as to have less space for my unfettered pen. From your letter I learn of your escape from a perilous storm, for you have not only sailed into port but are seated on the shore. My congratulations to you, since no news of you could have made me happier. As for me, however, know that I am safe in the midst of perils (O thick head of mine!) and so tranquil amidst the tempests that if I did not see others strewn about in the stormy sea and were not struck by the seafarers' clamoring, I would not realize that I was at sea. I sit at the helmsman's feet and stand on the heaving prow, not motionless but certainly unshaken, awaiting the end with a mind that considers nearly every wind as favorable and every port as acceptable. Thus my neglect of human affairs at first caused tedium, then laziness and security, and finally sluggishness; and were I not thought arrogant to attribute to myself what was written of Marcus Cato, at times I do seem to myself, particularly at this late hour when writing to you, to be in the same condition in which Brutus once found his uncle: sleepy, fearing for everyone, and sure of myself. How true this may be will be seen through experience; in fact, I hope that it will not be the case, for it is the foolish man who risks danger in his desire to know by experience. The fact is that I envy your ordinary clothing more than the wealth of Crassus, and I sigh over your rustic dwelling that I am forbidden to enjoy. Farewell.

Milan, 27 January, before daybreak and in haste.

*See VII, 8.

Fam. XX, 11.

To Stefano Colonna, Provost of St-Omer,* a friendly letter.

With profound and solemn pleasure I have read your letters; and I rejoice that you are convinced of my good will, which while lacking visible proofs, is revealed, shines forth, and appears in a number of ways; on the other hand, I am as certain of your good will as I am of my own. The suggestive brevity of your letters itself speaks eloquently of you; this Bergamesque Cicero of ours, enemy of the one from Arpino, likewise tells me much, but no eloquence can persuade me of your affection as much as does my mind in silence. I do wish to see you, as you surely must know without my saying so, and although the conscript fathers have no concern about our separation, I still see you quite clearly despite them. As for them, while they may delight in my absence (in this alone do we agree), I still see them in spite of themselves. But I speak as though I see them as most people do! I see within them wherever they may be, and though blind to everything else, I marvel at being so sharp-sighted in this: I see their minds and secret feelings and, perhaps unknown to them, I participate in their thoughts. For their actions are daily becoming more apparent not only to me but to the entire world, which until now pretends not to notice them. When it does, it will not put up with them, believe me. I should like to write more, but I have barely been able to reach this point; for some reason, today I have taken pen in hand more slowly than usual, and even before beginning to write, I was weary. Farewell, O distinguished sir, and remember me.

Milan, 1 May.

*See XV, 7.

Fam. XX, 12.

To his Lelius, an exhortation to remain calm.*

From your last two letters I have felt that you are deeply upset. Astonished, worried, and taking many factors into consideration, I reached the conclusion that nothing, whatever it may be, should make you so sad; for it behooves a man, especially at this age, to have become hardened to all of fortune's blows. The greatest remedy for all of life's adversities is the realization that nothing remains constant, everything human evolves and flees, so that a person recognizes upon careful reflection that on earth there is no occasion for joy or grief, no reason for fear or hope; what often used to charm or distress us, what used to threaten or flatter us has vanished, vanishing in the midst of our planning. All things, my dear brother, whether happy or sad, will pass like a dream, in the blink of an eye, so that upon awakening we shall be ashamed of having grieved or rejoiced over nothing or of having entertained hope or fear over nothing. I ask you, then, cease your sorrowing, becalm every movement unworthy of your seriousness, and if you do have reason to grieve for which I can be of assistance, ask me anything at all and I shall obey. Today I am writing you only about our Milanese friend who called me father and you son, though you are older than I and he could be our grandfather, for that charming old man has departed for eternal bliss not without considerable sadness on my part; though certainly advanced in age, he still was for me and for my cares a pleasing and friendly comfort. A good and noble man but not wealthy, he was not denied the supreme honor; he was laid to rest under the portico of St. Ambrose in the old stone sepulchre belonging to his family. I loved that man who I knew loved us, who often made special mention of you; he had almost returned to childhood and his speech would evoke laughter even among mourners. He constantly disputed with me and with all who were with me on matters of philosophy or the Catholic faith; he had a veritable cornucopia of arguments, deigning to yield to no man except myself, to whom he would yield not because of reason or intelligence but because of friendship. He had a tremendous faith in knowledge, and harried all men, but especially the religious, with trifling questions; reason could not defeat him, shouting matches could not weary him. Whomever he would verbally accost, he would first ask whether that person were a man of letters; if he received a negative answer, he would scorn him as though an irra-

*See III, 19.

tional animal and silently depart, shaking his head. But if the person admitted a knowledge of literature, the old man would say, "Time will tell," and promptly throw a question at him; whatever the response, he would jeer at him with flowing words and never-ending arguments. Often he would question a person as though in admiration, asking where his books were or whence he had acquired such profound knowledge on so many matters. Then, touching his finger to his forehead, he would say, "It is here, here, that I have my books and my knowledge; for books are but borrowed remedies for human frailty, invented for the sole purpose of aiding a failing memory." We all would laugh; for he said nothing that he did not believe, and with his opinions he lived very happily and joyfully. He would use only grammatically correct speech, although neither Priscian nor Aristarchus, even if armed, would be secure, so blatant were the barbarisms and solecisms with which he would go armed into battle. Finally, he recently began writing a book dedicated to you, which I wish were completed, for he would have left us an offspring of his intellect; but I am uncertain whether, following Virgil's example, he consigned it unfinished to the flames or, like Numa Pompilius, he buried it in the ground, or whether he did anything else with it. Three days before his death he came to me, sadder than usual, and when I asked the reason for his changed demeanor, he said, sighing, "Today I am completing my eighty-fifth year; how much time do you think I have? Perhaps twenty-five years, which would be too few." Smiling, I answered, "Have no doubt; you will enjoy thirty more." With these words he brightened and said, "That is good; that would be enough." And with this, he departed, nor did I see the man thereafter, for he did not seem to be dying or laboring under any illness but old age. Yet three days later, under my grieving and astonished eyes, he was borne to church in the evening, as is the people's custom, in order to be buried the following day. In a tale so mournful I have also related many humorous things so that you may both enjoy and mourn our friend's memory. For me, who delights in men of such character even amidst my many concerns, he had become not a frequent guest, as was his wont, but almost a habitual one. Finally, I gave as much aid as possible to his painful and declining old age, and as a very last favor followed him with moist eyes to the door of his tomb. Farewell.

Milan, 1 May.

Fam. XX, 13.

To the same correspondent, * *a plaintive exhortation for reconciliation with a friend.*

Perceiving from your letters your mental state and unaware of its cause, I urged you to maintain your usual calmness by scorning mortal and transitory things that hasten toward nothingness. But afterward I learned not without a deep wound to my spirit that the reason for your turmoil was that, angered by someone's arrogant words, you attacked your Socrates and mine, that Socrates whom you knew before I did. Now I understand why you wished to keep this hidden from me, knowing as you do that it would grieve me, especially because I had to learn of such a terrible thing not from you but from someone else. Oh, what shall I say or where shall I begin? I can think and speak only of the pain, and I am so grief-stricken as to be incapable of uttering a sound. May he who caused your disagreement and my grief never have a moment's pleasure! And so, my brother, am I of so little import, am I of so little worth to you that I was neither consulted by letter nor, if unworthy of that, at least informed by letter after the fact about your radical change of mind causing you to reject a friend who had been so faithful, so long-standing, so dependable, particularly since, as they are saying, it is I who am the cause of this bad situation? For I hear that a viper's tongue, injecting you with terrible poison, accused Socrates of nothing more than writing to me against you. Had you been willing to weigh and consider everything with your wisdom, which you possessed since youth and which should have increased with time, you would have realized that this was absolutely false and inconceivable. Would that you had thought of the story about Plato, who rejected and cast out the accuser of his friend Xenocrates, who had accused him of slandering Plato as you did with our Socrates; Plato responded that it was impossible for such a dear and beloved friend not to return his love. How could you have so readily believed what was said about your friend by someone unknown to me, whom I do believe is an enemy of both and whom I consider without doubt an enemy of truth? O precipitous gullibility that has upset thousands of friendships in the past! Would that I had the time to write what is on my mind, for I would now have much to say; instead I shall remain silent. In short, suspicion, the poison of friendship, does not dwell in a noble and lofty heart, and I am astonished how it has now stolen into yours.

*See III, 19.

So, your Socrates has spoken badly of you? Why, may I ask, or to what end? What had you done to him, or what had he gained in making you hateful to me, something neither he nor anyone else could do? Such insanity was unbelievable in such a discerning man. For though he may not have been born in Italy, no one was ever more Italian in mind and inclination; we two, more than anyone else, made him that way. And—oh, the shame of it!—the impudent detractor had no qualms about saying that Socrates had written unfavorably to me about Lelius. Now just imagine how believable the accusation of a foolish and unjust man would be against a wise and upright one! If you think carefully, if you cast out every emotion and veil of anger, if you envisage the entire period of time until the present during which we all acted not only in harmony but almost as if of one mind, you will realize that three great lies without any semblance of truth are embodied in a single word; once you have recognized them, truth will side with innocence, your very conscience will plead though I remain silent, and the accused friend will not need an absent friend's protection. Believe me, O Lelius, indeed believe yourself, since you know the minds and ways of us all just as you know your own, perhaps even more because we know the others more profoundly and reliably than we do ourselves; believe yourself and not someone else, believe the truth speaking to you within your own mind and not in the clamoring treachery of accusers speaking in your ears. Believe, I say (and I hope you already do believe), that Socrates would not write ill of anyone; if ever he were to do so, it would never be against you, and even if it were, he might do it with others but never with me. I shall speak the truth: I would have believed anything about you two except that one would accuse the other, especially of an offense against me or my reputation or my condition; this he could not avoid knowing since he clearly knows all about me. Therefore, what mental blindness would make a prudent man, though he might hate you (neither you nor others have ever had the least inkling of this), dare bring before an unfriendly court such a reputable defendant whom truth would excuse, and a judge would acquit without requesting documents or witnesses, thereby leaving him with nothing but the reputation of being an envious accuser? Such things, my dear Lelius, can be said—for the human tongue is unbridled although no animal needs a stronger bridle—indeed all such things can be said, but all need not be believed, nor listened to, frankly speaking. True friends, among whom the name of Laelius was always outstanding and illustrious, turn a deaf ear to accusations, rejecting everything that conflicts with true friendship. Yet it is not enough to reject falsehood; in this one matter is the distinction between true and false unacceptable. Whatever is said against a friend's faithfulness must not be believed, for when the decision has been made to be friends with someone, you must entertain no doubt about the friendship, otherwise the foundation of friendship, mutual trust, will be forever shaky. Therefore, Bias's advice, praised by Valerius, warning us to love in such a way as to be able to hate one day, may perhaps apply to a harlot's love but must be rejected in friendship, which, being defined by all wise men as something that can exist only among good men, must exclude all types of fraud and every kind of degenerate and unbecoming cunning. There must be no mistrust and no apprehension; since minds are joined by the glue of friendship and from two, as they say, are made one, it is right for each man to have the same trust in his friend as he does in himself. Therefore, much better and justifiably did Laelius, in Tullius's work, contradict that advice with the aid of reason and the authority of Scipio. It behooves you to hold the same opinion as he whose name, character, and friendship you have inherited—namely, not to keep hatred in mind as you love, but to love in such a way that you could not hate even if you wished. Friendship is a great and divine matter, but it is simple and needs careful deliberation only once; before loving, you must choose, and when the choice is made, you must love; choosing after you love is too late. An ancient proverb forbids us to do what has been done; following a choice, there is no room for mistrust or animosity, in short, for anything but love. In fact, how could you love someone today whom you are thinking of hating tomorrow? It is justifiable then to praise Plato's answer mentioned earlier and that action of Alexander the Macedonian that I often cite since it so meets with my approval. Though rash and precipitous in everything else, in friendship alone he was so constant that, as he was about to take a potion for an illness prepared by a doctor friend, he received a letter not from some stranger but from another close friend; it warned him to beware of the treacherous doctor who had been bought by an enemy's gold to poison him; he read the letter and concealed its contents until the accused person entered the royal bedroom to perform his service. Whereupon, rising and holding the letter in his left hand, the king immediately seized the potion with his right and, undaunted, drank it, and then gave the letter to the innocent and astonished doctor for him to read. He thereby deserved to be saved then and forever afterward from his followers' treachery; whence I conclude that it is shameful to listen to accusations against a friend, and even more shameful to be willing to believe them; whoever weighs the trustworthiness of a friend's accuser is already guilty of offending the friendship. But alas, how difficult it is to enjoy life's pleasures, how easy to lose them! Only in friendship, in which he deserved good fortune because of his enthusiasm for friendship and because of the integrity of his life, was our Socrates unfortunate. For some twenty-eight years he loved you, something no one knew better than you and myself; how could a good-for-nothing in one moment with a few false words snatch him from you, transforming him from a friend and devoted brother into an unyielding enemy? Forgive me, O my brother, during my lifetime there should never have been not only without cause but for any reason whatsoever such a disagreement among friends whom I considered united in mutual love and inseparable through the bond of my recollection.

I know not, O my brother, what to do now and, as God is my witness, I am more inclined to sigh and even weep rather than speak, so disturbing and upsetting do I find your disagreement. I shall nonetheless say what is on my mind. I could fill this page with oaths, but since people who swear about too many things are less likely to be believed, you may perhaps place credence, if I am deserving, in a simple statement of mine: Socrates has never spoken to me against you, but he has often said many good things. If I took the time, I could find many letters to me in his hand where he frankly declares that I have no other friend in the Curia save you alone; the others who may have once been, have left this life, their homeland, or their position. You he calls my protector, a constant helper with my affairs; and you are the only person whose trust has not felt the usual ravages of time and absence. His letters, both old and recent, on these and similar subjects, are in my possession, and I serve as their witness in his behalf. I do not know if that gallows bird has seen letters conflicting with them; but this much I do know: those letters did not reach me. You yourself will have to decide whom you would rather trust: a false and worthless accuser or a loyal and truthful excuser. Yet I do hope that my sighs will not occupy last place in your trust, these sighs, O my dear Lelius, that across so many lands and over the Alpine peaks carry to you my pious affection together with these anxious and concerned words. You will listen to me, my Lelius, and unless I am mistaken, you will pay heed. I thus ask, beseech, implore, and swear in the name of devoted friendship, in the name of our mutual love in which we seemed to yield to no one, in the name of all that ever was or could be pious, holy, faithful, pleasant, and lovable between us; or if this be too little, in memory of our most illustrious lord who certainly for his outstanding and truly imperial greatness of mind deserved to be called Julius Caesar by us, but because of his genuine devotion to this country has been the Camillus or Scipio of our day; and in the name of his illustrious but, alas, too perishable progeny who, as long as it pleased God, were so very loving toward us, giving us such sweet and dear pledges of their love; and above all, in the name of the ever remarkable and truly heroic and noble soul of our Ascanius, whom I shall always mourn, whose hasty departure deceived not only our hopes but those of Rome and of Italy, whose bitter death cut short the flower of renascent military virtue of old: for the sake of all these men, I say, for my sake and for your own sake I beg you to remove speedily this weight pressing upon me, which consumes me and torments me and grieves me. And if you do love me, or ever did love me, then I beg you, before this letter leaves your hands, to visit or send for Socrates, who is astonished at the great change in you and is now vexed by his ill fortune.

This I beg you, this is enough. Only do meet and reconcile your divided minds and persons; have no fear of one another since you surely did love one another, and if you do not wish to see me consumed by tears and sorrow, return to the harmony that you once enjoyed and do not throw my heart to the dogs. Now I shall know if you do love me as rumor has it; unless you do as I ask, I shall have been mistaken in thinking myself dear to you, whatever else you may write; but if I hear of your reconciliation, I shall be certain that my prayer has been answered, and that my good faith has restored your friend whom a stranger's treachery had taken from you. I shall not fear the voices of detractors and the remnants of your anger; the murmur of envy ventures to place many obstacles between those who are absent, but great is the efficacy of a renewed relationship: this alone do I beg, this alone am I pleading; if you do this much for me, I do not fear the rest. What it behooves you to do and what must be said will occur to you as a result of your devotion to and memory of such a lengthy friendship as well as the sight of your friend; in his eyes you will read what neither I nor Cicero can express. Farewell.

Milan, 30 July, at dusk.

Fam. XX, 14.

To the same correspondent, * *joyful felicitations for having listened to his advice and appeals.*

Increasing responsibilities and a waning life have made me later than usual in writing; and lest by chance you suspect something else, this results from those old and ever-present demands of my studies, which do not cool as I grow older but instead become more enkindled, as if I were still young. It is extraordinary that, while everything else bothers me, they alone provide me daily with new pleasure without a trace of boredom. Today I seem to have begun for the first time; the wise man's words are literally being realized in me: "When man brings his work to an end, then will he begin, and when he has completed it, then will he be beginning." My rather lengthy absence has also contributed, since I have spent a great portion of this winter in Padua and in "a corner of Venice," to use Livy's words; in fact, on this very day and at this hour I have returned to Milan, fatigued and burned by the winds and the cold. I have neither the materials nor the will to write, thanks to a dull pen, frozen ink, coarse paper, a frozen hand, and weather perverse beyond belief, which has made this horrible year one to be long remembered, as they say, for never within man's memory has so much snow fallen between the Alps and the Apennines. Many homes have been damaged in the cities, many trees in the country, great have been the people's laments in both the city and the country, which neither a flowering spring nor a fruitful summer nor a wine-producing autumn with all the delights and abundance of nature will be able to calm. This present year has equaled the cold and surpassed the snowfall during the winter of four years ago, that is, between the end of the year 1354 of our sixth age and the beginning of the following; it seemed that nothing could be colder or, so to speak, more wintry, when our Caesar accepted the iron crown here in the Basilica of Ambrose, and then set out for Rome to receive the golden one. You, who at that time were also in France, hastily joined him in his journey, or rather race, to that city, and thereby came to deserve his intimate friendship because of your character and intellect. But what am I doing? Do I not seem to be dealing with superfluous matters after saying that I lacked the time to write of important ones? Pleasure has this power, it does not feel the cold and heat, it loves work and spurns weariness; in short, it rejects nothing that allows it to do what it wishes. Note that while speaking to you

*See III, 19.

I have become unmindful of my weariness and of the winter, and even of my purpose in writing. But to return to the point, when I returned home to find by chance your messenger, I could not permit him, though he was in a hurry, to leave without a letter to you; and so, love for you overcame his haste and my work and the winter's rigor.

First of all, then, my dear brother, I have fully understood your account of your suspicions, nor am I as surprised as you may think that you could be persuaded by so much cleverness; nothing is impervious to the deceits of detractors, there is nothing that a throbbing and flattering voice cannot penetrate. Rather, what surprised me, what I praise you for is ridding yourself so quickly of the anger that had long been boiling and seething, an excellent way to aid your mental health. Why, O Lelius, do you ask whether, for love of you, I would dare argue against Aristotle? Perhaps this seems almost a sacrilege to many, whereas it is perhaps more of a sacrilege to want to follow him obstinately in everything. Certainly the great Cicero with his elegant refinement preferred at times to assume personal blame than to refute openly any error by that philosopher; for example, because Aristotle had said that all melancholic people are gifted, Cicero, who did not like the idea, jokingly said that he liked having a slow intelligence, clearly insinuating his feeling about the idea. Let us too follow Cicero's example. In his *Rhetorica*, Aristotle does affirm the correctness of the view that anger is much sweeter than honey. What else shall I say except that I am glad to have a dull sense of taste that does not allow me to feel this sweetness, and that I do wonder about this taste of Aristotle or of whoever said it first? For although bees, as they say, make the sweetest honey from bitter herbs, I repeat that I have yet to taste the sweetness of anger; indeed for some it is sweeter than honey, whereas for me it is more bitter than bile. This is my frank opinion. But if one must swear by Aristotle's words and consider whatever he said as though from a divine oracle, even to accepting the idea that anger may not only be sweet but even sweeter than honey, you still did well to reject that arrogant and monstrous sweetness, so harmful to the stomach, and to wipe away the rust accumulated in your mind through neglect. My gratitude to you for this, and my return to my previous love for you and to my previous opinion of your virtue are all easier for you to imagine than for me to express. In short, know that although you have done throughout my life much that pleased me, nothing ever pleased me more than your ready yielding with such good will and devotion, once your feelings were subdued and controlled, to my advice, which was truly sincere, yet so contrary to your opinion and feelings; thus, driven by your love, which brooked no delay, having scarcely read my letter and still holding it in your hand, you rushed to our Socrates to embrace and kiss him—and you embraced and kissed me as well. After your many tears and those of the bystanders, which burst forth from my heart to your eyes, the two of you reverted to your brotherly friendship. Now I know what I mean to you, something I did know before, but my old conviction is now reinforced by new proofs. I recognize my Lelius: he is as I hoped he would be; he will always despise detractors and often lament this wasted time. I knew that Socrates had long been pining away with laments and sighs, considering his disagreement with you among the deepest wounds of his life and the harshest injustices of fortune.

I pass over all of what follows in your letter; I believe it all, indeed I know it all, for I know your loyalty and the ways of the Curia. But in return I ask you to believe one thing, which you will not refuse me because of your affection. If I had to accept that weighty appointment, which is perpetual, inglorious, and tedious, as well as servitude under many men whom I do not like at all, in short, if I had to accept the position of Calvo da Napoli, a good and caring man and, as he was wont to say, a friend of mine, but neither lettered nor illustrious; if I had, let us not say to solicit with pleas, but to receive the cardinal's hat without requesting it, considering the present situation and the customs of that college, I would prefer to lose my head to a sword's blow and drench the soil with my blood. Believe me: if there be any truth on this earth, this is it, or to say it more emphatically, this is the truth itself. I have stated it in strong terms so that in the future neither you nor other friends will waste time laboring for this or a similar cause, or subjecting yourselves to my refusal of something that, if it were offered me, I would turn down. Twelve years ago, you will recall, when I was younger, more resigned to work and more liberal with my time, when the Curia's condition and the pontiff's good will toward me were different, I did not accept the cardinal's hat despite my friends' indignation. With what mind then, with what self-forgetfulness, now that I am elderly, would I now wish to assume another's burden, thus aspiring to something that could have been obtained more honestly and readily so much earlier, or that another would never have received if I had not yielded it to him? There are some young men who are calm and tranquil and some elderly men who are busy, just as many men whom we have seen were most chaste in their youth became lustful and wanton in old age. As for avarice, it is known to be a common malady of nearly every old man, whereas it is not for young men, for they are not, in Aristotle's words, lovers of wealth because they have not yet in his opinion experienced poverty. Do you perhaps wish me to change, like these examples, from a peaceful young man to a hard-working old man, or become like one who stays in bed when healthy but walks about when sick, or like one who snores all day but tells tales all night? I am not of this breed, O Lelius, since I have sought repose in all things, as it is written, indeed since youth I have always loved it to the point of gaining a reputation for laziness; at present I seek nothing else, I love nothing more, and without it any way of life is burdensome to me. Now that I seem to have it almost within my grasp, now that I am about to lower and tie the sails, I am called into the straits. I shall not listen to you, O my friends, instead I shall beg you to help me anchor my ship. My desire is known to all, and to you above all others. I have always sought an honorable poverty; no way of life is really more tranquil and more secure. Thus far, this has been denied me by the conscript fathers in their inviolable judgment, though they have never denied me wealth. I know the reason, and so I am not surprised: it is not that they do not want me to be wealthy, but rather that they do not want me to be happy. I shall obey and happily pursue my fate, for what man knows what is good for him. I shall find comfort too in the thought that whatever I am, I am not because of them, and I thank God who has answered my prayer, giving me the means for living without them. Let the opportunities then, for toil and rejection cease; you know where, you know how I wish to die. Is that not sufficient? If I cannot be poor, I shall be rich, although nothing prevents me from living and dying poor in spirit in the midst of my riches; for poverty alone is both easy to attain and dear to God. But enough about me.

I was happy to hear about Zanobi's promotion; I love the man and am certain that he loves me. I rejoice with him, indeed not with him but with his good fortune and ours, since amidst so many enemies of God and of men we shall have at least one friend; yet I do feel sorry for him and for the Muses, who perhaps may not be losing his great talent but sharing it with undeserving partners. Undoubtedly he has provided for his income, but not for his fame nor for his life nor, I predict, for his peace of mind. Behold how things turn out! Not long ago, he commiserated with me like a brother, gently reproving me for making the turbulent city of Milan my Helicon. With great affection he would say this, but without knowing Milan, I believe, and certainly without knowing my way of life here, full of leisure and freedom, solitude and peace. Even previously, he was wont to criticize my transalpine sojourn and wonder about this joy of mine so far from Italy when I, a man for my sins but nearly an angel for my peace of mind, was spending considerable time at the source of the Sorgue. I remember his very words and the barbs that he let fly. He used to speak thus, not foreseeing, I believe, that soon he would be voluntarily leaving Italy to establish his own Helicon so near Babylon, about which I know so much not through empty guessing but experience; but if I were to begin saying what I feel about this, I would never end. The fact remains that enough, and more than enough, hatred for me has been enkindled in that hell; through daily experience and observations he will comprehend what I have now left unsaid about his Helicon, and if I know him, he will often recall my words and sigh for the tranquillity of Naples and for Italy, having become perhaps wealthier but certainly busier and sadder. O how he would envy me if, just as I behold his storms from here, he could behold my repose and then realize that with the exception of intellectual interests we have nothing in common! Give him my best wishes, and farewell.

Milan, 9 February, in the evening.

Fam. XX, 15.

To his Socrates,* concerning the same matter.

It has been a long time, my Socrates, that we have ceased corresponding, that great cure for absence, because of our affairs and perhaps many other reasons; but the principal reason, I believe, was that we were running out of topics to write about. We should not be suprised that what happened to Tullius and Atticus has happened to us: no pile is so huge as not to be diminished and reduced to nothing by continually taking from it; whatever we knew, we have exhausted in my opinion under the yokes of our writings. The one subject now remaining to us is the renewed friendship and reconciliation at my urging between yourself and Lelius; from your letter and his, and from those of others as well, I have joyfully learned of it, indeed I am happier about it than anything else. It has gone well, thanks be to God and to you; He inspired your spirits and you did not deny access to the Holy Spirit. Both of you eagerly praise my style, which, though always unpretentious, was on that occasion improvised and hasty because of the season, the hour of day, and the messenger's impatience; yet it was so charged with affection and ardent devotion that I—how clearly I recall this, so help me God—could not hold back tears as I wrote. Before my eyes were you two, all your friends who were distressed over your disagreement, your triumphant rivals, and the bygone years spent in such harmony. This was the source of my inelegant style and my tears; what triumphed was not my talent, not my style, but my intention and devotion with the Lord's assistance. Praise, then, whatever you please; I shall praise only God, from whom all good flows, and your humanity that not only welcomed but greedily grasped my good advice. I recognize your noble minds so very devoted to me; may the Lord bless you for an action most worthy of you and for giving me a joy that I could not have found elsewhere. Farewell, O my Socrates, and remember me.

Milan, 10 February, before daybreak.

*See I, 1.

Fam. XXI, 1.

To Ernst, Archbishop of Prague, * why the truth has so many enemies.

In my mind I had conceived many things, and with my pen had written many others that I am keeping from you for reasons that will be explained; the person bearing these few words that you see and the many others that you will hear has taken it upon himself to deliver them to you viva voce, for he is most devoted to you and very friendly to me. Truth has always been considered noble and sacred, yet not always safe; in every age she has had enemies, but never more than in our own, the reason being that never before has virtue had fewer friends. No man hates truth unless he leads a wicked life; and while fear never compels a strong man to tell a lie, it does at times compel him to remain silent. Driven by a desire for truth I did not realize this either in the present or in the past until I could no longer refrain from speaking. In a conversation words cannot be retracted, but in writings that are too free, this can be remedied by either hiding or erasing what has been written. I have done the first, thereby hiding much that eventually I shall perhaps destroy or perhaps allow to live so that after my departure from this world they will emerge from their hiding places to reveal me as a disciple of truth, but hidden out of fear of the Jews. Who knows whether, with my impatient mind unafraid of shadows, I may not show the way to those who desire to know it? Though I am omitting matters about which I have yet to decide, know this much about me: no one is more devoted to you than I. I recall the attitude, the warmth, the words, and the kindness with which last year you welcomed me, a foreigner known to you only by name, as a member of the delegation sent to our emperor; I recall too how courteously you repeatedly said to me, "I pity you, O friend, for having come among barbarians." I confess to having seen nothing less barbarous, nothing more human than Caesar and some of the great men in his entourage whose names I consciously refrain from mentioning, outstanding and remarkable men, I say, worthy of special mention and, as far as it pertains to our discussion, men of consummate kindness and courtesy, as though born in Attic Athens. Farewell.

Milan, 29 April.

*Archbishop of Prague who had given Petrarch a warm welcome during his mission to the Emperor in 1356. As a high official in Bohemia he headed several legations, both papal and imperial. He played a central role in the drama of Cola di Rienzi. His close friendship with Petrarch led to several daring anticlerical letters from Petrarch, which he subsequently decided to include among his *Sine nomine*.

Fam. XXI, 2.

To Jan, Bishop of Olmütz, Imperial Chancellor,* a lengthy expression of gratitude.

If I did not understand and see more clearly than light what you think of me and how great is your love for me, I would surely be not only deaf but blind. For you reveal your mind to me not only in words but in deeds, which, it is said, cannot lie. What, I ask in the name of all that is divine, could be more delightful than your letter in which with unusual and engaging skill you force me, who am constantly distracted and, so to speak, covered with aimless cares, to think about and desire to see only you? What could be more kind—leaving aside other things that I conceive more readily in my mind than in writing—what, I say, could be more kind or more courteous than your words near the end of your letter, that Francesco's name will never be forgotten by Jan? You have allotted to my poor and unknown name an admittedly splendid and ample haven in your memory, appropriate for any distinguished man, where dwelling now in greater safety, it fears no difficulty or lack of hospitality in the transalpine regions. But surely it would never have occurred to you to say what you did, had you not truly felt it. Who does not see how much kindness this judgment reveals in you and how much glory it brings me? It is unnatural for so great a man to remember so steadfastly such a trivial matter, yet you thus demonstrate your own generosity and exalt me with your opinion of what I do. I thank you for your esteem as much as one can for human affections since it has often allowed me to enjoy the esteem of the most learned men. But revealing my entire heart to you without concealing anything within its chambers, I know of nothing about myself that merits your opinion. I am like the peasant who finds a valuable pearl; astounded by his unexpected good fortune, stunned by his find, and ignorant of its true value, he inquires of passersby their opinion about it. So for a while I too take pride first in your repeated praise and then in that of several illustrious judges, and—please do not laugh—I have somehow slowly gained in self-esteem. I am joking with you, O glory of mine, for I have no doubt that all this depends on your love and not on my merit; even if the entire world with one voice were to extol me, it would not dislodge my awareness of my own insignificance. Now what shall I say of those more blatant indications of your esteem, of your kind actions in my behalf? I shall not mention past instances that shall always remain in my memo-

*See X, 6.

ry, but what a great and rare privilege you recently extended to me! Although you had conferred it some time ago, you have now generously appended the secret imperial seal and the great golden boss whose very sight inspires in observers an immense sense of majesty and of glory, forcing honorable men to recall the greatest of empires and ancient Rome and the golden age. For on one side is our Caesar with crown and sceptre, seated on his lofty throne, flanked by the Roman eagle and his own ancestral lion; on the other is Rome, proud with her temples and walls, and in the very pallor of the gold, to use one of David's images, the holy and venerable image of the beloved city delights our eyes and sweetly steals upon us. For such a gift I have nothing to offer except pure gratitude. My thanks to Caesar, my thanks to you; I have never asked you for anything in vain: he made me a member of the Counts Palatine, adding other gifts, which he is wont to do for few men, and you with great enthusiasm decorated the majestic imperial gift and made it most imposing. But while I do declare my continual need for his favor and your benevolence, I am not in need of gold in the same way. Wherefore, while I accept unusual gifts, in particular your patronage, which you cautiously offered me in that letter, as your words indicate, so I ask you to accept the golden boss that I am returning with this excellent soldier, our Sagremor, a great admirer of your deeds and a sharer of my intimate secrets, who will supplement with his pleasing eloquence whatever this brief letter lacks. Live happily, and farewell.

Milan, 29 April.

Fam. XXI, 3.

To Cecco da Forlì,* an excuse for his failure to render the requested assistance, and an offer of consolation together with confidential advice.

Long after you had written it, I read that noble poem so worthy both of a response and of receiving the assistance that you sought; but I have neither the time to answer nor, if I did, the poetic ardor of youth to enkindle my mind with its usual flames, finding as it does satisfaction in rearranging collected works at which it has also become sluggish. Nor is it within my power to offer the aid that you seek. I do commiserate with you, yet I am aware of the words, "Why do you commiserate rather than give aid?" As I have said, the matter does not depend on me at all; if it did or had, I would not have waited until now for your requests, although they are by far the most reasonable that I have ever heard or read. My love and natural pity for you, and the atrocity of the affair, so goaded me from the beginning of your troubles that I needed not spurs but bridles. I call as witness to this truth God, who sees all things, my conscience, and the memory of this most faithful man. Since I am denied the fulfillment of my desire, I do what no power can deny, I fight with open and sincere conviction alongside the oppressed, and as one of yours I eagerly and anxiously await what fate will bring. There is nothing more for me to hope for or to say except Philo's weighty phrase, so applicable to this speaker's nature and to the present state of affairs: "It behooves us to be of good spirit because inevitably divine aid is forthcoming when human aid ceases"; and the words of Terence's old man in the *Adelphi*: "Man's life is a game of dice; if what is most needed is not thrown, then what falls by chance may be corrected with skill." I ask you, then, to glean from these sayings whatever comfort and counsel you can for your unfortunate republic. Farewell, and remember me.

Hastily, at dusk, 26 October.

---

*Well-known jurist and official of the papal states who was also known as a poet, scholar, and strong admirer of Petrarch. He often sought Petrarch's help in behalf of the cause of his lord, whose seigniory was one of the last pockets of resistance against papal intrusion.

Fam. XXI, 4.

To Bartolommeo da Genova, * *what the difference is between the customs and pursuits of the young and the elderly.*

From your letter I can imagine a friend whom I do not personally know; his age is budding and fresh, and his talent glowing, he is agile and quick, his mind is joyful, abounding in serenity, and he has a tremendous sense of friendship. Except for the very last, I partake of none of these traits, what with my years declining like the man who with great effort reaches the summit of a very rocky mountain and already begins descending, plunging with ease to the bottom after his demanding climb; a sluggish intelligence that is nearly cold, burdened and exhausted by the heavy weight of affairs; a mind rather sad because of its hatred of the world and its awareness of its condition, not because of approaching old age—which promises reason for joy, impending release, departure from a blind prison, and the end of a sad exile—but rather because of being freed too slowly from the chains of youth and somewhat later than I would like. Behold, my dear friend, how we proceed along different paths toward a single goal; or rather we walk almost the same pathway, but as happens, each along a different section of the road: I have been where you are, you will be where I am. Thus, an identical goal has created a friendship between us, while the dissimilarity of the wayfarers leads to such contrasting feelings that my silence, which you find astonishing, but which, in the manner of lovers, you pardon with specious excuses, may not only be excusable but necessary for me; rather I find quite astonishing that amidst the clamor of cares that haunt me I have managed to find the time to say anything. I suspect that this sounds harsh to your ears; but continue to live happily. When you arrive where I am now, you will understand that it is as I say; if now you scarcely believe me, you will then believe the facts and yourself. If you ever have need of anyone, then use me as you will, and consider me confidently among your friends. But forgive my silence, and do not expect from me frequent or lengthy letters; many things that once used to be of comfort to me—how human affairs do change!—are now a punishment. Farewell.

*Unknown young admirer of Petrarch and student at the University of Bologna.

Fam. XXI, 5.

To Jan, Bishop of Olmütz,* a recommendation for a common friend.

To Caesar has come Sagremor, a fine man, and, as I am often used to saying, truly worthy of his name, unless love deceives me, and of the praise of true friendship; not only is he a lover or a friend, but to use gladly your expression, he is a love, indeed all love, and not just any kind, but sacred love. He has, then, come to Caesar and to you, and his love spurred me to write with my usual frank confidence to Caesar about my feelings for this man. I am not going to repeat what I have written, nor do I have to, since as usual you alone will be the letter's interpreter and glossator. Let this suffice for you: if you ever have believed or will believe in me, believe that this man esteems and cherishes you, respects and venerates you with all his mind and soul and heart, and places you at the very summit of all that he holds dearest and honors. Either I am mistaken, or having often been allowed by right of friendship to penetrate the innermost recesses of his mind, I always found you there in first place, close to Caesar, or close to first; as for external qualities, no one I have known was ever a more ardent and eloquent admirer of your name and your affairs. It would be fitting and worthy of you, then, were you to reciprocate his love by proving that, just as no one can surpass you in intelligence or eloquence or virtue, no one can outdo you in kindness and love. I would say more if speaking to someone else, but I am speaking instead to one who hopefully understands me even when I say little or remain silent. And I shall conclude with the younger Africanus, "There you have a man worthy of you." Having said this, I remain silent over what you say about the style of your letters being so unequal to mine that either you feign stupor or, if it is sincere, which I cannot imagine, it results not from my style but from your fatherly indulgence. For could you really be stupefied by anyone's style, even Cicero's? Tell it to someone else who may believe you. Just as pride is considered more than it really is, so humility is considered less than it really is, and if it often seems great to others, to itself it always seems insignificant. As for the rest, since you insist on sending your gift, I accept it gratefully and happily, though to tell the truth, I do not wish to receive gold from you, having no need of it as I once wrote you, and contented as I am with your golden will. A cordial farewell, and keep your promise that neither place nor time can ever banish me from your memory.

Milan, 25 March.

*See X, 6.

Fam. XXI, 6.

To Ernst, Archbishop of Prague,* concerning the same matter.

The pressure of time prevents me from writing at length, but love for a man very dear to me and for the truth compels me to speak briefly. Here is that distinguished man who is very devoted to you, whom we so used to share that his person was at times yours and at times mine while his mind was always with both of us, and now he has really become all yours. Let others judge this as they please; but I fully realize how the comfort gained from his presence will now be missing in my life so that I am saddened at my loss, though happy at your gain. For either I am a bad judge or there is no greater fortune than to find a good man and no greater loss than to lose one. What else shall I say to you? Much could really be said, if I had as much free time as thoughts in my mind. May I dare say something to you that I ventured to say to our Caesar: if great obligation arises out of love and trust, then you, my dear father, and however many others there may be, owe a great deal to this man. He loves no one on this earth as much as he does you and Caesar; and were he not deserving of anything from you, it might still be worthy of your kindness and spirit, and of the men surrounding Caesar, to give this man such a welcome that he would deservedly be both yours and Caesar's. I shall say no more, considering it more useful, in Cicero's phrase, for you, rather than myself or anyone else, to speak with yourself, particularly about something so well known to you that it needs no further expansion. Enjoy good health, and even if there may be no other reason for deserving your esteem except my love for you, number me among your friends.

Milan, 25 March.

*See XXI, 1.

Fam. XXI, 7.

To the Emperor Charles, * *a recommendation for the same person so deserving of him and of the empire.*

Love makes even timid people daring. I believe that I have often said this, as I do even now and hope to continue doing, for I speak as one who has learned from experience: true love dares great things and fears tiny ones. But laying aside the fear of lovers and speaking only of their daring, without dealing with those things to which a mad love can lead the human spirit, I shall touch upon the power of a noble love, as it applies to the matter at hand, with a unique and recent example: how would I dare, except out of great love, to speak this freely to Caesar? The man who delivers this letter to Your Majesty is most worthy of you, truly deserving of your favor and kindness, for not only you but the entire empire in your name owes him a great deal. To try to say how much he loves you seems superfluous since I am speaking to you who can read the innermost feelings on men's faces. You know how often he came to you in the rain or the unbearable heat, how wisely and diligently he overcame every difficulty of time and of the roads in crossing the Alps, forgetful of himself in your service. At your arrival in Italy when, as I then said to you in person, an arctic cold had assailed you at our borders so that German soldiers might not dread our mild climate, we all saw how often in the dead of the night during that harsh winter he went back and forth in his concern for you and for your reputation; he thus seemed in some fashion to be trying to curb the rigor of heaven and earth by the ardor of his love and his faith, feeling within his burning mind nothing of what happened externally and living up to his fine name with his actions. For it was not by accident, I believe, that his name was bestowed upon him at the baptismal fount, when he was called Sagremor as a clear presage of things to come. For if every just love of neighbor is sacred, that love can surely much more properly be called sacred that is directed to the Roman emperor, a love truly anointed by the Lord, truly holy. Therefore, because he came into the world to dedicate to you all his love and all his spirit, it was proper that he, upon being reborn in the faith, should be given a name befitting his future vocation, which was ever present in God's mind. Many things could be said about this man that I believe are better known to you than to anyone, but I shall only narrate one story of a thousand. The year of your arrival you sent him to summon me to you in Mantua, a journey

*See X, 1.

that I undertook within a few days, and it happened that, after a stop one evening on the Adda's banks, I emerged from my dwelling the next morning before daylight, awakened by my own eagerness to hasten to you, amidst the complaints of my companions and servants because I was exposing at night my body, hardly robust, to the harsh snows, treacherous ice, and severe weather, when the extreme cold could scarcely be endured during the day inside with a fire. And behold, we had scarcely left the city when to our suprise we met this man who had left Cremona during the uncomfortable silence of the night and had already traveled twelve miles so as to reach Milan on that very day, the shortest of the year. And though his servants and companions were frozen with the cold and fatigued by toil, he alone continued, as though taking a short stroll over grassy terrain at daybreak on a summer morn, finding warmth in your name and in his thoughts of you. I recognized the voice—since darkness hid him from me—and called him by name; he eagerly approached and, good God, what news of you, what hopes, what joyful tidings he happily whispered in my ear to my great delight! For he was coming, O Caesar, to make easy your arduous journey, and in Isaiah's words, trying to have "every mountain and hill be made low and the crooked paths be made straight and the rough ways smooth"; and soon, with heaven favoring your resolution, this was all happily accomplished beyond all expectations. The following year we were both summoned to your palace in Bohemia, and during the long journey we spoke of almost nothing except you and the affairs of your empire. In sum, either he is too astute or I am too ignorant, but he holds you and your name and your well-being above other affections in his heart; he is more dedicated to you than to anyone else, as though obsessed that his uncertain fate depends exclusively on yours, and his ultimate desire is to live and die in your service. But I am dwelling much too long on such an obvious matter; please forgive me, for to speak of him and to address you is pleasing to me. I should now present my requests, except that he would lament a great deal about his fortune if you needed my, or others', requests in his behalf. I assure your majesty, O Caesar, which for me is almost a divinity, that this man is most worthy of your imperial favor. You know the man, my lord, but even had he always been unknown to you, I would still dare to maintain that it would not be unworthy of you to use the services of such a soldier, indeed it would be especially valuable to your immortal glory; thus while other rulers and nearly all mortals covet gold and are slaves of pleasure, the Roman emperor, foremost among men, despises such things from on high, finding time for other pleasures and other riches: an abundance of prudence, virtue, and especially illustrious supporters. So, O you who are our glory, there you have what I said earlier: love has emboldened me. Enjoy good health, O Caesar, and farewell, and think of yourself, of us, and of the empire.

Milan, 25 March.

Fam. XXI, 8.

To Empress Anna,* felicitations on the birth of a child, though a girl, and the occasion it affords to express many thoughts in praise of women

Happily and reverently I received your Serenity's letter, O most glorious Majesty. What shall I first admire about it? Should it be the great wisdom that it contains for such a young person, or the unusual and singular kindness in this moment of extremely good fortune with which you deigned to make me alone, though separated from you by nearly an entire world, a participant in your joy through your eloquent announcement and friendly letter? For this I render heartfelt gratitude together with you, not to Lucina as the Gentiles once did, being ignorant of the true light, but to Christ, the creator of light and of life and of all good things. He has cheered your youth with solemn fertility not only for yourself but for the entire empire; and I too respectfully rise to the occasion in this letter to thank you for this esteem, since I have nothing to offer you in exchange for so great a gift. Nor indeed is your joy, indeed mine and others', diminished because your first child is a girl, for as wise men are wont to say, better fortune often follows upon a weak beginning. Those who strive after great achievements begin humbly; this is what, I believe, nature has just done with you, and with this first happy childbirth of yours—she promises you many more happy ones. It is sufficient for me and for whoever wishes happy news of you and your illustrious consort to know that now you have become a child-bearing member of the Roman empire. You will not cease here, for what you have happily begun you will conclude most happily. In the meantime, one surely cannot despise that sex from which our heavenly Emperor received His earthly origin. In the words of that singular authority, Augustine, lest anyone perchance think that any sex was disdained by its Creator, He took on the form of man and was born of a woman; furthermore, earthly rulers, the foremost of men, and the divine Caesars who hold the highest position among kings, are born of woman. Add to this that the female sex is noble not only for child-bearing, but for

---

*Third wife of Charles IV, who initially seemed destined to continue the tradition of either sterility or female births that seemed to plague the royal family during the two earlier marriages, but eventually succeeded in providing the emperor with two sons, who were to rule as emperors of Germany. The high regard reflected in her sending Petrarch an announcement of the birth shows the extent of Petrarch's intimacy with some of the highest nobility of the time. This is the only letter addressed to a woman in any of Petrarch's letter collections.

its intellect, its manifold virtues, and for the glory and accomplishments of the empire.

To touch upon a few of the countless examples, among the most ancient Greeks Minerva, the inventor of the various arts, surpassed all men in intellect, thereby becoming goddess of wisdom; Isis, daughter of Inachus, was the first to give Egypt its alphabet; and among our people Carmenta, mother of King Evander, is said to have invented the alphabet that we use. A Greek maiden, Sappho, wrote works comparable in genius to the greatest poets; a certain Proba, wife of Adelphus, used Homeric verses for the Greeks and Virgilian verses for our people, being proficient in both languages, and summarized in chronological order in others' words but in her own verses the origin of the world, the vicissitudes of the patriarchs, and Christ's coming and life. I shall pass over the Sibyls, those divine women with a single name, who were prophetic and cognizant of the divine plan, although we do know from Marcus Varro's account that they were ten in number and of different lands and ages; we know, too, that they had made so many predictions about the end of the world and especially about the coming of Christ that, when the latter was fulfilled, this name common to all the Sibyls was included by our learned men among the names of the holy prophets. Let us now turn to other types of female glory. Orithya, queen of the Amazons, to pass over the other Amazons, is said to have been so knowledgeable and valorous in warfare that one of the twelve labors imposed by Eurystheus, a Greek king, upon the invincible Hercules was to seize the Amazon queen's weapons, a task that the king believed impossible. Of the same ilk is the well-known courage of Penthesilea at Troy and Camilla in Italy. Who has not heard of the conjugal love and mental fortitude of Queen Ipsicratea, who alone and through all kinds of misfortunes accompanied her Mithridates, king of Pontus, during the serious and lengthy wars that he waged against the Romans, not only while the situation remained uncertain but even after his defeat and his men's desertion? Neglecting her beauty, for which she was renowned, and changing her mode of dress, she trained her body, raised amidst royal pleasures, to ride horses and bear arms and perform similar kinds of labors, this spouse who afforded the only comfort to that unfortunate king in his extreme afflictions. Among the Carthaginians and the Spartans, among the Teutons and the Cimbrians, all bellicose peoples, well-known historians speak of women distinguishing themselves more boldly in some battles than men. These are great examples, but there are still greater ones. Semiramis not only ruled among the Assyrians but conspicuously extended her kingdom's borders after having done battle with the Indians and Ethiopians; according to some sources, she founded Babylon, but beyond doubt it was she who enclosed it with extensive walls. And when news of an unexpected rebellion in the city reached her as she was intent upon fixing her hair as women do, she was so overcome by mental fervor that, with one section of her hair well-arranged but the other still disheveled, she seized her arms and hastened to free Babylon; and fortune assisted her valor so that harmony was restored throughout the city before her hairdo was finished. A statue of the queen hastening in that condition, which stood in the city for many centuries, bore witness to this very deed. Among the Scythians, Queen Thamiras demonstrated such prowess that she slaughtered in a single battle the formidable and celebrated king of Asia, Cyrus, together with two hundred thousand Persians; and for revenge and consolation at the loss of her son, she offered a great many sacrifices to the spirits of the youthful dead, cutting off the king's head and submerging it in a skinbag full of blood as a reproach for his cruelty in having lived a life with an insatiable thirst for human blood. Over the Egyptians ruled Cleopatra, over the Persians ruled Zenobia, who wished to be called queen of the Orient, a woman of great courage, exemplary virtue, and the loftiest chastity, a quality lacking in Cleopatra and increased twofold by her rare beauty. Both invaded the Roman Empire with such force that the first made victory uncertain for Augustus while the second gave the emperor Aurelianus reason to fear battle and then to boast of his victory over her.

Lest antiquity claim all the credit, in our own time Countess Matilde possessed a considerable portion of Italy, and thus was not an insignificant emulator of the Roman Empire, waging battles with a manly spirit, and being severe with her own people, very harsh with the enemy, and very generous with friends; the Roman church bears special witness to her extravagant and more than feminine generosity. Perhaps of lesser renown are other examples that are either equal to or greater than these, indeed worthy of true praise. A certain daughter was often allowed into a prison by a sympathetic guard, but carefully searched lest she bring food to her wretched mother, who had been imprisoned and condemned to death, yet left to die of hunger out of pity; she astonished her mother by secretly offering her breasts to her; another woman performed the same service for her father, who was in an identical situation. Supposedly this happened either in Athens or in Rome, for the writers from whom I have taken the tales attribute them to one or the other; the deed is consistent with the customs of either city, and could have happened in both, particularly since some historians ascribe it to the daughter of Cimon, a great Athenian leader, while others ascribe it to a humble unknown. Leaving all suppositions aside, I shall abide by the facts. When astonishment arose over the fact that a life lacking food could be extended so unnaturally, and when the case was subsequently investigated closely by the guards, it was reported to the triumvir who supervised punishments, through him to the praetor who had passed judgment, and from him to the consul. Thus, through an effort worthy either of Attic kindness or Roman largesse, an acquittal was granted each parent because of the daughter's devotion. Whose heart, I ask, would not be touched by the spectacle of a starving old mother, and even more of a father consumed by hunger and old age sucking the breasts of his young daughter? We read too that the place was transformed from a prison into a small shrine consecrated to Piety in memory of that pious deed. And who has not heard about the faithful Spartan wives who, in order to speak for the last time to their husbands who had been found guilty of capital crimes, entered the prison by night with the guards' permission; at the time the punishment of the condemned men was to be carried out, they changed clothes with their husbands and covered their faces, feigning sorrow, so that their men were able to leave with the help of the early hour while they assumed the danger? And who has not heard about the maiden sister of King Leonidas of the same city who was the first to denounce the war threatening the fatherland, while men were procrastinating in deliberations? Who does not know that Ephesus and other Asian cities were founded by women, and that once a large region of Asia and of Europe was ruled by women? Who does not know that the Carthaginian empire in Africa was founded through a widow's valor? Who has not read that the Israelites were born of the union of one man with two women and a like number of maidservants, and freed through the courage of a widow who brought back the enemy leader's head in her lap? Even Europe, which, unless love deceives me, is the most beautiful and noble region on earth, has the name of a royal maiden whose maternal grandmother, Agenor's mother, in turn gave her name to Libya. Asia too, third in number but occupying half the world, bears a woman's name. Thus, the three regions of the world—an amazing fact that is a glorious honor for the weaker sex—have until now been named after three women, nor do I see any reason why this would not continue. What are the names of the Italian cities of Mantua, Parthenope, Gaeta, Lavinia, and the Greek Athens, not to list them all, if not women's names?

What shall I now say about Roman women who have been the most honorable and noble in the world? Certainly were I to begin naming them, I would never end; "for with this subject," as Cicero says in praise of Pompey the Great, "it is more difficult to find a beginning than an end." Who indeed, I ask, can find the proper words of praise for Lucretia, that most steadfast example of chastity? Although I do not altogether approve of the manner in which she took vengeance upon her body for another's crime, I still cannot avoid admiring her noble anger and her mind incapable of tolerating baseness. Who can worthily celebrate the virgin Cloelia who swam the whirling Tiber after evading an enemy guard in order to return to their homeland the band of maidens who had been taken hostage? Such valor amazed both her enemies and her subjects, making her worthy of honor and reward. Who can do justice to Cornelia, daughter of Africanus and mother of the Gracchi, who lost twelve children partially to illness and partially to the sword, the strongest of whom were killed by the people and thrown, unburied, into the Tiber before her very eyes? She thus endured so bravely a catastrophe and bereavement as would have shaken even manly spirits that she could not be moved by the tears of the mourning women, but preferred to call herself fortunate rather than wretched for having borne such sons, a lady worthy of having borne such children in my opinion and undeserving of having lost them. What can we say about Cato's Martia, whom antiquity called saintly, or about her daughter Portia, who at the news of her husband's death swallowed live coals for lack of any weapon in order not to survive him, thus dying very much in love with her husband and hastening to follow him? I shall pass over many of our young ladies whom I know and would like to mention since they are well known to you. Drawn not by earthly feelings, but by devotion, truth, chastity, faith, and the desire for eternal life, they endured harsh punishments and painful deaths with tender bodies but strong minds. Admittedly in these enumerations I have strayed considerably from my purpose so that this sex zealously defamed by some writers might not lack its due portion of praise in my writings, something that may seem haphazard but surely bears true witness, unless I am mistaken. But to arrive at the summit of my argument and to take leave of you, O illustrious Majesty, with the name of the loftiest woman holding your rank, what is comparable to Livia's virtue, or to her majesty or glory? She held the same place with Caesar Augustus as you hold today with his successor, our Caesar, sharing not only his bed but his deliberations and his entire life. Eloquent and affable above all others, she deserved the full and continuous love of her great ruler because of her devotion and prudence, which no other wife had previously deserved; I am convinced that you too have achieved this with the same qualities and will continue to do so. But lest our discussion bore you by its length, embrace joyously your daughter, whom heaven granted as a token of a more noble birth and a more complete joy, and as is worthy of you and of her, endow her with your ways, make her your admirer, and doubt not that a child whom Caesar has begotten of you will not only resemble her parents but will be worthy of the imperial marriage.

Milan, 23 May.

Fam. XXI, 9.

To his Socrates,* words of consolation and advice.

You have touched my spirit, I confess, and were it not for reason now blocking my laments and convincing me not to succumb to fortune, you would perhaps have moved me to tears. In your letter I have truly felt the truth of what orators maintain, that manly laments can arouse one's compassion more than feminine wailings. For had you tenderly complained about your difficult situation, had you effeminately deplored the violence of fortune, as most men do, I surely would have grieved, for who has ever happily listened to friends' misfortunes? But now, when I see you amidst the storms of human vicissitudes, still erect though angered by the winds, I feel a more profound love for you and better understand why you are undeserving of such blows by fate and worthy of a happier lot, unless love deceives me. I am most deeply moved and grieved by that section of your letter where, for reasons of health and your time of life, you express fear at leaving your homeland, where you would like to die, for you may then be forced to wander through foreign lands on untimely and fatiguing journeys, which would be a truly grim experience for you. What can I say? Shall I deny the gravity of these things when reason shows me their high seriousness? Shall I order you to be of iron when you are of flesh? Shall I warn you not to look at what stands before your eyes? Shall I urge you to forget your wounds when they are constantly being reopened by new blows? This is easier said than done, but it can be done if the spirit, lifting itself by prodigious effort, chomps at the bit, soaring on high to trample human concerns under its feet. I confess that such a thing could not happen without God's direct aid; this alone, this first and last, we must humbly invoke in all adversity, something the philosophers did not see though they investigated everything. The rest is well known: let fortune play its games, fearing her when she flatters us, jeering at her when she thunders at us, and scorning her when she hurls lightning at us; give her less credence the more she promises joy, consider her more inconstant the more she offers us, and believe that the more weapons she hurls at us the fewer she has; recall too that it is easier to subjugate her than to draw her into a stable friendship, that she usually yields before those who offend her, abuses those who believe in her, drives the weak onward, and oppresses the fallen; and that no weapon is better than patience in order to vanquish her. What is more, great misfortunes must be confronted

*See I, 1.

with a courageous spirit, for on this threshing floor of toils there is no hope of repose; life is not only military service but actual warfare, and whoever is born joins a battleline for which fortifications and guards are of no avail; there is no time for repose with danger always at hand and the battle interrupted only at nightfall, that is, at death. The only shield against fortune's blows is fortitude, for those who fear are like unarmed people and those who fear the most undergo the greatest danger; those who flee are oppressed, those who fall are crushed, those who stand firm cannot be trampled, and though the unwilling body can be cast down, the mind cannot without its own consent; nothing is difficult to the strong will, nothing unbearable to the wise person, nothing is sad unless it is believed to be so, for through the free will either pleasure or bitterness is fashioned, and all things depend on our judgment. For the strong spirit nothing is difficult, but for the weak everything seems difficult; happy people can, if they wish, be miserable and miserable people happy. One should not yield to difficulties, for all terrible things have an end, and through life's labors one can reach the repose of the tomb; whatever torments us passes on; life's battles are painful but short-lived, and enormous are the rewards gained from a minimum of exertion. Glory is above and shame below, pleasure is found in the open and virtue in rugged terrain; the mind rots amidst pleasures and brightens amidst labors, usually becoming rusty amidst softness and cleansed amidst difficulties. Nothing is so peculiar to man as toil; man is born for this, as the bird for flying and the fish for swimming. While the disreputable prostitute lies until noon in the arms of her loathsome lover, the saintly virgin rises alone at night shaking with cold; the sick man lies on his bed, the parasite sits at banquet, the warrior stands firm in battle; the sailor may be seen amidst the billows, the drunkard amidst goblets, and the soldier amidst the wounded; Thersites sweats under his blanket and Achilles under his armor, Sardanapalus is infamous for his sleep and pleasures, and Hercules famous for his labors; camp followers and panders snore while the commander remains vigilant; the seasoned athlete trains for still more strenuous matches. More esteemed by his king is the person who proves his loyalty in rigorous trials, and languid leisure is allowed only to those without hope of performing glorious deeds; with good fortune peace is uncertain and with adversity the struggle is honest. In life there are one good and one evil while the remainder is neutral, usually reflecting the mind of the one possessing it; wealth is a beautiful but weighty burden, mistakenly considered precious by the multitude rather than by the wise, while a golden chain is splendid but cumbersome. To be enjoying good fortune is to be on the verge of collapse, human power is nothing but an illustrious and preferred wretchedness, the course of a lofty life is nothing but a resounding and resplendent storm and its end nothing but ruin. The sword with a bejeweled handle does not wound any the less, the noose made of precious silk does not tighten any the less; every corner in the world is a homeland to man, nor is there exile anywhere except that created by impatience; when the spirit begins to desire heaven, it is in exile everywhere until it reaches where it longs to be; the wise man takes his belongings with him wherever he goes, unafraid of shipwreck, fire, or theft. What is called poverty is actually solace against anxieties and dangers, what is called exile is escape from countless cares; for the good, death is the end of toil and the beginning of a truly happy repose. A thousand other things of this sort, which for the most part seem incredible to the multitude, are still considered to be the truest and most certain by learned and experienced men; but since I might well be uselessly stuffing them into you, I shall turn immediately to other matters.

I hear that you are suffering persecution because of me; against you they direct the spiteful poison that they dare not direct against me. I shall see to it that they not harm you, but rather torment themselves in their own evil — a characteristic of evil — and feel more wretched the more successfully they operate against us. I shall not let it be said that our friendship has brought you more evil than good; violence cannot be done to you, so try not to become dejected at base men's threats. Console your afflicted spirit; it is not, nor will it be, miserable unless it makes itself so. Do you want to see to what an extent you are not miserable? Ponder how many men envy you; no one can be both envied and wretched. While they oppress you, stand firm; while they try to frighten you, keep the faith; while they oppress you, lift yourself up; to your mind and body cite Virgil's celebrated words: "Be patient and find salvation in the hope of better things"; or those other words: "O comrades, we're well acquainted with past evils. Worse than this you have suffered. God will put an end to all this too," that God, I say, who put an end to countless other sufferings. I beseech you not to afford your enemies and the enemies of all good men reason for rejoicing, and not to consider deserting your homeland, thereby leaving it to them. It is unworthy of a strong mind with solid foundations to be troubled by light breezes. At the time when spirits were undermined by the defeat at Cannae, Cecilius Metellus devised a plan to abandon Italy. The plan was brought to nought by the valor of Africanus, then a youth, who drew his sword and held it over the deliberators' heads, forcing them to swear not to desert their homeland, nor to allow others to do so. You, as a man, dare at fortune's first murmuring what he, as a youth, dared in extreme misfortune; dare to do within yourself what he dared against others, and dare to do against one person what he dared against many. Direct your sword against the confused movements of reason; force them to change their minds, if they favored a plan for departure; otherwise let your restless mind stand firm and compel it to abide by a wiser decision. Time brings changes with it, good fortune is never constant, many remedies come to those not expecting them, there is always time to despair since aid will be forthcoming perhaps from where you least anticipate it. As for me, it is my intention to share all things with you, in particular my friendships, an area in which I would certainly yield to no one of my class, whether it be in nobility, in charm, in trust, or in number of friends. Just now I wrote to that great friend about your affairs, as you requested; rest assured that his assistance will not be long in coming. Meanwhile, perhaps I shall come to you; pretend that it is Psyllus who is coming with a magic herb in hand in the hopes that its odor alone will silence the serpents' hissings. But if you have decided to retreat for a time from envy, you have in this tempest a ready port nearby. I know that you have a great desire for me, for although nothing can separate minds bound by virtue and, in Jerome's words, joined by the glue of Christ, whether it be location, time, forgetfulness, weariness, hope, fear, envy, anger, hatred, chance, prison, chains, wealth, poverty, illness, death, the tomb, the body reduced to ashes, therefore making friendships immortal, there is nonetheless a considerable sweetness in a living presence. Never before has this been so long denied us, ever since our first separation; already seven years have passed since I have been living in this royal city without you. Do come then; what is preventing you? Come, knowing that you are expected and longed for, knowing that you have been beseeched, but in such a way that you do not seem driven by fear of enemies, but drawn by the desire for your friend, which is the way it truly is. Lay aside all delay, make haste; you will be doing something for me as well as for yourself and for many others to whom you have long been dear, though not personally known, who held you in great esteem—which, believe me, your presence will not diminish. Come; do not allow laziness to overcome you, do not let anything frighten or delay you; arise, for the journey is brief. One of two things will happen; either I shall chain you here or you will free me of this place to take me back with you; whatever happens, your coming will not be useless, for you will certainly have seen me once again, visited Italy, and enjoyed in the meantime a little peace, with envy vainly raging in the breezes. The Alps now separating you from your friend will separate you from the serpents, and while now an obstacle to you, they will defend and protect you until the source of the poison runs dry, which I hope will be very soon. I ask you not to hesitate;

but whether you choose delay or a journey, do it with courage. My great hope is that God, enemy of the proud and leader of the humble, that God Himself, I repeat, will assist you and that, present or absent, I shall not fail to do whatever is in my power for you. Since I know, then, the gentleness and greatness of your spirit, I shall press you no further, lest what is friendship appear to be diffidence; only one thing do I ask, that you remember me and not forget yourself. Finally, to use Caesar's words, I order you to hope for the best. Live happily and farewell.

Milan, 23 June.

Fam. XXI, 10.

To Neri Morando of Forlì, * *felicitations at regaining his health, advice to flee a dangerous undertaking, and news about a serious mishap that had befallen him.*

I was grateful, as much as one can be during bad times, that news of your convalescence reached me before news of your illness; and for this I thank God, who threatens more than He strikes, who thunders more than He hurls lightning bolts, who often shakes us not to make us disheartened but stronger by reminding us of our condition. Never was a father's devotion so great that, when compared to the eternal Father's mercy, it does not seem to be sternness or even cruelty; He continually bestows His clemency upon us, often without our realizing it, a clemency that, if it ever ceased, would cause us to be as nothing; but it is quite clearly revealed when we are rescued from a serious and threatening danger. And when, I ask, are mortals not subject to danger? Certainly never and nowhere do we live without being in peril; and if at times we live without suspecting danger, it still is everywhere even if fear is not always present. Whence it happens that we do not always render thanks for escaping a peril, being of course ignorant of the situation and ungrateful for our salvation, as Maro says; otherwise never would our mind and tongue be idle since mercy never tires. But when there is an end to oppressive fear, then do we finally offer our thanks, then do we unleash our prayers. For this reason, you for your own health and I for that of a friend are bound to owe votive offerings to your Healer, the Savior of all mankind, not by offering profane sacrifices but a sacrifice of praise at the altar of the heart. There is little else to add. I often warned you not to submit your body, already so exhausted by unavoidable labors, to useless toil, and not to turn a mind born for letters to military weapons in which one encounters greater danger and less pleasure or glory; even though, to give credit where credit is due, I know no one today to whom the words attributed to the elder Cato by Titus Livy are more applicable, namely, "his intellect was so versatile that it could be said he was born for anything he undertook." Yet you will not deny that your own talent, if given complete freedom and loosened reins, would turn to letters despite being capable of any undertaking. But you, unmindful of my advice and of your welfare, betraying your intellect, constantly journey through heat and ice, rain and dust, briars and slime, without any recognition of perilous events or sur-

*See XX, 1.

rounding hazards. I beg you to reject the evil and clearly false opinions of men in order to follow nature, for she will lead you to your goal. At present you are pursuing other ends not because they please you, since nothing that is not decent truly appeals to you, but because you please others whom perhaps it may be better not to please. But enough about you; I now return to myself.

I live in the country not far from the Adda's banks, and since I know you to be as concerned about me as I am about you, you will be surprised, I think, to learn how I am presently living. You do know that I have long admired and loved Cicero above any writer from any nation or century, and in this as in many things I was in agreement with you. I have no fear of being any less a Christian for being a Ciceronian, for to my recollection Cicero never said anything against Christ; if perchance his teaching did, that would be the only thing about which I would not believe Cicero, Aristotle, or Plato. For how could I believe a man if I would not believe an angel, trusting as I do in the Apostle's advice to the Galatians: "Even if we or an angel from heaven should preach a gospel to you other than that we have preached to you, let him be anathema"? To return to Cicero, he does mention gods, reflecting the customs of his day, and he does deal with the nature of the gods in a large volume, but if attentively read, he ridicules and exposes the lot and their empty names more than he praises them; whenever he speaks seriously, he refers to one God, calling Him the lord and master of the world. And although, as I have often said in my writings, he almost feared the danger inherent in the truth, he somewhere openly admitted that it did not become a philosopher to say that "there are gods." Who, then, can prove to my satisfaction that Cicero is an obstacle or stranger to the true faith, or what is worse, who is so filled with envy as to judge him an enemy of Christ? Christ is truly our God, but Cicero is our prince of eloquence: I confess that they are different, but I deny that they are in conflict. Christ is the Word, both the power and the wisdom of the Father; Cicero has said much on the art of words, the virtues and human wisdom, all true and therefore doubtlessly pleasing to the God of truth. For since God is living truth, and since, as father Augustine says, "every truth is true because it derives from the truth," then any truth that one utters derives beyond doubt from God. I admit that Cicero could not know Christ, having passed away just before Christ became man. His fate is surely worthy of tears, for had this man of truly lofty and divine intelligence seen Christ or heard His name, in my opinion he would not only have believed in Him but with his incomparable eloquence would have been His greatest herald, as the apostle Paul, weeping, reportedly said about the other prince of Latin eloquence, the poet Virgil, upon visiting his tomb. But why seek the reason that Christ did not wish this to be so from Him whose will is the supreme reason? To the extent that human conjecture can rise to the loftiness of divine counsel, He did not seek, although He could have, power, earthly wisdom, or eloquence. His intention was not to persuade with words as rhetoricians do, but to teach the blind and the strays the naked light of the truth, and He chose the feeble of this world, as is written, to confound the powerful, to destroy the wisdom of the wise, to reject the prudence of the prudent, and finally to convert the world's wisdom into foolishness, and through the preaching of fools to bring salvation to believers. Had He done otherwise, the truth that He taught would appear not to be of celestial and divine origin but the work of human power and skill, and in the wisdom of the word, as the Apostle says, the cross of Christ would be lost.

But now listen to how I was tricked by Cicero about whom I started speaking, whom I always loved and cherished from boyhood. I have an enormous volume of his letters that with my own hand I transcribed some time ago while in bad health because the transcription proved difficult for the scribes. Despite my body's discomfort and the hard labor involved, my love and pleasure and my desire to possess it won out. As you have seen, so as to have the volume always close at hand, I usually kept it at the doorway to my library resting on the doorpost. As I entered the room, thinking of something else as I often do, it so happened that a fold of my garment inadvertently caught the book; when it fell, it struck me lightly on the leg a little above the heel. I picked it up and jokingly said: "What's this, my Cicero? Why do you strike me?" He said nothing, but the next day, as I again returned to the room, he again struck me and again I jokingly picked him up and put him in his place. Why go on? After being repeatedly injured, I decided to pick him up and put him higher, as if he did not deserve being near the ground. Although my skin was broken from repeated blows on the same spot causing a considerable sore to develop, I paid no attention to it, thinking about the cause rather than the effect, and thus did not abstain from bathing, horseriding, or walking. Can you believe what happened? Gradually, as if angry at being neglected, the sore swelled and then around it appeared a discolored and infected growth. So finally, when the pain began to affect not only my joking but my sleep and rest, when my neglect seemed folly rather than brave disregard, I was forced to send for some doctors. For several days now they have treated this wound that is no longer to be taken lightly since it is causing considerable pain and, according to them, some danger to the wounded leg. While I know that you are aware of my great confidence in their prognostications, whether good or bad, I must still suffer frequent hot applications, abstain from my customary food, and get an unusual amount of rest. I despise all of this, and especially being forced to eat gourmet delicacies. Now my recovery is proceeding so well that you too will be learning of my convalescence before my illness. One thing often irritates me: nearly every accident, every ailment, inevitably strikes this one part of my body that my servant, in joking with me while doing his chores, quite rightly calls my unlucky leg. Throughout my life it has often bothered me, and many times from boyhood onward it has forced me to rest, something I find most intolerable. What shall I say? I am not far from, if not actually recognizing, at least denying with less conviction the existence of fate since not only every man but even every part of the body and soul has its particular destiny. Indeed its existence is suspect because depraved and wicked minds usually give its name a bad meaning rather than because it is in itself true. If fate derives from the verb *fari* and if, as David says, the Lord "spoke once and for all," then what He said can surely be called fate. To add poetic eloquence to prophetic seriousness, in the words of Statius Papinius, "Unalterable and momentous is the weight of sacred words, and the fates obey their utterance." Thus fate and divine providence are one; whoever understands this as such is not mistaken, although because of the name's bad connotation, one must, as Augustine warns, retain the meaning but improve the word. But leaving aside all dispute on the word, with a pious and flexible mind we admit that there is fate, striving as we do in all things for truth and not victory, always eliciting from words some moral aid for the mind, ever ready not for a particular evil but for all kinds. For there is no adversity that does not threaten man while he lives. Death alone frees us from all these ills and from the dangers of life. In this mishap of mine, about which I have said more than enough, the accident certainly corresponds to its name; what is unfortunate is commonly called lefthanded or sinister, although I know full well that, in prophesying, the left is considered favorable, whence the poet says, "It thundered on the left," and thunder on the left is considered favorable because things on our left are on the right of heavenly beings, from whom all good fortune is to be expected. Nevertheless, this too has caused much contention among the Greeks, the barbarians, and ourselves because, as I have said, we consider the left to portend happy tidings while in auguries they consider the right. Since my ramblings have strayed far from my original argument, know by way of summary that this unlucky left leg has suffered another of its usual misfortunes but this time from an unexpected enemy. My beloved Cicero has now wounded my leg as he once did my heart. Farewell, O you who are healthy and unwounded.

15 October, at midnight.

Fam. XXI, 11.

To the same correspondent, * *concerning a very loyal and admirable friend of his.*

You have by now read enough about my trifling experiences, and my tale about the wound inflicted upon me by Cicero. But lest you think that Cicero is the only person admired by those who do not know him, I shall add one more incident that, though it may be an old story to you, may fill your heart with new wonder. From here I always have in view Bergamo, an Alpine town in Italy; as you know, there is another in Asia by the same name, which was once Attalus's capital and later inherited by the Romans. In our Bergamo lives a man with little literary knowledge, yet with a sharp intellect, which would have served him well had he devoted himself to letters when he could. He is a goldsmith, and outstanding in that field; but he enjoys nature's finest gift, in that he is an admirer and lover of fine things, a despiser of the gold that he daily handles, and of wealth, which he considers deceptive except insofar as it is needed. When this man, already advanced in years, happened to hear my name, he was immediately attracted by my reputation and seized with a burning desire to win my friendship. It would take too long to recount his many attempts to satisfy his modest desire, or the courteous compliments and flattery he extended to me and to my circle of friends in order to bridge the distance separating us and to approach me in a friendly and warm manner. Though I had not known him by sight, I did recognize his name and purpose since his feelings were written on his face and in his eyes. What do you think? How could I refuse what no savage or no wild animal would have denied him? Overcome by his charms and by his sincere and constant flattery, I embraced him wholeheartedly, for I would not consider myself human if I were callous in returning the affection of one who honestly loved me. But he began to exult, boast, and project his inward joy on his face, in his voice and in his gestures; as if having attained his fondest hopes, he held his head higher and suddenly seemed to become another man. Long before he had begun spending a sizable portion of his patrimony in my honor, displaying the bust, name, and portrait of his new friend in every nook of his house, and imprinting his image even more deeply in his heart. He spent a considerable sum in purchasing copies of any of my writings. Delighted by his warm and novel enthusiasm, I began without hesitation to give him writings that I had denied to much more impor-

*See XX, 1.

tant people. What more can I say? Gradually he renounced his former life and activities, his work and habits, becoming so much the contrary of what he had been that all of his friends were utterly amazed. Finally, despite my attempts at dissuasion and my frequent warnings not to waste his patrimony so late in life on literary study, he remained deaf and incredulous to my words; he abandoned his workshop, and began frequenting schools and cultivating teachers of the liberal arts with the greatest delight and expectation; with what success, I know not, but his determination is worthy of success, I believe, since he sought such a deserving goal with such energy and with such contempt for anything else. He certainly has a good mind and tremendous enthusiasm, and his city has always had an abundance of teachers; only the man's age seems to stand in the way, although we know that in similar circumstances, and not in vain, did Plato dedicate himself to philosophy at an advanced age and Cato to Greek literature in his old age. Perhaps for this very reason will this friend of mine be deserving of a place in some part of my work. His name, then, is Enrico, his surname is Capra, a swift and tireless animal, fond of leaves, and naturally inclined to ascend on high; whence Varro believes that *capra* with transposed letters derives from *carpa*, to nibble at twigs as does a goat. If anyone deserves this name it is our friend for this reason: if he had entered a woods in the morning, he would have returned in the evening, believe me, with udders and belly full. All this you have known for some time, but it is repeated here for others to know. What follows you have yet to learn. This man, then, who is as good to me as he is to himself, had long begged me to honor him and his household with my presence, and with a visit of at least one day, saying that I would thereby make him happy and renowned for all time. For several years I had resisted his request with some difficulty, but now, at last, his nearby residence as well as his pleas, entreaties, and tears so overpowered me that I yielded despite objections from my more exalted friends who believe his humble condition unworthy of such honor. I therefore went to Bergamo on the evening of 13 October, in the company of my host, who was constantly in fear that I might meanwhile change my mind. He thus sought, together with his companions, every possible way to distract my mind from the journey through conversation. As a result, we made the brief and easy journey without noticing it. A few noblemen accompanied me, being especially eager to learn what such an enthusiast had in store. Upon our arrival in the city, I was cordially greeted by his friends who came to meet me, as well as by the provincial governor, the captain of the people, and the foremost citizens, who all vied in inviting me to stay at the *palazzo pubblico* or at some gentleman's home, while he in the meantime stood by in great distress for fear that the many invitations would tempt me. But I did what I thought proper; with my companions I proceeded to my humble friend's home. There I found elaborate preparations, a dinner more suited to royalty than to an artisan or philosopher, a gilded bedroom, a plush bed in which he solemnly swore no one else had slept, or ever would, and an abundance of books, not those of an artisan but of a scholar and true lover of literature. There I spent the night, and never, I believe, have I ever spent a night with a happier host. In fact, he was so transported that his friends were alarmed for fear that he might fall ill or become mad or, as happened to many in times past, even die. On the following day I departed, loaded down with many honors and surrounded by a great swarm of people, with the governor himself and many others accompanying us farther than I wished. Late in the evening I was barely able to tear myself from my loving host, and at night I returned to my country home. This, my dear Neri, is what I wished you to know; let this be the end of my nocturnal letter, for I have been so carried away by writing that it is nearly dawn and the late-night quiet reminds me in my weariness to enjoy some early morning repose. Farewell and be happy, and remember me.

Written with a rustic pen, 15 October, before daybreak.

Fam. XXI, 12.

To Francesco of the Church of the Holy Apostles, * *on lengthening time's brevity and halting life's flight.*

I have determined to expand the narrow confines of life; you may well ask how that can be done. Truly fleeting is time, unrestrainable by any strategem; whether you are asleep or awake, the hours, the days, the months, the years, the centuries slip by. All things under the heavens from birth hasten and are led to their end with astonishing swiftness. There is no interruption, no stopping, and the days and the nights equally take flight. The busy and the sluggish are proceeding in like measure, and those who seem to be standing still are hastening. Unlike a ship at sea whose progress varies with alternating winds, the course of life is ever the same and extremely rapid; never is there any returning or standing still, for we sail onward in any kind of weather and wind. For some the road is easier and for others more difficult, for some it is longer and for others shorter, but for all the speed is the same. We progress along different pathways but with like footsteps, and through different byways we all seek the same end; nor has someone proceeded more slowly if he arrives at the goal later since his path was somewhat longer and the goal more distant, this goal that is beyond doubt close, even if it seems most distant. To this goal we impulsively proceed; every moment urges us onward, driving us unwillingly from this sea into port, as strange wayfarers who love the journey and fear the goal. In vain do we turn back, we must go forward and indeed arrive; the road is behind us, the goal is before our eyes. What therefore shall I do, and what is my plan for extending life? I shall tell you. First of all, I admit, we must train our minds to love the goal; for what, I ask, is healthier than to do willingly what we are compelled to do? When the mind has learned not to fear vain things, when it has learned to love natural things and even to welcome the inevitable, then will it confidently and eagerly anticipate what the human species anticipates so sadly and apprehensively. I believe that this can happen only to the person who has achieved all that he really wanted from life, a rarity indeed, and who is exclusively devoted to the pursuit of virtue. It is that kind of living after life's completion, mentioned by Seneca; nothing is more pleasant in my opinion than the kind of life that fears nothing, is disturbed and tormented by nothing, expecting nothing except what is certain to come and incapable of being stopped by any obstacle, a time when the remembrance of things past

*See XII, 4.

and the hope of things to come increase one's well-being in the present. Those who pursue their lusts do not attain this goal, for just as a useless or broken container is never full, so those who always begin afresh never reach an end, there being no end to something infinite; what is more, cupidity is ever vigorous and incipient, always attractive and infinite. Those, then, who follow her are undertaking an infinite journey, never resting nor able to find repose because their motivation, lust, knows no rest. The lives of such men do not end but break off and are cut down at inception, whereas the lives of those who have completed their duties are tranquil and happy; the lives of the first cease before completion whereas those of the second endure until perfected, and then begins a genuine and enjoyable life. I, who am of the group in the middle, have not yet completed life, but never will I prolong or spend it under the control of passion; I have some needs, indeed a great many, but they are still within limits; to complete what remains I need not centuries but a small period of time, whose very brevity frightens me; and thus I need to learn how to extend time, as I have said.

Again you may inquire how that can be done. It all depends upon the efficient management of this time; drunkards waste wines, besieged people economize even with water; abundance begets wastefulness, want begets thrift. Often toward the end it begins to become clear what should have been done from the beginning; indeed almost never do intention and ability coincide. The former is weak when the latter is vigorous, when the former is strong the latter fails; otherwise human affairs would be happier and the outcome of human endeavors would be more joyful. Now that I am beginning to understand, my ability is failing me; I would have preferred this sooner, but time's value cannot be impressed upon youthful minds. For whoever has in abundance makes poor judgments; moreover, for the purposes of this argument, to abound is the same as to believe that one abounds since all error exists in judgment and not in fact. No mortal has an abundance of time, but not everyone equally realizes its paucity. The mist of future time is evenly spread through all ages, and the healthiest youth knows nothing with greater certainty than the stooped and decrepit old man except that he hopes for more, and for that very reason more frequently and more gravely hope fails him, whereas he who hopes for less is often safer. Countless are the things of this world, countless are the men, but of all of them nothing deceives more than hope. Lest I be deceived in this at life's end, I am beginning to open my eyes; for it is better to know something later than never. Now I desire to be frugal, greedy, and tenacious with what I was at first extravagant and later liberal. The hour admonishes me, necessity compels me; this is no time for joking; unless we rouse ourselves to offer resistance, believe me, we shall be conquered in the midst of our struggles, and unless we rise up with all the strength of our will, we shall be crushed. And so, my situation and the obvious magnitude of the danger are now rousing me from sleep, as the trophies of Miltiades awoke Themistocles. Often half-asleep, with eyes closed but mind awake, I am drawn from my bed by anxiety, and without seeing the light that customarily is lit at night by my bedside, I go with outstretched hand through the darkness to rouse my servant who is nearby. Sometimes it happens that—you may laugh at this!—having opened my eyes and seen the light, I extinguish it lest my servant, coming and realizing that he has been disturbed in vain, might inwardly laugh at my silliness or imagine who knows what. That is the way I am, and although I regret the time wasted, I am not ashamed of my resolution. Oh, if only I had had such thoughts as a young man; at least I can rejoice that I do have them as an old man. Then would have been the opportune time for great undertakings, but this age too is not useless or despicable; and if I had to fail, I prefer to have slept in the morning than at night. For more serious are the concerns related to death; more dangerous is the final error; the hour of death decides about an entire lifetime. It is for this that we must prepare with a singular and crowning foresight; all our past time and study were to be directed to this end; and if we grieve at having spent them uselessly, let us at least collect the remains in order to allow perseverance to mend what idleness has destroyed. I am striving to do this with no fear of it being taken as a fault because I am being more frugal with an irrecoverable commodity; for though a tenacious hold on wealth is shameful, tenacity applied to other areas is praiseworthy. Who would not praise the monk's observance of his rites, a woman's determined chastity, the scholar's economy of time? This last I shall seek, this I shall hold fast, with this I shall compensate as I can for the ravages of wasted time; this I meditate upon, this I sigh for, and this I shall perhaps attain with God's aid and with a tremendous effort of the will. I shall take care that none is wasted, and if this cannot be, then as little as possible. I shall assign a time to sleep and pleasure, and not allow them to enter my domain. If pressed, I can appeal to virtue, that fountain of incorruptible judgment and that impregnable and unconquerable stronghold of reason. If these limits are called into dispute, to her shall I refer the problem, from her must I seek a decision. I would prefer to act without rivals, but that may be impossible; my body has given me these partners; I shall try to maintain a balanced sharing. If possible, I shall compel them to be content with one-third of my time. Augustus used to sleep for seven hours under luxurious and golden covers, and even then would not sleep the entire time since he would often be disturbed by his cares.

I shall make a pact with my eyes to be satisfied with six hours of sleep; two more hours may go for other necessary things, but the remainder must be for myself. You will comment, "You won't be able to do so." I made the agreement, I have proved able to do it; "Nothing is difficult for mortals," says Flaccus. So it is; sloth has made some things impossible for us, but nothing is totally resistant to virtue; many things could we do if we did not become discouraged before attempting them. Once upon a time, the story goes, someone tried to reach the heavens in flight, and another succeeded in living under the sea. These are rare instances, I admit, but we delight in such accomplishments since frequent repetitions commonly beget aversion while rarity produces delight.

You now know a considerable portion of my plan, to which must be added that with such a scarcity of time, I too, following in Augustus's footsteps, usually read or write or listen to someone reading or dictate to scribes while combing my hair and shaving; and what is more, that I have developed the habit of doing likewise while riding or dining, something I do not recall having read about Augustus or others. Thus, often while on horseback—this will surprise you—I have completed a poem and the journey at one and the same time, and when I am far from the crowds in either of my Helicons, except when prevented by respect for a traveling guest, my pen is always to be found at my rustic meals and the table never set without writing tablets. In the middle of the night I have often awakened to dim light, and grabbed the pen at my bedside before doing anything else, for fear of losing an idea, to write something in the dark that is barely legible with the return of light. These are my cares. To others I may perhaps seem boastful, but you understand my life and mind in this friendly discourse of ours; you will understand too that I am ashamed rather than proud of this account because obviously at this age I should not be concerned about anything but my soul. Yet this is how I am made, and I persuade myself that my exertions will even be useful to my soul. And thus, I continue onward, happier and more secure, and as they say, while aging I learn something new each day. You will ask, "And what do you still hope to learn?" A great deal indeed: I am learning how to leave youth behind willingly and—to mention something that I have always learned eagerly and never to excess—I am learning how to grow old and how to die. My success with the last two will be proved by my last day—of doubtful value is the evidence afforded by an act performed once in a lifetime. As for my first goal, I have made such progress that with the approach of old age I am daily more thankful for having been freed from shameful ties and a heavy burden; from all that I can now determine, it is my belief that old age is undeservedly defamed. What the public, the accuser of nature and excuser of itself, ascribes to years is not the fault of years but of laziness; every age is capable of virtue, vice, glory, and infamy, from the moment man first began to comprehend and to use reason. Moreover, just as winter is not in itself adequate for human life, yet is not an unpleasant season when ushered in by a bountiful summer, so too an old age that follows upon a lengthy period of laziness is an empty, sad, barren, and useless part of life, but if preceded by a youth of dedicated study, it is rich and fertile in good skills, useful and enjoyable. If it served no other purpose than to soothe the fires of earlier years, this would be sufficient cause, if I am not mistaken, for its being desired and loved. For who but an ingrate would not praise an age that promises better things, bringing to fruition what reason has thus far neglected through laziness, in short, an age that roots out the worst in man and substitutes the best? I return to my point and to the strange devotion to studies that keeps me so busy, my dear friend, that I seem to have just begun; if nothing more, it serves to distract me in the meantime from serious cares, to forget the times, to find pleasure and joy in living, and barely to feel what most disturbs other men. Let others, then, run after wealth, let others long for honors and pleasures; in study I find wealth, in this I find honor and pleasure. Even as a boy, this was my attitude except that then I used to proceed slowly at my convenience during the morning hours, whereas now so near to sunset I double my pace, as if driven, and recalling the many projects I have begun, I hasten on, certain of the toil and doubtful of the outcome. I do not deny that my resolution is tardy, but the later something is undertaken, the sooner its execution. Plentiful examples of outstanding men make my mouth water, forcing me to cast off my sluggishness and rousing me every night despite my weariness. I do not wish you to think that there is but one Themistocles or one Miltiades; there are many. Much remains to be added of greater importance and, hopefully, of greater certainty; for now, it is enough for you to know my present mental state, as you wished. With these means I strive to check, if at all possible, time's swift flight, stealing a few days from death by reading, writing, thinking, and remaining awake. For if, as great men have said, sleep is death, life is wakefulness; in this fashion I shall live at least a few more hours. Farewell.

Milan, 13 November, at midnight.

Fam. XXI, 13.

That you more often pursue the path of the few, only rarely taking the majority's path, does not surprise me: the first you do as a philosopher and the second as a man. No one is so devoted to knowledge that he does not return at times to common humanity, stooping to vulgar customs, although, to tell the truth, I had decided to write you today about the philospher's way, not the multitude's; thus, I already regret having begun in this fashion since you are always the same for me, always one of the few. The more the ignorant multitude acquires, the more it wants; but for a few men, the learned, the more they know, the more they desire to know; and thus, both the desire to possess and the desire to know are equally insatiable. Moreover, had you not received my previous letter, I doubt that you would be asking for this one. That one sip has made you so thirsty that, after learning about one part of my life, you also wish to learn about another: how I eat and dress, despite knowing something of both from other letters of mine. I suppose, however, that you fear a change of place or time might have changed my situation, previously described. I shall thus repeat my way of life and tell you whom I follow as models. There are some who cannot rest unless within walls embossed with ivory, on feather beds, or with a recently plucked rose; there are others who do not believe that their thirst can be quenched except by using golden cups adorned with gems. And so? What advantage comes from being of this number? I far prefer to abhor these things than to miss them. There are some for whom pleasure arouses bile and continued passion produces nausea; if I may boast to you, I am of this type because of my studies and my disposition. From my earliest youth I rarely sought choice food, shuddering at lengthy meals and banquets that went far into the night; and I always considered as my own the words that Flaccus adopted too late: "I delight in a simple meal and in sleeping in the grass by a stream." My words may astonish you, but I always disdained the pleasures and charms of wealth, not so much out of enthusiasm for virtue, which I would have liked to pursue even more closely, but out of contempt and hatred for such things because of what accompanies them—the fear of boredom and aversion for the kind of life thought to be happy by the multitude. But at times my mind and eyes rebel; emulation overcomes the mind, weariness the eyes, and when I now behold in a mirror those eyes that once so foolishly pleased

*See XII, 4.

me, and now are so often exhausted with dark circles because of nightly wakefulness, I ask myself in astonishment whether I am the person I see. But their rebellion is easily managed. As for my dress and other apparel, you once heard all about them from me when I lived at my transalpine Helicon. But lest you do gain a false impression of total frugality, remember that at that time I was a country resident, cultivating a rustic simplicity. One must admit, however, that places either transform or soften feelings that may not be staunch to the end, yet remain steadfast and unbending. The Persians crushed Alexander, Capua crushed Hannibal, whom Rome had not crushed, with the result that his bitter enemy could elegantly and properly say, "Capua was Hannibal's Cannae." Not simply the virtue of one man but often the strength of an entire people is weakened by changing location: Babylon weakened Macedonian vigor, Asia weakened Gallic prowess, and Spain and Africa crushed Roman power, not with a hostile sword but through the cowardice of its troops and the laxity of military discipline. This great and powerful people, of which I am hardly a part, is undoubtedly barbarian in origin; at the present time—see what a change in location is capable of doing—no other nation has more humane or more civil customs. Transplanted herbs change their juices, wild trees when grafted transform their original nature into another one because of a change in location. You see where I am heading, for I too—and why should I conceal my situation from you when I never have—seem almost another person in the country than in the city. Here I follow the ways of nature, there the ways of man; and in this I especially feel how distant is the goal that I should have already reached, namely, a uniformity and constancy of purpose, which, once attained, marks the attainment of one's goal—a peaceful and secure haven of life where the ship of fools cannot enter. Whether a victor, or unconquered in other things, I do battle in one corner of the battlefield; having bridled my gluttony and laziness, having stamped and even extinguished lust with divine aid, I am having trouble controlling less serious faults. In particular, only now am I beginning to persuade myself to wear a common and modest, even "philosophical" dress. The heavy yoke of old habits has weighed upon me, and shaking it off has required much of me, so you will see the progress that I have made in a brief time. Yet with a great deal still remaining to be done, my spirit and mind must now be armed rather against the shame of wearing worn-out clothes than against the vainglory of foolish dress, and perhaps one day I shall no longer have to do battle. Farewell, remember me, and I beg you to pray that I may live as I should like to have lived at the moment of death.

Milan, outside the walls, 7 December.

Fam. XXI, 14.

To the same correspondent, * *concerning his move from Ambrose's house to that of Simplicianus, and some observations on the life of Simplicianus.*

The date of the preceding letter could have made you wonder how, with the war in full swing, I went outside the walls, although you might have thought that, though living inside the city, I was writing you from outside the walls in order to escape for some reason and for some time the city's pressures and tedium; but that was not the case. To inform you of what happened, then, know that on 3 November I left Ambrose's house and its neighborhood where I have lived for seven years, and moved to the monastery of Simplicianus outside the ancient city walls, passing from the western to the northern side: such is my tremendous love for freedom, solitude, and tranquillity. Although, as matters stand, there is scarcely any hope for solitude here, still this house is so situated that from a concealed back door I can easily avoid the troublesome throng of visitors, a benefit that I did not enjoy in my other dwelling. For a mile or so, pleasant retreats are easily accessible; whereas if I wished to walk about the city, for miles along the walls there is extensive solitude since the multitude is nearly always crowding into the shops and squares. But this mile is entirely mine because a steep bank and rather thick hedges enclose it on one side, and though open on the other, it is naturally divided by a hidden and little-used grassy path where I, often alone or with a companion, meet no one. With the road winding very slightly, I am so free to go to and from sunny and shady spots that, were it not for the sight and noise of the nearby city, I seem in the midst of woods. This convenience and my wish to flee the public have persuaded me to leave the city; nor do I fear Ambrose's annoyance since in my thoughts I have not abandoned him and really have moved nearer to his father—for thus Augustine calls Simplicianus, "the father of Bishop Ambrose in receiving divine grace." Neither was I afraid of dishonoring myself by seeking a more peaceful life in his dwelling where Augustine mentions having gone for counsel. The first thing that I did upon arriving was to ask for the saint's story, thinking that the life of so great a host would be a source of considerable pleasure. The monks brought me a recent work by an unknown writer, a work with no authority, elegance, or order, although they understood it to be from Augustine's *Confessiones* where the saint is mentioned; but unlike what Augustine writes, everything in the work is not simply unpolished but disfigured and con-

*See XII, 4.

fused by the whim of this new man of letters. Astounded and irritated, I lay down the book, for what else was I to do? The harm has been done, and now for the multitude the life of Simplicianus is as written by that writer, yet far different in the eyes of Him who sees all. Whence there came to mind, while I was reading, a saying by a man of letters who was not an equally good man, that a saint's fame is only as great as his biographer's eloquence. Clearly poisonous words, but in keeping with what a poet or historian would say. For in Flaccus's words, "Hidden virtue is not much different from hidden sloth"; and in Crispus's, "The virtue of those who ventured great feats is only as great as the ability of those who extol them in words." The judgment of both these men is self-evident and true, while the man about whom we are speaking is suspected of hidden heresy: the first two deal with deeds where glory is sought through virtue, where the ultimate goal of virtue, according to a major poet, is to enlarge one's fame with deeds, a fame that without written records would be either insignificant or very brief; but the latter writes about saints who find glory not in the clatter of popular favor but in the Lord, whose names written in the book of life by the hand of God have no need of the skills of mortal writers. If every pen were to cease writing, if every tongue became silent, if every favor and remembrance of men vanished, the just man will still remain in eternal memory and the greatness of his celestial glory will spurn the narrow confines of thundering human discourse. In any case, Simplicianus, my host, truly great in the eyes of God but handled too intimately and roughly by his biographer, deserves a more refined work from which he would derive no advantage, but the reader would develop a desire for imitation and a fervor of devotion. But even were a suitable writer available, where would he seek the truth if it is unknown even in his own home? Through Augustine's testimony, it is known that Simplicianus was a good servant of the Lord, upon whom divine grace shone, that he lived from youth to old age most devoted to God, a man learned and experienced in many things who through long practice followed the way of the Lord; he was a good friend as well as a great and effective stimulus to the true faith to Victorinus, an illustrious Roman rhetorician and subsequently a pious martyr for Christ; and finally he motivated Augustine to Christian humility and to the hope for a better life, when he came, as I said, to him for counsel because of his reputation for great virtue; at a late age he was preferred above other outstanding men on the recommendation of the dying Ambrose to be the bishop of this city, which was even then great, and he discharged his new pastoral office with the greatest integrity and the highest sanctity in order to be worthy of such an honor. This is what I know so far about my new host; the remainder is known by his celestial host. I have written this to you with the pains of my body battling my mind as I lie on a very hard bed in the dead silence of the night. What else can I say? Everything is difficult for me, even rest. Farewell.

Fam. XXI, 15.

To Giovanni Boccaccio, * *a defense against an accusation by envious people.*

There are many things in your letter needing no reply whatsoever since we recently dealt with them in person. But I have chosen two that must not go unnoticed, and shall briefly give my thoughts on them. In the first place, you ask pardon, somewhat heatedly, for seeming to praise unduly a fellow countryman of ours who is popular for his poetic style but doubtless noble for his theme; and you beg pardon for this as though I believe that praises for him or for anyone else would detract from my personal glory. You assert that, whatever you say about him, if closely examined, redounds to my glory. You expressly add as justification for your praise that he was your first guide and the light of your youthful studies. This is a proper, grateful, accurate, and, to speak candidly, fitting acknowledgment; for if we owe everything to the creators of our bodies and much to our benefactors, what do we not owe to the parents and fashioners of our minds? How much more deserving of our gratitude are those who cultivated our minds than those who tended to our bodies is realized by whoever has a just perspective on both, for he will recognize the one as an immortal gift and the other as a perishable and mortal one. Continue, therefore, not with my sufferance alone but with my approval to honor and cherish that beacon of your intellect who has afforded you ardor and light for this pathway that you have been treading with giant steps toward a glorious goal; raise high with sincere praise worthy alike of you and of him that torch long buffeted and, I would say, wearied by the windy applause of the multitude. I have concurred with all such praise, for he deserves such commendation while you, as you say, feel obliged to perform this friendly office. I thus commend your poem of praise and join with you in extolling him. Hence nothing in your apologetic letter disturbed me except that I am still so little understood by you, whom I thought knew me so well. So then, I do not delight in the praises of outstanding men, and indeed do not join in glorifying them? Believe me, nothing is so foreign and no curse more unknown to me than envy; to show you how far removed I am from such a curse, I call God, who reads minds, to witness that scarcely anything in life distresses me more than seeing worthy men deprived of fame and reward. Not that I am complaining of the harm done to me or am hoping for gain, but I do deplore what is happening to public taste when

---

*See XI, 1. The unnamed poet discussed in this letter is Dante Alighieri.

I behold the reward owed the noble arts being given to the obscene ones. I am aware that, while the glory of deserving men stimulates in the mind an enthusiasm for such glory, true virtue, as philosophers like to say, is its own spur and its own reward, its own way and its own goal. Now that you have afforded me a theme that I would not have voluntarily chosen, I shall gladly dwell upon it so as to clarify for you and through you for others an opinion that has been not only falsely, as Quintilian remarks of himself and of Seneca, but insidiously and maliciously circulating about my opinion of this poet. Those who hate me say that I hate and despise him, trying to stir up the multitude against me, for he is extremely popular with them. This is a novel kind of perversity, showing a marvelous aptitude for hurting others. Let truth itself answer them in my behalf.

In the first place there can be no cause for ill will toward a man whom I have seen only once, and that in my early childhood. He lived with my grandfather and father, being younger than the first, but older than the second with whom on the same day and as a result of the same civil disturbance he was driven from his native land into exile. At such times, fast friendships often develop among victims of similar tribulations, and this was especially true of them since, in addition to a similar fate, they shared common interests and studies. But my father, compelled by other matters and by concern for his family, resigned himself to exile, while his friend resisted and began devoting himself all the more vigorously to his literary pursuits, neglecting all else and desirous only of glory. In this I can scarcely admire and praise him too highly when nothing—not the injustice suffered at the hands of his fellow citizens, not exile, poverty, or the stings of envy, not his wife's love or his devotion to his children—diverted him from his course once he had embarked upon it, when many other great talents, being weak of purpose, would be distracted by the least disturbance. This usually happens to writers of verse who need peace and silence more than other men since, beside the substance and words, they must also worry about style. Thus you will understand that my scorn for that man is someone's detestable and ridiculous invention because, as you see, there are no reasons for hatred and many for love, including our fatherland, our family's friendship, his talent and style, the best of its kind, which must always raise him far above contempt. There is a second accusation leveled against me: I never owned a copy of his book, although from early youth when one usually longs for such things I enjoyed collecting books. While always passionately hunting for other books with little hope of finding them, I was strangely indifferent to this one, which was new and easily available. I admit this to be so, but deny that it was for the reasons that they give.

At that time I too was devoted to the same kind of writing in the vernacular; I considered nothing more elegant and had yet to learn to look higher, but I did fear that, were I to immerse myself in his, or any other's, writings, being of an impressionable age so given to indiscriminate admiration, I could scarcely escape becoming an unwilling or unconscious imitator. Because of youthful boldness I considered this unworthy; such was my confidence and enthusiasm that I deemed my own talent sufficient for that kind of writing without anyone's aid. It is for others to judge if I were right about this. This one thing I do wish to make clear, for if any of my vernacular writings resembles, or is identical to, anything of his or anyone else's, it cannot be attributed to theft or imitation, which I have avoided like reefs, especially in vernacular works, but to pure chance or similarity of mind, as Tullius calls it, which caused me unwittingly to follow in another's footsteps. If you ever believe me about anything, believe me now; nothing can be more true. And if, as was the case, I did not do so out of shame or modesty, it must have been because of youthful vanity. Today I have left these scruples far behind; and with my total abandonment of such productions and the waning of my earlier fears, I can now welcome wholeheartedly all other poets, him above all. I used to submit my work to the judgment of others, whereas now I judge others in silence, varying in my opinion of them but deeming him the one to whom I would readily grant the palm for vernacular eloquence.

They lie, then, who maintain that I slander his fame, when perhaps I alone, more than many of these tasteless and immoderate admirers, know the nature of that unknown quality that charms their ears without penetrating their minds since the pathways of intelligence are closed to them. They are really of that herd branded by Cicero in his *Rhetorica*, "When they read fine orations or poems, they applaud the orators and poets without understanding why they were so moved by them, for they are incapable of knowing either where or what or how that certain something is that so delights them." If this happens with Demosthenes and Tullius, with Homer and Virgil, among learned men and in the schools, what can you expect to happen to our poet among the illiterates in the taverns and squares? Insofar as I am concerned, I admire and esteem him, I do not scorn him. I would venture to say in all honesty that, had he been allowed to live into our times, there would have been few with whom I would have been friendlier—provided his character matched his genius. On the other hand, there are none by whom he would have been more disliked than these silly admirers who never know why they praise or censure, who so mispronounce and mangle his verses that they could do no greater injury to a poet; and if my many concerns were not so pressing, I might even strive to the best of my powers to rescue him. As it is, I can only express my reprehension and disgust at hearing them befouling with their stupid mouths the noble beauty of his lines. Here may be the proper place to mention that this was not the least of my reasons for abandoning his style of composition to which I devoted myself as a young man, for I feared for my writings what I saw happening to the writings of others, and especially of this poet about whom we speak; I had no hope, then, that the tongues or minds of the rabble would be any more flexible or kind to my works than they were to those whom long habit and favor had made popular in the theater and public squares. Events have proved my fears well-founded since a few pieces that slipped from my youthful pen are constantly being mangled by the multitude's recitation, something that is so vexing as to make me hate what I once loved. Each day as I stroll, reluctantly and angry at myself, through the arcades, I find scores of ignoramuses everywhere and some Dametas of my own at the street corners usually "ruining my poor song with his screeching reed."

But now I have said enough about a trifling matter that I should never have taken so seriously, since this hour, never to return, ought to have been devoted to other concerns. But your excuse did seem to resemble their accusation; for, as I have said, many accuse me of hating him and others of scorning him whose name I have intentionally withheld today lest the rabble that hears everything without understanding anything would noisily maintain that I was defaming him. Still others accuse me of envy, and these are truly the ones who envy me and my reputation. Although hardly worthy of envy, I surely do not lack for people who envy me, something I once did not believe and only lately began to realize. Many years ago when enthusiasm played a greater role in my life, I dared to admit with a clear conscience, not in an ordinary composition but in a poem sent to a distinguished man, that I envied no man anything. But let us assume that for some I am deemed unworthy of belief. Yet how true can it be that I am envious of a man who devoted his entire life to those things that were only the flower and first fruits of my youth? How, when what was for him, if not his only occupation, surely his principal one, was for me mere sport, a pastime, a mental exercise? What ground, I ask, could there be for envy or for mistrust? In praising him you suggest that he could, if he wished, have used another style; I heartily agree, since I have the highest esteem for his ability, that he could do anything that he undertook; but what he did choose to attempt is clear. Suppose that he had turned to something else in which he enjoyed success—what then? Why should this have been a source of envy rather than satisfaction? Or how can someone who does not envy Virgil envy anyone else, unless perhaps I envied him the applause and raucous acclaim of the fullers or tavern keepers or woolworkers who offend the ones whom they wish to praise, whom I, like Virgil and Homer, delight in doing without? I fully realize how little the esteem of the ignorant multitude carries weight with learned men; or if they believe that a Mantuan is dearer to me than a Florentine, the fact remains that origin by itself without any other factor is not sufficient reason for esteem, although I do not deny that envy flourishes most vigorously among neighbors. Apart from these many things that I have said, the difference in our ages likewise does not support such charges since, in the elegant words of one who says nothing without eloquence, the dead "are neither hated nor envied." You will accept my solemn assurance that I delight in our poet's talent and writing, and never refer to him except with the greatest admiration. I have at times said only one thing to those who wished to know my exact thoughts: his style was unequal, for he rises to nobler and loftier heights in the vernacular than in Latin poetry or prose. Not even you will deny this, nor does it redound to anything but his praise and glory in the minds of sensible judges. Forgetting the present age inasmuch as eloquence has long since vanished and been buried, and speaking only of the age when it flourished, who, I ask, excelled in all its branches? Read Seneca's *Declamationes*: it is not conceded to Cicero or to Virgil, to Sallust or to Plato. Who would aspire to praises denied such great geniuses? It suffices to have excelled in one genre. This being the case, I ask the contrivers of calumnies to remain silent; but let those who perchance believe such calumniators kindly read this opinion of mine.

Having disposed of this matter, which has been troubling me, I come to my second point. You thank me politely and courteously for my great concern about your health without realizing that an expression of gratitude is unnecessary. For who is ever thanked for being concerned about himself and his own affairs? You, my dear friend, are part and parcel of myself. Though nothing in human affairs is truly sacred, more godlike, and more celestial than friendship, save virtue, I still believe that it makes a difference whether you begin by loving or being loved, and that those friendships should be more carefully fostered than those in which affection is merely received. Leaving aside the many instances in which I was overwhelmed by your kindness and friendly offices of friendship, I cannot forget the time when, as I was hastening across Italy in midwinter, you not only sent me affectionate greetings, which are like footsteps of the spirit, but came personally in haste to meet me, on the heels of your admirable poem, motivated by your great desire to see a man whom you had yet to meet. You thus revealed to me, whom you had determined to love, first the face of your talent and later that of your person.

What is more, it was late in the day and the light was already waning when, returning from my long exile, I was received within my native walls, and welcomed by you with respect and reverence far beyond my deserts. You renewed for me that poetic encounter of King Arcadius with Anchises when he said, "The mind burned with youthful love to address the man and clasp his hand." For although I did not stand as he did, above the others, but rather beneath, your spirit was none the less ardent. You led me not within the walls of Pheneus but within the sacred portals of your friendship; nor did I offer you "a fine quiver containing Lycian arrows," but my lasting and sincere affection. Though inferior in many respects, I shall never in this regard yield anything to Nisus or Pytheas or Laelius. Farewell.

Fam. XXII, 1.

To Pandolfo Malatesta the Younger, Lord of Rimini,* whether
he should take a wife and who she should be.

You ask my counsel on whether it is better to take a wife or remain
unmarried. I am grateful to you for thinking me a suitable adviser in
such an important matter. But if experience is the mother of art, you
who have experienced both states can much more competently address
the subject than I who have experienced only one, and thus must make
inferences about the other based on ancient writings or on reports from
contemporary married men or my own personal feelings! It is for this
reason that I have delayed my reply, fearful as I was of responding to
a judge such as yourself on such a controversial question. Yet, I prefer
to appear ignorant rather than discourteous or unconcerned about your
affairs. I have therefore laid aside all sources and arguments useful for
writing a book but not a letter; although some writers have written books
on this subject, I will briefly and simply summarize my opinion, whose
sincerity at least you will admire if not its substance. It is useful to
remember above all else Socrates' response to a young man who, having
doubts like yours, had asked him your very question, to which Socrates
replied "that he would eventually repent of doing either one of them";
he then gave his reasons, which I shall not repeat since they are well
known. By these words he quite clearly revealed his feelings about our
subject, yet the same thing can be said about a sizable portion of human
affairs because you will always find trouble, boredom, and danger whatever course you choose. Nor will you be surprised to learn that our
lives in which we so greatly delight are nothing but danger, boredom,
and toil regardless of where we turn. And what else may be expected
from life except what it contains? Who would seek frosty dew within
a burning furnace, or a fountain of fresh water in the middle of the sea,
or live coals under mounds of snow? Everything must be sought in its
proper place, and if sought elsewhere, even the most thorough search
proves fruitless. Since along life's pathways, so dark, rocky, and steep,
cannot be found true peace, pure joy, or certain security every time uncertainty arises about something (as is now happening to you and often
to others), once false hope is laid aside only virtue remains. Virtue will

---

*Well-known military commander whose feats had earned him a high reputa-
tion throughout Italy, especially in the papal states, Florence, and Milan, and whose
interest in humanistic studies had so attracted him to Petrarch that he commis-
sioned at least two painters to attempt portraits of the poet.

provide the means for directing and steering one's own counsel, and by depending upon it you will not stray; and though you may perhaps fail to attain your goal, still you will not fail to enjoy the glory of a free choice. And yet even in the selection of useful things, the process of seeking to determine what is advisable is most difficult; often something appropriate for you is not so for your home, your country, your friends, your patrimony, or for your reputation, your pleasure, your health and welfare; at such crossroads, I believe that in order to judge rightly the public good must be preferred to the private, and noble things to ignoble ones. Not to keep you in further suspense with my irrelevant remarks, I here draw the matter to a close. I am truly convinced that for you alone, for your rest and repose, it would be preferable to avoid marriage; but your family, your homeland, and your friends demand something else of you; and too, neither children nor age can be used as excuses since you have no children and are still young. What then? Since you have asked my advice, I am of the opinion that you should take a wife. For while I do believe that nothing is sweeter or more peaceful than celibacy, your own, and your family's position begrudges you such pleasure and peace. A higher station cannot remain tranquil any more than a lofty mountain or a swollen sea; it too is exposed to its own kind of winds. Nor is it fitting for you to say, "I care only about myself, give me your advice," since you were born for your country, for your relatives, and for your friends in Plato's esteemed opinion. Proceed, then, with Christ as your protector, take a wife, and in choosing her, let your judgment remain pure and removed from common fashion, so that you consider not so much her dowry and wealth as her family line and upbringing, not so much her elegant attire as her devotion, and above all, not so much her bodily beauty as her mind. Should she be from nearby or from a distance? That was your second question. My reply will conflict with the common preference for a wife from nearby; all things being equal, I prefer her to come from a distance. Others do seek the favors of their neighbors which are rare and costly; surely your destiny did not leave you in such need. I prefer independence of spirit and freedom from annoyances and even from hatreds very often caused by close neighbors. And as my final piece of advice, I believe that this could be useful: take as a bride either a judicious lady (for how could such a wife be unsuitable for you when she was perfectly suitable for King David, for the great Pompey, and for Caesar Augustus?) or perhaps an inexperienced young virgin, particularly if the marriage terms seem favorable to you. For a noble maiden, devoted to you from an early age and distanced from her people's flatteries and old women's gossipings, will be more chaste and humble, more obedient and holy; quickly casting off her girlish frivolity, she will don the seriousness of a married woman. In short, whether a virgin or a widow, once she joins you in the nuptial bed, hearing, seeing, and thinking of you alone, she will be transformed into your image alone and will adopt your ways, and once her friends and nurses are forgotten, she will devote herself only to the joys of marriage. This, O most illustrious sir, is my opinion, which I am hoping will be as useful to you as the degree of good faith with which it was given. May God Almighty favor whatever choice you do make. A cordial farewell, and remember me.

Venice, 11 September.

Fam. XXII, 2.

To Giovanni Boccaccio, * *that often in writing it is easier for him to err in what he knows well; and concerning the law of imitation.*

Soon after your departure and despite my distress, because I still do not know how to remain idle (yet, to tell the truth, everything that I do is nothing or very nearly nothing), I detained as a personal favor our friend to have him help with the work that I had begun with you: revising the transcripts of the *Bucolicum carmen*, a copy of which you had taken with you. As I conferred with that good man with his old-fashioned ways, not a slow-witted friend but a really slow reader, I noticed several short words repeated more frequently than I wished as well as some other things in need of more polish. Thus, I urged you not to hasten your transcription or to give a copy to our Francesco, knowing your interest in all that I possess, especially my writings; indeed, were your love not interfering with your judgment, they would be unworthy of your fingers or your eyes. I thought that I could easily make the corrections in a few hours after returning to my country dwelling, where I was preparing to hasten on the first of July; but I was mistaken. The frequent, and almost annual, revolts in Liguria kept me in the city despite my great love of the country and hatred of cities; very recently, since my fear was beginning to appear greater than the actual danger, around the beginning of October, which was quite late, my confidence managed to overcome the bothersome delay, and I arrived at the Adda's banks, which for the time being is the site of my solitary retreat. I have now been here eight days where constant rain and an inclement autumn, or rather an early winter, promise an all too short respite. Nevertheless, during this brief interval, which forbidding skies and inclement weather threaten to cut short, I have concentrated on revising that poem, and in the process realized that a reader's slowness aids a corrector's labor. Unquestionably if a polished, quick, and intelligent reader makes the material being read a delight, then a slow, hesitant, and obtuse reader helps to uncover and detect errors. Nor, by Jove, does this differ from anything else. Give a faulty horse to a skillful rider, experienced in horsemanship, and faults remain hidden; with an inexperienced rider, they all will be evident. Entrust an unjust cause to a distinguished lawyer and he will skillfully obscure the injustice; bring an inexperienced lawyer to court and and the unfairness of the case will be revealed along with the defender's ineptitude. Perhaps you forget the decision of Mar-

*See XI, 1.

cus Cato the Censor to replace at once the academic Carneades, leader of a philosophical delegation sent to Rome by the Athenians, giving as his reason that it was not easy to grasp how much truth or falsehood there was in anything he said. That truly is the way it is: an expert's skill conceals all defects. While our friend was reading, I saw what I had not seen while you were reading, and I have now really learned that when pleasure is sought from a work, one must have a quick and pleasing reader, whereas when corrections are sought, the reader must be slow and awkward. In any event, whatever changes I wish to make in the poem are indicated separately so as not to fill this letter with boring details.

There is one thing that I thought must not be kept from you or excluded from this letter, something that was unknown to me until today, and still is unbelievable and astonishing. Whenever we write something new, we often err in what is most familiar to us, for it deceives us in the very act of writing; whatever we have slowly learned we know better. You will ask: "What are you saying? Isn't this a contradiction? It is impossible for opposites to be both true; how can you write that what we know better we know less, and what we absorbed more slowly we know more firmly? What Sphinx or enigma is this?" I shall explain. Something similar happens in other areas, as, for example, when something hidden more carefully by the head of a household is less readily available, or when something buried more deeply is uncovered with greater difficulty; but these apply to material things, with which I am not dealing. So as not to keep you in suspense with circumlocutions, here is an example. Only once have I read Ennius, Plautus, Felix Capella, and Apuleius, and then it was done hastily and quickly, brooking no delay except as one would in unknown territory. Proceeding in this fashion, I saw many things, culled a few, retained even fewer, and these I laid aside as common property in an open place, in the very atrium, so to speak, of my memory. Consequently, whenever I happen either to hear or use them, I quickly recognize that they are not mine, and recall whose they are; these really belong to others, and I have them in my possession with the awareness that they are not my own. I have read Virgil, Flaccus, Severinus, Tullius not once but countless times, nor was my reading rushed but leisurely, pondering them as I went with all the powers of my intellect; I ate in the morning what I would digest in the evening, I swallowed as a boy what I would ruminate upon as an older man. I have thoroughly absorbed these writings, implanting them not only in my memory but in my marrow, and they have so become one with my mind that were I never to read them for the remainder of my life, they would cling to me, having taken root in the innermost recesses of my mind. But sometimes I may forget the author, since through long usage and continual possession I may adopt them and for some time regard them as my own; and besieged by the mass of such writings, I may forget whose they are and whether they are mine or others'. This then is what I meant about more familiar things deceiving us more than others; if at times out of habit they return to the memory, it often happens that to the preoccupied mind, deeply intent on something else, they seem not only to be yours but to your surprise, new and original. Why do I say you would be surprised? Surely, you too will readily admit to having experienced something similar. I have really spent a great deal of time trying to identify my sources; I call to witness our Apollo, the only son of the heavenly Jove and true God of wisdom, Christ, that I have not been eager to plunder, that I have refrained from intellectual as well as from material thefts. If anything contrary to this is found in my works, it results from an intellectual kinship in the case of authors whom I have not read (as I wrote you in my previous letter) or, in the case of others, from the type of error or forgetfulness that we are now discussing. I grant that I like to embellish my life with sayings and admonitions from others, but not my writings unless I acknowledge the author or make some significant change in arriving at my own concept from many and varied sources in imitation of the bees. Otherwise, I much prefer that my style be my own, uncultivated and rude, but made to fit, as a garment, to the measure of my mind, rather than to someone else's, which may be more elegant, ambitious, and adorned, but deriving from a greater genius, one that continually slips off, unfitted to the humble proportions of my intellect. Every garment befits the actor but not every style the writer; each must develop and keep his own lest either by dressing grotesquely in others' clothes or by being plucked of our feathers by birds flocking to reclaim their own, we may be ridiculed like the crow. Surely each of us naturally possesses something individual and personal in his voice and speech as well as in his looks and gestures that is easier, more useful, and more rewarding to cultivate and correct than to change. Someone may comment, "And what do you think of yourself?" Not you, my dear friend, who know me well, but one of those who observe others, being totally secure in their silence and safe from critics, have learned to direct stinging barbs against our every word. Let them carefully listen since they bluster only on the basis of what they hear. I do not resemble Juvenal's description, "A distinguished prophet not of public vein, who usually repeats nothing that has been said, nor strikes a poem with common and ordinary coin," whom the writer himself did not wish to identify but simply to imagine. Nor am I like Horace: "I was the first to plant free footsteps along an untrodden path," or "I first revealed Parian iambics to Latium"; nor am I like Lucretius: "Alone do I wander over the remote pathways of the Muses, previously trodden by no man"; nor like Virgil: "I love to climb gentle slopes to the heights where never had earlier footsteps gone to the Castalian fount." And so? I am one who intends to follow our forebears' path but not always others' tracks; I am one who wishes upon occasion to make use of others' writings, not secretly but with their leave, and whenever possible I prefer my own; I am one who delights in imitation and not in sameness, in a resemblance that is not servile, where the imitator's genius shines forth rather than his blindness or his ineptitude; I am one who much prefers not having a guide than being compelled to follow one slavishly. I do want a guide who leads me, not one who binds me to him, one who leaves me free use of my own sight, judgment, and freedom; I do not want him to forbid me to step where I wish, to go beyond him in some things, to attempt the inaccessible, to follow a shorter or, if I wish, an easier path, and to hasten or stop or even to part ways and to return.

But in my excessive wandering I have been distracting you unduly. At issue today is the tenth eclogue of my pastoral poem where I had written in a certain section, "Solio sublimis acerno"; upon a later rereading of the verse, I noticed its close similarity to Virgil's words in the seventh book of his divine poem, "Solioque invitat acerno." Consequently, you are to change them and substitute the following, "E sede verendus acerna." For I wished the Roman imperial throne to be of maple because in Virgil the Trojan horse is of maple; and thus, as in theology wood was the first cause of human misery and later of human redemption, so in poetry not only that same wood in general but that same tree in particular caused the ruin of the resurrected empire. There you have the gist of my thought, nor is there need of further explanation.

In the same eclogue was a passage that was oddly overlooked because of my familiarity with it, and thus I made a mistake that would not have happened had I been less familiar with it; nor was it a passage merely resembling another, but identical. The same happened to me as to the person who cannot see a friend right before his eyes. The passage read in this fashion: "Quid enim non carmina possunt?" Finally coming to my senses, I realized that the end of the verse was not mine; but for a while I did not recognize whose it was for the simple reason that, as I said, I had made it already my own; but at length I discovered it in Naso's *Metamorphoses*. Therefore you are to change this as well, replacing it with the following: "Quid enim vim carmines equet?"—a verse that is inferior neither in expression nor in content. Let this then be mine even if it must be mine as corrected; let the other return to its master and be Naso's, for I could not steal it from him if I wished, nor would I wish to if I could.

Although I do know that some ancient writers, Virgil in particular (as when he boasts of having taken away Hercules's club), not only translated innumerable verses from Greek into Latin, but transferred them from foreign works into their own, not out of ignorance—since one cannot imagine such illustrious and evident examples being stolen from this or that source—nor, one gathers, for the sake of stealing, but rather for the sake of competing. In any case, they either had greater freedom or a different mentality. As for me, if forced by necessity, I would allow myself to use another's words knowingly, but for the purpose of looking better. If out of ignorance I ever do sin against this principle, make certain that I hear about it: I shall readily recognize your good faith and return what I have stolen. The two verses that we have been discussing fall into this category; and if you find more, feel free to correct them or admonish me in a friendly way. For you or any of my friends cannot do anything more pleasing for me than to show a truly friendly, free, and intrepid mind in correcting my errors. No criticism is more welcome than one that censures my ways: I stand ready to rectify most willingly my style and my life not only upon the advice of friends but also at the barkings of my rivals, provided amidst the shadows of envy there shines a glimmer of truth. Live happily, remember me, and farewell.

Fam. XXII, 3.

To Barbato da Sulmona,* forwarding his "Epistole metrice"
dedicated to him.

For some time now, my dearest Barbato, I have had many doubts as to whether to send you at last my *Epistole metrice*, which were long ago dedicated to you, or whether to withold them and keep them carefully hidden; the former would have satisfied your desire, the latter would have served my reputation. I am well aware of the expectation and ardor of your mind, which in matters of this kind usually wishes to know only whether the writings are mine. At the mention of my name, you straightway, in the manner of Pythagoreans, let authority take the place of reason, allowing the veil of your great love to diminish your keen judgment. In truth, the letters are such that, either because of my age when they were written or because of negligence, they cannot be safely exposed to the judgment of outsiders. In rereading them, I am so drawn back in memory to that period that against my wishes I seem a boy again and the same as I once was despite my striving ever since then to be another person. In fact, memory is a most powerful faculty of the mind that at the slightest reason often becomes so strong that it grabs us by the hand, thereby compelling us to go where we would rather not go and detaining us there despite our reluctance. Finally, having considered everything and being more concerned about my reputation than about you—I beg you to forgive me—or about myself, I had decided to keep them; and I would have done so except that nearly all my writings, as I say in the preface, are known to the public. Now in order to safeguard the very reputation that I have been discussing, it would be better not to keep them at home so that the ones now scattered around in the possession of friends and, I suspect, full of errors, may be corrected as much as possible by using these as norms. What else shall I say? I am giving you what I would have gladly withheld, not because I dislike anything of mine becoming yours, but because I do dislike the idea of them reaching others through you, something that cannot be avoided; nor do I give them to you because of my promise, but because I must. In this I am complying not with my good faith but necessity, for in order not to be compelled to act, I willingly submit to the test of fame, which I can no longer avoid with hiding places or silence. In every necessity there is but one remedy: consensus. Farewell.

*See IV, 8.

Fam. XXII, 4.

To the same correspondent, * *that the inconvenience of absence can be mitigated by using an imagined presence as a remedy.*

Ah, how often, my dear Barbato, have I lamented not only life's countless misfortunes but this one in particular: though so alike in spirit, we are so apart physically and socially that we may not see each other as we grow old, nor be allowed to converse even once before departing this life or rather this death. For although it is not difficult to effect an imaginary meeting as is the case with the unattached mind, especially with those who love sincerely, although among good men friendship always remains fresh, I know that you are no less dear to me, nor I to you, than on that first day in the royal palace in Naples when we were joined in friendship in the presence of that excellent king who is now in heaven. Surely his divine genius would never have brought together dissimilar spirits under a single yoke unless he had observed some notable affinities in us, for though you were much more cheerful than I (something you alone deny), all else was the same—our studies, age, habits, and thought. As I was saying, despite all this, and despite the fact that no place or time has any hold on our minds, it would please me, and I believe you too, if our destiny would allow us actually to see one another some time, "to hear our live voices and respond" in Maro's description, and to encourage one another in what remains of our lives and in facing its end. If destiny denies this, it will be realized in our minds and imaginations, something that cannot be forbidden us; you will embrace me in your thoughts and I shall do the same; no day will pass, no night, no study, no conversation, no joy, no toil, no repose will take place for one without the other. The book that one of us picks up, the other will open; wherever one of us looks, the other will read; wherever one of us sits on the ground, the other will be beside him; as often as one of us begins speaking to himself or to another, he will perceive the presence of his absent friend listening carefully; finally, whatever one does, wherever he will be or will go, the other will be close at hand. And since man's end can be concealed, though not avoided or even delayed, when one dies, the other will accompany him in memory in the belief that he is still alive, nor will he be mistaken, for he truly is living through the grace of Him who is the source of life, and with pity he will be awaiting the survivor who has not yet begun to live. When he does join his friend, then, if we cannot make it come

*See IV, 8.

to pass sooner, we shall finally be united without fear of separation, then we will both be able to look down upon the smallness of your Naples and my Rome and our Italy, which now are large enough to keep us from meeting again, once we separated; indeed it prevents us not only from seeing one another personally but through letters, and thus, this short stretch of land separates us as though one lives on the Indus and the other on the Iberian sea. The mind, noblest part of creation and sublimest work of nature, can neither be forced nor contained; it flies across mountains and seas, opens prisons, breaks chains, crushes locks, and is present whenever and wherever it wishes. The jump from the Alps to the Apennines, or from the Tyrhennian to the Adriatic is a simple thing, for such are the boundaries separating us, insignificant indeed, yet what does it matter how short the distance if it is impassable? Often devotion has urged me to make the difficult journey in order to attain, like Aeneas, what I mentioned previously: to behold you and hear your voice. More than once I have tried to make up my mind to fulfill this longing of many years; almost nothing on earth do I desire more than to see you in Rome once again, and the few friends who are still living. This promise that I made you some time ago has so far not been kept, not because of the difficulty of the road or the weight of my cares, but because of the dangers of war that have regularly recurred nearly every spring for a number of years now. I have yet to lose hope, and it may well be that, when I cease expecting, it may be close to fulfillment; for just as every evil is the more difficult the more unexpected it is, so every good is the sweeter the more unhoped for it is. Meanwhile let us bear absence manfully since it only separates mortal things, and with the ingenuity about which I have spoken at length, let us counter this violence of fortune. Farewell, and remember me.

Venice, 20 April.

Fam. XXII, 5.

To Philippe, Bishop of Cavaillon,* an exhortation to pursue a quiet life and to avoid hardships.

Countless are the hardships and dangers from which almighty God has freed you and returned you to us! My unworthy spirit cannot render Him fitting gratitude for His kindness, but in its devotion it renders what it can! How fearful I have been that the Rhine, the Meuse, and the Moselle, having dared to offend our Rhone, Sorgue, and Durance, by seizing their distinguished resident, would forever keep you for themselves! But although a lengthy deferral is nearly a theft, you still have been detained a long time, not abducted, from your country, which now implores you through my words to forsake her no longer. You have come and gone and traveled about long enough. Once I said, and it bears daily repetition, "Evening draws nigh, one's lodging must be considered." This, I repeat, I have often said and even written, but never at a more opportune time, for the idea of resting may be useful for the young but is necessary for the aging. Oh, if only I had the time, how much subject matter would emerge from this theme! But you understand me just as well whether I speak or remain silent, for nothing I can say, let alone think, is new to you, although in this not only I but Cicero as well warns in vain. Though most learned in all good disciplines, in this one alone have you outdone yourself and your ability by shaping his firm skill for yourself upon the anvil of experience with a skillful hammer. Indeed never is security more welcome than in times of peril, never does a restful life appear so sweet than in times of hardship. If this is true, what advantage is there in undergoing new experiences so often when they always seem to increase perils without enlarging knowledge? Constant exposure to questionable events reveals a rashness hardly suitable to your learning, your profession, your age, and your stature, or to your character and customs. And while at one time you did manage to avoid such rashness, do not now allow a defect that you were able to elude in youth to afflict you at an age when the need for possessions is less and the need for judiciousness is greater. Such a suspicion is inevitable in the case of one who exposes himself to danger and difficulties. Nor does your superior's authority offer an excuse since you would be excused only if it were really forcing you; but the Roman pontiff, despite his long enjoyment of your faithful and effective service, still has many suitable men for such an office. Would that

*See II, 1.

there were not so many driven by the goads of avarice and the winds of ambition to confront any danger, who fear no journey and no part of the world where empty honors and perishable riches abound! Yield to the new recruits, O illustrious veteran, and let them yield to you in turn. Have you ever seen at one and the same time someone weary of sitting and another weary of walking? Have them change places, and both will be content; the same will happen to you, for they are eager for work and you for repose, and a single act will settle the situation for both. But if the ˙pope's order is pressing—for it is the nature of employers to be domineering, considering only themselves and their advantage—let your eloquence and your talent come to your aid, let your health and your age be your excuse (I teach you not to lie but to escape), pretend to be a little older than you are. As in many other areas, so with age it is customary to pretend in one way or another, since reliable witnesses are lacking. Your midwives, nurses, and even parents have died; the evidence of one's face and hair is deceiving, for the person who speaks about himself, especially if he overdoes it, is believed. Pretend to have a feeble and delicate body unaccustomed to heavy toil with hidden defects, since the demands of your office are real with no reason for feigning them. Never has a bishop left his see as saddened and widowed as yours was. You so won your flock's favor that without you it may not return to its happy pastures; in your eyes and on your tongue lies the peace of your diocese. Your small, devoted, and gentle flock, totally dependent as it is on its shepherd's words, does not recognize another's voice, and thus, it is not so much a matter of being entrusted to another as of being forsaken and lost. Not from the one who draws you away, but from you yourself must come the justification; his responsibilities are no greater, but they do apply to more and greater people, whereas you must answer for your flock and none other. I admit that he can compel you who are part of his flock, but believe me, he will never do so if you refuse in good faith; he will not wish to add to his responsibilities your slight one and become your debtor. Vigorously and clearly explain to him your own danger and that of your flock; you must not omit anything, and if the truth is insufficient, use your imagination, for pretense in support of the truth cannot be called a falsehood. You must make every effort to be free, to be your own, to be saved, and to be happy. Some writers censure Ulysses for feigning insanity in order to avoid military service; and obviously if the pretense is true, the accusation is just because a soldier wished to abandon Greece, which needed his aid and counsel amidst its many preparations for a very just war. But there are no criticisms of the simulated fear of Thamyris, queen of the Scythians, of Caesar's dissimulated fear, of the simulated passion and terror of Ventidius, of the simulated illness of Themistocles, or of the feigned departure of Claudius Nero and many others; through these artifices they sought honor for themselves, safety for their armies, and freedom for their native land. Your pretense hurts no one and will bring to you peace of mind and avoidance of perils, and to your native land tranquillity and joy. Your many long labors did nothing for your welfare or that of your people, or for your freedom or for that of the universal church in whose behalf just and strong men must labor and die, but—allow me with my usual frankness to speak the truth to the one whom I have never said anything not on my mind, nor remained silent about what was, and allow me to prick your mind confidently and boldly where it needs attention—you are endeavoring to serve another's ambition and to fill a bottomless abyss. Do you who have always been totally devoid of ambition and desire for power now wish to become the slave to another's avarice, and you the master of your own feelings, to yield to another's? This, I am certain, is not your intention, nor is it my advice; you were born to a greater office than being someone else's agent. I ask pardon for my frankness and openness; for me you will be a true bishop, a true pastor, only when you cease being an agent. Such a lowly position is unworthy of you, and if you refuse it, others will be found to whom it would be better entrusted. Show the pontiff that you cannot do what is asked of you, show him that others both do and aspire to what you flee; beg him to give them their coveted tour of duty and you a well-earned discharge; in short, refuse with firmness. He will think more highly of you, and if your refusal is displeasing, he will esteem your virtue and admire your steadfastness, and he will cease asking; for it is true, as Seneca states in his *Declamationes*, that no one repeatedly requests a favor of someone who has refused in no uncertain terms. This, O dear and illustrious father, I would not dare say to someone such as yourself unless, on the one hand, your modesty and kindness, and on the other, my love, faith, zeal, and fear did not encourage me. For I fear these journeys of yours, so frequent and difficult, so distant and lengthy, and—this I view as worse than death—I dislike your risks in which I myself feel endangered. Cease, I beg you; now is the time.

What is more, my great desire to see you once again may be more readily imagined by you than expressed by me. Since you have known me intimately from my early years, I shall tell you my accomplishments during these seven years since our separation. When age had removed nearly all attractions of earthly loves, it produced in me a boundless kind of perfect love: I once admired much that I now scorn and loved others that I now yearn for; and consequently as I grow older each day, the more I alternate between hot and cold. Perhaps before I die God will satisfy this noble desire of mine, and when I am least expected, I shall arrive. Oh, if only I could suddenly appear amidst your books, oh, if only I could do so on the grassy bank of that limpid river, or under the high cliff whence rushes forth with such a roar our king of headwaters! In the meantime, my and your Socrates is there; I beg you to embrace him, as is your wont, and through him me, with the arms of your paternal spirit, and to do for him and with him whatever you would do for me. And so farewell, remember me as usual, but think of yourself even more than you customarily do.

Milan, 9 August.

Fam. XXII, 6.

To Zanobi da Firenze, concerning the arrival of the Grand*
Seneschal of the Kingdom of Sicily.

Your Maecenas has visited my Augustus and, I might boldly add, me too. Making little of his status, he twice visited my library, and neither the crowd nor the press of affairs, and finally not even the difficulty of the road stopped him. Although earlier I lived just within the city limits, I now reside outside in a healthy, isolated, and uninhabited area. It was here that our illustrious man came, and with his official insignia removed, as the great Pompey once did at the small home of Posidonius, and just as respectfully, he entered my modest residence with head uncovered, nearly genuflecting as though a student of Parnassus at the shrine of Apollo and the Muses. His behavior was such that it evoked in me and in the illustrious men who were present a shiver of devout embarrassment at such a noble humility, and near tears at such devotion—so great were his dignified expression, his courteous ways, the solemnity of his silence and then of his words. He examined my humble books, nurses and companions of my idleness, first in general and then one by one with such care that you could imagine nothing more pleasing; there was much conversation on a variety of subjects but especially of you. Nor in truth did he make his stay brief, as travelers usually do, but so lengthy that it could be said he was compelled to leave. In short, he made this place such as all future centuries would wish to visit, such that not only a Roman or a Florentine guest, but any friend of virtue, whoever he may be, would pay homage to it while passing through here. What shall I say? The entire royal city was delighted with his coming and brightened by his majestic bearing; he was marvelously welcomed by the lords and by the people, but above all by myself. He also did something that I considered impossible: he increased the affection that I had long felt for him and also accomplished something wonderful and rare among mortals, that my opinion of him whom I had long known but had thus far never seen was not only undiminished by his presence, but even increased, something that had not happened with almost anyone else and I had rarely read about. Live happily with such a friend, farewell, and remember me.

Milan, 17 August.

---

*See XII, 3.

Fam. XXII, 7.

To an unknown correspondent, a sharp rebuke to a stubborn
youth, denying him permission to return.*

I could care for you, if you could care for yourself, or better if you
did not hate yourself. "What man," you may say, "has ever hated himself?
Who has ever not cared for himself above all else?" I know that this
is the multitude's conviction, and I am well aware of Paul's words and
of Cicero's maxims. It is difficult to deny that excessive love of ourselves
is the cause of nearly all ills. There is little question that from this proceed thefts and adultery, from this come the robberies and similar acts
to which excessive self-love so drives us headlong that we cannot bear
to be without what gives us pleasure; and therefore I maintain that many
love themselves to excess, whereas few in just measure. I ask, How may
one be said to love himself in just measure, that is, moderately, who
voluntarily seeks an everlasting death? How can one love oneself when
his unforgivable conduct is destroying him? And finally, how can one
love oneself when he hates his Creator? For he who loves himself must
love Him who made him; if he hates his Creator, he certainly does not
love himself. This truth is very apparent not only within ourselves, whom
we intimately know, but with external things as well. Who can enjoy
the trees' shade and the lyre's music, and yet despise the roots and the
instrument? Who can love a river and hate its source? If a loving husband respects his father-in-law, who has given his daughter nothing more
than her name and her share of sinfulness, what must we owe God,
who created our wife, our children, and everything that we love, who
created us and our souls with which to love ourselves and others? With
confidence and conviction I repeat that one who hates God must necessarily hate himself because, as I was saying, excessive self-love is hatred. It
is opposed to the welfare of the loved one whom true love considers
its goal; false love tends toward the opposite, which is nothing but hatred.
I too might avoid spurning you, had you not spurned God and men
and your own soul; I could be patient with you, had you not abused
my patience for much too long; I could be kinder to you, had you not
dared to trample foolishly and spitefully upon my indulgence (or shall
I say, my good nature or softness?), or had you not opposed my daily
and nocturnal activities with your daily and nocturnal laziness and sluggishness, or my nightly vigils so well known to you with your continual
and languid sleepiness so similar to death, or my cultivation of friends

*See XVII, 2.

and my constant and continuing enthusiasm for friendships with your silly laughter and scorn for men whom you did not deserve to see or hear, or finally my character, life, customs, studies, in short, all of my life with your behavior and actions so contrary to them. Consequently, whatever pleasure my mind provided me—which may lack total innocence and great virtue yet is aware of its good will—your spirit opposed with an equal amount of grief and ill intention, which you could not conceal, nor knew how to, nor really wished to out of complete contempt for my actions and ideas. Thus appeared the immeasurable dissimilarity of our natures, which, if men's opinions were well founded, should be very similar; thus appeared the remarkable clash of all our aspirations.

I bore all this as long as possible, but with such distress that of all the burdens imposed by the world and by life, none was, or could be, more troublesome and unbearable; in fact, the staff that I had procured for my feeble old age became a great weight and pitfall. Still for many years I tolerated this with fatigue and anger, something that now astounds me; but compassion strengthened my patience, and a slender hope that your life would change prevented my disgust. When this too vanished, not simply weary but broken and overcome by your evil habits, I drove you from my home as an unworthy burden. If you now seek an end to your exile, you must realize that it will end when you cease sinning; my love is vanquished, my hope drained, my patience destroyed, and my house cannot endure you, nor my walls welcome you, my roof protect you, my ears listen to you, my eyes see you. Thus, as long as you remain what you were at your departure, you should be ashamed to hope or to desire to return. To receive a welcome, return as another man, in different dress, with a different mentality, a different gait, other gestures, a different bearing to your head and body, another tone to your voice, a different twist to your eyebrows and nod of your head. Take care not to return with anything that made you odious even to those who would naturally hold you dear, especially that disdainful arrogance with which you are shamefully swollen, for nothing is more unworthy of or more unbecoming to your condition, which, as long as it remains unchanged, is nearly the most abject and contemptible in the world. Do you think that by scorning your Creator, God the Father of all, your fellow men, especially those who love us, and your soul and salvation, you thereby become greater and more celebrated? You would be more puffed up, yet, I ask, what will ever result from that arrogance of yours except a ridiculous mouse? Even less, I say; for ridiculous things bring smiles, make our sides shake, and provoke humor; your arrogance is perhaps ridiculous to others, but it promises you genuine sufferings and the material for eternal death. For you are swollen like a lethal serpent and not like a ridiculous mouse, and yet you consider yourself happy as you are! But you are mistaken, you have seriously erred, you are blind, I say, to the path of true glory; and what is worse, you enjoy your misdeeds, O wretch that you are, and glory in your dishonor without understanding the consequences of your straying. You further hoped that your conduct could perhaps remain hidden or even be pleasing, and I admit that you applied this vainest of hopes to me principally because everyone is more loving toward his own. As though it were always true that "the judgment of lovers is blind"; as though it were not sometimes truer that no judgment is harsher than a lover's! For those who love may demand so much of their dear ones that their sensitive feelings are often offended by the slightest trifle. Would that you had fulfilled perhaps not all but at least your simplest duties, would that you had remembered to be, if not a gentleman, at least a man, or if you did not wish that, certainly not an animal! But you became lost in your meditations to the point of reaching a deadly self-forgetfulness and fatal trance from which you may not merely be absolved by being called or berated but you must be aroused by fire and sword. Awake, you madman, rouse yourself, and behold where you now lie; let your eyes not cease weeping over your lost time, your hands not cease striking your arrogant breast, your tongue and spirit not cease invoking forgiveness. "Some god gives ear to those who repent," says Naso. What could express more truth and piety, if only it were said of the true God? Indeed, some God does give ear to those who are repentant and contrite, that God of whom the Hebrews said in amazement, "What is He saying?" when He remitted their sins. Knowing that only God can do this, they were astounded at a man doing it, being unaware that the man was also God, who not only hurls men's sins behind His back but also "into the depths of the sea," who "distances our iniquities from us as far as the east is from the west," and who "is near to all who call upon Him in all sincerity." He will be with you if you truly invoke Him, if you lay aside your arrogance, repenting of the past and fearing the future, despairing of yourself and hoping in Him. Though He has often and quickly brought many a man to justification, having no need of time in order to do so, nonetheless you may require lengthy purgation; filth hardened over a long period of time is not so easily washed away. You may consider yourself fortunate if your return to the straight path takes no longer than you spent in error, for straying is usually simple whereas returning is not. You must follow the course over which you wandered so afield of justice's pathway; you must repeat your digressions and retrace your steps, thereby doing everything in reverse. In place of unbridled license you must cultivate moderation, while in place of your contempt for God and men you must, for greater security, spurn the world, yourself, and that inciter to sin, your flesh, your most mortal enemy, which shamefully goaded you to revolt against me and—what is far more serious and deplorable—against your God. With me it matters little, but I should like to see you return first to God's good graces, since I shall not willingly receive under my roof an enemy of my God. If you appease Him with due respect—for He is gentle and placable beyond belief—I shall easily forget my hurts, many though they are; and whomever the Lord has forgiven, I as His servant shall not deny my pardon; nor can I forget the words in Ecclesiasticus: "Despise not the man who is turning away from sin, nor reproach him; remember that we are all in the state of sin."

But enough of this. I have written more than I intended, for today compassion has overcome anger. These things I offer you, unhappy boy— but it was my duty to indicate again and again to you the right path lest your sins seem to cast upon me a suspicion of guilt, if after you had fallen so low, I were to enclose myself in silence, a mute observer of your headlong plunge—these things, I say, I offer you as remedies and suggestions for your lost life and abandoned hope, insufficient for your desperate and inveterate sloth, but perhaps even now they may prove useful if not rejected. Upon careful consideration of your situation there appears to me no prognostic of salvation, yet some hope is still offered by your age, but even more by the clemency of the offended Lord, through which He often makes friends of enemies; He can effect in you as much as He has for many others, provided you open yourself to Him and remove any obstacle. It is you who will see to this; as for my role, I seem to have fulfilled it with a thousand words and now in writing, yet with what success, I repeat, will in the long run depend on you. Henceforth I am resolved to remain quiet, awaiting the outcome in silence; if you survive I shall rejoice over your salvation, if you perish I shall find comfort in my conscience, which, despite your stubbornness and ingratitude, has often pursued you with loud warnings and then with silent prayers, even unto the grave. Consequently, unless of course I am mistaken in my judgment, indeed not simply myself but everyone save perhaps your accomplices, you will never, living or dead, have just cause to reproach me. As for your eagerness to return home not out of love for me or for virtue, but rather perhaps because of the inconvenience of your exile, I could with real justification cite Augustus's response to Tiberius in exile on Rhodes when he begged to return in order to see his relatives, that you not worry about your beloved ones whom you so readily abandoned; but I shall respond differently. When you not merely think but know that you have become as I have asked (and in these pages you will see the reflection of your spirit as in a mirror), only then and no sooner may you hope with my consent to behold my face, which you scorned despite its kindness and good nature, which now is no longer as it was, but as you deserve and I consider fitting. For I know what ruined you: it was my indulgence; I shall see to it that I no longer make you wicked through compassion or ruin you through love. Consider these words to be spoken not "by the oracle of Pythian Apollo" as Cicero says, but by the lips of Christ Himself; nothing is more certain, nothing is more true.

Milan, 30 August.

Fam. XXII, 8.

To his Socrates, * on the differences between one guest and another.

Toward evening our Bolanus arrived in the midst of a tremendous downpour and an even greater outpouring of words. What can I say? At his noisy arrival, this solitude became a veritable public square. You know what I mean; he is the weightiest of men, not with the weightiness befitting a wise man, but with the weight of a ponderous man. Why describe him to you? You know him all too well. I do not have the back of an elephant or a camel; the very sight of him makes me weary and, in the words of Flaccus, "my ears droop like an unruly jackass," and I begin to perspire in spite of being cool. What could I do or where could I turn? The time and the place, the rain and ordinary politeness induced me not to let him depart, although that was my intense desire, aside from my wish that he had not come. I was encouraged by a certain reserve that is comely in many people but unnatural in him; he thought his companions too numerous, and indeed they were, and he was afraid that a hermit's house could not host such a crowd. For a while my fate hung in balance, and my night's activities and repose were in jeopardy; I was saved by the thoughtfulness of one of the guests who by repeated taunting and admonishing caused him to leave despite his inclination to remain. Noticing this, I began to feel safer and wished to appear more gracious by urging them to spend the night. O the artful ways of men, to plead for one thing when you desire the contrary! But that is our nature. Anyway, he refused, alleging or feigning other obligations. Why prolong this? If you think that I tugged at his coattails, you are mistaken; I let the man go, and was happier than one who shakes off a fever. Surely you have been worried as I spoke, being in doubt as to the outcome; but now, having removed your concern, and wishing to fill you instead with pleasure and envy, you should know that not long afterward, at the hour the ancients called the first torch, there arrived that most delightful friend of ours. O what a difference! There is no animal as varied as man; one is worth nothing whereas another has infinite value. My house quickly changed aspect, and I began to fear what I had previously hoped for, that he had to or wished to depart; I was grateful to the night and to the clouds that forced such a guest to spend the night. Nor was there need for chains, for I was as anxious to have him stay as he was of staying, and thus we spent not only that night together, but several happy days. Joy, however, has this peculiari-

*See I, 1.

ty: it suddenly ends, and with that nothing remains; and even this would be bearable except that sorrow then replaces joy. He departed, and I remained behind more dejected than had I not seen him. Strange as it may seem, what I feared for the first, I hoped for the latter, and where the first made me happy, the latter saddened me. Farewell.

Fam. XXII, 9.

To the same correspondent, * *that he prefers to do good to evil men than evil to good men.*

You inquire about the outcome of my troubles with that flattering, deceitful, and, on occasion, violent and threatening man. Why deny the truth, why not instead admit with Cicero to a "softness and weakness of mind"? I could never resist his tears and entreaties. I must confess this; while he was speaking I felt something tender and feminine steal into my heart, and was close to bewailing my own harshness and to assuming the roles of offender and offended. But then these thoughts occurred to me: "Who is speaking with you, what has he done, what did he desire and will, what did he strive to do, what would he have accomplished had his evil purpose not been blocked? Did he not join with many others in doing you harm, has he shown any shame or repentance, how little is there standing in the way of his designs except his impotence, how false are his tears, how insincere his flattery, how forced his entreaties? What kind of spirit and mind does he possess, what manner of wolf lies hidden inside this lamb?" While mulling each of these questions, I gradually stiffened, changing into stone and diamond. Would you believe it? I now became another man, totally unlike my real self; reason ordered me to refuse pardon to that awful man since ready indulgence uplifts good men but provokes evil ones, and my well-justified anger was supported by the opportunity for prompt punishment. But my kindlier nature won. I thus forgave him with this condition, that henceforth he may be neither my friend nor my foe; he will doubtless fulfill the first, while the second depends on him as long as he never again entertains any hope for an easy pardon. And thus the matter stands; I would prefer to maintain a middle course, but if I must make a choice, I prefer to be good to the wicked than harsh to the good. I beg you to pardon my pardoning, and farewell.

*See I, 1.

Fam. XXII, 10.

To Francesco of the Church of the Holy Apostles, * concerning the blending of sacred and secular studies.*

In one of your letters I noticed that you would like to see me combine the sacred with the secular, stating that this would please even Jerome; for great are the charm of variety and the beauty of symmetry that you declare derive from the power of such juxtaposition. What can I reply? You must form your own opinion since you really are not easily deceived or mistaken, except that those who love are wont to be deceived readily and gladly. Putting all this to one side, then, I shall speak of myself and of my recent but already strong enthusiasm for sacred literature, to which I have devoted my writing and my mind. Let the arrogant laugh who are revolted by the austerity of divine eloquence, as the modest dress of a chaste woman offends the harlot's eyes accustomed to cosmetics. I believe that with the Muses's assent and applause and with Apollo's support I can devote my riper years to more important matters after devoting my early years to youthful studies. Nor can it be considered unbecoming if, following my many years of rising from bed to sing the praises of vainglory and the empty fame of men, I should now rise in the middle of the night to sing the praises of my Creator, to interrupt my sleep and repose for Him who does not slumber or sleep as He watches over Israel, who, dissatisfied with universal custodianship, watches over me personally and is concerned for my welfare. I am clearly conscious of this as are all others capable of gratitude. He thus protects each person as if forgetful of the others, and rules over all as if unconcerned about individuals. In short, I have it firmly fixed in mind to spend, if it be granted from on high, my last years amidst these studies and occupations. For when or how could I better depart this life than by always loving, remembering, and praising Him without whose constant love I would be nothing or wretched, which is less than nothing, without whose love my wretchedness would have no end? I have loved Cicero, I admit, and I have loved Virgil; I was taken by their style and genius more than by anything else; many others, too, from that band of illustrious writers I have loved, but these two were such for me that the first was like a father, the latter like a brother. Admiration for and intimacy with their genius achieved through lengthy study led me to such love that you would think this kind of affection scarcely possible toward living men. I loved among the Greeks Plato and Ho-

*See XII, 4.

mer, whose talents when compared with their Latin counterparts often made me despair of sound judgment. But now I must think of more serious matters, for I am more concerned with salvation than eloquence; I used to read works that gave me pleasure, now I am reading works that are good for me. This is my present state of mind, and it has been so for some time. Nor am I just beginning, and from my graying hair I can see that I began none too soon. Now my orators shall be Ambrose, Augustine, Jerome, and Gregory, my philosopher shall be Paul and my poet David, whom, as you know, many years ago in the first eclogue of my *Bucolicum carmen* I so compared to Homer and Virgil as to leave the victory undecided. Until the present the old power of deeply rooted habit has stood in the way, yet personal experience and the glowing revelation of truth allow no room for doubt. But if I do prefer these, I do not reject the others as Jerome maintains he did despite his apparent approval of them in subsequent writings. I seem capable of loving both at the same time, provided I distinguish between the ones preferred for their style and the others preferred for their substance. What, I ask, prevents me from behaving like the prudent head of a household who devotes part of his furniture to practical uses and another to ornamentation, and assigns some servants to care for his son and others to entertain him? Furthermore, wealth is composed of both gold and silver, and when you have recognized the value of both, you avoid being deceived by either, especially since the ancients demand nothing of me save that I not let them fall into oblivion; and happy about my devoting my youth to them, they now allow me to dedicate all my time to more important matters. Despite my having already come to this conclusion, I shall act with much greater confidence thanks to your encouragement. If circumstances demand it, I shall make use of Maro and of Tullius for style, and not hesitate to borrow from Greece what Latium may seem to lack. But with regard to living, though much that is useful has come from the ancients, I shall still use the others as advisers and guides to salvation since their faith and learning have no trace of error. For me the greatest in terms of merit will always be David, who is the more beautiful for his simplicity, the more learned for his purity. I desire to have his Psalter always at hand and within sight while awake, and beneath my pillow while sleeping and at the point of death, in the belief that this would be no less glorious an act for me than were Sophron's farces for the greatest of philosophers. Enjoy good health, remember me, and farewell.

Milan, 18 September.

Fam. XXII, 11.

To Guglielmo da Verona,* a recommendation for a friend who had late but passionately turned to intellectual pursuits.

When you come to know this man, you will come to love and admire him. It is a long tale, but suffice it to say that he has become very friendly and devoted to me for good reason and, though tardy, he was so swept up by the passion for learning that he neglected family cares and abandoned his business, in which he was quite prominent, to dedicate himself completely to letters. And now he thinks of nothing but schools, books, and teachers, spending his sleepless nights and hectic days in this alone. I beg you to welcome him and support his resolve; there is nothing more godlike than to encourage just desires. And what do you think he is striving for? He seeks not wealth or power, not honor or pleasures, the multitude's fetters and the mind's poison, but books, the only safeguard for his isolation and the solace of his life; and he would venture nothing without your direction and advice. Once you understand his aspirations, you will sigh to yourself, "Had you only begun earlier!" Farewell.

*See IX, 15.

Fam. XXII, 12.

To Albertino da Cannobio, physician, * *that trustfulness is a sign of a good mind; concerning the disdain for property, the worthlessness of servants, and the inevitability of death, against which there is no remedy but serenity.*

In your letter I read nothing but pleasant news, for although it seems to express some needless fear, it all emanates from the springs of pure love, about which the teacher of love has written, "Love is something full of uneasy fear." Whoever seems free from care is not a lover, you may be sure; although virtue has no fear for itself, it does fear for others as happened to Marcus Cato during the riots of the civil war. But to avoid beginning with the last point in your letter, I shall follow your order and later return to this subject. I am glad that my excuse, unlikely as it may appear to the multitude, though basically the truth, has found your ears open and your mind receptive. The sign of good will is trust; he who constantly lies is wont to believe nothing, while he who never lies is wont to believe anything. Nearly always a person judges others as he sees himself, unless perchance something unexpected arises forcing him to change his mind. So common has this been in our day that what the Psalmist said with exaggeration, "Every man is a liar," was never so true and so evident in any other age, and amidst the countless liars it is difficult to say how to believe those few who do speak the truth. You acted nobly, then, by showing trust in a friend who was not deceiving you; unworthy hands have so drained me that I must now appear destitute and poor to worthy people. This is difficult, but so it is; what cannot be changed must be borne.

As I see it, I am no better a householder than a politician; the love of solitude and of literature has completely deprived me of all that, nor do I entertain any hope of changing my ways in the future. Despite my daily attempt to learn something, it is too late to develop a skill utterly unknown to me; and so, let my private affairs go as they will or as they can, provided that I escape safely even though stripped naked. Returning from a journey only to see his possessions laid waste, Anaxagoras said, not at all moved by the damage, "I would not be safe had these not perished." Philosophical words indeed, profound and magnificent. What does it matter if I am near or far when my possessions are

---

*One of the few members of the medical professions admired and respected by Petrarch. His concern over Petrarch's health during the plague that was threatening Milan in 1360 was deeply appreciated by Petrarch.

seized and destroyed? Admittedly I speak neither with exactness nor according to the precepts of Bias, for my true possessions cannot be seized and destroyed, and I have called mine what belongs to fortune, following a popular error of speech rather than my own judgment, a weakness of the vernacular. What does it matter, I repeat, where I may be when my possessions disappear, if even within my own room I fail to protect my transitory possessions, as though I were dwelling beyond India and in distant Taprobane?

Those who are called my servants when they are my bitter enemies seized the opportunity by using their guile and abusing my indulgence; and with brazen wickedness they reduced me, quite unsuspecting, to the point that upon awakening to what was going on and realizing the danger (for by then almost nothing remained except my body and my books on which those greedy and famished scoundrels might have vented their rage), I turned to any hiding place, no matter how cramped, in order to escape them. Had I continued living in that large, secluded house, there would be danger from my servants, about which I have spoken, or danger from my very solitude if I threw them out. Whereas a few occupants in a large dwelling make for solitude, moving them into a cramped one makes for a crowd. Thus I have been for a time compelled to change my lodging and in large measure my way of life, yet not without serious consequences to those who forced me to do so. When their fury, spurred by greed and jealous rage, so intensified that they were undeterred by my presence or by my words, threats, or pleas, they struck one another with their own weapons, causing their own deaths, and finally, losing all patience, I disowned them. I used a paternal expression because I had truly been a father to them, whereas they were not sons to me but rather plotters, assassins, and domestic thieves. Now let them reap the fruits of their crimes, for they obviously considered me not only drowsing but insensible, and for that very reason, persuaded of perpetual impunity in their prowling and their outrageous thievery, they sought from their villainy only the vain pleasures of the gullet and of lust. They thus deserve what they get: unless I am mistaken, they will soon be starving; for they have already laid aside their arrogance, pleading humbly and dejectedly to return. If they manage this, they will regard it as a pardon for past offenses and a license for future ones, and I shall not only be ridden with the usual injuries, affronts, and annoyances but even deprived of any satisfaction deriving from making useless complaints. It would be easier to persuade me to surrender to any enemy than to compel me to tolerate their laziness and barbarity; for an enemy to strike you is a common and well-known calamity, but for you to feed him is surely a strange and extreme form of wretchedness

Now what, I ask, do you think of all this, my dear friend? Gladly would I flay this type of thief with an immortal satire except that often in the past and present much has been said of these paltry and evil gallows birds unworthy of a pen destined for better things!

Anxious and concerned you invite me to your country and to the truly healthy foothills of the Alps, far from this air once so esteemed yet now tainted for reasons unknown to me. You surely act out of your customary generosity, and in your insistent plea shines a love for me brighter than the midday sun. Yet ponder, I ask you, how it would be for a person who, though unlearned, enjoyed from childhood the works of learned men, to consider fleeing or delaying death in his riper years. To be sure, limits have long since been imposed on us and on all who are or who will be, limits that cannot be avoided, just as they cannot be reinstated once they have been passed, nor anticipated before they are reached. Lest you think that only our own writers or Sacred Scripture speaks convincingly of this, listen to the foremost leaders of secular letters and of Roman eloquence. One states, "Death is certain, and it is uncertain as to whether it will occur this very day"; "no one is so foolish, even though he be young, as to hold that he will live until evening." Another writes, "Each man has his particular day; the duration of a man's life is brief and irretrievable." I could cite many other authorities on these truths, but they are well known with no lack of witnesses, and too, true testimony is not provided by number but by authority. Aware of all this, what else can I do except await death or proceed cheerfully and undaunted? For to die joyfully is our utmost happiness, to face it with excessive terror our greatest weakness; to remain fearless amidst things that appear frightful and to gaze upon death with steadfast eyes is truly the proper course and duty of a real man. If fleeing death is stupid in a young man and ridiculous in an old man, then it is useless in any and all cases. Whether we go toward death, as some would hold, or whether it comes to us, as others think, it can happen and frequently does that we meet it while in flight. Not always, then, but very infrequently, does death happen to be what or where we think; indeed, it is often different and elsewhere since most men are overtaken in a place and by a death other than they feared. Flaccus said it very well, "The unforeseen power of death has swept away nations, and will continue to do so." Were I to flee the plague, which has thus far terrified rather than invaded this city, how very numerous and varied would be death's arrows in pursuit of fugitives, and though I may dodge a number of them, I expose my life to another! The man who fears the sword perishes in a shipwreck, while another who avoids a storm at sea is slaughtered by his enemy on shore; the man who flees war is killed by a fall from his horse, while still another who avoids labor dies in sluggish repose. You know that Alexander of Macedonia, invincible in battle, was overcome by drink; Pompey the Great, who survived Thessaly, fell in the Egypt that he had given to another, and a hostile army proved kinder to him than a follower's house; Julius Caesar, victorious over foreign enemies, was undone by domestic ones; Augustus, who feared lightning, died of disease and old age; Domitian, who abstained from mushrooms, was felled by the sword, while Claudius, who was well guarded against the sword, was killed by a poisonous mushroom. Africanus the Younger, unharmed by the hostile armies of Numantia and Carthage, met death in the conjugal bed, as had happened long before to that illustrious Greek king, conqueror and destroyer of Troy. But why continue? Why do I assemble examples of unexpected death when I ought rather to try amassing rare examples of the opposite instance? How few men die as they imagined, being mistaken as to the time or the place or even the manner of their death, and sometimes in fleeing a false danger collide with a real one! Flight from one peril is often the cause of another; the fear of an evil has driven many into another, according to Isaiah's prophecy, "He who flees at the sound of terror will fall into the pit, and he who climbs out of the pit will be caught in the trap." As death is the most certain of all things, so all that surrounds it is most uncertain, and nothing is so doubtful as that occurrence of which there can be no doubt. I shall not even add death by famine, debauchery, honest toil, and shameful sloth, since among these things there is a tremendous difference. Provided there be no stench of guilt, no twinge of conscience, no fever of passions, no swelling of pride, no blemish of infamy, death is one and the same in and of itself. No one can truly escape it; it threatens all equally, whether it be the wealthy king, the poor farmer, the feeble elder, the robust youth, the young man in his prime, the tender boy, or the child at the breast. All things must die, and all things are equal in this one respect despite countless differences in others; there is no privilege of age, of place, of dignity, or of fame. Let us look death in the eye: why do you calculate its arrival, O mortal animal who are about to die, why do you tremble, why do you look outside of you? For the real discerner external appearance matters not at all; the object must be examined in itself in order to determine its true value. If, then, the day and place of our death has been established for all those who are born, why our concern about location and time? We have already been warned about both. If I were to hear Jeremiah saying, "He who remains in this city shall die by sword or famine or pestilence; but he who goes out to the Chaldeans shall live and his soul will be safe," I would unhesitatingly flee to the Chaldeans. On the other hand, if Moses were to speak and say by divine decree, "Beware ascending the mountain or touching its base; anyone who touches the mountain will die," I would venture to urge you to descend forthwith from the mountain. Now I hear neither one, but rather the woman of Tekoa saying to King David, "We must all die, and we are then like water that is poured out on the ground." This being the case without exception, what will flight afford except useless toil and a fear of death worse than death itself? Fear is truly swift, but death is swifter and fortune even more so; it will be more to our honor to be found standing firm than forestalled in flight. Let us with serene spirits, then, await on earth what has been decreed for us in heaven, lest like small birds entangled in lime or snares, we become more entangled by trying to fly.

As for your promise to be my constant companion, it is once again proof of your deep love for me, worthy of your profession and of our friendship. But by Jove, while the art of medicine does contribute something to maintaining health and curing minor disease, it still stands by helplessly before final things. Hence that flight of doctors and that despair at curing the ill, a real sign of human ignorance or of weakness serving as a warning to have faith only in that Physician who does not abandon His patients in crises, about whom it is written, "Even though I walk in the shadow of death, I fear no evil, for you are at my side." O powerful Doctor who rends the shadow of death simply with the sun of His sacred presence, allowing no one who walks with Him to be afraid, who cures with words and not with herbs, indeed not only cures but revives! For He is not of those about whom it is written, "Will you work wonders for the dead or will the physicians revive them?" He is the most high, who created this medicine on earth for the good of mankind, reserving another kind for Himself uncreated and eternal with His divine substance by which He might resurrect the four-day stench from hell and save the human species from eternal death. I surely do not deny that friendship is a great comfort in life and in death, and whether it be absent or present I do not refuse it, I embrace it; and although in every respect I do like you, yet it is more as a friend than as a physician that I enjoy you. Therefore, considering your wishes more than my danger, and thinking of you as a friend more than a physician, I would most eagerly accept your invitation except for physical obstacles and other kinds of impediments; I would come to visit you and your solitude, which for me has always been a desired and praiseworthy haven from life's storms, but not in order to avoid death, mindful that in times passed and present the raging plague struck the lofty Alps and the Noric strongholds, in the poet's words. If the Alps were truly impervious to death, believe me, so great a will to live is inborn in mortals that you would now be dwelling in tight quarters and I in roomy ones. Farewell.

Milan, 26 October.

Fam. XXII, 13.

To Pierre de Poitiers, Prior of St-Éloi in Paris.*

Last year as a participant, though unworthy of that great office, in the delegation to the most serene and gentle king of the French, and in conversations with you of which I never have enough—I would daily find greater pleasure in them the longer I had been forced to do without them—I learned from you that, from among the various things that I said in their presence, the king himself and his firstborn, the celebrated Duke of Normandy, a young man of unquenchable spirit, were struck by my words on fortune. This I had noticed from their intense concentration as I was speaking; I saw them straighten and listen attentively to me at the mention of fortune. As I understand it, they are amazed and astonished, as if in the presence of a new prodigy, by fortune's enormous inconsistency; as often with the small and the great, it has recently so smitten the very greatest that a once fortunate realm, the object of much envy, is now worthy of pity. At that time I answered you that no one should be surprised if either fortune or any benefactor of the kingdom were not only to destroy it but to take back what had been given, and that furthermore we must hope in Him through whom kings reign, who does not slay but punishes His sons, and ministers to us on the basis of our illness, at times perhaps too harshly but always compassionately and to good effect. Consequently, on that festive day when my colleagues and I were invited to dine with the king, the discussion afforded the royal youth the opportunity to ask you, along with some distinguished and learned men chosen for this purpose, to request me to express my thoughts on fortune after dinner. This was reported to me late that evening by someone concerned and worried about my reputation; although I was unprepared for such discussion and deeply involved in other matters, it was nonetheless not easy to refuse him. Therefore, not wishing to be surprised by something unforeseen and hasty, without any books I collected my thoughts as best I could amidst my many preoccupations. My opinion could be given in one word—being now and always in agreement with the belief that fortune is nothing but an insignificant and empty word, though I usually follow the multitude's

*A Franciscan turned Benedictine, also known as Pierre Bersuire, who was highly acclaimed and respected as a scholar and philosopher in Avignon and whom Petrarch had met some twenty years earlier. He was present during Petrarch's mission to the French king in 1361 in behalf of the Visconti who wished to send felicitations to the ruler on the occasion of his release from imprisonment at the hands of the English.

habits of speech by often referring to her, yet I did wish to give a more sophisticated version in order not to offend greatly those who believe and declare her to be a goddess or "the mistress of human affairs." On the following day, as you know, with the king very busy paying homage to us or indeed to himself, and with the duke, eager to satisfy his own desire, reminding the king of it every now and then with words and gestures, the hour allotted to the conversation was put to other use; and I thus departed, freed from the burden of a response and happy about not having to speak in public against the public's opinion, but also saddened not to have heard the opinions of such learned men on the subject, inasmuch as I was much more prepared to learn than to teach. The remainder of the day, from noon to evening, was spent with you and with those three teachers in my room, where you had politely gathered to speak about this subject and about various others. After my departure from France and from the royal city, often thinking warmly of you and your affairs during the journey over the Alpine ice of that terrible winter, I wrote you in the gloomy, uncomfortable rooms of the inns a lengthy letter, which then was not sent for lack of a reliable messenger. But now, with the offer of this well-known religious who is so devoted to both of us, I have with some difficulty transcribed the same letter that had been put aside and neglected. In it I said nothing about fortune, but many things about why I think your kingdom of France and our kingdom of Italy are reduced to their present condition; and while they are admittedly not weighty or elegant, they are all true, such as would perhaps please you who delight in reading my trifles. Farewell, and remember me.

Padua, 6 September, in haste.

Fam. XXII, 14.

To the same correspondent,* concerning the inconstancy of fortune, which derives from changes in social and especially military customs.

Astonishment is a sign of inexperience: we marvel at the unusual and feel no surprise at the familiar; do not marvel at all, then, for the objects of your wonder are trite and common. Human affairs are in constant flux, and as with everything else, military glory is transitory, transferring its favor from one people to another. In all we see there is but one kind of stability: instability; but one kind of trust: deceit; but one kind of repose: perpetual movement. I do not ask you to look very far, but simply to examine your country and your times. In my youth the Britons, who are called Angli or Anglicans, were considered the most cowardly of all foreigners; now the most bellicose, they have routed the French, long crowned with martial glory, in such frequent and unexpected victories that those who had been unequal to the faint-hearted Scots not only have treated the greatest of kings wretchedly and unworthily, which I recall with deep sadness, but have destroyed the entire kingdom with fire and sword. As I recently passed through your kingdom on an official mission, I could scarcely recognize it as the same one I had previously visited. Everywhere were dismal devastation, grief, and desolation, everywhere wild and uncultivated fields, everywhere ruined and deserted homes except for those spared by being within the walls of a fortress or a city, in short, everywhere remained the sad vestiges of the Angli and the recent, loathsome scars of defeat. What else can I tell you? Paris itself, the capital of the kingdom, is disfigured with ruins up to its city gates, quakes with fires, and shudders at its wretched misfortune, while even the Seine, which flows within its walls, seems to bewail and dread the city's fate, as though aware of its misery. Now see how, once again, the base region of Illyria has gradually raised its head, venturing to measure itself against martial Germany. Do you not see how, beyond everyone's wildest guess, the fleeing archers of the Danube, after a couple of avowed successes gained as much by a slow enemy's diffidence as by their own bravery, have become so confident as to dare oppose and terrorize the Teutons? From experience one can grasp not only the truth of Lucan's words, "The sword has power, and any strong people wages war with swords," but also those of Iulius Capitolinus, "No measure is more effective against the Germans than speedy archers." But this is the steadfastness of fortune, thus do mortal affairs proceed; absolutely no

*See XXII, 13.

one can call anything his own or enduring. If you wish a shorter definition or an earlier authority on this subject, listen to Crispus: "Fortune," he says, "changes along with customs, and power is always conveyed from the less to the most able." Beyond any doubt, whatever can be said in general about this is included in that brief statement. As wealth is passed on among men, so are powers, talents, virtues, and names — what belongs to one will become another's. If gold, a most weighty substance, is unstable, how transitory and flighty do you think fame is? It too is but an empty and fragile breeze; though inconstant and uncertain, it has retained for itself this one quality, fixed and certain — it follows virtue and flees sloth. This is why, according to Iustinus, "amid Greek vices arose the Macedonian repute that had been base and obscure." This was why Carthage, founded by exiles on narrow lands purchased for a price, became widely feared on distant shores; and from this came the city of Rome which rose from thatched huts to head and ruler of peoples. What caused these vicissitudes if not in the case of Carthage a laziness due to prosperity and an extravagance corrupting its original character because of awareness of its fame; while in the case of Rome its alert diligence as well as a spirit born of difficulties, willing to endure toil, hungry for glory, and disdainful of pleasures, a spirit that once under control becomes an easy victor over all, yet also open to conquest from all quarters, dissolving into extravagance and folly, were it to weaken and begin to yield? It would be easy to demonstrate this with the three peoples that I just mentioned, the four whom I previously mentioned, and many other kingdoms and peoples as well, were it not such a lengthy matter and so well known, indeed no other is better known by mankind. This is that transferal of power from the less to the most able, which I called Sallustian, and that change in fortune that accompanies a change in mores. The foremost victor over armies and the destroyer of power is pleasure, against which only virtue has succeeded; whoever is armed with her resists pleasure, does not surrender to any enemy, and inscribes his name on an immortal trophy. You know Scipio's decree in Numantia, a famous and well-known decree whereby harlots, peddlers, and camp followers were expelled from his camp. Or to put it briefly, pleasure was sent into exile and virtue was summoned as aid, whereupon victory, a companion of virtue, likewise followed. In imitation, Metellus with similar resolve and purpose in Numidia also exiled pleasure, thereby restoring the army's strength and paving the way for the Roman legions to achieve a victory that had long eluded them.

Do not expect me to speak about the discipline of our military, or about their conduct, the ordering of their camps, their leaders' foresight, their soldiers' strength and moderation. You may think that you are entering the brothels of harlots and the taverns and bistros of gluttons rather than the camps of military men. They cannot really be called anything else, nor is their barbaric drunkenness due to any old wine; unless they abound in imports, they complain of shortages, failures, and intolerable thirst, in which they find sufficient justification for flight and surrender. This is how military art has progressed; thus has military ambition proceeded from weapons to wine ladles! The question is not how they fight, but how they drink and become inebriated. Allied in this with their enemies, they fight it out entire nights and days with their fellow soldiers, and that soldier is deemed the glorious victor who is more extravagant and has a greater capacity for wine. In this type of man (would that they were the only ones!) Seneca's prophecy has come true. He says, "Some day intoxication will be held in honor, and to hold the most wine will be considered a virtue." Do you expect great things from such principles and practices? Such are the consequences that rightly befit drunkards. The unfortunate Italians pretend not to notice or see this, and these hordes of thieves pass their time in our country not to do battle but to plunder and drink. It is an ancient evil. We read that that people first crossed into Italy drawn by our abundant crops and especially by the tastiness of our wine. Would that they would not do so today so eagerly, and that they would find us at our borders forbidding their entrance rather than being imitators of their madness! The outcome is that gradually all things degenerate, our ancestral customs, our language, our dress, our home life, and our military life, and, as I am wont to lament in vain, with our encouragement this Italy that you know so well though you have never seen it, will be strangely transformed into a savage barbarism that even our enemies will pity. I do not understand how we could justify this horrible event to our fathers, though we find in it such insane delight. But I have spoken of this often though insufficiently. Now I shall return to my point.

Is it any wonder, then, that in our country the Empire is dead and liberty oppressed, or that in our world today peace is not enduring and wars are endless, since we are incapable of living in peace or ever ending a war with these mercenaries? How, I ask, can they be victorious who do not wish to be so, who really consider victory a defeat? They are afraid of returning to their own country, and with good reason, for they have tasted the sweetness of Italy and fear the war's end, the end too of their drunkenness and licentiousness; although even if they wished, they could not defeat the enemy, being degenerate slaves overcome, captured, crushed, and disarmed by their vices and conduct. What would the ancient Roman army of virile soldiers now say who usually carried on their backs weapons, rations for several days (and not the tasty meals so carefully prepared nowadays, but the hardest of breads!), and building materials, with which to satisfy their hunger in the evening and to protect and fortify themselves at night against blind enemy assaults? Those were soldiers accustomed to hearing from their leaders whenever someone made too little progress with such weight, "Soldier, when you have learned how to protect yourself with a sword, you will no longer have to carry building materials," and whenever a soldier was having trouble carrying an enormous shield, they would hear, "You bear a shield that is too large, but you ought not to complain since you make better use of the shield than the sword." No mention was made of feasts or wine; every stream, though muddy, gave nectar-like drink to the thirsty soldiers; there was no room for pleasures since virtue, the desire for glory, and a fear of shame abounded. They served under stern commanders who could not bear softness in themselves or in others, and they viewed them not as teachers of dissipation but examples of sobriety; not to follow such examples was considered conduct unbecoming soldiers. Even the enemy was aware that Julius Caesar was extremely moderate in his drinking and quite indifferent to his meals, an adversary then no less of his gullet than of his enemy, and that even in peace he would not refuse ordinary meals or even unpleasant and unsavory ones. They had learned too that Augustus "was particularly fond of hard bread, tiny fish, bovine cheese squeezed by hand, and unripe figs," that Hadrian lived sparingly like a soldier, usually eating "camp food in public, namely, lard, cheese, and watery wine, following the example of Scipio Emilianus, Metellus, and his father Trajan." Such things famous writers have reported about these men, not to mention lesser ones. And truly, who would not feel shame at being enslaved to such disgraceful masters as the throat and belly upon hearing that the great emperors lived in such fashion?

Furthermore, those soldiers customarily expected reward or punishment according to the nature of their actions, for nothing remained hidden or unobserved under the eyes of such judges. They would see statues of illustrious warriors, and the oak, turreted, or grassy crowns; they would hear that because of the incredible, astounding battle in which Cesius Sceva had singlehandedly checked the momentum of the entire British army with his breast and shield, he had been honored with a centurionship by the distinguished judge of martial valor under whose eyes the deed had occurred; that Lucius Dentatus had been rewarded because of his innumerable and unbelievable victories with not one soldier's spoils but with that of an entire legion; that, on the other hand, some legions had been branded infamous because of their cowardice and deprived of their horses, arms, furloughs, and the opportunity to do battle. For they knew very well that the one who is involved with things worthy of reward is inclined to give rewards, whereas the one who needs no forgiveness is reluctant to forgive, or if he has erred, he usually shows no mercy upon himself. Their backs were thus always ready both for the enemy's booty and for deserved punishments if the situation warranted, and their ears always prepared for honest praises and just reprimands. They knew the response of Pescennius Niger in Egypt to those begging for wine: "You have the Nile and you want wine?" They knew too his reproach to others defeated by the Saracens who noisily demanded wine, insisting that they would not fight without it: "You ought to be ashamed of yourselves; those who are defeating us drink water." Pescennius admittedly had Marius in mind, being one of his greatest imitators and admirers, thereby recalling his answer to his army's request not for wine but water: "You are men; you can see it over there," he said while pointing to enemy camps holding the riverbanks. The soldiers' bravery was so enflamed by his response that they found neither wine nor water for their thirst since, as Florus narrates, "the battle was fought so valorously that the Roman conqueror drank as much blood as water from the bloody river." What else could the demanding leaders answer their soldiers on the battlefield when the kindest of princes, Augustus, at home and at peace, according to Tranquillus, "restrained with sharp words those complaining about the scarcity and price of wine, telling them that his son-in-law, Agrippa, had made adequate provisions of the finest water so that the people would not be thirsty?" They recalled too that Niger himself was so temperate that not only did he forbid the military to use money so that, should the soldiers' backpacks fall by chance into enemy hands, barbarians would not become arrogant over booty taken from our troops, but he also forbade bakers to follow the army, as well as the drinking of wine, ordering all to be satisfied with vinegar and hard bread. Elius Spartianus writes as follows about him: "Under him the soldiers never took wood, oil, or accepted services from inhabitants in the provinces; as tribune he accepted nothing from the soldiers, and allowed them to accept nothing; and as commander he ordered his troops to stone two of his tribunes whom he heard had accepted donations." Nor had they forgotten another admirer of Marius, Cassius Avidius, who, as Vulcatius Gallicanus reports in his history, "every week always inspected the soldiers' arms, clothing, footwear, and leggings; he removed all delicacies from the camp, and ordered the soldiers to spend the winter under animal hides," carrying nothing "but lard, hard bread, and vinegar in their campaigns"; moreover, he would inflict severe punishment whenever he found any hidden delicacy. Consequently, it was only right that the prefect whom the emperor had put in charge of supplies, in writing his opinion of Cassius, should use these words: "You have chosen well, my lord, in appointing Cassius to lead the legions in Syria, for a strict leader is absolutely necessary to soldiers trained in the Greek manner. Doubtless he will shake all the flowers from their heads, necks, and breasts. Not much is needed, nor is much being spent." These were the prefect's words to the emperor about Cassius, under whose leadership "all soldiers were required every seven days to practice archery and exercise with arms. For he would complain that while athletes, hunters, and gladiators would train, soldiers did not, whereas their future hardships would be lessened if they were accustomed to them." Finally, according to the same historian, "while he was in charge of the army, without his knowing it, a band of auxiliaries led by his centurions killed three thousand Sarmatians who were carelessly roving on the Danube's banks; upon their return with an immense booty, he ordered the centurions who had been expecting a reward to be seized and crucified, a punishment reserved for slaves, saying that they might have been caught in a trap intended to destroy respect for the Roman name. And when a serious rebellion had arisen among the troops, he proceeded into their midst unarmed and said, 'Strike me if you dare, and to the disorderly breakdown of discipline add the crime of killing your leader.' This resulted in such an increase in discipline among the Romans and such terror among the barbarians who had observed that even those who were victors without permission were condemned at the Roman commander's order that they requested a one-hundred-year peace from the absent Antoninus," who was then Roman emperor. In short, this is that unusual man whom Marcus Aurelius Antoninus, wisest of emperors, selected with sound and mature judgment to reform the corrupt and wretched conduct of the legions, the man to whose exemplary sternness he renders exceptional witness and praise in a personal letter.

I have said much about Cassius because I had read a great deal about him and because, being so different from our modern military commanders, he seemed a suitable model with which to reproach the defects of our time. In this Maximinus resembled him, though he was cruel and barbarous in other matters; his biography narrates that "every fifth day he would order his soldiers to exercise, to fight mock battles among themselves, and daily to inspect their swords, breastplates, helmets, shields, tunics, and weapons, actually overseeing such things himself and behaving like a true father to the soldiers." I was also thinking of Probus, who, as Flavius Vopiscus observes, "never allowed soldiers to be idle, and had them perform many public works with their hands, saying that they were not to consume military provisions gratuitously." But I am setting aside examples of lesser importance and omitting Quintius Cincinnatus, who as dictator deprived Minutius of the consulship for allowing himself and the Roman army to undergo an enemy siege near Mount Algidus. I am likewise not mentioning Calpurnius Piso, who as consul ordered the cavalry commander, who had surrendered his arms to the enemy after suffering various affronts, to stand throughout the campaign from morning to evening in the front line with a torn, ungirt toga and naked feet, to prove that he preferred respect for the Republic and military discipline to recognizing his bonds of kinship to the commander. Therefore, while I may bypass these, I cannot overlook the unparalleled severity of Manlius Torquatus, who killed his unusually able son because he had fought against the enemy without his orders, although he had done so successfully and with distinction. The same may be said of the even more rigid cruelty of Postumius Tuburtus against his son for the same reason, although his reputation may be less certain. Nor was the harshness of Papirius Cursor inferior except that he did not visit his wrath upon his son but upon Quintus Fabius, cavalry instructor, whom the dictator wished to have decapitated because he had fought against his orders despite the fact that he had been successful and valorous. And he would have done so had public compassion not tempered his planned severity. So it was not the valor or dignity of an extraordinary event, not the fear of a rebellious army, not the tears of an aged father, not the authority of the Senate, but ultimately only the pious entreaties of the Roman people that freed a most noble and courageous young man from death. They doubtless knew that under such a leader the army had been so troubled and frightened because he was destroying the soldiers' bodies and spirits with constant labor and fear, and that, according to Livy, when some cavalrymen dared "to ask for a lessening of the labor because of the successful campaign, he ridiculed them thus, 'Lest you say nothing was granted you, I dispense you at least from wiping your backs when you dismount from your horses' "; and another time when the praetor of Preneste "out of fear led his men too slowly to the front line," he summoned the lictor with his battleax, then jokingly confused and chided the praetor with the threat of death, and then dismissed him. Quintus Messius also comes to mind, who – and I marvel that Livy could have overlooked him – during the Second Punic War in the battle of the Trebbia ordered five cohorts that had been thrown out of their assigned post by the enemy to recapture it at once, not because he was confident that it could be done, but to punish their failure with a firm hand and to let death be punishment for their abandoned post. He added in his order that any of them who sought refuge in camp was to be killed as an enemy; and this sharp spur brought on by extreme necessity incited their spirits and overcame their bodily exhaustion, their despair about the undertaking, the harsh terrain, and the enemy's numerical superiority, and thus what had seemed impossible to a resolute commander became possible for defeated soldiers. This calls to mind Julius Caesar, who, as Tranquillus recalls, "often singlehandedly regrouped wavering battlelines by standing before the fleeing troops, restraining them individually and turning them bodily to face the enemy, with some of them so upset that he once threatened with his spear a wavering standardbearer, while another one left him holding the standard as he tried to detain him." I confess that it is difficult to serve under such leaders, but glory made such severity bearable, and what personal danger and hardship had made frightening, became desirable through virtue alone. Rare were the deserters and fugitives in those days; confidence and fear restrained weak minds. A good example of such discipline was Fabius Maximus, who cut off the hands of all fugitives before sending them back, thereby giving warning to those who were contemplating flight. Another was Africanus the Elder, who had against his will so armed his spirit, which was naturally gentle and kind, with the necessary firmness that, during the course of that terrible war that was to earn him such glory, he had the leaders of defections tied to a stake, scourged until dead, and decapitated; and once Carthage was conquered and the war ended, he ordered those who had deserted and had been apprehended likewise decapitated if they had Latin names, and Romans crucified because theirs was the greater infamy. There was also Africanus the Younger, who, after Carthage had been conquered and destroyed, exposed deserters to wild animals to be mangled during the public games celebrating the victory. And Emilius Paulus, who was victor in the Macedonian war, ordered those who were guilty of similar shameful deeds trampled by elephants. These are all sound and memorable examples, provided the judgments of the illustrious leaders and men are viewed in conjunction with their desire for virtue and glory, and not from the viewpoint of envy, which is the worst of judges, and which tries to impose upon justifiable harshness the name of arrogant cruelty since it always sees everything in the worst light. At this point I would like to add a noble saying by Valerius Maximus, which he applied to examples such as these: "Military discipline requires harsh and immediate punishment because power resides in arms that, when deviating from their rightful use, will become oppressive unless they are suppressed."

Such dedicated trust was expected not only of commanders and armies but also of allies. For who would dare deceive, steal, plunder, or whatever, once they recalled the soldiers sent to protect Reggio who had shamefully slain its foremost citizens and cruelly seized the city for themselves? According to Livy they numbered some four thousand men whom the Senate ordered, one by one, to be scourged, decapitated with axes, and left unburied, forbidding any mourning for them. Then, too, they would bear in mind that the same Pescennius Niger, as is written in his life, "ordered decapitation for ten members of the same maniple who had eaten a chicken stolen by one of them," although he subsequently mitigated the rigid sentence for fear of an insurrection of the entire army, which interceded on their behalf. It was different with Cassius, about whom one reads: "Soldiers taking anything from citizens in the provinces were crucified on the very spot of their crime." And to bring to an end examples of such severe punishments, who, I ask, unless he despises virtue and glory, would not be moved and thereby abstain from harming his allies after reading the exceptional homage to moderation in Cicero's oration in praise of the great Pompey? "His legions," he says, "went even to Asia, conducting themselves so well that not even the hands, let alone the feet of this great army are said to have harmed any private citizen. Daily reports and letters tell in detail how the soldiers are passing the winter; not only is no one forced to spend anything on a soldier, but that is not allowed even if someone wanted to; for our forebears wished to find in the homes of allies and friends refuge for the winter and not an excuse for greed." Thus speaks Cicero, and his words carry no less weight than others' opinions. And not only did they behave with integrity toward their allies but with trustworthiness toward the enemy by observing all treaties and pacts. Hence the consuls Veturius and Postumius surrendered voluntarily to the enemy because they had made peace with the Samnites against the orders of the Senate and the Roman people, and thus saved public trust through personal danger, even though the enemy did not accept their surrender. Hence, the ten captured at the battle of Cannae, who were sent to the Senate by Hannibal to ransom or exchange prisoners after swearing to return if unsuccessful, were sent back to Hannibal by the Senate when one of them, or all of them according to some reports, had remained quietly in Rome after completing their mission. If the deceit of these and others is justly reproved, so the trust of Atilius Regulus maintained until his cruel death will be praised for all ages; while it is wonderful to defeat an enemy with weapons, and even more so with piety, it is shameful to deceive an enemy except with military skill. I could now cite examples from foreign nations, but my one purpose in initiating the present discourse was simply to discuss the Roman army, and no people—and I say this without intending to offend anyone—can equal them in this kind of glory.

With soldiers trained in such camps and an army accustomed to such discipline, what could ever be so difficult that could not be overcome, what so hard that could not be broken, what so high that could not be climbed? To those with all types of experience, nothing new or fearful can happen; experience is the mother of arts, and habit removes the fear of perils. No battleline composed of such men was small, for what was lacking in numbers was made up by the soldiers' obedience, the leaders' authority, the strength of spirit and experience of both, and a dedication to a military discipline considered dearer than life and cultivated as something divine. No one was so deaf as not to hear the sound of the bugle calling the troops to battle or signaling retreat, no one so stupid as not to understand such calls; no one was so slow or timid as not to obey the order at once, for together they would rush upon the enemy, together they would make a stand, together they would strike, and together they would withdraw from the battlefront. Great is the power of united valor, almost nothing is more invincible than many brave men fighting as one when virtue and experience in war unite them as one. Such an army conquered fearsome Hannibal, crushed magnanimous Pyrrhus, and led Syphax to prison, Perses to fetters, Mithridates to death; such an army divested Antioch of its kingdom, Cyprus of its wealth, pirates of the open sea. It was such an army that sank the all-powerful Punic fleet in its own waters, that compelled Jugurtha to pay the price of parricide and treachery, that divided Great Britain with a wall, joined the Rhine's banks with a bridge, checked the Danube's whirlpools and force. It was such an army that at first found difficult the crossing of the Ciminian forest but soon opened the Alpine summits, penetrated the glades of the Ardennes and the Pyrenees and the recesses of the Hercynian forest, crossed the snowy Caucasus and the rocky Atlas, traversed hot Libya, navigated the murmuring Euripos and glowing Euxinus, the risky Syrtes and the swollen ocean. It was such an army that captured Spanish Carthage in a single day, while in the other Carthage it enjoyed the same outcome but after greater effort. It was this same army that destroyed Numantia, Jerusalem, and Corinth; that seized Syracuse, Capua, and Taranto as well as Spain, France, Germany, Africa, and Asia. But what am I saying? With its valor and arms it overcame Italy, Europe, and the entire world, and ordered it to be content with one ruler. It would have been ever victorious and unconquered had not pride detracted from that victory, and had not success, as I said, always led to extravagance and corruption, turning its sword finally against its own breast, and had it not taken vengeance upon itself for the wrongs done to a conquered world.

Such were those forces; but ours, replete with thieves and plunderers, take booty more often from our allies than from the enemy, and trust more in flight than in valor and in spurs more than in swords. They deceive more freely than fight, and more often violate their word than battle the enemy. At home there is no one to avenge crimes and no Senate to chastise cowardice; in their ranks there is no Fabius, no Africanus, no Emilius Paulus, no Pompey the Great, no Julius Caesar, finally no Niger or Cassius, instead commanders who by example favor and excuse any and all military misbehavior, with the result that no crime is punished and the least worthy is given not only greater license but even a reward. Innocence is derided, abstinence is called fear, trust foolishness, but fraud is called prudence and skill; modesty is defamed as filth, frugality as avarice, chastity as inhuman. Today virtue finds more enemies than treachery once did; thus not only is it dishonored but scarcely secure, and if it perchance avoids hatred, it falls into contempt. And thus, the greatest good is either stifled or ridiculed. But how can our leaders control their armies except in this way, or with what nerve can they correct others when they themselves need so much correction? Nature does not allow anyone to give what he does not have. In Cicero's words, "A general cannot control an army if he cannot control himself, nor be severe in his judgment when he does not want others to be severe in judging him." Consequently, with drunken leaders what can our intoxicated soldiers do except what follows from intoxication? They snore, perspire manfully but feverishly, not as soldiers but as women or buffoons. They become old in their tents, they love joking, they gobble meals, they give themselves over to gambling, they are immersed in pleasures, they are surrounded with detestable bands of harlots, and neglecting orders, they wander about like bees when their hives have been destroyed. Each is his own commander. They love dark places, idleness, the idea of war to which they know they are indebted for their stipend, although they hate war itself, and yet feel no shame in discussing it as though they were experts. Lazy, ignorant, cowardly, garrulous, they possess arms and horses not to serve their masters or protect their country or gain glory, but for gain, for fancy, and for pleasure; they are loaded with gold to impress their ladyfriends and to offer a more splendid booty to the enemy. They never vie with their leaders in virtue, but being similar to them, they compete with them in sleep and drunkenness, and prove worthy disciples of their teaching in the hope of soon becoming teachers to equally weak talents. Those who are perhaps dissimilar they despise, envy, and accuse, and it is a miracle that among so many fools the few wise men do not lose their minds; nor is it surprising that amidst so much evil it is dangerous to act uprightly. With such a situation, cease wondering not so much at the fact that as one people falls another rises, and that when the latter falls the former rises—which, as I have said, derives solely from changing customs—but rather that we who consider uniformity an evil are continually being forced to change, and that our situation having reached an extreme continues to subsist not on a foundation of virtue but by its own bulk, revealing through gaping fissures the impending collapse of the great structure. It is quite astonishing too that the causes are not equal to the effects; nor can it continue for long that with such leaders, such soldiers, and such mores, destruction is not already close at hand and that in the meantime, during the respite, we are involved in unending war, peace is dead, virtue in exile, and the state enslaved and wretched, torn to shreds from within and without. Farewell.

27 February, en route.

Fam. XXIII, 1.

To an unknown correspondent, indignation and complaint against whoever ought to be crushing what are called societies of thieves, now roving throughout Italy.

I speak out of compulsion, for love of country drives me and thrusts into my heart burning goads that do not allow me to remain silent. I know that I speak in vain, nor do I find any comfort in the Ovidian saying, "The loss of words is unimportant," since nothing is more serious to a lover of silence. And so I speak, but compelled to do so, as I said, and I speak to you: who you may be, alas, I know not. O Brutus, great avenger of liberty and chastity, who dethroned the authors of shameful slavery and the teachers of lewdness, following them even to the underworld with your avenging sword, would that you were alive—I would speak to you! O glorious Camillus, who extinguished the transalpine fury dripping with our blood in the still smoking embers of our homeland, would that you were alive—I would speak to you! O great Scipio, who forced Hannibal to return home after an Italian campaign of seventeen years, miraculously destroying him with the assistance of valor and fortune, would that you were alive—I would speak to you! O Paulus Emilius, who led onto the Capitoline before your chariot the Macedonian kings, exalted because of their ancient empire and rebellious against Italy, teaching them to submit to the yoke of the Roman Empire, would that you were alive—I would speak to you! O Marius, a peasant in the words of your compatriot Cicero, but a real man who overcame the barbarian invaders of Italy, forcing them into such retreat that their thirsty army could drink both blood and water from the bloody rivers, and who with astonishing speed then turned to another region of the world in order to crush the Cimbrian madness so thoroughly that their conquered lands scarcely held the number of dead, and Rome the long lines of captives, would that you were alive—I would speak to you! O great Pompey, who quickly subdued the shameful bands of plunderers threatening Roman ships and Italian shores and raging over all the seas, and then put them in chains, would that you were alive—I would speak to you, and I would beg you to cleanse now, just as you once cleansed all the infected seas, if not all lands, at least your Italy so pitifully stained with a new band of plunderers! O Julius Caesar, who speedily crossed the Alps without waiting for an enemy attack, rapidly fording the Rhine, the Rhone, and the Garonne, and then either through good fortune or valor passed with your victorious army through Germany, France, Britain, and Spain, would that you were alive—I would speak to you! O

Caesar Augustus, who beheld from your lofty throne the kings of the earth and delegations from all nations at your feet, indeed the entire world suppliant and prostrate, and happily closed the temple of Janus after restoring peace to the land and sea, would that you were alive—I would speak to you! O noble couple, Vespasian and Titus, worthy of one another, the son of the father and the father of the son, who in a single chariot, a sight never seen before, achieved a glorious vengeance for Christ and the acclaimed triumph over Jerusalem, would that you were alive—I would speak to you, and I would urge you once again to avenge the wrongs committed against Christ! O powerful Trajan, who with great fervor revived the Empire's members already languishing from old age, and rejuvenated them beyond all expectation (never was the Empire so immobile and decrepit, never your fervor so needed), would that you were alive, I would speak to you, and I would ask you to assist the dying homeland, mindful that you are Italian even if born in Spain! O good Theodosius, who with a small band of men protected by divine aid, with the elements fighting for you and the winds conspiring with you, miraculously and incredibly turned against the enemy their own barbarian arrows drawn from enormous quivers and intended for us, resulting in their massacre, would that you were alive—I would speak to you!

What shall I now do? I need to speak and I find no one to speak to. I shall cast my words into the wind so that perchance a spirit friendly to good men may carry the words from my lips to a noble ear where they may bear fruit, as is my desire more than my expectation. For what hope remains? What is happening, O exalted Jesus? Where are Your eyes with which, beholding us from on high, You made us renowned and envied throughout the world? You surely beheld this great upheaval of fortune, this unexpected power of fate—or what other words shall I use to express what weighs upon my sad spirit? You surely witnessed the small band of our fathers bearing our victorious banners everywhere, at times to the north and at times to the south, to the east or the west, bridling avarice here and suppressing swollen pride there, appeasing the vile movements of anger here and placing a yoke on raging lust there; in short, always and everywhere doing something whereby the glorious vestiges of our magnificent passage might survive, and the subdued world would honor its acknowledged head or, if that were delayed, would yearn for it in silence. How many of our ancestors' works shine over all lands as the stars scattered in the heavens. How many remarkable acts, how many examples of virtue, how much fame, how many tales of deeds, how many cities and colonies throughout the world, how many menacing monuments in awesome marble still persist in conquered lands! Who could enumerate them all? The world recognizes them unwillingly, the world recalls them resentfully. What then is the matter? Why do I complain, why do I lament, whom do I blame? Behold a small band of thieves emerging from a thousand caverns, roaming throughout Italy, mistress and conqueror of all lands, who demand as their own province the queen of all provinces. Alas, who is there to save us from shame, now that it is too late to think of safety? Who will cover our faces with the veil of deception or ignorance now that there is no one to assist us in our ills? May we at least be allowed to be unaware of our sufferings or, at least, to be blind to the foul scars of our wounds!

I wished to speak to you with humility, O great man, whom I dare not name, so that you may come to our aid, something you seemed able to do since it is especially within your power, but I see that you have turned a deaf ear. Since it is futile to speak to any man, I turn my prayers to You, the ultimate and greatest hope of mortals. If we have used Your kindness, O creator of all things, without sufficient acknowledgement, if we have arrogantly raised our heads perhaps higher than we should for Your great and divine favor, and You wish to punish us with ill fortune, change the course of events. For fortune is Yours, fate is Yours, and Yours are human vicissitudes: we ruled arrogantly, let us serve humbly. If we never fought as thieves, then remove this band of thieves from us; if we offended You and our liberty displeases You, at least look with disfavor upon their killings, sacrileges, pillagings, thefts, adulteries, and rapes. Put an end to so many evils and reveal Yourself master over them who have said in their hearts, "God does not exist," and assist, O dear Father, Your own who are perhaps undeserving, yet who hope in You, tearfully invoking Your name and sincerely confessing that there is no other to fight in our behalf except You, our God.

1 September.

Fam. XXIII, 2.

To our present Caesar,* first a personal expression of sincere gratitude for his friendship, then a bitter rebuke in behalf of the abandoned republic and empire, and finally a vehement exhortation.

Your letter made me happy, O Caesar. But how could it be otherwise, inasmuch as mere recollection of you is wont to make me happy. I know not whether to attribute the fact that I have become so dear to Your Imperial Majesty to your kindness, to my good fortune, or, to speak openly, not so much to the solar influence under which I was born, but rather to the munificence of Him who made the sun and stars, Almighty God – indeed a famous astrologer predicted, while I was still a boy, that I would enjoy the special friendship and remarkable kindness of nearly all the princes and illustrious men whom my age would produce. The clearest evidence of this, O magnanimous emperor, is your recollection of me, which, despite such a long time and such a distance, still remains so alive that, almost as an equal, the greatest of men considers it worthy to return the affection of the most humble of men. A truly remarkable portent in an age where you can observe that anyone gaining even a little prominence is wont to become too proud and to belittle or oppress with his harsh arrogance those in inferior positions. Silently taking account of this, I understand the great value of your esteem for me; for if, as is customary, you too were to adopt an attitude equal to the loftiness of your position, you would not have deigned to make my acquaintance; but fortune does not puff up or narrow, exalt or cast down a generous and truly imperial heart. Therefore, you have deemed me worthy not only of friendship but of kind letters which do not and will not occupy last place among those possessions of mine that do or will bring me any claim to glory. For if the acquaintance and intimacy and letters of Caesar Augustus brought glory to Virgil and Flaccus, why shall I not glory that I too, their successor not in talent but in time and perhaps in the minds of men, have also deserved something similar from the successor of their Caesar? I have received no less an abundance of kindness and letters from you than did those two writers from their emperor; and if they surpass me in intimacy, that derives rather from my mental laziness and even more from my love of country than from your lofty position, which, though more sublime than any other human condition, you readily and willingly are wont to downgrade, and to exalt instead those who are worthy of you or who honor your name.

*See X, 1.

Perhaps you will laugh at my weakness, recognizing how far I still am from true philosophy. At one time I could remain far from Italy, but now I certainly cannot for long without being troubled, be it because of the unique sweetness of one's birthplace or because of my conviction, which may not be true but is firmly and solidly planted in my heart since youth, that no land under the heavens is comparable to Italy for natural beauty and for its inhabitants' qualities. Had I not been deeply persuaded of this, I would have doubtlessly been more flexible and would have yielded to you upon realizing that you desired my unworthy presence; and more recently I would have yielded to your brother-in-law, the king of France, truly the kindest and most gentle of kings, who not only with fervent pleas but with a friendly gesture tried to detain me, and who later sent insistent letters to your faithful representatives, asking them to persuade me, despite my resistance, to return to him. In short, he omitted nothing that might interfere with that astrologer, so accustomed to lying about many things, appearing to speak the truth about me. Nor was I unaware that refusing an invitation of that exalted king appeared arrogant, yet the more powerful pull of which I have spoken – my love of country – as well as, to be perfectly honest, the mental burden that my already declining years makes even heavier, so constrains me that I find it difficult to change residence.

There is in addition that conviction of mine, as mentioned, concerning Italy's preeminence that alone gave me the courage to make frequent appeals to you and to dare exhort and reprove you because you seemingly assigned last priority to what Mother Nature, in my judgment, had assigned the first. And if you continue in this fashion, lest you complain of not being forewarned, I shall venture even in my writings to single you out to posterity. I therefore ask you, O Caesar, what are you doing? What are you thinking about, why are you delaying? Do you hope to earn glory without toil? It is surprising that such a powerful mind, such a penetrating intelligence has become not blunted – for I do not fear that – but quite rusty from idleness. Eleven years have passed, unless I am mistaken, since my first criticism of your delay, at a time when I was unknown to you but desirous of knowing you and devoted to the empire; and if at that time you not only accepted but praised my frankness, surely now that we are older there is more reason for me to be frank, and less reason for you to offer excuses. Reread what I wrote you at that time. You will realize how much more fittingly each of my accusations might now be repeated since you may be losing a great opportunity and since the faster life passes, the less of it remains. Do you not sense the passage of time and the swift flight of life? Do you not realize the necessity to devote your time first to the pursuit of virtue and to your conscience, and then to your glory and to the judgment of posterity? Do you not think that when you have departed and relinquished your throne—which necessarily must occur—you can entertain no hope of return, nor can your successor's valor, as that poor old lady once told Trajan, compensate for your shame? "When you are finally dead and Minos has proclaimed his solemn judgment of you, O Torquatus, neither your race, nor your eloquence, nor your piety will restore you to life," says Flaccus. Do you not hear Virgil, "The first and best day of life is the first to flee wretched mortals"? Or the same author saying, "Every man's hour is appointed: brief and unalterable for all is life's duration; but to prolong fame with deeds, this is the work of valor"? Do you not hear Flaccus once again, "Day treads upon the heel of day, and the new moons hasten to wane; and you on the threshold of death let out contracts for sawing marble, and unmindful of your grave, construct buildings"? Do you not hear Lucan, "The hour will come that will overthrow all leaders: you hasten to your death"? And when the same author says, "Oracles do not make me secure, but certain death does: both the timorous and the strong must fall. Thus decreed Jove"? Do you not hear Statius, "Use your life to acquire eternal glory"; or again when he says, "You know that the cruel fates never unwind the warp"? Do you not hear Juvenal, "The little flower speedily hastens to complete its narrow and terribly short span of life: while we drink, while we seek crowns, perfumes, and women, old age steals upon us unobserved"? And if perchance you believe that old age will overtake you late and will long endure, if you pay little heed, as many do, to the loss of time, do you not hear this same author who once said, "Old age in a nobleman is like a miracle"? If that were once so, what of today? And if in a nobleman, what can we expect in an emperor? Search the chronicles: many old men became rulers, but few grew old as rulers; if the life of all mortals is brief, it is especially so for rulers, burdened as they are by the internal warfare of worries and encircled by external snares. Therefore, if sluggish delay is detestable in everyone, it is most detestable in an emperor who has more to do and less time to do it, and, as is often said, has a longer road and a shorter day. And so, O Caesar—for from here I sense the happenings there because love is a wonderful spy and observer—you are wasting your life in deliberations. Unless transformed into action, such deliberations remain barren thoughts and useless cares. "I shall begin tomorrow, I shall move the day after." Why not today, I ask? Is it perhaps that tomorrow will be more serene and today is more cloudy? And yet, as you heard, the greatest of poets calls the first day the best; the first is the present, since nothing remains to us of the past except recollection, nothing is gained in deliberating over impossible things, and nothing can be expected of the future save expectation and the charms of a false hope. Granting that today and tomorrow may be equal in all else, can it be denied that this day is more present and thus more certain? Whether we reach the day that is to come is truly in doubt, and it is just as certain that when this day departs it will never return. Why do we always seek what is absent? Let us embrace the present, striving not to allow it to flow uselessly away from us. While doing this is beneficial to all, it is essential for you, O Caesar, since without it, regardless of your tremendous industry or your virtue, you may never settle the empire's accounts. "And to whom," you will say, "am I to render an account of the empire?" To yourself, O Caesar, and I have no doubt that you will often require it of yourself. Do you consider such an accounting of little import? No rebuke is more severe than the one directed at oneself, and none more wholesome. But you should also render an account to this age, which looks up to you and fixes its gaze upon you alone, as well as to the coming centuries, whose opinions will be more enduring and less inhibited, and finally to that eternal Emperor Who appointed you overseer of this temporal empire, not simply to occupy a throne or wield a sceptre or assume the empty power of empire, but to exercise authority, to rule, and to help the afflicted. Why do you back away, why waste today while awaiting tomorrow? There is no room for tomorrow in today's needs; do today what is needed, for if something must be done tomorrow, either you will do it or someone else; other leaders will not be lacking for other times, and even if they were, you would never be blamed for another's indolence. So take care not to fail in your time; and what is more, that tomorrow that keeps us in suspense and inactive, that is thought to be a sure thing, has already passed, for no day save the first has been anything but the tomorrow of another day. Do you wish to listen to a young poet's words? " 'This will be done tomorrow.' The day after would do. 'What? You give me a day as though it were a great concession!' But when the new dawn arrives, we have already wasted yesterday's tomorrow; here is another tomorrow reducing our years, and always a little beyond reach; for although it is near you, although it revolves under the same cart, in vain do you run in pursuit since you are the rear wheel on the rear axle." What then? Did the young and inexperienced Persius perceive more clearly human blindness while our more mature age refuses to see it? We must open our eyes, we must set our minds so as not to be deceived and entangled in errors that cannot be set right. Why else have I now been soliciting poets from door to door if not to move you with the testimony of others, thus compensating for what my voice perhaps lacked in authority and persuasiveness? Never was there a poet or philosopher who did not say and feel the same, for though in disagreement about many things, they all agree about this. But even if all remained silent or denied it, surely the matter speaks for itself, as they often say, and if anyone were to turn a blind eye, he will feel its truth despite himself; experience will not be denied, and truth rushes upon those who would not see. Therefore, though you may disregard all the rest, and I doubt that you could with your great intellect and incomparable judgment, did you not even notice that in your letter to me the sixth year of your reign has passed? And so? Are you perhaps waiting for the fifty-sixth? That happened only to Caesar Augustus, and I wonder if it is desirable; it certainly must not be anticipated.

You came to Italy following my exhortations, O Caesar, and I seemed to participate in your glory, realizing that even a spirited steed needs a spur; you came, I say, and as I had promised you, confident as I was of heavenly assistance, you found everything accessible and smooth where you expected troublesome obstacles. You entered Milan, then Rome, where you received the double crown, and after giving new hope to the people and the cities, you suddenly returned to Germany. Why was that, or what mental lapse or terror overcame you? Did you perhaps fear the minor uprisings of a few seditious persons? But everyone ought to know that one who is considering a sea voyage must anticipate stormy weather. Were you unaware that no sea is without waves, no mountain without winds, no empire without cares? I omit the Scipios, who, deserted by their armies, overcame their soldiers' treachery sometimes with the traitors' deaths and at other times, when the situation demanded it, even with their own; and I do not mention Alexander, who suppressed his men's insurrections, secret plots, and conspiracies; instead you may perhaps be more receptive to your own predecessors. Beset by his entire army, Julius Caesar not only showed no fear but with great presence of mind and indomitable valor, proved himself worthy of being feared, and by punishing only a few and by shaming an entire legion he looked after the safety of all and his own dignity. We also read that, in imitation of him, the Roman emperor Alexander meted out punishments to his soldiers and discharged from service entire legions in revolt, doing so with remarkable confidence, sometimes with considerable danger, as when he said to some angry soldiers who were threatening him with weapons, "Lower your hands, which ought to be raised only against the enemy, if you are strong; for they do not frighten me. If you kill a single man, you cannot escape the Republic, the Senate, and the Roman people, who will avenge me." Caesar Augustus, assailed by countless ambushes, eventually put an end to them with just sternness or with gentle compassion. I omit others lest I bore your busy mind with long stories, and I return to you.

After escaping many perils not only alive but with glory, what did you ever see or hear that managed to cast down from the calm stronghold of imperial serenity a man such as yourself, the offspring of a great lineage, so accustomed to great events and to observing human affairs from lofty heights? Nothing ought to seem too great or too serious to a mind unafraid of assuming the might and weight of an empire. You reached the summit of human achievements on the day you accepted the emperor's name and title; why then do minor events disturb you when you remained undaunted by the very greatest? Perhaps you will reply that it was not fear that drove you from here, but rather love that drew you there. Why should you not enjoy the same rights that I enjoy, namely, to love your country? I am not opposed to this, indeed I urge you, O Caesar, to love your country; but as Cicero would have it, either virtue derives from *vir* or *vir* derives from virtue; nothing can be of greater value to man than this, nothing more welcome, and if it is lost, he will have lost not only his greatest possession but even cease being what he was. Though your country be critical of you, then, your indomitable virtue recalls you, ordering you to ponder your duty, namely, the empire. For if, according to Cicero, Laelius expresses the opinion, in speaking of less important matters, that under no circumstances "should a man of constancy allow any interruption of his duty," what shall we think of the highest and greatest of duties? There is no excuse for your forgetting the empire; other cares may embellish you, this one renders you perfect and makes you a true emperor. There is no comparison between this duty and others: you can perhaps defer or overlook others, this one, as long as you remember who you are, must always cling to your bones and to your heart; for in the other direction lies decorum, here duty, which you are forbidden to neglect not only out of concern for glory but out of respect for your faith. As for your assertion that you should be allowed the same as I, it cannot be; I may do many things that you cannot do, just as my servants are allowed much that is forbidden to me. The greater the office, the lesser the freedom, and you know that the more steps you ascend, the more you must descend. Are you, O Emperor, aware of what the founder of the Empire said? "Where good fortune is greatest, there freedom is least." In what can you better love or honor your country than by promulgating its name far and wide? If Alexander had remained within Macedonia's borders, the Macedonian name would not have become so well known. Who do you think loves his wife more, the man who embraces her night and day, forgetful of everything, or the man who spares no journeys or toil so as to nurture her honorably and abundantly? It can happen that a great love may be similar to hatred. Never did Africanus love Rome more than when he left her behind to go to Carthage. Tender feelings and inconsequential advice by wives, children, and ordinary friends have always been in conflict with lofty designs; one must block his ears like Ulysses in order to sail into the port of glory, avoiding the reeflike sirens. What is more, this country that you call yours was indeed yours, but now no longer is since the day you first acquired the empire; though born in one country, you acquired another once you were born again. You have heard that the same Alexander the Macedonian, upon receiving royal power, issued an order that he be called king of the world, not king of Macedonia. I cannot deny that, though he was precipitous in many things, in this one act he revealed greatness of spirit. Until now you have not done likewise for lack of a successor to the empire, which would seem deserted at your departure, and which would fall into foreign hands, should anything perchance happen to you. A propitious providence has now eliminated this just or unjust excuse, for it granted you and the empire the child sought through your venerable consort's prayers. Bohemia now has its king; you as king of Italy and of the world, now confident of the world that you leave behind, must seek your fatherland and your throne. For although in the Apostle's opinion you do not have here on earth an enduring city, still if you do have a homeland, it is Rome, fitting abode and true fatherland of the Caesars, indeed the homeland common to all, the capital of human affairs, the queen of the world and of all cities, so abounding in noble examples that only to visit her readily inspires the spirit, freeing it of all paralysis. So now what excuses will you advance or what chains can you henceforth say are restraining you? After your sworn promises, whatever they were, to the Roman pontiff, you are being kept from entering Rome as if by an impermeable wall or an impassable mountain; in such wise is an empire taken from the loftiest of princes and a prince from the loftiest of empires, and your liberty from you, the greatest of all losses. You did swear under oath—would that you had not!—but you did; you must obtain a dispensation. Why hesitate about something so simple? When one person binds another, often the same person or someone else can release him. What does it matter how you regain your liberty provided it is returned to you? He who bound you will set you free; if he does not wish to do so, there will come another who will; how does not matter provided he wishes to; your virtue will generate love, your glory admiration, your success fear, for there is no man who does not love, admire, or fear a prince who is just, famous, and successful. Take the first step. According to an old proverb, all roads lead to Rome. If you remain paralyzed, every fetter will hold you back; if you move, all the snares encircling you will fall away, and you will emerge not only with your liberty, but fittingly as master of the world and ruler of men, demanding freedom for yourself and the entire human race. A sick boar may be held fast by its illness, but to subdue a healthy and growling boar requires much labor. Shake off your sluggishness, and instantly all things will be easy for you; otherwise that very sluggishness will serve as chains. No one has ever beheld a lion caught in a spider's web or an eagle in bird lime; why, then, do your eagles now hesitate and your lions remain silent? He who considers himself unworthy of liberty is easily drawn into slavery, but he who knows himself to be free will sooner be deprived of life than liberty; indeed not even then, for to be stripped of life is natural, to be stripped of liberty is folly. What now is that arrogance depriving a Roman prince of his liberty when he is the author of public liberty, so that where all things ought to belong to him, he himself is not his own? How can he be free and master of himself if forbidden to go wherever he wishes, much less forbidden even to cross the threshold of his own home and, to tell the truth, relegated as far from it as possible?

You understand, O Caesar, not only what I have said but what I meant to say; for many other things come to mind except that I fear they may be superfluous for you and even dangerous for me; in the name of truth I have already attracted enough hatred, and to seek enemies consciously is pure madness. And so enough for today; how effective my words have been will depend on you. As for me, if I proceed no further, it is enough for me to have performed my duty faithfully toward my own age and toward posterity as I have often done in the past, and if I ever fell short, this day has compensated for it. Yet I have still to touch upon the concern that always ought to move your spirit to serious and pious enthusiasm, often filling your eyes with tears. For does not the image come to your mind, whether asleep or awake, of the widowed, helpless, captive, enslaved, and wretched Jerusalem, seeking and expecting assistance from no one but you? Meanwhile you allow your eyes to sleep, your eyelids to doze, your days to slacken. It is time to awaken, O Emperor, rather it has already passed; make haste, give double spur to your virtue so that by hastening you may compensate for your sluggishness. Arise, I say, arise now, O Emperor, arise, and listen to the outcry of Rome and of the world summoning you; rub your eyes and look around, O Emperor; you will see much in need of reform, and will then realize that this title was not bestowed upon you to help you find repose. In every one of my letters to you, there is but one style, one theme—exhortations, reproofs, and the prods of lamentations and words. I beg you, do something daring so that I need not always exhort you and urge you on, but instead sometimes even restrain you, reining you in rather than ever spurring you onward. One of Aristotle's maxims that I consider quite powerful states that whoever has habitually erred toward one extreme must struggle to reach the opposite, "as do those who straighten bent sticks," to use his own expression; for in this fashion they are more readily drawn to the center and to a straightened position. Thus far I have written according to the dictates of my heart, now I must reply to your letter; since you wish the response to remain secret, and I wish everyone to know these things, I shall keep the two apart by sending under separate cover what you request of me. Farewell, O invincible Caesar, and ponder often, I beg you, what is the duty of a man and what that of a prince.

Milan, 21 March.

Fam. XXIII, 3.

To the same correspondent, * *a rather urgent recommendation for a friend.*

I determined to remain silent, but writing to you compelled me to speak as much out of respect for you as out of love for the person for whom I write. This soldier of yours and friend of mine was already confidently recommended to you in one of my letters, not because I did not know either you or him or myself sufficiently well, but realizing that Your Majesty regarded my humility with some favor, I thought it my duty not to remain silent about something that I knew related to your honor. I said then and I repeat now, O Caesar, that you owe a great deal to this man, and not only you but the empire. I shall not reveal why; his concern, faithfulness, and diligence are known to you; he places his hope in no other but you. This man so deserving of you constantly and painfully exposes himself daily to many dangers, becoming wealthier only in age; if each day he grows older, why does he not daily also become richer? I beseech you to forgive my frankness and self-assurance, since without considerable self-assurance so much frankness would never suggest itself. It is up to you, O Caesar, to tread upon the wicked and to raise the good; do make it possible for this trustworthy and noble man who passed his youth toiling so much in behalf of your glory to find repose in his old age under your guidance and protection.

*See X, 1.

Fam. XXIII, 4.

To Bonincontro, * *felicitations on his escape, albeit late, from the storms of the Curia into the haven of private life.*

Now, O excellent man, you are beginning to live, though it is late in life. Rejoice, for it is already enough even to have made a start before you stopped living; as Anneus says, "Some men will finish before they begin." Now without the clamor of trumpets or the crush of cares you are enjoying a fresh, peaceful, and tranquil sleep; now you pass joyful days and secure nights; now you are sailing into port and looking behind you, and undaunted you perceive the wild and dangerous storms. I congratulate you for your present condition, as I used to pity you for your previous one, although it perhaps seemed to the multitude the happier one. You could have died among the storms and in war, whereas now you will surely die in peace, and you will live in peace. Recognize this hidden gift of Divine Providence; released from bonds of long habit, perhaps unwillingly—since man's spirit is often ignorant of circumstances and inclined toward danger—you have been returned by a favorable wind to your homeland so as to ascend more freely to the eternal homeland, whence we are now exiles. O how much better you have fared than you hoped! With ears closed, you have safely passed amidst sea monsters and the sirens' songs, and in your undamaged ship skillfully avoided Scylla and Charybdis and the Curia's billows and reefs. Now you dwell in your homeland, now you are making your way to the other fatherland, now you are finally your own. O you who are enviable and blessed, if only you would recognize what you were and what you are! Farewell.

Milan, 27 January.

---

*Nothing is known about this correspondent except that he was a notary and a man of letters.

Fam. XXIII, 5.

To the same correspondent, * *that one must confront old age and death not only with courage but with joy.*

I hear that you are rapidly sliding into old age. What am I saying? Rather you are ascending to it; for old age is lofty, respectable, and, as everyone agrees, venerable. Do you want to know its real loftiness? Having passed beyond the slippery journey of youth and the clouds of passions and anger, it is nearer to heaven, disdainfully looking down upon whatever any other age looks up to. Although it does cause the shoulders to become stooped, it also exalts noble minds, and although those who consider only the body with their eyes' mistaken judgment view it as a bent and depressed time, it is really sublime and erect. Thus, only they lament old age who have placed every hope and happiness in their body; you must rejoice at having reached an age more concerned with the spirit than with the body. For what you did with the greatest effort and exertion in youth, as though rowing against the current, you now do effortlessly as an old man, as though sailing in the second waterway of your years with the aid of what once used to restrain you. I might at this point proceed to examine in detail all the torments and discomforts that seem to attend old age, very gladly dedicating this pen and this one short day to you who used to dedicate so many to me, were it not for the fact that old age was sufficiently defended and praised by Cato in Cicero, and that I believe that by growing old with such great courage you could not be induced or incited to grow old with any firmer spirit: for one can ascend no higher than the summit. Placing these things aside, then, I pursue another matter. Can you imagine how gladly I read that section of your letter that says you are awaiting death undaunted? O learned man, and words so worthy of you! Those who know not how to live, fear death; you who led such a life that your birth was not useless to you, to your country, or to your friends, why, I ask, should you fear death when it can deprive you only of a weary little body along with many labors and much fatigue without doing any harm to your soul or to your name? While death does indeed mark the start of punishment and the end of pleasures for all evildoers, for good people, among whom I confidently include you, it is the end of toil and the beginning of a better life. Therefore, go securely, as you are doing, and be fearful of nothing. Old age and death are liberators of the human species: the first moderates the innumerable and nearly incurable diseases of the spirit, the second destroys them; the first re-

*See XXIII, 4.

moves us from evils and struggles, the second introduces us to the true good and to eternal peace. I would perhaps not dare to speak this way about death, which I see defamed by many, except that Plotinus, the prince of Platonists, not to mention others, and after him several of our teachers, especially Cyprian and Augustine, said that it was the mercy of God that made us mortal; to use Plotinus's very words, it was a compassionate father who made our chains mortal. Old age is therefore good, it is near you, it is already with you, and death is even better than you expect. For just as "the death of sinners is the worst," as the Psalmist says—I speak of those who do not repent but delight in sin, for if the matter were considered too hastily, all men are sinners—so too death is the best thing for the just man. Without doubt it is now approaching; just as at no age is there any certainty about life's duration, so at this age there is no uncertainty about death's proximity.

A great good unknown to the multitude is now within your reach; live up to your name, encounter this good not only undaunted but exulting, and once you have encountered it, do not be saddened as are most mortals for whom dying, or better, yielding to nature, is a punishment, but rather go happily as do the few, as if embracing some great gift of God. Assume that you have been led by favorable winds through the many storms of life into a port and not against a reef, and be unafraid of what is unavoidable, even though it be an evil. We shall all depart, everyone must necessarily leave; but let us go fearlessly. For fear is not real but a mental attitude, not a universal distress but a weakness in individuals; otherwise we all would die in fear. Nor shall we go unaccompanied; from all lands and all ages there will be an infinite crowd in front, behind, and around us, and all those who have been born or will be born will tend toward a single goal over different paths. From our mothers' wombs we all are destined for this journey; those who are puffed up because of their youth or their office, who have forgotten their condition and have foolishly grasped at the hope of immortality, must either follow or precede us, and all the more sadly the more deeply they have sunk their roots here, or the less cultivated and ready they find the terrain there. Wherefore, since the end of everyone's life is veiled in a dense cloud, since for everyone the inevitable is certain, since furthermore nothing is certain and secure for anyone, we must so prepare our minds as to expect calmly on this very day and at this very hour whatever the passing of so many years may threaten. What, I ask, does it matter whether today or tomorrow or even right now or a little later there comes to pass what must in any case happen soon and cannot be postponed? In vain does human cowardice seek these subterfuges and delays; eager to live, it despises the time already lived in the manner of ungrateful people who feel a loathing for something that they had unseasonably sought. That is the way it is: we all desire a lengthy life and yet nothing is enduring on this brief journey. But let it be so, let us suppose that in some way this desired longevity is attained; yet once that very unusual point is reached when death's hand will have broken the long thread, what, I ask, will the person who has lived a hundred years have that is any more than the one whom death snatches directly from the breast to the grave, seeing that for both the end is at hand and time has ceased? Often on their deathbed I have heard aged persons say that they seemed barely to have lived an entire day; and indeed between the shortest winter day and Nestor's long life there is little difference in length and no difference in results when both reach their goal and, so to speak, arrive at eventide. Yet, the situation is as I said, and that much more is made of the hope for a longer life than for life itself can easily be gathered from the prayers and laments of fools; but the wise do not indulge in unjustified complaints or in empty prayers because of their conviction that happiness does not result from the length of life but from its worthiness, not from the aid of fortune but of virtue.

Such being the case, let us conclude. I could have heard nothing more welcome from you than the news that such is your mental state. Were I to learn that you had inherited enormous riches (or shall I say instead were obsessed or oppressed by them?) or were even made the king of Italy, what would I say? How brief, how passing a joy! Kingdoms, wealth, and whatever else fortune allots she knows how to reclaim. Let us imagine a more generous fortune who is friendly until death, who lets her revolving wheel come to a halt as a result of some special favor: nevertheless, even then, death, which cannot be touched by such liberality, forces empires to be abandoned, wealth to be laid aside, and us to return naked whence we came naked. But neither fortune nor death can hold sway over your spirit, which will accompany you to the end and beyond, raising you on the wings of virtue to heaven, whence it came. I too, O magnanimous sir, so that you may also rejoice, am striving with great effort to develop a similar spirit, and now seem almost to have succeeded. Meanwhile I live on in good health, if there be any good health or real life for mortals. Certainly if I dare to boast along with the Greek legislator, I daily grow old while learning and daily fear less that inevitable and dreadful hour, being ready to follow you in old age and in death, or since there is no order in dying, if it be granted from on high, to precede you in death without, I believe, any fear or hesitation. But as long as we are here, make use of me, I beg you, as though I were yours; and if perchance you desire anything from me, let yours be the responsibility of asking and mine the pleasure of obeying. Farewell, and remember me.

Milan, 23 February.

Fam. XXIII, 6.

To Jan, Bishop of Olmütz, Chancellor of the Imperial Court, *
that the more someone loves us, the less must we pay attention
to his praises.

How can it be that my lord and teacher should call me his lord and
teacher, unless, forgetful of himself, he remembers only the one whom
he loves, imagining him to be as he would want him and striving to
exalt him; and if unable to do that, he belittles himself and finally tries
in every way to make him his equal? Unless you raise your friends from
the dust and place them above yourself, you believe that you have done
nothing for them; but the higher you raise me, the more humble I
become, for the kindness of such a man will never cause me to forget
my condition. I once chose you as my lord; indeed it was not my choice
that made you my master, but the power and vigor of your intelligence.
Therefore, do with me henceforth as you will; it is up to you whether
to raise or lower what is yours, it is up to me to know myself and what
is mine, believing any opinion about me less than my own and trusting
less in another's praise of me the more the praiser loves me. I thank you
nonetheless for your devoted affection and courteous esteem, and I consider you happy for such kindness and me fortunate for such an opinion. Much now comes to mind, but my days are very full and time
is short; and besides, with my many lengthy letters to Caesar I shall be
keeping your eyes sufficiently occupied as well as your tongue, which
hopefully you will use to bring them to his royal attention, and to seek
forgiveness for my ardent and busy pen if at times it may bite the bit
to excess. I also send you my *Bucolicum carmen*, which no one except
you has had in its entirety, although many have seen it. I should also
like you to have the gloss or rather the glosser at the same time, something
I cannot begin to hope for until our Caesar has been aroused by the
many loud outcries from myself and from the entire world. The remainder
you will learn from the person delivering this brief letter, who knows
everyone's business, in particular my own. I shall say nothing more, for
you know all there is to know about him except that among your supporters, many though they are, none speaks more favorably of you. A
cordial farewell, O you who are our glory.

Milan, 21 March.

*See X, 6.

Fam. XXIII, 7.

To the same correspondent, * *a recommendation for a friend.*

As you must have gathered from my many letters to you, the love that you bear me is so well known here that everyone who needs favors from you believes that he likewise needs my intervention. Today I want to recommend to you and through you to the emperor what I consider a just request of a nobleman very dear to me because of his virtue, a young man of keen intellect and nimble eloquence, who comes to Caesar's feet at his uncle's bidding. Caesar himself, I believe, loves his entire family; as for you who have ever been the helper, guide, and support of all good men, this man desires nothing more than to be and to be called one of yours. Men cannot be similar to God by procreating, but they can by loving, helping, encouraging, sustaining, having compassion, and inspiring. Cicero expresses this most admirably, "In nothing do men come nearer to God than in looking after the welfare of other men." And what mortal is closer to God than the loftiest of men, Caesar? He who is at the summit of human nature must necessarily be closest to divinity, and no one is nearer to Caesar than yourself. Now this man whom I am recommending is an assiduous person who can ascend with little assistance and, if fortune is supportive, does not lack natural abilities; but being still young, he is not yet what he will become. But what am I saying, or to whom am I speaking? When you see the man, you will perceive what he is and, unless love fails me, you will understand what I am saying. Farewell.

*See X, 6.

Fam. XXIII, 8.

To the Emperor Charles, * *an expression of gratitude for the gold bowl that he had sent, and an expression of some hope that he will answer his invitation to visit him.*

Your letter, which was more courteous than either of our stations warranted, reached me, as you may know, O Caesar, some months after being written, together with a precious bowl made of gold with designs in high relief, to use Virgil's words, which you deigned to send me with a munificence worthy of you but not of me. O amazing lot not only of men but of all things! A vessel remarkable for its substance and for the artist's talent, but above all made immortal by Caesar's lips, has passed from your table to mine! I shall not use it every day but only for offering toasts—I would say at the altar if we observed the same customs as the ancients. Presently displayed on festive tables as a rare object, it will serve as ornamentation on feast days; I shall keep it among my treasured possessions, I shall show it to admiring and celebrating friends, together with your splendid letter, which I shall save as long as I live as a certain witness of your kindness and of my truly undeserving good fortune. For as often as I shall want to show your kindness and my good fortune, it will be summoned as witness. In short, I shall always glory in your double gift, and would attempt to express my gratitude if either I had sufficient ability to express my deepest feelings or you had need of words to realize the love of your faithful followers. What shall I now say about the letter itself? You, O Caesar, who command kings and reign over peoples, request my presence! I am more moved by your requests than by your commands since your virtue is greater than your power. But what is to be done? My spirit is ready to act, yet the situation is very complex. Have the futile outcries of my many letters, I ask, come to this, that summoned so often and so long, awaited with anxiety by so many, you finally call to yourself, desire, and await the person who has been summoning you, as you admit with such dignified kindness in your letter? What, O Caesar, is to be done in this situation? You summon me to Germany and I summon you to Italy; you are above me in authority, I above you for the cause that I espouse. You summon me to an honorable and admittedly enjoyable pleasure, I summon you to a virtuous duty so necessary and urgent that you seem to have been born for it alone, since its realization will assure you happiness in heaven and fame with posterity. Though

*See X, 1.

my cause is superior, I should like to yield to your command; but much stands in the way, in particular this season so in conflict with my nature that during this period I seem not to be living but languishing and suffering. If I have always found it troublesome, imagine how it would affect me now when I fear the heat less and the work more? Never was I so young as to be unaware of growing old, indeed I knew it without feeling it; until now, as a sleeping person is borne along in a boat, floating with the current, I proceeded without feeling it. But now, O Caesar, I am gradually beginning to feel my age, and daily become more frail and slow. Furthermore, although you are supreme, although that faithful servant of yours whom I have long been serving seems not only ready to give me leave, but if I know him, willing to come along also at your command, I still must receive his permission as long as I am under his patronage. But this is not so important since, as I have said, he would in my opinion deny his lord nothing. Rather what do I do with my books, which, while not too numerous, suffice for what I lack in intelligence and learning? Though they would perhaps be a burden rather than an ornament, still through long habit I am so fond of them that I would not know how to do without them. To transport them, as you know, O Caesar, is a serious problem not only because of the difficulties in crossing the Alps and the labor of a lengthy journey, but the fear of thieves and the countless perils of the road, which often call to mind a Hebrew sage who said with pregnant brevity that all things are difficult. It is truly so, and let him who doubts this live until old age, for he will then understand it; one who has grown old understands it; otherwise he has not grown old, believe me, but has rather vegetated, traveling the lengthy road with eyes closed. Amidst these many difficulties and doubts, I shall still say what I believe: if by summer's end I receive the consent of my lord, your faithful servant, and find a companion for the journey, I shall come there to remain as long as you like, drawing consolation for my lack of books and friends as well as for the absence from my homeland in the greatly desired presence of Caesar's person. Live happily and farewell, O Caesar, and remember me.

Padua, 18 July.

Fam. XXIII, 9.

To the same correspondent, who summons once again with greater insistence, and the increasing possibility of his complying.*

You have won, O Caesar, and your kindness has shattered my argument concerning the difficulty of the long journey and the sluggishness of my aging spirit. I waited and delayed, saying silently to myself, "He has perhaps forgotten his request and my promise; meanwhile I shall rest, indulging my nature, my age, and my weariness." For I am truly weary in body and mind, O Caesar, weary of men and weary of tasks, and finally weary of myself; as that tired old man says, "I have become a burden to my own self," or rather, to tell the entire truth, I am feeling my weight. I hope that amidst the many burdensome cares that daily flow from the entire world into your heart, as waters from all directions do into a great sea, you would easily forget my insignificant name. For me, save for your empire, to which I owe everything, nothing is truly dearer than rest, which I have never found despite my meticulous search for it everywhere since early youth; and what is worse, I never hope to find it as long as I look for it in the storms of this life. And yet, I do not despair of finding it in its own domicile; to seek it up there where it dwells on high is most difficult for a wandering spirit distracted by a variety of matters, and what is more, crushed by its own weight and inclined toward the earth. I am really trying, often giving myself encouragement with David's words: "Turn, O soul of mine, toward your rest because the Lord has been kind to you." Trusting not in my own power and looking about for external aid, together with the same king, I say sighing, "Who will give me the wings of a dove so that I may fly and find rest?" Meanwhile I embrace this laborious repose granted to me while meditating on and sighing for the other. Thus, I frankly confess my guilt to you, whom I want to know my mind just as well as my appearance. Although no one would I see more gladly than you, particularly if heaven allows me to behold you on your throne, and although no one would I obey more faithfully than you, especially if you ordered me not to the ends of the earth but within this Italy that awaits you, I did have it in mind in weighing and considering all the possibilities to try to fool you with my silence and with your forgetfulness. Oh, what have I said? Whom have I fooled? My lord who rules the universe! The deceit seemed useful to me since I knew not how I might be of service to you and since, as I have said, I was most desirous

*See X, 1.

of rest. But I see that all is in vain; for just as you have a keen intellect and mature judgment, so do you possess a tenacious memory, O Caesar. In this, as in many other things, you resemble that first Caesar, whose memory Cicero invokes, saying that it was so formidable that he usually forgot nothing but wrongs. Since this is the situation, there is no further room for pretense, for I cannot fail to hear the Roman emperor summoning me for the third time. I did not immediately obey your first summons not from insolence—as God is my witness—but from laziness. And now, O Caesar, you summon me once again. I shall come, and would that I find you prepared to visit those who have summoned you not once, but again and again, day and night without interruption. Farewell, O Caesar, and keep in mind your glory, Italy, and your empire.

Milan, 21 March.

Fam. XXIII, 10.

To Jan, Bishop of Olmütz, Chancellor,* concerning the same subject, and that a mind aware of its own insignificance must not allow itself to be diverted from its humility by the praises of others.

You are astonishing, my lord, you are truly astonishing; for what, I ask, is more wonderful than such remarkable and lofty humility in one whose excellence dominates all that he does? You constantly disparage yourself in all that you say when nature, fortune, and the Lord of both nature and fortune, Christ, have raised you on high, when the greatest of men, Caesar, loves you, when the nobles admire you and the people adore you, when the Roman empire cherishes you and knows not whether to consider you foremost among its wise men or among its eloquent orators. Yet you heap undeserved praises upon me, who am scarcely known to my neighbors, you push me into the limelight, and you raise me to the stars with your words. What can I say? I know that eloquence is all powerful in the minds of listeners, but it has no rightful place in matters dealing with basic truth. You may adorn me with the flowers of your eloquence, but you cannot change me, were even Cicero, Demosthenes, or Maro to praise me. And though I may be dazzled by others' opinions of me, could they tear out my eyes so that I not see myself as I am? It is within your power, then, as I seem to have written you once before, to give me, who am yours, whatever value you wish; it is within my power to know myself, to believe no one who judges me, especially someone who holds me as dear as you do. Being fixed to the earth, I am not easily shaken by such winds, and if I am, I am not uprooted; aware of my insignificance, I have faith only in those who without hatred or envy criticize my life and my reputation; in short, if I did not know you so well, or if another said what you say, I would believe that I was being ridiculed. But far be it from me to suspect from such a man, so gracious toward me and of such proven honesty and notable virtue, anything other than what is honest, straightforward, and sincere. I do believe that you say what is on your mind, but what is on your mind is not in me. As an admirer of your insight on other matters, I rejoice in your error, which derives not from a faulty intellect, but from the noble roots of love, devotion, and refinement. To conclude, please note that I am on my way there since this is what Caesar and you would like so much; and I come not, as you say, to teach, but to learn from your teaching and example, if we are

*See X, 6.

to believe that Plato, Aristotle, Xenophon, and all that ancient and noble family of philosophers learned as much from Socrates's conduct as from his teachings. Most enduring in the soul is what enters through the eyes rather than through the ears. The duration of my stay, however, will be decided by those who have summoned me; but I do hope that our emperor will quickly grant me leave once he realizes that I must henceforth think of myself and the other life, and will transfer me to the payroll of the heavenly Emperor. Lest you be surprised by my slowness, you know my ways; you are not to imagine a swallow flying through the air, not a stag climbing the mountains, but a tortoise crawling with difficulty. Farewell.

Milan, 21 March.

Fam. XXIII, 11.

To Giovanni da Bergamo, attorney, * *who is journeying across the sea to receive military honors at the sepulchre of Christ, an attempt to dissuade him from such a project.*

I prefer to send you advice rather than a satire, for the first is full of my sincere love whereas the latter, as are man's ways and minds, is not without hatred. If what I advise you against has already been done, I shall censure you; if it has not as yet happened, now is the time for you and me to try to avoid it. I surely would prefer to see you praised a thousand times than rebuked even once, and without doubt you desire the same thing, since the desire for glory follows virtue just as does glory herself. Those who tend in this direction, then, must observe constant vigilance with every step along life's pathway, lest anywhere along the way the mind should waver or deviate. I hear that you desire to go to Jerusalem in order to visit the sepulchre of the Lord; I say that I hear this, and I approve and praise it, and I who loved you very much am now compelled to love you even more because of this pious intention of yours. For what is greater in a man than piety, or what is more ancient? Or what is a more justifiable piety than to repay in some measure the great love of the One who has willingly shed His blood, risked His soul, and given His life for you; or if a better occasion does not present itself, at least to bathe with grateful sobs and pious tears the places where He neglected Himself for love of you? But what certain rumors are saying about you I do not praise, namely, that you have decided to accept while there the so-called golden spurs and a knight's insignia and title. Admittedly this custom is in vogue, but I know not whence it came; the Poet does make mention of iron spurs, but nowhere do I remember his mentioning golden ones. But let us assume that a man's true virtue resides not in his mind but in his dress, and his power not in his sword but in his spurs, and that unless they be of gold, a man cannot be strong. This, I believe, derives not so much from authoritative sources as from a foolish and transitory vogue. If your lineage, age, and condition tempt you toward this military honor about which I am speaking, I am not surprised, driven as you are by custom and public opinion. But I urge you to consider before departing the appropriateness of strutting about with bright golden spurs on a well-groomed horse in the very place where your Lord and Master bore the crown of thorns, submitted to the cross,

---

*An unknown correspondent except for the information contained in this letter indicating that he was an attorney and of the nobility.

and accepted death for your sins and those of mankind; and that in the very place where blood reddened the holiest of brows at whose nod the heavens revolve, the winds become still, and the seas are calmed, whose standard the blessed angels await and the damned fear, your spurs should gleam with a golden hue. But do as you please; I have given you some friendly advice, and similarly I do not wish to lack an exemplum. Godfrey (a commander and hero so acclaimed by word of mouth and in nearly all the French courts that among the three most famous members of the three orders of outstanding Christians he ranks third in writings and paintings) went to the Holy Land, captured it, subdued it, and brought it to the worship of the true faith, succeeding much more in retrieving our heritage from a powerful enemy than in protecting it for posterity against a cowardly enemy. But I pass over this, for the complaint is not new to me and altogether unequal to my strength. Turn your attention now to the following: under no circumstances would that victorious commander of truly royal spirit be persuaded to assume a king's name and garments, for he refused to wear a golden crown where Christ had worn a crown of thorns. O sublime modesty! O man worthy above all others, if only for this reason, to avenge the wrongs committed against Christ! If he, victorious and armed, by invoking Christ's thorns refused to allow gold to touch his triumphant and deserving brow, what boldness or spirit causes a man in our time who is but a humble and troubled pilgrim, and not a victor over those lands, to adorn his wet or dusty heels with gold? I shall not go on, nor is there need to. And although I may displease a number of those who have done or are about to do the opposite, I really am not saying anything prescriptive, but simply offering counsel. My advice is for you to cease doing what you have begun, advice that I wish were as wise as it is sincere. And if you trust a friend, even assuming the necessity of carrying a sword with a golden handle in order to attain glory, or to rein in or spur onward a horse with gold, or, as we have already said quite often, to possess golden spurs when neither Scipio nor Caesar ever had them, it would still be more noble for you to return a decorated victor from a just and pious war fought for your country's welfare and undertaken in the name of justice, than from the sepulchre of Christ, whence I would prefer to see you return safely in humble garments, shedding tears of joy. Farewell.

Fam. XXIII, 12.

To Guido, Archbishop of Genoa,* that endurance of pain is preferable to pain in itself; and that furthermore many things useless to those who obtain them are of benefit to others.

No one wishes, or ever wished, to be unhappy, for that is against nature; on the other hand, we do not lose the desire for happiness even though happiness itself may be lost. Indeed we especially wish to be happy when we are most wretched since the desire for good increases with the presence of evil; and if ever we seem to desire something else, only this do we desire, nor can anyone wish for anything else. Even those people whose actions interfere with their desires still wish for it, but their ignorance makes them act contrary to the desires, as do wayfarers who often in their travels abandon the very destination that they had sought in their minds. Even those who sin do things that make them wretched, but in the belief that satisfying their lust brings happiness. And those who turn their hand against themselves may thereby flee unhappiness, but are deceived by not realizing that their flight from short-lived miseries leads them to eternal ones. Certainly no one ever faces death voluntarily except out of hatred for a wretched life or out of hope for a blessed one: this is a pernicious hatred and a foolish hope, for the first falls into what it flees while the second abandons what it hopes for. Of course, as the mind cannot wish for affliction, and even if it could, that would not be the desire of a sane mind, so its tolerance when the situation warrants it is a sign of prudence, and achieving it is a partial happiness. It would indeed be complete happiness not ever to endure wretchedness or harshness or adversity while always abounding in joy and security. But since this is not to be expected in this wretched and tearful exile, the closest thing is to bear every vicissitude with a strong spirit and to ward off fortune's blows with the shield of patience. While pondering this, if I felt distressed over your bodily illness, so much the greater was my joy over your serenity and over your mental soundness and vigor; for there is more good in the latter than evil in the former, or rather, speaking as a Stoic, there is a great deal of good in the latter and no evil in the former, although it does entail some annoyance. Yet it is easy for a healthy and sound person to philosophize to others about illness and pain; it is more difficult, however, to comfort and free oneself from feeling his own pain. Not every bed contains a Posidonius, who was visited, when seriously ill, by Pompey the Great, at that time feared

*See V, 16.

in Rome and considered fearsome throughout the world. When he who had been arrogant with kings showed himself humble to the philosopher, Posidonius wondered how to return such an honor, and so amidst his torments and pains he discussed this famous theme with Pompey, who listened in wonder: that virtue is the only good and vice the only evil. When pain interfered with his words, repeatedly addressing himself, he would say according to Cicero (if I recall both the sense of the words and the words themselves): "O pain, you accomplish nothing; for though you may be troublesome, I shall never admit you to be evil." Do you see where the power of this opinion lies? It lies in the difference between what is certainly evil and what is troublesome, just as they say that there is a difference between what is good and what is useful. If, then, virtue is the only good, and nothing is evil that is not opposed to the good, since only vice stands alone in contrast to virtue, nothing whatsoever is evil except vice. But let us lay aside these fine distinctions to speak as others do, especially since these judgments are rejected by the multitude or by common sense, and even the other school of philosophers under Aristotle's leadership dissented with much clamor.

It is easy, as I have said, for a healthy person attending a sick person to dispute and to advance petty theories with subtle argumentation, or to spout forth resounding problems; but pain is relieved with warm lotions and not with words, although even with words it too may be soothed and alleviated. Often a friendly rebuke or manly admonition has incited shame or desire to the point of not feeling the pain inflicted upon the body; but at such times words do carry weight if the listener is properly disposed and the speaker has authority. This can be truly sizable when whoever is speaking adds experience to intelligence so that having undergone at some time something similar he can use himself as an example of what he is asking of someone else, yet it is greatest and most perfect when the speaker is suffering as he speaks, for he is not advising but demonstrating, and his present pain gives authority to his courageous words. Consequently, to produce the greatest tolerance, those words uttered while in severe pain are the most effective of all. Such considerations have endowed me, who am perhaps not a sufficiently serious adviser, with authority and confidence, since I believe that my distress while writing to you is no less painful than the gout besetting and burdening you, which you are enduring so manfully and bravely; and so, if confidence and tractability do not fail us, we each can be a fitting teacher or pupil for the other. At present I have assumed the teacher's role, and when you wish I shall become your pupil; to be sure, I am speaking of a matter particularly close to home, and saying nothing except from personal experience. With greater confidence than I would wish, I am speaking about pain while writing to you in great pain, so much so that on days such as these, in recalling the words of Posidonius, I doubted his opinion and remained hesitant. For if the argument advanced earlier is true, why is not this one equally true, I ask? If bodily pleasure, health, and well-being are good things, and if whatever contrasts to the good must be considered evil, it follows that any physical affliction, illness, and pain are evils. Therefore, I do not easily accept as much as I admire the author's constancy, for basically I find that, though Stoic reasoning has often appealed to me, my heart is with the Peripatetics. But let us not torment our minds with futile disquisitions on bodily pain; let us leave these scholastic subtleties at the threshold, reserving them for another, perhaps less hectic, time. Amidst your sufferings and mine, I felt special joy at discerning in your letter the word *patience* not only written but actually carved in words. For whatever the endless disagreement among philosophers, in this alone do all philosophers, all experience, and truth itself agree: in difficulties, whether they are called evil or disagreeable, the one remedy is patience. Indignation, complaints, unmanly wailings and lamentations, aside from being unseemly in men, do not alleviate but only aggravate pain. Similarly in prosperity, whether one wishes to call it a good or a convenience, there is one remedy, moderation, that may bridle the assaults of exuberant pleasure. I have had it in mind, of late, to write more extensively on both these remedies, and now have done so; you would have received the booklet except that I am weary of writing and have no one to help me. My friends, whether absent or involved in their own affairs, cannot offer me assistance from afar, and as experts we know how much good will, consistency, and intelligence dwell in copyists; they promise a great deal, they corrupt everything, they complete nothing. Whence in many of us—I feel this to be the case with me and I imagine it to be so with others—the flame of new inventions is quelled for fear of someone's carelessness defiling our noble writings. That industrious young man of mine, whom I educated for twenty-three years amidst many difficulties so as to be in my later years of assistance in my works as well as a domestic honor and pleasure—O mistaken prediction of a blind mind, which must be erased from my other letters to you!—that young man is the only hardship of my life, the only shame, the only grief, altogether contrary to my hopes, capable of learning if he desired, yet an enemy of virtue, with very bad habits, indolent, envious, stubborn, and rebellious, a slave of his passions, and a follower of his appetites. But all this must be borne lest the patience about which I speak and which I praise in others seem lacking in my personal affairs. I dare not say that I shall tolerate the situation happily, but I shall do so willingly in order not to appear compelled. Nor can I myself expect pardon considering that the greatest and most fortunate of men, Augustus, bore three tumors in his bloodline, as he used to say, and I, a man born for hardship, cannot bear one. Thus abandoned by all, I turn my attention to the words of the learned Phrygian so as to gather my harvest with my own scythe, deprived as I am of any anticipated and desired assistance; but in this I have less than Aesop's old man because he had a son and I have no one. Therefore—I often complain of this each time the occasion arises—every labor and effort revert to my little fingers now so weary and worn, every burden weighs down my feeble and laden shoulders, and this too must be borne with courage. Thorny pathways lead upward to the place for which I yearn; never was I so young as to believe that repose would come my way, although I have often sought it—and today I am shocked by this—where it was not, unhappy and with my mind wandering, as though feeling my way through the shadows. All this I have said to avoid the accusation that I have not yet sent you something personal that, while not a complete cure, does provide some solace and, as you read, some distraction and beneficial forgetfulness of your ills.

But, to return to the letter's main subject, I am sorry about your illness, yet pleased with your patience, and I wonder whether it may not be considered a desirable evil since it is doubtful that something could rightfully be called evil that has led you to experience for yourself and to enjoy peacefully so much good despite the many inconveniences. I urge you to continue in this fashion, do not allow yourself to become weary, persist, and amidst such ills encourage, strengthen, and uplift your spirit. You will need no assistance except from heaven; He will be present, extending His hand to you in your suffering as often as you direct to Him with Christian devotion those poetic words, "Redeem me from this doom, O unconquered one," provided that you do not doubt or despair or fall exhausted to the ground, but turn to heaven and remember to beseech His aid who desires even more than you to come to your assistance, and knows how best to do it in ways hidden to man. Sometimes deferral of a vow is of great benefit: it is our duty to desire health, let us leave the manner and the time up to Him whose will never varies, whose judgment never fails, whose power never diminishes. Despair not of His assistance even when He may appear forgetful of you; for it is written of Him, "In your wrath remember compassion." With trust, confidence, and righteousness, repeat those memorable and devout words of the sore-covered elder: "Slay me though he might, I shall hope in Him." Repeat this, do this, think this, hope this; you will be able to do all things, not in yourself but "in Him who comforts you." Finally, be persistent as usual in your actions, all the more resolutely the closer you are to the end. The journey is brief, and nothing brief is difficult, for a short road though steep does not bring on weariness, whereas simply to look at a longer road wearies, though it may be level. And what do you think? A large portion of our day is spent in false pleasures and real hardships, amidst uncertain hopes and certain dangers; yet how little of the journey remains! Believe me, eventide approaches; while we speak and look about us, the day passes without our noticing it. Let us observe the sun: we shall realize its end is near, even though hidden, it is still near; as happens to most wayfarers, especially those who ride, the host will be at the doorway before we know it, and our final home will receive us. Consequently, we must proceed with cheerfulness and prudence, and complete the remainder of the journey with undaunted spirits, relieving the labor with the hope of finding repose. At this point in our discussion, I must say that I prefer that custom of wayfarers of going more slowly as they approach their resting place so as to cool the heat built up during the hot day; and thus they consciously check their speed, slowing down their heated horses, and in this fashion arrive at their destination with no visible signs of haste. We too, who have crossed the mountainous terrains and dusty roads of adolescence and youth with glowing spirits and have now returned to the firm and level plain, must temper our anxiety and check our impulses. Let us reach our goal so tranquilly and peacefully and fearlessly that those who see us in the evening will scarcely recognize us to be the same ones who hastened at midday. If even now toward the end we encounter some difficulty, may its brevity, I repeat, help us to surmount it. I am so happy that you have been doing this on your own that I could scarcely be happier about a noble action of my own. What particularly adds to my joy is your acknowledgment of having found useful one of my letters written many years before to that old religious who in his correspondence had complained of being afflicted by the gout, poverty, old age, and above all by his desire to see me, who had been away for so long. Of such ills, you suffer only two, the first and the last, and I shall completely free you of the latter once the din of battle has ceased for good; I do wish that I could also free you from the first so that you would no longer have to suffer. Already you have given more than enough proof of your courage, and although patience is to be sought, as I was saying at the beginning, still, as even the most conservative philosophers admit, pain must be borne, not desired. For this I really praise you, toward this I urge you to direct yourself since I cannot do otherwise; I am flattered too that you found my letter useful, yet whether it was as useful to the person for whom it was written, only he knows. I subsequently saw the man only once more for a brief moment in the fortress of Palestrina, where he seemed to be struggling with more than his usual joy and patience against his discomforts and old age. He expressed his gratitude by saying that because of me he was growing old without complaint and at peace, and fearlessly awaiting that terrible day; not long afterward he passed away. It is well known that something prepared for one person may benefit others: a father seeks wealth for his son, but someone else, and what is worse an enemy, enjoys it. I have noted in wonder that this happens not only with things subject to fortune, but even with those over which she is said to be powerless. It is such a shameful and yet common occurrence that to be astonished at such things is in itself astonishing. Since you are usually not wearied by our prolonged discussions, and since the matter requires some examples, I shall press onward.

I shall not speak of those who instructed their sons in the art of politics or warfare only to benefit everyone except those whom they had really wanted to benefit. I believe that this happens even more frequently in letters, where it is rare for the son of a great man to equal his father since nature so alternates things that any man owes what he is to God and not to his father. I could list generals, rulers, and emperors as evidence, but time is short; I shall limit myself to those writings that have proven useful to countless men throughout the ages yet had little effect upon those for whom they were written. Aristotle wrote his book on ethics for a certain Nicomachus, who was either the writer's father, as some say, or his son or his friend; in any case, he was of so little account that even now many scholars question who he was, although Cicero affirms him to be Aristotle's son; he is really not known except for the philosopher's concern, and indeed not even for that. So utterly unknown is his name that Aristotle himself shed no light upon it. Amazing as it may seem, Seneca wrote to Nero concerning clemency; how effective the book was on the one for whom it was written is known throughout the world. Macrobius wrote for his son Eustachius his commentaries on Cicero and the *Saturnalia*, ponderous volumes; in the proem to the first volume he expresses the wish that everything he himself had read during his lifetime would become for his son a storehouse of learning and a sanctuary of knowledge. What else is there to say? He devotes his genius, his knowledge, his eloquence, his hard work to him, making him his heir and beneficiary not of meager wealth or a limited estate but of all the possessions of his mind; a remarkable inheritance, but an obscure heir unknown except for being mentioned in his father's dedication. Virgil wrote the elegant and enjoyable *Georgicorum libri* for Maecenas, but it is doubtful whether he produced a farmer; and certainly

Horace did not make him a stable or modest man when he wrote for him practical letters full of counsel, as well as his highly serious satires. Can it be said that after so many warnings and so much advice, he strove any harder, spoke more maturely, or was more stable when prosperity caused his flighty mind to waver? It would be tedious to cite more individual cases, so I pass on to a final one. The great Cicero wrote a delightful and elegant exhortation to his brother. Did he divert his mind from wrath, to which he was inclined, or did he check his irrational activity? He also wrote *De officiis* for his son Cicero, who resembled his father in nothing but name. O how rich in elegance and seriousness those works are! Filled with wholesome precepts, no section is without incentives that he uses to rouse the young mind, inciting it at least to imitate the splendor of the family's renown. And so? He who was able to placate and influence Julius Caesar, so hostile to party politics, so proud of his victories, and so irritated by the offenses committed against him, whose eloquence so often swayed judges, the public, and the Senate, who you would say could move even stones with his voice, was unable to influence a young man so unlike his father. In this alone did he prove unsuccessful and unequal to his other accomplishments that had brought him such fame and success in life. But no man is endowed with blessings alone. Happiness alternates with sadness, light with dark, peace with turmoil, fortune with misfortune, while a close examination of most human affairs would reveal a minimum of good and a maximum of evil. To you, my dear Cicero, there befell a great deal of good, boundless glory, but a degenerate son, and truly, in the words of Elius Spartianus, for you "it would have been better not to have had children," since you had one who scorned the duties that he had read in those books I mentioned and that, one must assume, he had often heard viva voce—a voice that truly lives above all others in my mind as it did in Seneca's—viva voce, I say, from his father's mouth; he subsequently became renowned not for the art of living but for the art of drinking, capable of imbibing two measures of wine at a time. Truly an outstanding son of such a father and a brave avenger, able to deprive his slayer, Antonius, not of his life or power or wealth, but of his fame as a drinker and his reputation as a drunkard, something that Antonius complains of in a book on his drunkenness. O monstrosity born under an evil star, O incredible diversity of nature that from such light there should emerge such darkness! Alas, Marcus Tullius, outstanding man but unfortunate father, how enthusiastically did you strive to create another Marcus Tullius! Instead you created a Marcus Bibulus. Enough of my weeping as though in Cicero's presence. I turn to you, O father, and to the matter at hand. If, as I said, the efforts of so many men often proved ineffective in assisting those for whom they were intended, they were often of value to others after thousands of years, and will continue to be so, including perhaps ourselves. If by chance, to make myself one of their number, that letter of mine, whether it was useful or, as I suspect, useless for the one to whom it was sent, has proven after so much time helpful to you, I rejoice, and I bless that pen and that day I wrote it. But today I am detaining you too long; please forgive me since I seem to be with you. Farewell.

Milan, 1 December.

Fam. XXIII, 13.

To his Socrates, * *that we must bear with equanimity the fact that others reap the fruits of our labor, since it is a common occurrence.*

You cannot bear someone else taking advantage of your labors. Set your indignation and your astonishment aside: life is full of such tricks, and ordinary things must not surprise us since you will find them always the same. Only a few things are of service to those who do them; often the greater the labor, the less the reward is. The founders of the greatest cities lie beneath thin marble slabs, the cities themselves are governed by foreigners; one man builds a home, another inhabits it, and the architect sleeps in the open; one man sows, another reaps, and the sower goes hungry; one man sails, another is attired in goods shipped by sea, and the sailor is unkempt. Finally one man weaves, another wears the material, and meanwhile the weaver is unclothed; one man fights, another seizes the rewards of victory, and the winner is left without honor; one man digs for gold, another spends it, and the miner is needy and wanting; one man collects gems, another wears them on his fingers, and the jeweler is poverty-stricken; one woman bears a son in labor, another gladly marries him and makes him her own, and the mother is abandoned. Daylight will fall before we exhaust such examples. For what else does Maro's verse mean when he says, "So you do not build your nest for yourselves, O birds?" The rest is well known. Besides, there is a popular old saying that he who cultivates the greater number of vineyards drinks less wine. Nor are the words of the prophet king without meaning: "Because you will eat the fruit of your handiwork, happy shall you be, and favored"; nor the words of his son: "For every man to eat and drink and enjoy the fruit of all his toil is a gift of God." I say that the gift is rare and remarkable, for so it appears that both father and son wanted it to be understood. Therefore, may he who has obtained it be filled with gratitude, may he who has been denied it perhaps find consolation in its common occurrence and in the belief that no unusual injustice has been inflicted upon him. And may the words of the same Solomon not be overlooked: "When one labors with wisdom, learning, and skill, and must leave his property to another who has not toiled over it, this too is vanity and a great misfortune." A great one, I admit, but a common one. And so, each time you wish to blame nature or fortune, consider first whether you alone or you along with a thousand others are being made to suffer whatever it is that is bothering you, lest

*See I, 1.

you appear to be an agent of all the complainers against Divine Providence should it be an evil common to all or to many. But enough about your complaints. Regarding the matter for which you so profusely thank me, as if the sole defender of your fortunes, since I do not wish my words to increase or decrease my merit, I shall add nothing to Terence's words in the *Andria*: "I rejoice at having done something for you, or doing what pleases you; and that you have been grateful for it, I render thanks to you." Stay well and farewell, and remember me.

Fam. XXIII, 14.

To Jan of Olmütz, Chancellor to Caesar,* a friendly letter.

Your letter caused me no little astonishment, for it was first of all written in a style unfamiliar to me: you address me in the plural when I am but one person, and thus wish that I were whole and not divided by many warring and contrasting ideas. I shall not change my style, which all learned men once used, and which I have in turn been using for a long time, for I abhor the flattery and sheer silliness of the moderns; for this reason I modestly and in a friendly way boast to you about having been the first, or at least the first in Italy, to transform the effeminate and feeble style of our predecessors by restoring its manly and wholesome qualities. And so shall I do with you unless I hear that you would really prefer otherwise. I note too that none of my recent letters has reached you since you have answered none of them, and you rightfully express surprise that without keeping you informed, as I usually did, my situation has so changed that I have moved my fortunes and dwelling elsewhere. The truth is that I did not leave Milan for Venice, but with the intention of coming to Caesar and to you; but fortune ended not only the journey itself but also the return. What did I do? I followed Terence's advice because, unable to do as I wished, I began to wish what I knew could be done. And so, looking around and considering many things, I chose a nearby inn and, as it were, a public port of mankind, carrying with me nothing more than my books and my pens. I made certain of having these and many other things come to your notice, but evidently I was not sufficiently fortunate with my messengers. This one of yours, whom I rejoice in having become mine and therefore ours, will not fail us, I dare say, for at this very moment he has in his haste to depart compelled me, busy as I am, with gentle urging and profound sighing, to write something or other to our Caesar. Farewell.

*See X, 6.

Fam. XXIII, 15.

*To Caesar himself,** an exhortation and a supplication to return to Italy.*

I fear that the frequent protestations contained in my letters to you may give me the reputation of being insolently arrogant or ridiculously insane since I am burdening and disturbing the tranquillity of your serene heart with what amounts to stormy gusts. For who am I, or where do I get such nerve? Beyond any doubt I speak from a clear conscience, which I make use of only for your affairs and no one else's, O Caesar, being fully aware of your circumstances, of mine, and of the situation. Although David's words often come to mind, "What do I have to do with heaven, and what have I wanted from you on earth," I find comfort and strength in your kindness and integrity that seeks the bitter truth rather than flattering and charming words. I believe that I am intimately known to you, O most prudent of emperors, not because I have given any great proof of my worth, but because I am confident that my faithfulness shines through to you as a result of knowing one another intimately. And thus, I have no fear of offending someone whom I dearly love, even were I to exhort or reprove him in all sincerity; certain of your opinion, I pay little heed to others', particularly when they are false. And if no innocence is so great as to avoid censure, I prefer my faithful impudence to reproval for faithless silence, though nothing really remains for me to say. I seem to have drained my mind and made my throat hoarse in summoning you to your throne, O Caesar; no longer have I a tongue or a pen, long have my pleas been scorned, weary is my voice, dried my tears, finished my sighs, and now I speak only from the heart. I do hope that you will hear me, albeit hoarse and silent; for the more silent I seem, the more loudly I am speaking, night and day beseeching, imploring, begging, and reproaching you. It has happened to me as to a deluded lover who, after exhausting all arguments capable of persuasion, can only call out his beloved's name with his lips, indeed not even with his lips but from his heart. For me and for all your followers, this alone remains: to hold you in our mind as an image of our deity, but one who takes no notice of or shows no concern over our wretchedness. If our spirit is willing, we are lacking in ingenuity, except that prostrate in humility we call out to you not once but a thousand times; there are moments when naked voices and naked feelings have replaced ingenuity, when the constant repetition of

*See X, 1.

a dear name has been far more effective in influencing minds. O most glorious Caesar, bear my insolence with patience and with an even more understanding mind, but without anger at those who continually invoke you; it is punishment enough not to have listened to me. Famous and sweet is Caesar's name, one feared by all peoples and rulers, truly a name that means salvation for us; allow it to sound sweetly on our lips, whether we invoke it aloud or silently. Even in silence, hear the voices of your supporters; your Italy is summoning you, O Caesar, with such shouts that, if they are heard at all, would move not only their own prince but the most distant kings of India. Your Italy, I say, is summoning you, O Caesar: "Caesar, Caesar, O Caesar of mine, where are you? Why do you abandon me? What makes you delay? Were I not immobile, enclosed on the left and on the right by a double sea and at my shoulders by the Alps, I myself would long ago have sought my Caesar beyond the Danube." Farewell, O Caesar, and awaken: the day is at hand.

Venice, 11 March.

Fam. XXIII, 16.

To Jan, Chancellor, * *personally, that you must not forgo what you are capable of doing, even though you cannot do what you would like.*

And so, because you cannot write what you would like, you write nothing? I beg you, do not add insult to injury since for me it is much more painful to be deprived of your letters to which I had become accustomed than to do without the realization of a doubtful hope. For the latter perhaps promised my body material comfort in keeping with the insatiable and infinite longings of the mind, but certainly not a necessary comfort; the letters afforded me internal nourishment and comfort. I anxiously urge and implore you not to consider depriving me of them, for your sake, for your leader whom I have always venerated, and who is so worthy of such veneration, and for whatever love you have ever felt for me. Is it because you cannot give me what you wish that you are taking away what you used to give me? Or is it because you are unable to be generous that you do me harm? Is this not similar to killing a sick person whom you cannot cure? Take care, O dearest father, ever so pious toward me, if I might use a Latin expression, lest your piety deviate for excess of affection. You wished to make of me something extraordinary, and you did not succeed; no one can prohibit you from loving me as an ordinary man. I am requesting nothing new; so do what you are wont to do, and since I who am yours wander alone in this large city (which may surprise you), and since I myself once rightly called Venice another world, do not forsake me, removed as I am from the rest of the world, but revive my thirsty soul with your desired letters and comfort me with your holy and pleasing words. Lastly, I request with good reason that if I have had no change of mind toward you, you view me as before when you wished to make me someone else. Certainly I know that you continue to be well disposed toward me, yet if your affection remains the same, why is the effect different? You are sorry, I suppose, that for the first time your requests to Caesar in my behalf have not prevailed. Do not have regrets, I beg you, for I have none; let my friends be troubled for whom I had made the requests, for I am now satisfied with little. If I consider my own nature and myself, I am not only sufficiently wealthy but too much so, to the point of being the object of envy. And if by chance I still lack something, old age is already at my threshold as a welcomed guest, and behind her

*See X, 6.

is death, the great leveler, who brings with her the greatest of all wealth, namely, not to feel the need for anything more. I am grateful, then, for your good will, and I ascribe my failure to fortune, not to you or to Caesar, to whom I have always been dear beyond my deserts, and who will soon either grant me what he now denies me or perhaps, in keeping with his lofty prudence, help me by denying it. After all, despite his constant refusal of my final request, he still has bestowed so much on me in the past that as long as I live I feel obliged to worship his very footsteps. But enough of this.

The messenger delivering this letter is a dear friend, half-German and half-Italian, a bright and energetic man quite proficient in letters and the principal arts. In his determined pursuit of fame (and I assure you that if he finds imitators, he will bring considerable renown to your university), he has left Padua to go to Prague, eager to learn and to teach, in need of nothing but your favor. If, as a foreigner, he could personally meet you, it would be of great assistance, something he hopes to achieve through my letter; were he to prove worthy of such favor, and if he appeals to you, may your kindness, which you refuse no good man, be extended to him. Live happily, and if pure love has any merit, send me some response so that I may rejoice at not having yet been removed from the stronghold of your memory.

Venice, 27 August.

Fam. XXIII, 17.

To Ugo, Count of San Severino, * concerning the courtly dogs at the royal palace in Naples.*

Today, O illustrious sir, I finally received and gladly read your letter that was long awaited and perhaps often noisily lamented. Its style was marvelously in keeping with my taste; indeed I recognized in your account the courtly mores that I have long known and despised. So as not to take too long, which is forbidden because of my uncertain health and my many occupations, please know that insofar as the illustrious queen is concerned, my prayer has been granted, and I am her debtor in every way. I know not how true it may be, but I am certainly convinced that her generous, noble, and beneficent mind would not willingly deny anything worthy of herself and of me; but she has placed "her feelings and her power under the jurisdiction of Photinus." I am sorry for her, for you and for the few good men, and finally for Italy, where I find it most disturbing to see Egyptian monsters ruling; I do not feel sorry for myself, however, since distance causes those matters not to affect me. Many years ago during a stay in your Naples, which then wavered between happiness and wretchedness, I foresaw as though with my own eyes and predicted and wrote about all this evil according to the dictates of my mind. Consequently, I shall revere with eternal devotion that divine and heavenly king who was then snatched from earth to return to heaven, who in his old age honored my youth beyond any merit of mine but short of his desires and intentions with displays that may not have been splendid yet surely were rare; and I shall continue celebrating his name and his remains and any blood descendant of his. I promised him this, I know that I have fulfilled this promise and hope to continue doing so at least in spirit; for this reason there is no need for new favors due to their abundance in the past. And I say the same to you too; what was in your power to do, you certainly did, although envy in its customary fashion may have replaced love, yet for me an ineffectual trust is much dearer than an effectual faithlessness. But as for the court dogs, no words of mine would be more effective than Caesar's: "I like nothing better than that I be myself and they be themselves." Certainly in my poverty I am wealthy, not so much in my own judgment but in the judgment and consensus of many; they are needy and indigent in their wealth, and I wish that they could be suffer-

---

*A high official of the court of Naples who eventually was given command of all royal troops.

ing even more, for then they would know how much more peaceful and happy one day is for me than an entire lifetime for them, beset as it is with the worst concerns, oozing with filthy pleasures, quivering and faltering in its expectations, deceived by empty joys, crushed by genuine sorrows, frozen with terrors, burning with passions. There is no one among them with whom under any circumstances I would exchange my way of life. Though it is possible to be wretched amidst golden vessels, it is also possible to be happy amidst earthen jars, for in order to live happily potter's clay is no more base than gold, nor is Samos inferior to Corinth. Farewell, and if you wish to be a good man, attempt to be unlike them, taking care lest their contagious mores contaminate you.

Fam. XXIII, 18.

To Niccolò Acciaiuoli, Grand Seneschal of the Kingdom of Sicily, * *concerning his magnificent feat.*

With my entire soul I reverently embrace you, O man most rare in every age and unique in ours, and legally lay claim to you as to a discovered treasure, whether in my presence you open your hallowed mouth in lively conversation or in your absence you employ the golden style of mellifluous words at times in military or vernacular style, at times with exquisitely eloquent words and thoughts, as you now have done more loftily and divinely than seems possible amidst the clattering of arms. Despite its endless streams and varying flavor, I recognize the unique source of your divine intellect; and I marvel wonderingly who this man might have become had he nourished his great mind only with such studies, seeing that he is still remarkable despite the minimal amount of time dedicated to them; and this he had to steal secretly and randomly from his most weighty responsibilities in order to indulge in such activity. I pass over those major preoccupations worthy not of my feeble pen but of Homeric celebration, not of a letter but an entire book, as for example your military prowess in battle or your skill in law or the civil justice with which you enforce the peace. Until now, Naples and praiseworthy Campania have witnessed your skills, now Sicily has joined them along with Arethusa now joyful and Etna now more lukewarm and Charybdis now more peaceful, all out of respect for your presence and admiration for your deeds. I salute you for your manifold virtues, and above all for the modesty that marks all your mental qualities, you who expect to enjoy among posterity a fame no less from these trifles of mine than from your own personal greatness, as you so often confessed to me in your letters. This is perhaps an honest yet nonetheless serious error, based as it is on love. As for me, the favor of such a man will bring me glory, perhaps not with posterity, which may not even know my name, but at least with my contemporaries; moreover I not only hope but know that for me it is a source of joy and honest pleasure. When you offer your greatness to a man of my insignificance, when you affirm that my affection, and all I have attempted to do for our prior of the Holy Apostles, perhaps not very effectively but certainly faithfully and sincerely, redounds to your glory—perhaps you are not mistaken—and you resort to your customary expression of grateful commemoration, you honor not me but yourself, thereby seeming perfect

*See XI, 13.

in every respect; accordingly, if the occasion warrants, I shall make use of your frequent and splendid offers with the utmost confidence. But enough about you. The person about whom we are speaking is not one to whom I may be outwardly devoted, for he is truly a part of myself, one of the few whose ways and mentality in this fleeting life are acceptable to me and have become deeply rooted in my heart. Last of all, I anxiously beg you to keep me informed of your situation and any change that you may have exerienced after the king's death; how I wish that you had been as able to instill the royal virtues in him as you were able to facilitate his path to the throne. In vain did we devote ourselves to this end, I with my letters and you with your words. An evil man expressed this excellent thought, "Virtue is not increased by words"; how true this is, if no responsive spark is struck in the listener's mind. Oh, if only he had shown greater sensitivity to your warnings (please forgive this outcry of grief from my mind and pen!), for then he would surely have enjoyed a happier life, a less wretched death, a greater fame. Farewell, O you who are an honor to me and to the fatherland.

Padua, 8 June.

Fam. XXIII, 19.

To Giovanni Boccaccio, * *concerning a young man who has been assisting him with transcriptions; and that nothing is so correct as not to lack something.*

One year after your departure I happened to come across a young man of considerable talent whom I regret you do not know, though he knows you very well, having often seen you at my Venetian dwelling, which is also yours, and at the home of our Donatus, on which occasions he observed you attentively as is natural at his age. So that you too may know him from a distance as much as possible, and mentally see him in my letters, I shall tell you that he was born on the Adriatic coast at about the time, I believe, of your stay with the former lord of that region, the grandfather of the present lord. Though of humble origin and fortune, the youth's moderation and seriousness are worthy of an elder, his mind is sharp and agile, his memory rapacious, capacious, and most importantly, tenacious. In eleven consecutive days he committed to memory my *Bucolicum carmen,* which, as you know, is divided into twelve eclogues; every evening he would recite one of my eclogues to me, and on the last he recited two without stopping or hesitating, as though reading from a book. What is more, he also possesses a wonderful power of invention, something rare in our times, a fine enthusiasm, and a heart that loves the Muses. Already "he is composing songs," as Maro has it, and if he survives and, I hope, develops with the passage of time, "he will become something great," as Ambrose's father prophesied of him. Many things can be said about him; I shall limit myself to a few. You have already heard one; now listen to his excellent grounding in virtue and knowledge. The multitude does not love and seek money as much as he hates and rejects it; it is futile to get him to accept money, for he scarcely accepts the wherewithal to live, and he vies with me in his love of solitude, his fasting, and his vigils, and often surpasses me. What else can I say? His character has so recommended him to me that he is no less dear to me than a son, perhaps even dearer, since a son — such are the ways of our young men today — would wish to rule, while this one is eager to obey and to follow not his own inclinations but my will, doing all this without self-interest or expectation of reward, but simply out of love and perhaps the hope of becoming a better person through our friendship. More than two years ago he came to me — would that he had come sooner! — but his age would have made that impossible. Amidst the confusion of scattered copies and personal cares,

*See XI, 1.

I had nearly despaired of my prose letters on familiar matters, whose value will hopefully be as great as their number, after four friends who had promised assistance abandoned the project in midstream; instead this young man by himself has now brought to completion, indeed not all, but enough to form a volume of modest dimension; and if I insert this letter, they will number 350. God willing, you will see them sometime, written in his hand, not with that pompous and fancy lettering so typical of contemporary scribes or rather painters that from a distance appeals to the eyes but from up close confuses and wearies them—as though it were destined for something other than reading, and, to cite the prince of grammarians, as though the word *litera* does not derive from *legitera*—but in neat and clear lettering, affecting more than just the eyes and lacking, you might say, nothing in orthography and nothing at all in grammatical skill. But enough of this.

To arrive finally at what was first in my thoughts, this young man has a decided leaning for poetry; if he continues along his present path and eventually realizes his potential, he will compel your wonder and delight. Until now, given youth's natural shortcomings, he remains vague and still undetermined about what he wishes to say; but he expresses very nobly and beautifully whatever he does wish to say. Thus, he often happens to compose verses that are not only melodious but serious, charming, and well considered, the sort of work that you would ascribe to an experienced poet had you not known the author. I am confident that he will strengthen his thought and expression, forging a personal style from his extensive reading, not necessarily avoiding imitation but concealing it so that his work will not resemble anyone else's, and appear to be bringing from the writers of old something new to Latium. But now, as is the way of youth, he delights in imitation, and at times is so enraptured by another poet's sweetness and so entangled, contrary to good poetic practice, in the rules of such a work that he becomes incapable of freeing himself without revealing the originals. He admires Virgil above all, appropriately enough; for though many of our poets are praiseworthy, he alone is supreme. So enamored of Virgil's charms is he that he often inserts bits taken from him into his own works; but I who happily see him developing before my eyes and becoming the type of poet that I should like to be, warn him in a friendly and fatherly fashion to watch what he is doing. An imitator must take care to write something similar yet not identical to the original, and that similarity must not be like the image to its original in painting where the greater the similarity the greater the praise for the artist, but rather like that of a son to his father. While often very different in their individual features, they have a certain something our painters call an "air," especially noticeable about the face and eyes, that produces a resemblance; seeing the son's face, we are reminded of the father's, although if it came to measurement, the features would all be different, but there is something subtle that creates this effect. We must thus see to it that if there is something similar, there is also a great deal that is dissimilar, and that the similar be elusive and unable to be extricated except in silent meditation, for the resemblance is to be felt rather than expressed. Thus we may appropriate another's ideas as well as his coloring but we must abstain from his actual words; for, with the former, resemblance remains hidden, and with the latter it is glaring, the former creates poets, the second apes. It may all be summarized by saying with Seneca, and Flaccus before him, that we must write as the bees make honey, not gathering flowers but turning them into honeycombs, thereby blending them into a oneness that is unlike them all, and better. I often speak thus to him since he is ever attentive as though listening to a father's advice. The other day it so happened that as I advised him in this fashion, he offered the following objection: "I understand, and I admit it to be as you say, but I have used others' words, to be sure few and rather rarely, following the practice of many writers, including yourself." Full of amazement, I said: "If ever, my son, you discover anything of the sort in my poems, you may be sure that it was an unintentional oversight. For although cases of this sort, where a writer makes use of another's words, are to be found by the thousands in poetry, I myself have always taken the utmost pains, when composing, to avoid traces from my own works and especially from those of previous writers. But where, if you please, is the passage justifying your accusation?" He answered, "In the sixth eclogue of your *Bucolicum carmen* where a verse near the end concludes, 'atque intonat ore.' " I was astounded, for as he spoke I realized what I had not noticed while writing, that it is a verse ending in the sixth book of Virgil's divine poem. I decided to inform you of this, not because of any possibility of correcting the passage since the poem is widely known and disseminated, but so that you might reprove yourself for allowing another to be first in pointing out this slip of mine, or that you might now take note of it, had it escaped your notice so far, and might realize that such things happen not only to me, admittedly a scholar seriously lacking in learning and talent, but to all men, however learned; so unequal to the task are they that all their human inventions possess an element of incompleteness, since perfection is reserved for Him alone whence comes all our knowledge, all our potential. Lastly, I ask you to pray to Virgil with me for forgiveness, asking him not to be annoyed if, just as he stole many things from Homer, Ennius, Lucretius, and others, I inadvertently took, but did not steal, a little something from him. Farewell.

Pavia, 28 October.

Fam. XXIII, 20.

To Francesco Bruni, Florentine rhetorician,* an agreement to enter into a new friendship.

Considerable proof of your virtue, O illustrious sir, has been given me by that magnanimous man so worthy of trust who recently returned bringing me the name of a new friend as a noble gift; included among the many things that he said about you, whom he clearly loves and proudly names, was your desire for my friendship. In fact when anyone asks whether you know me, your usual response is that you have seen and met me, thereby trying to conceal with a polite lie the embarrassment that you have often felt until now of not having known me, your contemporary and fellow citizen, whom you esteem and love without really having met. I thank you for your affection and for your natural error; an error with an admirable origin is not shameful. A kindly nature and a mind disposed to love have caused many to go awry in their judgment of things; it is nonetheless preferable to love many undeserving persons than not to love one who is deserving. That gentleman insisted that because of your great affection for me I should write something in a friendly vein since for some reason you were hesitant to write me first. I refused first because I had no subject to write on and then because I was unaccustomed to addressing people unknown to me. This is why almost everything that I have written as correspondence takes either the form of a response or is addressed to close friends; and moreover, I was really no more daring than others or less suspicious of this novel kind of writing than you. But what do you think he did? Do you think that he perhaps remained silent, convinced of my words? On the contrary, he approached the lord of this city, also a great friend of yours, and led him by the hand to my home with the clever idea that in the presence of such a witness—rather I should say master, for he too came to beg me, and a prince's request is an order—I would not dare refuse anything. Unaware of their purpose, I sat down with them among my books. There many subjects were discussed, and finally you. Only then did the one who had begun the discussion begin pressing and the other unexpectedly broke forth in support. I recognized the trap, but what could I do

---

*A Florentine who, though late in striking a friendship with Petrarch, became one of his most devoted correspondents in his later years, despite the fact that they never met. He was named Apostolic Secretary, following Petrarch's refusal of the post, and received many letters from Petrarch containing strong exhortations for the return of the papacy to Rome.

against two such men? Unable to resist my good friend's flattery and the weight of the lord's words, I yielded; following their departure a short while ago, I seized my pen, mindful of my promise, in order to write whatever occurred to me. But since I could think of nothing new, besieged as I am by responsibilities and laden with cares, I thought it sufficient to put down chronologically what had happened and how the matter had developed. And this is how it ends. You desire, I understand, my friendship, truly a small wish, but the more modest your desire, the more discourteous it is to reject it. I am thus satisfying your request; take armfuls of what you sought, count me confidently among your friends, and if I can be of any use to you, simply ask; if I cannot, at least you will occupy nearly last place among my friends and acquaintances and among the letters of my younger years. For you may not realize that you have run into a friend and a pen that are getting along in age. But if there is still a bit of life in me, it is the least silent inasmuch as "old age is more loquacious," as it seemed to the excellent Cato the Elder. Without doubt, then, you will more frequently be a part of it; meanwhile, bear your lot with equanimity, placing no blame on your intercessor, who conducted himself admirably and as a true soldier in your behalf, nor on me who obeyed him with some reluctance, but on yourself, if you manage to get somewhat less than you hoped for. And may you ever fulfill all your desires as easily but be more fortunate in your choice. Farewell.

Padua, 8 September, at the ninth hour.

Fam. XXIII, 21.

To Caesar,* a final exhortation.

Weary of the past and distrustful of the future, I had, O Caesar, laid down my pen quite exhausted and rebellious as a result of its exhortations to you. In difficult moments, the hope of success nourishes and refreshes the spirit, but once such hope is removed, who is so insane as not to prefer repose to fruitless toil? A sacred love compels me to return to my writing, whether it be your soldier's name (*Sagremor*) or that sacred enthusiasm inherited from my ancestors, which I have always fostered for your majesty since my acquaintance with you, and since childhood for the majesty of the Roman Empire, an enthusiasm that lives in my heart and increases day by day, or, which is more likely, both of them together. For my love would not have turned once again to a futile undertaking after my many vain cries and efforts, nor would this soldier, though a knowledgeable and eloquent friend, have influenced me, had he not found within my soul the still living embers of my old allegiance, which he could ignite with the tinder of hope and the gentle bellows of his charming words. Excusing your slowness with many valid arguments and whispering in my ears, which are ever eager and credulous with regard to your happiness and glory, impressive explanations about the noble concerns on your mind and your truly imperial involvements, he dissolved with the warmth of new hope the old ice of distrust. Come then, O Caesar, and with the aid of God, who did not commit His empire to you in vain, rise and fulfill with courage and joy, while you can, the noble task that you have postponed; for a glorious ending will excuse a slow beginning. All are in agreement that you have been delayed by lofty counsel since the Italian harvest was not sufficiently ripe for Caesar to use his sickle to advantage, although our hunger murmured impatiently at all delay. No untimely undertaking is done well, nothing good is late; and true are the words of Caesar Augustus, "Whatever may be done well enough, may be done fast enough." Seize this occasion, O Caesar, while you can, for you will not always to able to; act, I beg you, O Caesar, for I have not yet forgotten how to invoke your name or how to plead for your honor. Although also one of the impatient ones, for a time I had become lukewarm because of the unfortunate delay; yet behold that I am becoming warm once again. Do not extinguish a second time my beautiful hope and the hope of many others, since hope too often crushed is revived only with

*See X, 1.

difficulty. If any cloud has hung over your name, if any shame has befallen you from the dark beginnings, it all will, believe me, be wiped clean by the splendor of the completed undertaking; but as I said, it all will be transformed into glory because, whether it be error or wise deliberation, men will view it as wise deliberation rather than error. Often a noble ending has rendered glorious a slow beginning but never has a dark ending been illuminated by a bright beginning. Though you began in a manner that made us grieve, may you now end in the manner that we wish. You will deserve the name of Fabius Maximus, you will be considered a procrastinator but a wise man, more concerned about the public good than popular fame. Let Minutius surpass you as he pleases in windy loquacity provided he admit himself unequal to you on the strength of experience; let ungodly enemies say of you what Hannibal said of him: "I have always expected that cloud to burst forth from the mountains with great thunder." But if—and may divine mercy not allow it—the end too is sluggish, who among your contemporaries or posterity will ever be able to excuse you? I beg you, O Caesar, listen to me, an insignificant man, but one who loves you, is concerned about you, and is hopeful for you. You are no less mortal than I or anyone else among your subjects: time is fleeing never to return, fortune is unstable, life is brief, the hour of death is uncertain; there is but one remedy: economize with time, do not have faith in fortune, prolong life with good works, and have the body and mind ever ready for death, an impossible task for one who has not completed his primary duty. Though the end of life is uncertain, it is certain that it cannot be too distant; when it does come, nothing will remain of all your wealth and empire except what you have earned through a good life for the eternal life of your soul and the immortal glory of your name. As I often said in the past, you were born to be emperor, a magnificent and lofty calling; faithfully fulfill its duties if you wish to have it said that you lived well. Otherwise, what is the use of your having spent the last hours of your life in splendor? This you could have accomplished even without the empire, perhaps more easily since there would have been less envy toward you and less labor required of you. Another and greater task awaits you: undertake it without allowing its magnitude to frighten you; there is nothing that the empire's majesty cannot accomplish, armed with prudence, justice, and power. But if perchance heaven denies your seeing this task to completion, I still believe it much better and more useful to die in a glorious undertaking than in languid idleness; it was this that made your grandfather celebrated in every century. So there, O Caesar, I have now, as often in the past, anxiously expressed not with flattery but in all honesty, not with elegance of words but with clarity of thought, what has been on my mind, what I pray to God and to you I have not said in vain. Farewell, O you who are our honor, our joy, and our hope.

Padua, 11 December.

Fam. XXIV, 1.

To Philippe, Bishop of Cavaillon,* concerning the incredible flight of time.

Thirty years ago—how time does fly! and yet if I cast a glance backward to consider them all together, those thirty years seem as so many days, so many hours, but when I consider them singly, disentangling the mass of my labors, they seem so many centuries—thirty years ago, then, I wrote to that venerable and worthy elder, Raimondo Subirani, who rightly held the title of jurisconsult that many hold under false pretenses, as you well know. Possessing both the appearance and competence of a wise man, he used his independence of mind to an extreme until the end of his life, in the name of truth and justice opposing even the Roman pontiff with a noble and unyielding spirit. For this reason, while others inferior to him enjoyed many honors, he alone enjoyed the glory of remaining behind; but he held on to his post amidst praises and with his customary dignity without advancing or seeking advancement. So I wrote a friendly letter, as was my wont, to this elder who had begun to feel such affection for my extreme youth and my budding mind as to cultivate and favor it with example, counsel, and words. In that letter, which stands because of its date at the beginning of this collection quite a distance from this one, I even then confessed to a dawning recognition about the flight and swiftness of my young life. I now find this astonishing, but what I wrote was true. And if my words were true then, how do you think they now apply when what I had foreseen has come to pass? The flowering time of life and the roseate sheen of youth shone in my eyes, in Maro's words, but I was reading Flaccus too: "When the unexpected stubble of your pride comes and your locks flowing down to your shoulders have disappeared, and your color now vying with the ruddy roses has changed, O Ligurinus, to a shaggy visage, you will utter, 'Alas,' whenever you behold your altered features in a mirror." I would read in the other Satirist: "For the little flower swiftly hastens to wither, which is the briefest portion of this short and wretched life. While we are drinking, while we are seeking perfumed garlands and maidens, old age steals upon us unperceived."

These and similar things I would read, admiring not only the grammar and skillful use of words, as is customary at that age, but perceiving a hidden meaning in the words unnoticed by my fellow students or even by my teacher, learned though he was in the elements of the arts. I

*See II, 1.

would listen to Virgil proclaiming his divine words, "The beautiful first day of our lifetime flees wretched mortals, illnesses follow and sad old age, and the sufferings of a merciless death"; and elsewhere, "Brief and unalterable for all is the span of life"; and again, "But meanwhile time flies, and it flies never to return." Scarcely did he seem able to express to his own satisfaction the flight of time and its irretrievable loss, except by constant repetition. I used to listen to Ovid, who was for me a more serious authority and incorruptible witness, the more licentious his Muse; he would say, "Our lives slip away and furtively abandon us, and nothing is more swift than the passing years"; and in another place, "Time flies by and we grow old with silent years, and the days flee with no bridle to check them." I would listen to the same Flaccus just mentioned, "Time runs madly onward," referring to youth, and then for any age, "Alas, O Postumus, my Postumus, the years glide swiftly by, nor does righteousness delay wrinkles and approaching old age, or invincible death"; and once again, "Life's brief span does not allow us to entertain far-reaching hopes." And still again, within a brief period "are cut short far-reaching hopes; while we speak envious time will be gone"; and further on, "Fresh youth and beauty are disappearing behind us, with withered old age banishing sportive loves and ready sleep"; and lest I were ever to expect its return, once it had fled, I would hear him say, "Neither Coan silks nor costly gems will restore to you those days that time in its flight has laid away and locked up forever in the archives known to all." But I am lingering too long on Flaccus. I would hear Seneca saying: "Our bodies are dragged along as by a river; whatever you see rushes on with time; nothing of all we see endures. Even while speaking these words I am changing." I would hear Cicero, "Time flies," and again, "Who is such a fool, even if young, as to maintain that he will live until evening?" Shortly thereafter he says, "It is certain that we must die: and it is uncertain whether it will be this very day." And again he would repeat the same thought, "Is it given to anyone to know how his body will be, I do not say within the year, but this evening?"

I omit others, for it becomes wearisome to pursue particular opinions of individual writers, and childish rather than mature to pluck little flowers; but you often plucked at your leisure and by the thousands these and similar flowers either from my writings or from these authors' fields along with me. With what youthful zeal I plucked from them for several years before becoming familiar with other kinds of writers may be seen in my surviving works from that period, and especially in my marginal notations on certain passages whereby I would conjure up and precociously reflect upon my present and future state. Diligently I would note not the verbal facility but the substance of the thought—the distresses and brevity of this life, its haste, tumbling course and hidden deceits, time's irrecoverability, the perishable and changing flower of life, the fugitive beauty of a rosy face, the frantic flight of unreturning youth, the deceits of a silently stealthy old age, and finally, the wrinkles, illnesses, sadness, toil, and implacable cruelty and harshness of indomitable death. All these that appeared to my companions and contemporaries as nothing but dreams, to me—and I call all-seeing God to witness—appeared real and almost present, and whether mine was a true handsomeness or youthful self-deception—since nearly every young man sees himself as very handsome even though ugly—whenever I heard or read those pastoral words, "O fair youth, trust not your brief, bright bloom," I thought that they applied particularly to me. I know that I am speaking the truth; and He whom I have called to witness knows this very well; but reconsidering the matter, I am even more surprised that with such thoughts and concerns I was still led so astray by youthful loves and errors. I understand: the mist of earth clouded my sight and raging youth extinguished the earlier light of my spirit. But I am glad to have begun to see the truth. Truly happy is he whom no error leads astray, but since total happiness is rare, he too is happy for whom a divine light still shines amidst the dark clouds of error. What do you think now? See how what once seemed to be now truly is; I now comprehend that life's flight is so swift that it can scarcely be measured with the mind, and while the swiftness of the mind may be unequaled, life itself is still swifter. I feel that each day, each hour, and each minute propels me toward the end; each day I proceed toward death, indeed—as I had begun to realize while still young—each day I die; in fact I came close to using the verb in the past tense inasmuch as I have accomplished a large portion of what I was to do; what remains is minimal, and is happening, I hope, at this very moment as I speak with you. Truly ancient is my conviction that those maintaining that any one age can endure are either deceiving others or surely deceiving themselves. O you who promise so much to this poor little body, be generous to it in all else, but do not promise it a stable condition. Faithfully, carefully, prudently care for it and offer it all that is in you; drive away recurring diseases; postpone old age, which is subject only to death's power; resist death, which will come soon enough; keep in check youth, which will chomp at the bit, escaping its rider; but beware of believing that you can ever hold on to it. For if life is brief, which is the foremost maxim of your profession, how could any of its parts be of long duration? They would surely be so if they could remain still, but every age flees and rushes on, none stays still; every age, I say, rushes with equal gait, yet each is not measured in the same way because the motion of the ones ascending or descending is more visible. These things that I pondered earlier I now know and see, and you too will see them if your eyes are not shut. For who does not perceive life's speed, particularly if he has crossed beyond its midpoint? I recall that at that time I looked as far ahead as possible; there was very little behind me. What stood ahead was somewhat more, as experience taught me, but it was uncertain and subject to endless misfortunes, for my friends, wearied by the journey, abandoned me in its midst, and I saw myself so often alone amidst such misfortunes that I reached the present day only after considerable distress. Between me and my contemporaries, and even my elders, was this difference: to them the journey seemed certain and endless, to me it seemed in fact short and doubtful. In frequent conversations and youthful disputes concerning this, my elders' authority prevailed, making me almost suspected of madness. For I did not know how to express what was on my mind, and even had I known, my youthful age and novel opinions seemed to win little favor. Defeated by words then, I took refuge in the stronghold of silence; and yet even these opinions of both sides were silently reflected in our actions. For them, elders as well as youths, these consisted in long-range planning, burdensome marriages, toilsome military service, perilous journeys, and greedy pursuits; for me — and I call Christ as witness — even at that age I entertained hardly any hope, for fortune had already begun to deceive my youthful thoughts. Thus whatever happened to me that seemed rather fortunate, which praise God was considerable, occurred beyond all hope; if meanwhile I hoped for something too ardently, it did not happen, perhaps so that I would learn not to hope. And indeed this I learned so well that, though daily enjoying additional gifts of fortune, I receive them with gratitude but with no additional faith in hope than if I had received nothing. My one quarrel with friends is their long-range propositions to me who am not far from death, and these, as I said, I used to reject even when young. This natural weakness, or natural goodness, saved me from marriage and other troubles of life toward which I was pushed by my parents' love and by my friends' advice. Nevertheless, in order not to go contrary to my parents' desires, who had so many hopes for me who hoped in nothing, I bent my back under the rod of studies in civil law, where everyone, except myself, expected me to reap enormous benefits. I knew well what I could or would achieve in that field, nor did I distrust my intelligence, but I could not bear to use my mind for profit. Thus, once left to myself, I wearily removed that burden from my shoulders, determining to continue in my own fashion my interrupted journey without hope and without worry, but since then achieving and suffering much beyond my expectations. Lest perchance the ignoramuses accuse me of despair in my remark about lack of hope, I speak only of those things subject to fortune; in all else I hold great hope, sinner though I am.

It has been pleasant to recall these things with someone who has known me from my earliest years. Nor does it seem to me that I have strayed much from my subject since my long-standing awareness of life's brevity has led to all these considerations in which, I believe, I have made some progress while going through life. This age differs from that age in that, while I then trusted in the words of the wise, as I said, I now put my faith not only in them but also in myself and in my own experience; then I would look only forward as I stood doubtful and insecure on the threshold, now looking backward and forward, I see confirmed what I used to read; I experience what I imagined, I behold myself hastening so swiftly to my end that it can barely be described or easily imagined. In this regard I have no need of poet or philosopher; I am my own witness and my own sufficient authority. Within a short time, my features and attitudes have changed as well as my customs, my concerns, and my studies. Nothing is for me as it was then; I am not referring to the time when I wrote you that letter, but to the moment I began writing this one. Now I proceed, and just as this pen moves, so do I, but much more rapidly, for my pen obeys the mind's sluggish dictation whereas I follow nature's law, and thus hasten, run, gallop to my end, already beholding my goal. I dislike what pleased me, and I like what displeased me. I used to take pleasure in myself, I loved myself. What shall I say about now? I hate myself. But I am lying; no one ever felt hatred for his own flesh. Shall I say, "I do not love myself?" I do not know how true that may be either. This much I can say with assurance, "I do not love my sins, nor do I love my ways except insofar as they have changed for the better and improved." But why hesitate? I hate my sinfulness, my evil habits, and myself as I am, for I learned from Augustine that no one can become what he wishes unless he hates himself as he is.

Having reached this point in the letter, I was wondering what more to say or not to say, and meanwhile, as is my custom, I was tapping the blank paper with my pen. This action provided me with a subject, for I considered how, during the briefest of intervals, time rushes onward, and I along with it, slipping away, failing, and, to speak honestly, dying. We all are constantly dying, I while writing these words, you while reading them, others while hearing or not hearing them; I too shall be dying while you read this, you are dying while I write this, we both are dying, we all are dying, we are always dying; we never live here except when doing something virtuous to pave our path to the true life, where in contrast no one dies, everyone lives and will live forever, where what once pleased will ever be pleasing, whose unutterable and infinite charm can scarcely be contained in the spirit, where there are no change and no reason to fear its ending. Often I recall and cite an interesting example from natural history: the Hypanis is a northern river that flows into the Pontus on the right of the Don; there, according to Aristotle, are born tiny insects that barely live a single day. How much longer, I ask you, is our lifetime? They too, as ourselves, live for a longer or shorter period of time; some die in the morning while still young, but others die at noon in the flower of their youth, and still others at sunset, already advanced in age; others die in the evening when truly old and even more decrepit if during the summer solstice. As Cicero remarks, "Compare our longest period of life with eternity, and you will find in it almost the same brief life as befalls those little creatures." That is the way it is, by Jove, nor do I believe there to be any more effective way to grasp life's brevity. Let us divide time as we wish, let us multiply the number of years, let us invent names for the ages, yet man's entire life is as a single day, and that not a full summer day but a winter one, in which one dies in the morning, another at midday, another a little later, and another in the evening; one is young and blooming, another physically powerful, still another parched and wasted. The Psalmist says, "Like grass one springs up in the morning, flourishes at noon and passes on; in the evening he falls, wilts, and fades." Many die as old persons, and if we believe wise men, everyone dies old because life's end is old age for everyone. Few, however, die in their prime, no one has lived a long life unless he first acknowledges there to be no difference between a very brief and a very long but finite amount of time. Regarding this I can add nothing to my early opinion except, as I said, that I had previously believed learned men, now I believe myself, now I know what I once believed. For they learned merely by living, seeing, and observing, and proclaimed it to their followers as one warns travelers about an unsafe bridge. The fact remains that today I never read that letter without astonishment, at times even saying to myself, "That mind possessed something of a noble seed, if only you had cultivated it with greater care at the proper time." I wanted to write these things to you for this reason, O most prudent of men, not to send you anything new—for if you have yet to learn such things, I could hardly hope to make you believe me—but to jog your memory and mine, beset with mold and entangled in daily concerns, to induce you to join with me in scorning this brief life and in tolerating inexorable fate, which you would doubtlessly have done had I remained silent, and also to shape our minds so that we, enclosed as we are within these confines and aspiring to the noble life beyond, consider with a glorious disdain all that fortune may spontaneously offer us; this, thank God, we have often done. Farewell.

Fam. XXIV, 2.

To Pulice da Vicenza, poet, * *concerning the contents of and the occasion for the following letters addressed to Cicero, Seneca, and others.*

While an overnight guest in a suburb of Vicenza, I found a new subject to write about. After my departure about noon from Padua, I happened to reach your city gates as the sun was setting; while I stood deliberating whether to stay there for the night or to push onward since I was in a hurry and there was still a good deal of daylight remaining, suddenly—for who can remain hidden from loving friends?—all my doubts were resolved by your arrival in the company of several eminent men, with whom the city abounds. You so ensnared my wavering spirit with your cheerful and interesting conversation that, even as I planned to proceed, I lingered, and no sooner had the day waned than night was upon us. On that day as on past occasions, I discovered that nothing so robs us of time without our perceiving it than conversations with friends; friends are the great thieves of time, although no time ought to be viewed as less stolen, less lost than that which, next to God, we spend with friends. Without recounting all that happened, you perhaps remember that someone made mention of Cicero, as so often happens among learned men, which at once put an end to our random conversation. To him alone we all turned, discussing nothing afterward except Cicero; we rallied around him, taking turns celebrating him in palinode or in panegyric, if you prefer. But since in human affairs nothing is perfect, and no man exists undeserving of criticism or even a modest critic, it happened that while I expressed almost unreserved admiration for Cicero, a man I loved and honored above all others, and amazement too at his golden eloquence and heavenly genius, I had no praise for his weak character and his inconstancy, which I had discovered from various bits of evidence. When I noticed the astonishment of all present at my novel opinion, and especially that old man whose name escapes me but whose face I remember well since he is a fellow townsman of yours and a venerable scholar, it seemed an opportune time for me to fetch from its box the manuscript containing my letters.

When it was brought in, it provoked even more discussion, for along with many letters to my contemporaries, a few are addressed to illustrious ancients for the sake of variety and as a diversion from my labors; and thus, an unsuspecting reader would be amazed at finding such outstand-

*Little is known of this correspondent except that he was a poet and scholar involved in the writing of historical chronicles of the time.

ing and honorable names mingled with those of contemporaries. Two are addressed to Cicero: one expresses reservations about his character, the other praises his genius. When you had read them to the attentive onlookers, a friendly argument ensued, in which some agreed with me that Cicero deserved the criticism. Only the old gentleman became more obstinate in his opposition; so taken was he with Cicero's fame and so filled with love for him that he preferred to applaud even his errors and to accept his vices together with his virtues rather than condemn anything in a man so worthy of praise. Thus, his only response to me or to others was to contrast the splendor of Cicero's name with everything being said, thereby substituting authority for reason. With hand outstretched, he repeatedly exclaimed, "Gently, please, gently with my Cicero!" When asked whether he thought that Cicero could have erred, he shut his eyes, and as if smitten by the words he would turn aside groaning, "Alas, are they denouncing my Cicero?" as though we were dealing not with a man but with a god. I then asked whether in his opinion Tullius was a god or a man; immediately he responded, "A god," but then realizing what he had said, he added, "really a god of eloquence." I said, "Quite so, for if he is a god, he could not have erred; still, I had not heard him called a god, but if Cicero called Plato his god, why should you not call Cicero yours except that our faith does not allow us to fashion gods arbitrarily?" He said, "I was joking; I know that Tullius was a man, but with divine genius." "This," I said, "is certainly better, for Quintilian called him a divine man in eloquence; but if he were a man, he surely could err, and in fact, did." As I said this, he shuddered and turned away as though the words were directed not at another's reputation, but at his own. Indeed, what could I say, being myself such an admirer of Cicero? I congratulated the old gentleman for his great devotion and ardor despite its Pythagorean flavor, I rejoiced in his reverence for such genius and in his awe that made any suspicion of human weakness in Cicero almost a sacrilege, and I marveled at finding a man who loved him more than I did since I had always loved him above all others. The old man held the same deep-seated opinion of Cicero that I recall having as a boy, and even at his age was incapable of entertaining the thought that if Cicero were a man, it followed that in some things, perhaps not in many, he must have erred. This I now believe in part and know in part, although up to the present no one else's eloquence has so delighted me; nor was Tullius himself, about whom we are speaking, unaware of this, having often and seriously deplored his own faults. Unless we admit his awareness of them, in our eagerness to praise him we deny him self-knowledge and modesty, which are significant reasons for his renown as a philosopher. That day following our lengthy discussion, given the late hour, we rose and departed without settling the question; but you made me promise, since time was then too short, to send you a copy of both letters so that, after considering the matter in depth, you could become either a mediator between the factions or possibly a defender of Cicero's steadfastness. I commend your spirit and forward the requested letters, fearing, strange as it may seem, to be the winner, and indeed wishing to be the loser so that you will realize that by winning you will be assuming a greater task than you think. For in a similar conflict, Anneus Seneca asks you to be his champion since the following letter in fact criticizes him. I have dealt lightly with these great geniuses, perhaps boldly, but lovingly, sorrowfully, and, I believe, truthfully, in fact somewhat more truthfully than I wanted to. Many things delighted me in their writings, a few troubled me; it was the latter few that prompted me to write with a vigor that I would perhaps not have had today, for although these letters are relegated to the last book because they are so unlike the others, I had hammered them out long before. The fact is that I still mourn the fate of such men, but I grieve no less over their faults; and please note that it is not my purpose to condemn Seneca's private life or Cicero's attitude toward the Republic. Lest you confuse the two cases, I am now dealing with Cicero, whom I know to have been a most vigilant, worthy, and effective consul, always the most patriotic of citizens. And yet? I cannot praise his inconstancy in friendship and his serious and destructive quarrels upon slightest provocation, which availed neither himself nor anything else; his inability to understand his own position and the condition of the Republic, strange indeed for a man with his keen mind; and finally his childish mania for wrangling, all of which are so unseemly in a philosopher. And remember that neither you nor anyone else can pass fair judgment on these matters until you thoroughly and slowly read all of Cicero's correspondence, which suggested this controversy. Farewell.

13 May, en route.

Fam. XXIV, 3.

To Marcus Tullius Cicero.

Francesco sends his greetings to his Cicero. After a lengthy and extensive search for your letters, I found them where I least expected, and I then read them with great eagerness. I listened to you speak on many subjects, complain about many things, waver in your opinions, O Marcus Tullius, and I who had known the kind of preceptor that you were for others now recognize the kind of guide that you were for yourself. Now it is your turn, wherever you may be, to hearken not to advice but to a lament inspired by true love from one of your descendants who dearly cherishes your name, a lament addressed to you not without tears. O wretched and distressed spirit, or to use your own words, O rash and ill-fated elder, why did you choose to become involved in so many quarrels and utterly useless feuds? Why did you forsake that peaceful ease so befitting a man of your years, your profession, and your fate? What false luster of glory led you, an old man, into wars with the young, and into a series of misfortunes that then brought you to a death unworthy of a philosopher? Alas, forgetful of your brother's advice and of your many wholesome precepts, like a wayfarer at night carrying a lantern before him, you revealed to your followers the path where you yourself stumbled most wretchedly. I make no mention of Dionysius, of your brother or of your nephew, and, if you like, even of Dolabella, all men whom you praise at one moment to the high heavens and at the next rail at with sudden wrath. Perhaps these may be excused. I bypass even Julius Caesar, whose oft-tested clemency proved a haven of refuge for those very men who had assailed him; I likewise refrain from mentioning Pompey the Great, with whom you seemed able to accomplish whatever you liked by right of friendship. But what madness provoked you against Mark Anthony? Love for the Republic, I suppose you would say, but you yourself confessed that it had already collapsed. But if it were pure loyalty, if it were love of liberty that impelled you, why such intimacy with Augustus? What would your answer be to your Brutus who says, "If you are so fond of Octavius, you seem not to have fled a tyrant, but rather to have sought a kindlier one." There still remained your last, lamentable error, O unhappy Cicero: that you should speak ill of the very man whom you had previously praised, not because he was doing you any harm, but merely because he failed to check your enemies. I grieve at your destiny, my dear friend, I am filled with shame and distress at your shortcomings; and so even as did Brutus, "I place no trust in those arts in which you were so proficient." For in truth, what good is there in teaching others, what benefit is there in speaking constantly with the most magnificent words about the virtues, if at the same time you do not give heed to your own words? Oh, how much better it would have been, especially for a philosopher, to have grown old peacefully in the country, meditating, as you write somewhere, on that everlasting life and not on this transitory existence; how much better for you never to have held such offices, never to have yearned for triumphs, never to have had any Catilines to inflate your ego. But these words indeed are all in vain. Farewell forever, my Cicero.

From the land of the living, on the right bank of the Adige, in the city of Verona in transpadane Italy, on 16 June in the year 1345 from the birth of that Lord whom you never knew.

Fam. XXIV, 4.

To the same correspondent.

Francesco sends his greetings to his Cicero. I hope that my previous letter did not offend you; for as you are wont to say, there is truth in what your contemporary says in the *Andria*: "Indulgence begets friends, truth only hatred." Accept then what may somewhat soothe your wounded feelings so that the truth may not always seem hateful; if we are irritated by true criticism, we rejoice in true praise. Allow me to say, O Cicero, that you lived as a man, you spoke as an orator, you wrote as a philosopher; and it was your life that I censured, not your intellect and your tongue since I admire the former and am astounded by the latter. Moreover, nothing was lacking but constancy in your personal life, a desire for the tranquillity necessary for the practice of philosophy, and withdrawal from civil strife, once liberty was spent and the Republic buried and mourned. Note how different is my treatment of you than yours of Epicurus throughout your works, but especially in the *De finibus*, where you approve of his life and ridicule his intellect. I do not ridicule you at all; I pity only your life, as I said, and applaud your talent and your eloquence. O great father of Roman eloquence, not I alone but all who bedeck themselves with the flowers of Latin speech are grateful to you; for it is with the waters from your wellsprings that we irrigate our fields, frankly admitting that we are sustained by your leadership, aided by your judgments, and enlightened by your radiance. In a word, under your auspices, so to speak, we have achieved whatever writing skills and principles we possess. In the realm of poetry we followed another master since necessarily we had to follow one supreme guide in the unencumbered ways of prose and another in the more restricted paths of poetry; we were moved to admire one who spoke and one who sang since, and I beg the indulgence of you both, neither of you could serve both purposes; in your waters he was unequal to you, and you to him in his measured flow. Possibly I would not have ventured to say this first, however much I felt it, but before me the great Anneus Seneca from Cordova said it, or borrowed it from someone else. He laments that the obstacle to his knowing you was not your ages but the fury of civil strife; he could have met you but never did, yet he was always an admirer of your works and those of that other writer. According to him, then, each of you is confined to his own realm of eloquence and is bidden to yield to his colleague in all else. But I am keeping you too long in suspense: you would like to know who the other master is. You know him; you must remember his name: it is Publius Virgilius

Maro, a citizen of Mantua, about whom you prophesied great things. For we read that, struck by one of his youthful works, you sought the author's name; you, already advanced in years, saw him while he was still young, and expressed your delight with him, rendering a judgment from the inexhaustible fount of eloquence, which, though mingled with self-praise, was truly honorable and splendid for him: for you called him "the second hope of great Rome." At your words, he was so pleased and committed them so deeply to memory that twenty years later, after your earthly journey had long since ended, he inserted your very words into his divine poem. Had it been given to you to see the work, you would have rejoiced at discerning from the first blossom the promise of the real fruit to come; what is more, you would have congratulated the Latin Muses either for having left a doubtful superiority to the insolent Greek Muses or for having won a decisive victory. There are defenders of both these opinions; and if I have come to know your mind from your works, which I do seem to know as though I had lived with you, your choice will be the latter, and as you gave primacy in oratory to Latium, so would you give it the poetic palm. Doubtless you would have ordered the *Iliad* to yield to the *Aeneid*, something that Propertius did not fear to affirm from the very beginning of Virgil's labors. For in his work on the fundamentals of poetry, he openly declared his feelings and hope for those works in these verses: "Yield, O Roman authors, yield, O Greeks; something greater than the *Iliad* is born." So much for the other master of Latin literature, the other hope of great Rome; now I return to you.

You have heard my opinions about your life and your talent. Do you also wish to hear about your books, how fortune has treated them and how the public and scholars view them? Some splendid volumes still exist that I can hardly list, much less peruse with care; moreover, your works enjoy an immense reputation and your name is on everyone's lips, but rare are those who study you, whether because the times are unfavorable or men's minds dull and sluggish, or, as I think more likely, because greed has bent their minds to other pursuits. Thus, some of your books, I suspect, are lost for us who still live, and I know not whether they will ever be recovered: how great is my grief, how great a shame for our times, how great a wrong to posterity! It was not degrading enough to neglect our own intellects to the detriment of the following age, but we had to destroy the fruit even of your labor with our cruel and unpardonable negligence. What I am deploring with respect to your works has also happened to many works of other illustrious authors. But since at present I am dealing only with yours, here are the titles of those whose loss is most to be deplored: *De republica, De re familiari,*

De re militari, *De laude philosophie*, *De consolatione*, and *De gloria*, although my feeling is one of faint hope for the last ones rather than total despair. And furthermore, even of the surviving books, large portions are missing; it is as though after winning a great battle against oblivion and sloth, we now had to mourn our leaders, and not only those who had been killed but those who had been maimed or lost. This we deplore in many of your works, but particularly in *De oratore*, the *Academica*, and *De legibus*, all of which have reached us in such fragmentary and mutilated condition that it would perhaps have been better for them to have perished.

In conclusion, you will wish to know about the condition of Rome and of the Roman state, as well as the appearance of your homeland, the degree of harmony among its citizenry, to whom power has been entrusted, and by whose hands and with what wisdom the reins of government are held; also whether the Danube, the Ganges, the Ebro, the Nile, the Don are still our boundaries, or whether in the words of your Mantuan poet, someone has arisen "whose empire shall reach to the ocean's limits, whose fame shall end in the stars," or "whose empire shall expand beyond the Garamants and Indians." I surmise that you are most eager to hear these and similar tidings, owing to your patriotism and your love of country, which led to your death. But it is truly better to pass over such subjects in silence, for believe me, O Cicero, were you to learn your country's condition, you would weep bitter tears, wherever in heaven or in Erebus your lodging may be. Farewell forever.

From the land of the living, on the left bank of the Rhone, in transalpine Gaul, in the same year, on 19 December.

Fam. XXIV, 5.

To Anneus Seneca.

Francesco sends his greetings to Anneus Seneca. I should like to request and obtain pardon from so great a man for expressing myself more sharply than befits the reverence owed to your profession and to the peace of the grave. For whoever has seen that I did not spare Marcus Cicero, whom, upon your authority, I called the light and wellspring of Latin eloquence, will have no reason for complaint if I do not spare you after having spoken the truth about others. I enjoy speaking with you, O illustrious man, in whom every age has been wanting, about whom our own age has permitted ignorance and total oblivion. For my part, I daily listen to your words with more attention than one would believe, and perhaps I shall not be thought impertinent in wishing to be heard by you. I am fully aware that among the illustrious names of all times yours must be included; had I not been able to obtain this from any other source, I should still have learned it from a great foreign authority. Plutarch, a Greek writer and tutor to the emperor Trajan, compared the famous men of his country with ours, opposing Marcus Varro to Plato and Aristotle (the Greeks called the first divine, the second a demon), Virgil to Homer, and Marcus Tullius to Demosthenes. He finally ventured to address the controversial question of which country had the greater military leaders, nor was he restrained by the respect owed to his important pupil. In one area alone he was not ashamed to admit the inferior genius of his own people because they did not possess anyone on a par with you in moral philosophy; great praise indeed, especially coming from a proud man who had compared his Alexander of Macedonia to our Julius Caesar. I know not why unstable nature so often mars with a serious flaw the most perfect bodies or minds, whether it is because our common mother envies mortals any perfection, the more so, the closer we seem to approach it, or because amidst so much beauty every defect becomes noticeable. What on an ordinary face might be a simple wart, on a beautiful face is an ugly scar; much light is shed on opposites by contrasting them. But you, O venerable sir, and, if we believe Plutarch, incomparable teacher of morals, review with me, if you do not mind, the great error of your life. You happened to live under the cruelest ruler of all centuries, and like a peaceful sailor you guided your ship laden with precious cargo toward a dangerous and stormy reef. But I ask you, Why did you linger there? Perhaps to prove your skill in such a terrible storm? None but a madman would have chosen this course, for if it is the role of a brave man to face danger, it is not the role of a prudent man to seek it. But if prudence is also given a free choice, there would be no need for bravery, for nothing would ever happen requiring its assistance; it is rather moderation with all its power that will check and control excessive joy and desires. Since, too, the vicissitudes of life are countless and man's life is subject to many things that undo our best-laid plans, we must oppose to mad fortune an invincible virtue, not from choice, as I said, but following the inexorable and iron-clad laws of necessity. But shall I not appear a fool if I continue preaching virtue to a teacher of virtue, attempting to prove something whose opposite cannot possibly be proven, namely, that it was not wise to tarry among the shoals? I would surely win whether the judge be yourself or anyone else who has learned to sail the sea of life tolerably well. If you strove to reap glory by overcoming difficulties, you would have enjoyed even greater glory had you extricated yourself in order to bring your ship safely into some port. You saw the sword continually dangling over your head, yet were not frightened, nor did you foresee the outcome of such a dangerous situation, especially when you must have realized that your death would have reaped no benefit or glory, truly the most wretched of all deaths.

You had fallen, O unfortunate man, into the hands of a person who could do whatever he wished, but who could wish only evil. Warned by a dream at the very beginning of your close relationship with him, you still accepted in good faith with eyes open a suspicious tranquillity based on specious reasoning. Why then did you tarry so long in his household? What did you have in common with your inhuman and bloodstained disciple or with a court so different from yourself? You may reply, "I wished to flee, but could not," offering as excuse that verse of Cleanthes that you are wont to cite in Latin: "Fate leads the willing and drags the unwilling." You may, moreover, cry out that you did wish to renounce your riches in order to sever the bonds that held you, or to free yourself in utter destitution from such a shipwreck; this was known even to ancient historians, and I who follow in their footsteps could never pass over it in silence. But if in those days I concealed my innermost thoughts when speaking in public, now, when my words are for you alone, do you think that I shall suppress what indignation and love of truth urge me to say? Come now, approach more closely, that no stranger may overhear us upon realizing that time has not deprived us of a knowledge of your doings. We have a most trustworthy authority, Suetonius Tranquillus, who is swayed neither by fear nor by favor when dealing with the most illustrious men. What then does he say? That you kept Nero from "any knowledge of ancient orators" so as to keep him all the longer as your admirer. You thus strove to become favored by someone to whom, true to your mission, you should have made yourself contemptuous by developing or at least pretending to have some kind of defect in your speech. The root of your misery, then, was inconstancy, even vanity. You coveted the empty glory of studies, O stubborn old man, too joyfully, not to say childishly. Your consenting to teach a cruel tyrant could have resulted from bad judgment or error, or some kind of fate, since in our eager search for excuses we attribute our faults to fate; but this desire of yours was certainly the fault of your judgment; you cannot accuse fortune, for you obtained what you desired. But where were you heading, O wretched man? Once you had so led that insane youth to admire you that no possibility remained of freeing yourself or leaving him, should you not have borne with greater resignation the yoke that you had voluntarily assumed, and at least have refrained from branding your master's name with everlasting infamy. You surely knew that tragedy is the most serious of all compositions, as Naso says; all know how biting, how virulent, how vehement is the tragedy that you wrote against him, and since the mind hankers for truth, it was all the more damaging, the more it spoke the truth. Yet perhaps it is true that the tragedy was not by you but by another of the same name. For the Spaniards themselves maintain that Cordova produced two Senecas, and a passage in the *Octavia*—that is the tragedy's title—lends support to this suspicion; and if we accept this opinion, insofar as it pertains to the matter at hand, you are acquitted of this charge. As for the style, whoever the author may be, he is by no means inferior to you, although he does follow you in time and in reputation. A writer's intellectual power is diminished in proportion to the inadequacy of his attack against infamy, which, in my opinion, is the only justification for that notorious play. I believe that no bitterness of thought or expression could equal the infamy of that awful man's deeds, if such fierce inhumanity can be imagined in a man; nevertheless, consider whether it was fitting for you to write it, you the emperor's subject, the master's servant, the disciple's teacher—in short, to write about him as you did when you customarily flattered him, even deceiving him with your flattery. Read once again your books dedicated to him on clemency, read once again what you wrote to Polybius on consolation; if the waters of the swirling Lethe have not destroyed your books or the memory of your books, I believe that you will be ashamed of your praises for your pupil. For I do not know how you could have written such things about such a man with such affrontery; I, for one, cannot reread them without a sense of shame.

But here you will once again counter by adducing the youth and disposition of the prince, which promised better results, trying to defend your error by his sudden change in behavior, as if these arguments were unknown to us. But consider in turn how inexcusable it was that a few insignificant short works of a hypocritical prince, or his soft words of false devotion, should have warped the mind and judgment of a man such as yourself, at your age, with your experience and learning. I ask, what deeds of his pleased you, which, in the words of historians, "were partly blameless and partly worthy of considerable praise," that is, before his headlong plunge into crime and scandal? Was it perhaps his love for chariot racing or for playing the lyre, to which we learn he was so curiously dedicated that at first in secret before his slaves and the squalid poor, and finally in public, before all the people, he would parade about as a princely charioteer; and as a renowned lyre player he would worship the lyre offered to him as though it were a god? At length, elated by all these successes and dissatisfied with his Italian triumphs, he went to Achaia, and puffed up by the adulation of Greek musicians, he declared that only the Greeks were worthy of being his listeners, ridiculous monster and savage beast that he was. Or did you consider it a surer sign of a great and conscientious ruler the consecration on the Capitoline of the first growth of his beard and the first covering of his inhuman face? These surely are the acts of your Nero, O Seneca. At an age when the historians still number him among men, you try to set him among the gods with commendations worthy neither of the one praising nor of the one praised, and, to mention something that may not shame you but certainly does me, you do not hestitate to rank him above the greatest of princes, the divine Augustus, unless it is perhaps because you believe it worthy of greater glory to have tortured the Christians, truly a holy and harmless sect, but one that appeared to him, as to Suetonius, who reports it, guilty of a "new and dangerous superstition." He had become the persecutor and cruel enemy of all piety. I do not, however, suspect you of this, and for that reason I am even more surprised at your conduct, for his earlier deeds were too frivolous and vain, while his later ones were abominable and dreadful. Such must also have been your opinion since one of your letters to the apostle Paul not only implies but declares it. And I am sure that you could not have viewed it otherwise once you had listened to his sacred and heavenly teachings and embraced a friendship so divinely offered to you. Would that you had been more steadfast, would that you had not in the end been torn away from him so that together with the messenger of the truth you might have died for the sake of the same truth, for the promise of eternal reward, and for the glory of the great apostle! But driven by my words, I have proceeded too far, and thus understand that I have begun my sowing too late to entertain any hopes of a good crop. Farewell forever.

From the land of the living, in Cisalpine Gaul, on the right bank of the Po, on the first day of August, in the year 1348 from the birth of Him whom I know not whether you ever really knew.

Fam. XXIV, 6.

To Marcus Varro.

Francesco sends his greetings to Marcus Varro. Your rare integrity, your diligence, and your illustrious name compel me to love and revere you. There are some whom we love for their good works and merits, who, unlike others who seriously offend our sight and smell, teach through their learning and charm by their example, and though they have departed hence "to the common abode," as Plautus says, continue to be of service to the living. You are of little or no service to us, not through any fault of yours but because of time, that destroyer of all things. Our age has lost your books; and why not, when it is desirous only of gold? Who was ever a good guardian of despised things? Though zealously devoted to the pursuit of knowledge, you did not for that reason avoid an active life, gaining distinctions in both areas and the well-deserved esteem of those most eminent men, Pompey the Great and Julius Caesar. You served as a soldier under the one, and wrote marvelously learned books for the other, two sharply contrasting activities amidst the concerns of war and public office. It is of great credit not only to your intellect but to your resolve to have had both body and mind in perpetual motion, as well as the power and desire to be useful not only to your own age but to all succeeding ages. Your carefully prepared books have not been deemed worthy of being passed on to posterity through our hands; our neglect has vanquished your industriousness. Never was a father so thrifty that his extravagant son could not squander within a short time his accumulated savings. But why now enumerate your lost books? Each one is a stigma upon our name; it is better, then, to remain silent, for a wound reopens at being touched, and pain, once allayed, is renewed by recalling the injury. Yet—O incredible power of fame!—your name lives on though your works are buried, and while almost nothing remains of Varro, Varro remains nonetheless a very learned man by general consent. Marcus Cicero did not fear to assert this "beyond all doubt" in those very books in which he argues that nothing must be positively affirmed. It is as if the splendor of your name had dazzled him, and while speaking of you he seems to have lost sight of his principal argument. There are some who would limit Cicero's testimony to the narrow bounds of Latin literature, and consider you as the most learned of the Romans. Others extend Cicero's opinion to include Greek literature, especially Lactantius, a Roman outstanding for his eloquence and his piety, who affirms that no man had ever lived who had been more learned than Varro, not even among the Greeks. But among your numerous supporters are two who are truly famous. The first one I have already mentioned, your contemporary and fellow-citizen as well as fellow-disciple, Cicero, with whom you exchanged much correspondence, thereby devoting your leisure time to a useful occupation in keeping with Cato's precepts. If his works have survived longer, it is perhaps due to the charm of his style. The second supporter is a very holy man with a divine intellect, Augustine, African by birth but Roman in language, whom I wish you could have consulted about your books dealing with divine matters. You would surely have become a great theologian since you dealt so accurately and analytically with the theology that you knew. But so that nothing be kept from you regarding your circumstances, despite the fact that you are known to have read "so many things that we marvel that you had time to write, and wrote so many things that hardly anyone could read them all," still none of them survives or at best they are only in fragments. I saw a few of them some time ago and am tortured by the memory of having tasted their sweetness only with the tip of my tongue, as the saying goes. But the works themselves, and especially the books on divine and human matters, which greatly increased your reputation, I suspect are still in hiding somewhere. Searching for them has wearied me for these many years, since nothing is more distressing than a prolonged and anxious hope that remains unfulfilled. But be of good cheer, and grasping in good conscience the fruits of your uncommon labors, grieve not that mortal things have perished. You knew that they would perish, even as you wrote; it is not given to a mortal intellect to create immortal things. What does it matter whether something that is destined to perish, perishes immediately or after a hundred thousand years? There is a throng of illustrious men whose works resulted from dedicated labor similar to yours and who enjoy no greater fortune, whose example should serve to convince you that you must bear your fate with greater equanimity. It may help to mention certain ones of these, since even the mere recollection of famous names is a pleasant task. They include Marcus Cato the Censor, Publius Nigidius, Antonius Gnipho, Iulius Hyginus, Ateius Capito, Gaius Bassus, Veratius Pontificalis, Octavius Hersennius, Cornelius Balbus, Masurius Sabinus, Servius Sulpitius, Cloatius Verus, Gaius Flaccus, Pompeius Festus, Cassius Emina, Fabius Pictor, Statius Tullianus, and many others too numerous to list. They were once famous men but now are obscure ashes, and except for the first two their names are barely known. I wish that you would give them my best with my words but with your lips. As for Julius and Augustus Caesar and as many others as are of that same rank, even though they were devoted to studies and very learned, and you were very intimate with some of them, it would seem more fitting for me to send them greetings through our emperors, assuming that these are not ashamed of having destroyed the Empire that had been established through their diligence and courage. Farewell forever, O most prudent of men.

From the land of the living, in the capital of the world, Rome, your fatherland, which has become mine, on 1 November in the year 1350 from the birth of Him whom I wish you had known.

Fam. XXIV, 7.

To Quintilian.

Francesco sends his greetings to Quintilian. A long time ago I had heard of your name and read something of yours, and I wondered where you had acquired your reputation of possessing keen insight; later I became acquainted with your intellect when your work *De institutione oratoria* came into my hands, but, alas, mangled and mutilated. Knowing how time destroys all things, I said to myself: "You do as usual; nothing do you faithfully preserve except what is better lost. O insolent and slothful age, in such condition you hand down to me men of genius while paying your respects to the unworthy! O sterile and detestable times dedicated to learning and writing much that would have been better left unsaid, you failed to keep this work intact." But your book allowed me to form a correct opinion of you, for I had long erred in judging your work and am now pleased to have put an end to my error. Seeing the dismembered limbs of a beautiful body, my mind was overcome by admiration and grief; perhaps someone now possesses you in your entirety who is doubtlessly unaware of his guest's renown. May whoever had the good fortune to discover you know that in his possession is this object of great value, which, if he is at all wise, he will consider among his greatest treasures. In these books—I know not the number but they doubtless were many—you dared to probe once again a subject already treated with the highest skill by Cicero in his old age, something that seemed impossible to me; following in his footsteps you acquired a new renown not from imitation but from your own learning, which gave birth to your remarkable work. The orator so carefully formed by him is so molded and fashioned by you that Cicero seems either to have neglected or not to have noticed a great deal. One by one you so diligently gather the many things overlooked by your master that you can be said to have surpassed him in diligence to the same degree that he surpassed you in eloquence. While he leads his orator through the difficulties of legal actions to the highest summits of eloquence, training him for victory in judicial battles, you go further back, leading your orator through all the twists and pitfalls of the lengthy journey from the very cradle to the impregnable stronghold of eloquence; this is pleasing and delightful, compelling our admiration, because nothing proves more useful to aspirants. Ciceronian splendor enlightens those already advanced and reveals to the strong the way to eminence, whereas your diligence assists the weak as well, and like an experienced nurse of intellects nourishes the tender child with the milk of humility. Lest flattering truth seem suspect to you, I must change my style; Cicero's words in his *Rhetorica* apply in your case: "For the orator it is of very little importance to speak about his skill, and of the highest importance to speak with skill"; I do not endow you with one of these qualities and deny you the other one, as Cicero does with Hermagoras, about whom he was speaking. I concede both of them to you, but the latter to a lesser degree and the former to such a remarkable degree that it now seems hardly possible for a human mind to add anything to what you say. When this magnificent work of yours is compared to your other book entitled *De causis* – by not having perished it shows all the more clearly that our age is especially neglectful of the best things but not of mediocre ones – it becomes sufficiently clear to discerning minds that you have performed the office of the whetstone rather than that of the sword, and have been more successful in polishing the orator than in shaping him! I wish that you would not take this in bad part, but understand that it is true of yourself as of others that an intellect is never so competent in all things that it may not be surpassed in some way. I admit that you were a great man, but you were supreme in teaching and molding great men. And if you had come across a suitable candidate, you would have produced someone greater than yourself, being as you were a learned cultivator of noble intellects.

There was, however, a considerable rivalry between you and another great man, Anneus Seneca. Your age, profession, and birthplace joined the two of you, but envy, that plague among equals, separated you. I know not whether in this matter you might appear the more moderate inasmuch as, while you refrain from praising him fully, he speaks of you with great contempt. If I may be considered any kind of judge between such illustrious parties, although I have a greater fear of being judged by an inferior than of being worthy to judge those who are superior, I shall still express my opinion. He was more versatile, you keener; he used a loftier style, you a more cautious one. What is more, you praise his genius, his dedication, and his breadth of learning, but not his taste and judgment. You say in fact that his style is corrupt and vitiated by every fault. On the other hand, he numbers you among those whose fame is buried with them although your fame has not yet disappeared and you neither died nor were buried while he was still writing. He died under Nero, whereas you, following his death and Nero's, came to Rome from Spain during Galba's reign, and there after many years, accepting from the Emperor Domitian the task of educating his sister's grandchildren, you were made sponsor of their youthful customs and studies. Having enjoyed great success in both fields, you performed your duty, I believe, in the best way you could. Nevertheless, as Plutarch wrote to Trajan shortly thereafter, the indiscretions of your youthful charges reflected upon you. I have nothing more to write. I hope to see you in your entirety, and if you are anywhere in such condition, I beg you not to hide from me any longer. Farewell.

From the land of the living, between the right slope of the Apennines and the right bank of the Arno, within the walls of my own city, where I first became acquainted with you, and on the very same day, 7 December, in the year 1350 from the birth of Him whom your master preferred to persecute rather than know.

Fam. XXIV, 8.

To Titus Livy, historian.

Francesco sends his greetings to Titus Livy. I should wish, if it were permitted from on high, either to have lived in your age or you in ours so that either the age itself or I as a person would become better through you, and, as one of your admirers, I would be disposed for the sake of seeing you to travel not only to Rome but indeed to India from either France or Spain. But now I am allowed to behold you in your books, not indeed in your entirety but as much as has not yet perished through the sloth of our age. We know that you wrote 142 books on Roman affairs. Alas, with what enthusiasm and labor! Scarcely thirty of them survive. What a wretched custom it is to deceive ourselves willfully! I said thirty because it is common for everyone to say so, but I find that one of these is missing. They are twenty-nine, that is, three decades: the first, the third, and the fourth, which does have the full number of books. I busy myself with these few remains of yours whenever I desire to forget these places or times, as well as our present customs, being filled with bitter indignation against the activities of our contemporaries, who find no value in anything but gold and silver and pleasures. If these are to be considered among good things, then not only the dumb beasts but even inert matter enjoy a fuller and more perfect good than does rational man. But this is a lengthy and well-known subject. Now it is rather the time for me to express my gratitude to you for a number of things, but especially for the fact that you often make me forget present evils by transferring me to happier centuries. As I read I seem to find myself with the Cornelii, the African Scipios, the Laelii, the Fabii Maximi, the Metulli, the Bruti, the Decii, the Catos, the Reguli, the Cursores, the Torquati, the Valerii Corvini, the Salinatores, the Claudii Marcelli, the Neros, the Emilii, the Fulvii, the Flaminii, the Atilii, the Quinti, and the Camilli, and not with these cursed thieves among whom I was born under an evil star. And if I could only possess you in your entirety, with how many other names would I seek solace for my life and forgetfulness of this hateful age! Since I cannot find them in your works, I read of them here and there in other authors, and especially in that volume where you are to be found in your entirety but so abridged that most of the subject matter is lost though the number of books is correct. I should like you to give my greetings to your predecessors, Polybius, Quintus Claudius, and Valerius Antias, and all those whose glory was dimmed by your greater splendor. Among the more recent authors, greet for me Pliny the Younger of Verona, your neighbor, and Crispus Sallust, who was once your rival. Tell them that their nightly vigils enjoyed no more happier a lot than yours. Farewell forever, O supreme preserver of the memory of past deeds.

From the land of the living, in that region of Italy and in that city where you were born and are buried, in the vestibule of the temple of Justina Virgo, and standing before your gravestone, on 22 February, in the year 1351 from the birth of Him whom you might have seen or heard, had you lived a little longer.

Fam. XXIV, 9.

To Asinius Pollio, orator.

Francesco sends greetings to Asinius Pollio. When I conceived the project of contacting through friendly letters a number of distant masters of eloquence who had been the rare ornaments of the Latin language, I did not want to remain silent about your name because, in keeping with the testimony of great writers, I considered you equal to the very greatest names. But since your fame has reached us almost stripped of details and has been aided more by the writings of others than by your own (a fact deservedly numbered among the shameful losses of our age), I have very little to say to you. I congratulate you, holder of the consulship and recipient of a triumph, as much for the glory of your lofty intellect, your polished eloquence, and your many other endowments of body, mind, and fortune, as for your particular fortune of having grown old under the best of princes, one who was dedicated to letters and virtues, and thus was a competent judge of your accomplishments. O happy are you to have filled the just measure of your life in Augustus's reign, and to have brought an illustrious life to a peaceful close at your Tusculan estate in the eightieth year of your life. You escaped the bloody hands of Tiberius, into which fell the orator, Asinius Gallus, your ill-fated offspring, who, we read, was killed by him with dreadful punishments. It was fortunate that amidst such great wretchedness when your fate was already beginning to waver, a most opportune death overtook you, which freed your eyes at least from such a dismal spectacle. Only a few years more, and you would have been the sad spectator or participant in your son's fate; his death, if certain wise men are right in holding that the dead are affected by the lot of the living, diminished your happiness to no slight degree. The law of true friendship does not allow me to pass over one matter in silent pretense, a law that binds me to the ashes and fame of the illustrious dead of every age no differently than if they were living. What displeased me, then, was that you chose to be such a bitter critic, not to say harsh censurer, of Marcus Tullius, whose name deserved rather to be especially honored and exalted in your writings. But if freedom of judgment supports your position – and I do not deny you that freedom even though I do not approve of your judgment – your denunciation could certainly have been used more moderately – but my words come too late. Since you often use that same freedom against the master of the world, you may easily deserve forgiveness from others. I grant that it is rather difficult amidst so much indulgence by fortune for one to restrain his mind and his tongue; but your advanced age and great learning compel me to make greater demands of you. They also oblige me to censure you more severely for your actions than either your son, who in following his father's footsteps agreed with you, or Calvus and the others who shared the same opinion. Nor indeed am I so forgetful of my own situation as to deny you the same right against that contemporary of yours, so well known to you, as I have enjoyed after these many centuries against a man of such reputation and so far removed from me in time. There is no man who is perfect. Who will forbid you, a man of such eminence, from noting a shortcoming in your neighbor's conduct when I from a distance have found things to criticize in his writings? But when you question his reputation for eloquence, or wish to wrest his preeminence in eloquence, allotted him by heaven and conceded without question by almost all of our world, see to it that the wound that you have inflicted is not too deep. Beware, and let Calvus beware with you, lest you undertake against that man a useless battle for the primacy in eloquence as we can now plainly see as spectators of your struggle. You have long since been defeated in the allocation of such primacy, but you still struggle and resist in vain, nor does your arrogant insight allow you to see the truth. I confess that you would have been great men had you been able to acknowledge one greater than yourselves. But when human pride raises itself through false judgments above what it really is, it subsequently, through the use of proper judgment, sinks to a lower level than it might have deserved. A large number of mortals have lost their own glory in their appetite for another's glory. But if perchance envy prompted your actions, despite the fact that you both had many associates in your pride and envy, nevertheless I can accept it less readily in you than in Calvus. He certainly had no little cause for both envying and hating Cicero, whereas I see no reason whatsoever for hatred on your part. Indeed to me it seems all the more a pity that envy, so accustomed to crawling on the ground, should have seized upon such a lofty intellect. Farewell forever, and give my greetings to Socrates, Demosthenes, and Eschines among the Greeks and to the orators Crassus and Antonius among the Romans, as well as to Corvinus Messala and Hortensius, provided that the former with the encumbrances of his flesh laid aside has regained his memory, lost two years before his death, and that the latter has not lost his.

From Insubrian Milan, on 1 August in the year 1353 of this last era.

Fam. XXIV, 10.

To Horatius Flaccus, lyric poet.

O you whom the Italian land hails king of lyric poetry,
to whom the Lesbian Muse did grant
her lyre with its harmonious strings;
you whom the Tyrrhenian stole from the Adriatic,
and Tuscany from Apulia, and whom
the Tiber claims as its own from the Aufidus,
scorning not your obscure and humble origin;
sweet is it now to follow you through secluded woodlands,
to perceive the shadows and bubbling waters in the vales,
the purple hills, the green meadows,
the cool lakes and dewy grottoes.
'Tis sweet to follow you whether you propitiate Faunus
with his roaming flocks, or hasten to visit
fiery Bromius, or celebrate with silent rites
the golden goddess, favorite of the god of wine;
or sing of Venus, ever in need of both, or the plaintive
laments of the nymphs and nimble satyrs, and the Graces
with their rosy and naked bodies, or the glory and honor
of indomitable Hercules and other descendants of incestuous Jove:
Mars with his helmet, Pallas with her dread aegis
and its Gorgon-head; the sons of Leda, submerged
beneath the waves and protectors of vessels;
cunning Mercury, inventor of the lyre; golden-haired
Apollo, whom you flatter with words while he bathes
his glittering locks in the waters of the Xanthus;
and his sister distinguished for her quiver
and unsafe for beasts; or the sacred dances of the Pierides.
Your pen carves ancient heroes in something
harder than marble, and, if there be any, new heroes as well
in words of everlasting and eternal praise
such as time cannot erase. Thus only the excellence
of poets through their enkindled studies
transmits perpetual images whereby we perceive
as though alive those demigods, Drusus and Scipio,
and others through whom renowned Rome imposed
her yoke upon vanquished peoples. Apart from these,
as a sun outshining all with vivid light,
stands the progeny of the Caesars.

As you modulate your song and precede
me in my anxiety, lead me, if you will, over
the oar-furrowed sea, or to the cloud-enshrouded
mountain summits. Lead me too through
the streams of the flowing Tiber, where the Aniene
bursts forth with its banks cutting across fields,
once so dear to you when you were among the living,
and whence in my musing I have now woven these words for you,
O Flaccus, our glory; lead me through forbidding
forest darknesses to the icy Algidus, to the warm
waters of Baiae, and to the lakes of the Sabines
and the flowering countryside to Soracte's peak
white with snow. Lead me to Brundisium along
remote bypaths; I shall hardly become weary
and shall gladly partake of friendly gatherings
with bards who come to greet us. Neither
time nor place shall swerve me from my purpose;
I shall go with equal vigor whether our great mother earth
be swollen with crops, whether the dew be dried
by scorching sun, whether the branches groan beneath
the weight of fruit, or whether the earth bristle
sluggishly with ice. I shall come with you to visit
the shores of the Cyclades, the murmuring of the
Thracian Bosporus, the remote wastes of torrid Libya,
and the stormy cold of the distant Caucasus.
Wherever you may proceed, whatever you may do,
pleases me; whether you diligently rouse, while seated,
your faithful friends, exalting virtue with worthy praises;
whether you assail vices with deserved sniping, and smiling
artfully attack folly with gentle bite; or whether
singing sweetly you fill your song with tender words
of love; or with martial style you upbraid the lust of
the old wanton; or when you condemn the guilty city,
its people, and their words and savage frenzy;
or when you sing of your Maecenas throughout your work,
whether beginning or end; or when you scorn the ancient bards
or let the ears of magnanimous Caesar resound
with your fondness for the more recent ones.
And I am pleased when you apply for Florus your file
to a jagged song or a swollen poem; or teach Fuscus
the rules of country living and the evils of
an agitated city, or why the wild steed is

the servant of man; or teach Crispus wealth's true value.
I find delight in your gentle urging of Virgil
away from his deep griefs and toward joyfulness
and short-lived laughter when spring is nigh;
when you warn Hirpinus of the flight of time, and
Torquatus and Postumus as well in a similar ode;
or when you write of the passing nights and flying days
or of old age stealing upon us with silent step,
or the brevity of life, or death that hastens with
flying footsteps. Who, too, would not listen
enraptured when you assign to Augustus an abode on
the stars; or when you weave a tunic for Mars
made of iron, even of adamantine; or when
you wend your steps as victor along the sacred way
and hill with captives bound to chariots by chains
of gold? Or when a haughty queen avoids such pomp and
is barely terrified by the rigid asps; or when
you recall how the laws of hospitality were broken
through the treachery of the Phrygian shepherd, or
how Paris was not placated by the threatening prophecies
of Nereus; or when the golden shower deceives Dane,
or the royal maiden, amidst her remarkable cries,
is borne away on the back of the horned adulterer?
You are always pleasing, whether joyful, agitated,
or even sad and angry, or when you reveal the various
suspicions of a rival lover; or when you rightly curse
viperlike hags, and the ignorant multitude;
when you sing of Lalage; or when defenseless and alone,
with unruffled brow, you put to flight the desperate
wolf; or when you escape the fall of the ill-omened tree,
and the waves stirred up by an Eolian tempest.
When I saw you reclining upon the fresh turf, listening
to the bubbling of springs and the songs of birds,
or plucking little flowers from the grassy meadow,
or binding vine sprouts with pliant hosiers,
or plucking the lyre with gentle fingers, and
changing the measures with your white plectrum,
and soothing the stars with varied song; when I beheld
all this, my eager mind suddenly fell prey
to a noble desire that spared me not till I had
followed you o'er the waves of the double sea and among
the reefs and monsters on land and sea, till

on the confines of India I saw arriving the gleaming steeds
of the Sun, and in the evening plunging into the distant ocean.
With you I shall roam with eager mind across the shores
of the North Wind and the regions of the South Wind,
whether you lead me to the Fortunate Isles, or drag
me to wave-resounding Anzio, or take me to the citadels
of Romulus; so do the pleasing strains of your lyre
attract me, so does the sweet bitterness of your pen soothe me.

Fam. XXIV, 11.

To Publius Virgilius Maro, epic poet and prince of Latin bards.

O luminary of eloquence, other hope of the Latin tongue,
illustrious Maro, whom Mantua rejoices to have begotten
as a Roman offspring who will be an ornament to the Roman name
throughout the centuries, what earthly tract, which circle
of Avernus keeps you from us? Does swarthy Apollo
pluck his harsh lute for you, do the black sisters
inspire your verses? Or do you dutifully charm the Elysian
groves with your song and inhabit the Tartarean Helicon,
O most splendid of bards? And does Homer, who was of one mind
with you, roam with you? And do Orpheus and other poets
wander alone through the meadows, singing the praises
of Phoebus, all but those whom a self-inflicted and violent
death and servile homage to a cruel lord have banished to
another region? Such was Lucan, who was driven willingly
to his death, offering his artery to the doctor out of fear
of a more painful and bloody punishment and a shameful death;
such was Lucretius, whose death and savage fury, they say,
compelled him to dwell in places apart. Who then are your
present companions, how is your life, I would gladly hear.
How far from the truth were your dreams, and how far has
wandering Aeneas emerged from the ivory portal? Or rather
does a peaceful region of the heavens contain the blessed
spirits, and do the stars smile upon the peaceful shades
of the illustrious, following the conquest of the Stygian abodes,
and the plundering of the Tartarean regions by the coming of
the Highest King who, victorious in the great struggle,
crossed the ungodly threshold with pierced feet, and
in His power crushed the eternal bars of hell with His
pierced hands, and tore the gates asunder from their
horrid-sounding hinges? All this I should like to know.
If any shade from this world of ours should perchance
visit you and your silent world, receive from him news
I have sent about the three cities dear to you
and the fate of your three works. Unhappy and
bereaved Naples mourns the death of Robert, and a
single day has destroyed the fruits of many years. Now
her people await anxiously its doubtful destiny, and
the crimes of a few are being visited upon an innocent

population. Excellent Mantua is shaken by the endless
disturbances of her neighbors, yet, supported by her
high-minded leaders, she refuses to submit her unconquered
head to the yoke, truly enjoying her own native lords
and ignoring foreign rule. It is here I have composed
what you are reading, and have enjoyed the friendly repose
of your rural fields. I wonder by what path in your wanderings
you sought the unfrequented glades, through what meadows
you were wont to stroll, what river shore you pursued,
what recess in the curving banks of the lake, what shady
groves, what forest strongholds. And I wonder too what
hilly turf you sought, where in your weariness you pressed
your elbow upon the grass or upon the bank of a charming
spring. Such sights bring you vividly to my eyes.
You have heard the fate of your native city, and
the degree of peace that surrounds your tomb. What is happening
in Mother Rome? Ask not this, consider it better
not to know. Therefore lend your ear to better things,
and learn of the great success of your works. Tityrus,
though old, still blows upon his slender reed-pipe, and
through your fourfold cultivation your fields still glitter;
your Aeneas lives and is loved and celebrated throughout
the world. With much effort you strove to raise him
to the stars, but death, envious of such solid
foundations, opposed your attempts. Already the Fates
were pressing upon your unhappy Aeneas, and he was
about to depart, condemned by your own lips,
when the mercy of Augustus once again snatched him on the brink
of destruction from these second flames. Augustus was
not moved by the dejected spirits of his dying friend,
and justly will he be praised for all time for having
denied your last wishes. Farewell forever, O beloved one;
and greet for me our elders, the Meonian and the Ascrean.

Fam. XXIV, 12.

To an unknown correspondent, * *a reply to a lengthy and highly informative letter addressed to him in the name of the poet Homer from the realm of the dead.*

Francesco sends greetings to Homer, the prince of Greek poetry. For some time now I have meant to write you and would have done so except for my feeble command of your language. For I have enjoyed little fortune in learning Greek as happened to you with Latin, which you were wont to use with our authors' assistance, and which, through their descendants' negligence, you seem to have forgotten. Cut off from either means of communication, I had remained silent. One man has once again restored you to our age in Latin dress; and by Jove, your Penelope did not wait for her Ulysses any longer or more anxiously than I have for you. Already I had gradually lost all hope, for, aside from some opening lines of several of your poems, in which I viewed you as one beholds from a distance the uncertain and shimmering look of a desired friend or a glimpse of his streaming hair, nothing of yours had reached me in Latin—in short, I had no hope of seeing you at close quarters; for that little book that commonly passes as yours, though of uncertain authorship, and though it has been derived from yours and is ascribed to you, is certainly not yours. If he lives long enough, this man will restore you to us in your entirety; for he has already begun to let us enjoy fully not only the outstanding fruits of your divine works but also the charms of conversing with you. I recently tasted the Greek flavor of one of these in Latin dress, which made me plainly see the capabilities of a vigorous and keen intellect. Therefore, although Anneus Seneca writes that Cicero loses his customary eloquence in his poetry, and that Virgil's usual felicity of expression abandons him in his prose, and although the one interpreted many of your sayings while the other imitated you in even more things—both still remain the princes of Latin eloquence—nevertheless, I truly believe that only when compared with themselves rather than with others does each appear unequal or inferior. Otherwise, I have read verses by Cicero that are not disagreeable, and prose letters by Virgil that are not unpleasant. I am now experiencing this in your case as well, for although poetry is also your primary and particular specialty, and although, following a certain Jerome who is a skillful user of our language, I wrote that, once translated into either

---

*The identity of the correspondent who wrote Petrarch a letter purporting to be from the shade of Homer continues to remain a puzzle.

Latin or Greek prose, you seemingly are transformed from a very eloquent poet into one scarcely able to speak, yet now, surprising as it may appear, I find you pleasing though translated into Latin prose. I therefore wished to preface this letter with these thoughts so that there would be no surprise at my speaking to Virgil in verse but to you in prose. I spoke to him directly, but am replying to you; and so, in his case I have employed the idiom that we possess in common, in your case I have used not your ancient language, but a new tongue used in the letter addressed to me, a tongue that I employ daily, but I suppose is strange to you. And yet, why do I say "speak" to both of you when whatever anyone may say to either of you is mere "prattle." You are unapproachable, you are more than mortal, your heads pierce the clouds; still, as a child, I find it pleasant to babble with eloquent masters. But enough on the subject of style. I now come to the contents of your letter.

You complain of certain matters when you could justifiably complain of everything, for what is there, I ask, in human affairs that can escape just complaint? When, however, laments become ineffectual, they somehow cease to be justifiable; while lacking a just cause, they are without their desired effect, which consists in offering some remedy for the present and making provision for the future while condemning the past. And yet, since they can at times relieve a grieving soul, they must not be considered completely useless. Thus, your lengthy letter, O great one, abounds in such laments, but I wish that it had been longer since nothing ever seems too long unless accompanied by tediousness. Touching briefly on particular details, I must say that my mind, in its eagerness to know and to learn, experienced a boundless and unbelievable joy in seeing what you wrote about your teachers; they were previously unknown to me, I admit, but henceforth, to the merit of their great disciple, I shall venerate them. I found delight, too, in what you wrote concerning poetry's origins in the distant past and concerning the most ancient cultivators of the Muses, among whom, along with the well-known inhabitants of Helicon, you place Cadmus, son of Agenor, and a certain Hercules, who may or may not have been Alcides. Finally, I delighted in your words about your homeland, whose identity is very doubtful in our minds, remaining unclear even to you Greeks. I also enjoyed what you wrote about pilgrimages to Phoenicia and Egypt in search of knowledge, where several centuries after you famous philosophers traveled, including Pythagoras, Plato, and the most learned and venerable Solon, who gave laws to the Athenians and in later life became a devotee of the Pierides; during his lifetime he admired you, and after his death I imagine that he has become your intimate friend. Lastly, I enjoyed reading about your books, a large number of which even the Italians, your nearest neighbors, do not know. These barbarians who surround us—would that we could be cut off from them not only by the lofty Alps but by the ocean's breadth—these barbarians, I say, have barely heard of your name, not to mention your works; let this serve as proof of the insignificance of this mortal fame to which we aspire so longingly. With such good news you have, however, mixed the bitter grief of the loss of your works. Unhappy me, thrice unhappy, and even more! How many things perish! Indeed, how little survives of all that our blind activities have accomplished under the revolving sun! O labors and cares of men, O brief and lost time, O vanity and pride over nothing! What are we, what do we do, what do we hope for, who indeed can now entertain hope in the dim light when the supreme sun of eloquence has suffered an eclipse? Who dares complain that anything of his has been lost, who can dare hope that any fruit of his labor will endure? A considerable portion of Homer's sleepless toil has perished, not so much for us—for no one loses what he did not possess—as for the Greeks, who in trying not to yield to us in anything, surpassed us even in our sloth and in our neglect of letters. They have surely lost many of Homer's works, which were for them as so many rays of light emanating from one of their two brightest stars; and so their blindness has made them unworthy of glorying in the possession of such a light. I was also deeply moved in reading your account of your end. For although that story of your death was widespread among us, and I myself, following that tradition, repeated it with some uncertainty in one of my works, I was nonetheless pleased, and, with your leave, still am pleased to entertain a better opinion of you and of Sophocles than to believe that in such divine intellects two highly disturbing passions of the mind, grief and joy, should have held such sway. As for Philemon's death, which is truly ridiculous if we accept hearsay, I have finally learned a more serious version: his death followed a period of unconsciousness due, not to excessive laughter, as is usually related, but to the power of profound meditation. But I return to you and to your fate, which you lament profusely and vehemently. Calm yourself, for I am certain that you can if, once free of your passions, you return to your true self.

You utter many complaints about your imitators, about your ungrateful and ignorant denigrators, with just cause if you were the only one to suffer such insults, and if, furthermore, what disturbs you were not common human traits. You must therefore resign yourself, for though you are admittedly the greatest in your class, you are not alone. As for imitators, what shall I say? In beholding yourself soaring so high on the wings of fantasy, you should have foreseen that imitators would never be lacking; it must be a source of delight for you that many wish to resemble you, but not many can. Why should you not rejoice, being assured of always occupying first place, when I, the least of men, rejoice, and not only rejoice, but even boast that I am now held in such esteem that there may be someone, if indeed there is, who wishes to follow and imitate me? I would rejoice even more should my imitators be such as to surpass me. I pray, not to your Apollo, but to my God, the true God of genius, that if anyone considers me worthy of imitation, he may overtake me with easy effort and even outstrip me. I shall believe myself truly fortunate and effective to discover among my friends—for no one is imitated unless he is loved—many who are my equal; and I shall believe myself even more fortunate if they surpass me, and from imitators become guides. For if a father's desire is for the son of his flesh to become greater than himself, what should an author desire for the child of his intellect? You who fear not that anyone be greater than you or overtake you, bear your imitators with patience, even though in the *Saturnalia* there is the unsettled controversy on the question of superiority between yourself and the one about whom you most complain, Virgil; what is more, some among us consider the issue a doubtful one, while others assign the crown unequivocally to Virgil. This I report to you not so much in support of or in opposition to either opinion, as to let you know posterity's varying opinions about you. Before continuing, it behooves me, O finest of guides, to defend Virgil, whose soul, according to Horace, is among the purest ever seen on earth. Not only true but commonly known is your statement about his imitating you, as well as many other things about which you maintain silence, perhaps out of shame or modesty; the main points are discussed in order in the *Saturnalia* along with his witty retort. Once rivals accused him of stealing some of your verses, to which he replied that it was a sign of power to have snatched the staff from Hercules; I have no doubt that you understand the veiled sarcasm of this witticism. But in order not to accuse one whom I was about to defend, as many do, I am in full agreement with all that you say. Yet I cannot calmly listen to your complaint that there is no mention of your name in his works despite his being overladen and bedecked with your spoils, while Lucan, as you correctly recall, acknowledges his indebtedness in grateful terms to the bard of Smyrna. I should even like to lend further support to your complaint. Flaccus often, and in noble words, mentions you; in a certain passage he expresses his preference for you over the philosophers, while elsewhere he assigns to you the foremost place among poets. Naso makes reference to you as do Juvenal and Statius. Why continue listing those who make mention of you? Nearly all of our writers have not been forgetful of you. "Why then," you will say, "should I bear the ingratitude of him alone from whom I should deserve the great-est gratitude?" Before responding, I shall add yet another element to the dispute. Lest anyone believe that perhaps he was similarly ungrateful to all, know that he mentions Museus, Linus, and Orpheus, and not merely once, and others, too, such as Hesiod the Ascrean and Theocri-tus the Syracusan. Had there been any envy in him, he would never have done so; nor does he fail to mention even Varus and Gallus as well as other contemporaries. What then? Have I not aggravated your resentment all the more despite my promise to lessen or remove it? Without a doubt if I stopped with this. But details must be attended to, and, whatever else is done, all the evidence must be brought to bear, particularly if judgment is to be passed. Naturally, with Theocritus as his guide in the *Bucolica* and Hesiod in the *Georgica*, he named each in his proper place. "And why," you will say, "having chosen me as his third guide in his heroic poem, does he make no mention of me in his work?" He would have done so, believe me, having been the gentlest and most modest of men, and, as we find written of him, "a man of irreproachable life," were it not that death interfered. Though he men-tions others where it was opportune and convenient, for you alone, to whom he was much more indebted, he was reserving a special place selected after careful consideration. And what was this, do you sup-pose, if not the most prominent and distinguished place of all? He thus was waiting for the end of his outstanding work, where he intended to exalt your name to the heavens as his guide in sonorous verses. Where, I ask, is it more fitting to exalt one's guide than at journey's end? You have good reason, then, to mourn his premature death. The Italian world mourns with you, but there is no reason to reprove your friend. That it is so you may glean from a similar but recent example; for just as he did with you, so was he imitated by Papinius Statius, whom I mentioned, a man renowned for his remarkable intellect, and possessing singular charm and sophistication. Yet he did not openly acknowledge him as his guide except at the end of his poetic journey. Although in a less conspicuous place he had declared himself the inferi-or in style, it was still at the close that he openly and in good faith paid the full debt of his grateful mind to the *Aeneid*. If he too had died prematurely, he would not have mentioned Virgil, just as Virgil did not mention you. I wish that I could persuade you that it is as I say. For it is surely so, unless I am mistaken, and if perchance it were otherwise, the more reasonable opinion should be preferred in doubtful matters. Let this suffice in defense of Virgil's major works; and if you turn to the *Iuveniles ludi*, clearly his first youthful creations, you will find your name therein.

It now remains for me to touch upon other minor complaints sprinkled throughout your letter. You complain of being mangled by your imitators; that had to be so, since no one was capable of grasping you in your entirety. You are indignant at their insulting you while being clothed in your spoils, but such is the common practice; no one can be truly ungrateful unless he has received some special favor. You lament that your name, once held in great honor by the early jurists and physicians, has now become subject to their successors' contempt, and you do not understand the reason. These men are truly very different from their predecessors, for if they were of like stamp, they would love and cherish the same things. Let your indignation cease, and your sorrow as well; be of good cheer. To have been displeasing to evil and ignorant men is the first sign of virtue and genius. The radiance of your genius is so brilliant that half-blind eyes cannot endure it; it is with you as with the sun, for which it is not considered a disgrace but the highest praise that feeble eyes and nocturnal birds flee from it. Among the ancients, and among the moderns as well, if even a faint spark of pristine valor still survives in any one of them, you are considered not only a holy philosopher, as you yourself say, but, as I have noted, greater and superior to any other, one who has concealed with a charming and transparent veil a very beautiful philosophy. How monstrous men view you is of no interest to you, or rather it is of the greatest interest, for you should wish not to please those whose scorn is the first step to glory, while the next step consists in not being recognized. Now lay aside, I beg you, your anxiety and sorrow, and return to the Elysian fields, which were your early abode, one worthy of you, from which you say you were driven by such absurdities. It does not behoove the mind of a wise man to be crushed by the affronts of fools. Otherwise, what or who would put an end to such an evil, considering the words of the Hebrew sage, "The number of fools is infinite." Truer words could not have been uttered, as is attested by any street, home, or public square.

What you next complain about so bitterly seemed laughable and utterly amusing to my ears, for even sweets taste bitter to the man with a bitter palate and stomach. You weep, when it would have been more fitting to rejoice, because a common friend, whom you consider a Thessalian and I a Byzantine, has forced you to wander or, if you prefer, to be an exile within the colorful walls of my native city. Rest assured that he has done this and continues to do it in good faith and out of the most sincere love for you. Primarily for this reason, he has become very dear to all the admirers of your glory, who, though quite rare, still do exist. See to it, then, that you not become angry with that very person to whom we all, as your admirers, render thanks in your name and ours, since, heaven willing, he will restore you to us and to the Ausonian Muses from whom you were snatched. And do not be astonished that the Fiesole valley and the Arno's banks have begotten only three friends. It is enough, it is more than enough, it is more than I hoped, to have found in such a mercenary city three friends of the Muses. Yet do not despair, the city is large and populous; if you search for a fourth you will find him, and to these I can add a fifth who is deserving, crowned as he is with the Penean or the Alphean laurel. But I know not how transalpine Babylon stole him from us. Do you think it of small account that five such men should be gathered at one time and in one city? Search in other cities. That Bologna of yours for which you sigh, though a most magnificent seat of learning, contains only one even after a thorough search; Verona has two; Sulmona one; and Mantua one, unless divine things have directed him away from earthly concerns, for he has deserted your banners to seek refuge under those of Ptolemy. How astonishing that the head of the world, Rome, has been emptied of such inhabitants except for one! Perugia contains one who might have made a name for himself were it not that he neglected himself and abandoned not only Parnassus but the Apennines and Alps as well, and now in his old age roams throughout Spain scratching away on parchments to earn his livelihood. Other cities have reared still others, but all those whom I have known have migrated from this mortal dwelling to that common and eternal city. You can thus see what I would like: that you not continue lamenting that he has led you to a land that today may possess few friends and admirers for you, but surely more than any other. Do you not know how rare men of this ilk have always been even in your country? For in our day, unless I am mistaken, this friend of ours is the only one in all of Greece. There was another, formerly my teacher, who, having raised my highest hopes, forsook me by dying at the threshold of my studies, although he had already abandoned me previously when, by considering his own interests rather than mine, he was able to advance with my assistance to an episcopal office. This being the case, be satisfied with these few friends, and forgive this enfeebled age as you would have pardoned a more flourishing one. Once there were a few, now there are very few, and soon I predict that there will be none who will prize noble studies. Abide with these few as eagerly as you can, and do not take it upon yourself to exchange our river for any larger one. You are not a sailor nor indeed a fisherman; in point of fact, if the rumor is true, and I wish it were not, your discourse with such people was not very auspicious. You liked the small Castalian fount and the low and humble Helicon. May our Arno and our hills be pleasing to you, where noble springs of intellects gush forth and the delightful nightingales build their nests. They are few indeed, I admit, but if, as I have said, you search near and far, they are many. Aside from these, what do you hope to find among the people except fullers, weavers, and smiths, not to mention imposters, publicans, thieves of various kinds, and thousands of kinds of cheats, hostile factions that are never lacking in deceit, anxious misers and their vain dealings, and the rank and smelly dregs of the mechanical arts? Among these, as an eagle among the night owls, as a lion among pigs, you must bear with courage their jeering, saying what Ennius, who was so inferior to you, once said: "I flit about in life on the lips of learned men." Let unlearned mouths ruminate their ignorance and their tasteless chattering; what matters it to you or to your situation that they either do not know you or ridicule you, when their praise is a respectable kind of blasphemy? But, as I am the least in intellect and in years, let me appear last and let our conversation turn to me. In your present adversity you request my assistance. O cruel and unkind fate, would that there were some power in me with which I might boast forever of having aided so great a man, an honor greater than I have yet attained or hope ever to attain! I call to witness Christ, who was unknown to you, that, save tender pity and loyal advice, I have nothing with which to come to your aid. For how can one who cannot help himself help another? Perhaps you have not heard that your disciples as well as yourself were reviled out of hatred for your name and declared insane by an assembly of insane? If this happened to you in your own age and in highly cultured Athens, what do you think will happen now to other poets in other cities devoted to the pursuit of pleasure? To the ignorant multitude I appear to be one of these; this astonishes me and I wonder why it is so. I wish that their reasons were sound, but it matters not how justifiable the reason for envy if envy itself is real. Do you seek refuge on my bosom? O insensate turn of fortune's wheel! Can this be true of you for whom no royal palace would be sufficiently spacious or resplendent were loftiness of intellect to bestow material honors just as fortune dispenses power. But it is not the case, and genius so often spurns the turrets and castles of the ignorant and delights in the isolated hut. For my part, although I may not be worthy of such a guest, still I have you in Greek in my home and, as much as has been possible, in Latin, and shortly I shall possess all of you, if your Thessalian would complete what he has begun. Know, too, that in order to consign you to a more secure place, I have prepared in the depths of my heart a retreat for you with great feeling and reverence. In sum, my love for you is brighter and more glowing than the sun, and my esteem so great that there can be none greater. This, O guide and father, I have done for you because

I was able to; to free you from the multitude's scorn would result in detracting from your uniquely sublime praises, certainly something beyond me and anyone else, unless there be someone who can put an end to the multitude's madness. Although this may be possible for God, He has yet to do so, and I believe that He will not. I have said many things as though you were present, but now upon emerging from these vivid flights of the imagination, I realize how far removed you are, and I fear that it may prove annoying for you to read so many things in the shadows, except that your lengthy letter was written from there. Farewell forever, and when you have returned to your place, do give my greetings to Orpheus and Linus, Euripides and the others.

From the land of the living, in the midland between the very limpid rivers Po, Ticino, Adda, and others, from which some say Milan derives its name, on 9 October of the year 1360 of this last era.

Fam. XXIV, 13.

To his Socrates, * *conclusion of this work.*

Just as this book began with your name, so will it end. You now have, my dear Socrates, what you wished, a volume of my trifles weaving together all sorts of things in a variety of styles, a work that will deservedly offend delicate ears. And yet, since man's spirit is capricious and changeable, tending to have its own preferences, perhaps there will be those who may not care for its contents, but who will like its very variety. Others will forgive me if they recall that I was led to it not voluntarily but by friends' entreaties, and that it results from my desire to please them. Nor have I been deterred by the opinion of critics or by my other duties or by the irreparable loss of time, so brief and so uncertain. If anything displeases you, you must ask not my pardon but your own, saying, "This is what I wanted; he could not deny me anything, having taken me more into account than himself." No better friend is there than the one who disregards his own reputation in a friend's behalf. Many men, including the worthiest, hold their reputation dearer than life or riches, and if this is sacrificed for a friend, then beyond any doubt he would sacrifice lesser things should the occasion demand. I began this work as a young man; I am completing it in my old age, or rather I am continuing it since it is the only one that death alone can end. What other end can I expect for my conversations with friends but the end of life? Or how could I possibly remain silent with them while still alive if I plan to speak to them with my cold lips from the grave? I have arranged this work not according to subjects but chronologically, with the exception of the last letters addressed to illustrious ancients, which I consciously brought together in one place because of their unity of character, and with the exception of the first letter, which, though written later, preceded its companions to serve as a preface; nearly all the others are arranged chronologically. Thus, the reader may, if he wishes, follow my progress and the course of my life. I confess, however, that in my desire to avoid repeating myself or some phrase two or more times I was unable to fulfill my original promise. I really tried, but a plethora of things interfered—the variety itself and the compelling distractions of a mind meanwhile intent on other matters. Since many other chores require the help of my pen and summon me to other tasks, since I know not how long I have to live, and this work has already grown enough and can hold no more without expansion beyond the proper

*See I, 1.

size for books of this sort, I have decided to insert into another volume any letters excluded and out of order here; and if I do write others, which will take their title from my age, they will be collected in another volume, provided that you, my dear friends, are still determined not to be deprived of any of my works, and provided, too, that I continue to give precedence to your wishes over mine. In the course of your fervent pleas you ought to have seen to it that, while you applaud all my works without distinction and wish nothing whatsover of mine to vanish, and while in your desire to please me you widely publicize things of mine that in my private judgment are not deserving, I not fall into the hands of critics who scorn every one else's works but their own, and, in esteeming and admiring these, are happy in the approbation of their own little circle. It is, my dear friends, to their criticism that you expose me defenseless and unarmed. I certainly cannot complain of your affection for me since nothing is dearer, but, as with everything else, there is a proper limit to love lest in wanting to do good, one does harm. You are too indulgent toward me, too well-disposed; you grant me too much, you press me too hard, in your love you pursue me too closely. Finally, I turn to you, most worthy reader, whoever you are, and I beseech you, in the name of our common enthusiasm for learning and your concern for your own reputation, not to be disturbed by the variety of subjects and the humility of my language, bearing in mind what I said about this in the preface to this work. Farewell.